Bricks Without Straw

A Comprehensive History
of African Americans in Texas

Written and Edited by
David A. Williams

EAKIN PRESS ★ Austin, Texas

Library of Congress Cataloging-in-Publication Data

Bricks without straw : a comprehensive history of African Americans in Texas / edited by David A. Williams.
    p.   cm.
Includes bibliographical references (p.   ).
ISBN 1-57168-041-1
1. Afro-Americans — Texas — History.   2. Texas — History.
I. Williams, David A., 1925–
E185.93.T4B74   1996
976.4'00496073--dc20   95-46442
                                                                    CIP

Contents

iv

Preface

Bricks Without Straw was planned as a collection of essays and articles designed to make the unique culture, history, and contributions of African-American Texans known to a broader audience. This collection makes a rare quality publication about the cultural, social, political, and economic history of African-American Texans. It is designed to be used as supplemental material for secondary and higher education, as a library reference, or as a general reference book for the serious and casual reader.

The book covers the period from the appearance of the first non-Anglo explorer on Texas soil to the appointment of the first African American as president of a major university in the University of Texas System. The emphasis is on individual and collective achievement. The treatment is of traditional and nontraditional roles of groups and individuals and their involvement in Texas history. Exploration, colonization, revolution, the Republic, reconstruction, the depression, the war years, the modern period, and contemporary years are covered. The overall aim is to introduce the reader to the variety of individuals and institutions that are historically significant and relevant to the total Texas history scenario.

Students and casual readers are provided with information of exemplary participation by African-American Texans in important periods of Texas history. This provides a basis for stronger self-identification and appreciation for the total heritage of the state.

Non-African-American students and casual readers are afforded an opportunity to learn that important historical periods of Texas include the contributions of African-American Texans. This promotes a wider appreciation of the value of individuals of other ethnic groups and counteracts biases based on misinformation.

All readers are afforded the basis for greater understanding and appreciation of the multi-ethnic contributions to the building of Texas.

— David A. Williams

Introduction

Historians generally agree that African Americans are not newcomers to Texas. They arrived with the first Europeans, continued to come in growing numbers for three centuries, and today make up about 12 percent of the state's population.

There is a new day dawning in Texas history. Until very recently, little or no attention has been given by historians to the contributions of African Americans to Texan culture and history.

The African American experience in the Texas environment for the last one and three-quarters of a century represents a record of survival despite bondage; a record of outstanding achievements and contributions to the Texan heritage despite overwhelming odds.

African Americans were among the early settlers. Some came alone while others came with Austin's "Old Three Hundred." The records of the military posts or the fortified settlements in the areas under Spanish control reveal the ethnic representation of the early Texas population.

Local records from 1778 show that among the presidios, villas, and the five missions around San Antonio, there were 514 families: 759 men, 613 women, 373 boys, 300 girls, 4 male slaves, and 11 female slaves, totaling 2,060 persons. Of the men, 324 were Spaniards, 268 Indians, 16 mestizos, and 151 of mixed races or blacks. Free persons of African ancestry were numerous, and their means of livelihood were not limited to farming. They were merchants, teachers, shoemakers, carpenters, teamsters, miners, laborers, and domestic workers.

Status of African Americans changed sharply with the founding of the Republic. They could not remain in Texas and own land without special permission from Congress.

This permission was granted in a number of cases to freedmen who played important roles in the Revolution. Others remained illegally, but the social attitudes changed more slowly than the laws, and they were unmolested.

From statehood to the Civil War, the situation of African-

American Texans deteriorated rapidly. With the end of that war came emancipation and an opportunity for political and economic preferment. However, the majority of the population at that time was a conquered people. During the occupation and reconstruction, some of the growing bitterness toward the conqueror was transferred to the African Americans, and the racial chasm became a gulf.

From the end of the Civil War until recent times, the African-American Texan's greatest opportunities were in the church, the schools, and in fraternal organizations. Only an exceptional few were able to achieve success in business and the professions.

In the past fifty years the situation for African Americans in Texas has improved, legally and socially, at a steadily accelerating pace. By 1996 many long-closed doors of opportunity had been opened and a number of African Americans in Texas had attained positions of wealth, prominence, and power in the state and nation. Not all of the problems have been solved, not all of the enmities and prejudices have disappeared, nor is opportunity yet wholly equal. Now, as in the days of the Republic when the trend was in the reverse, attitudes of the people as a whole change at a slower rate than the laws. The trend, however, is clear and discernible. As we near the twenty-first century, it must be realized that the true history of Texas will never be told until the contributions of African Americans are included to make the circle complete.

Section I

Chapter 1

Spanish Colonial Period to Statehood

1528–1845

African Americans are not newcomers to Texas. A few arrived with the first Europeans. They were actually people of color who were in fact Moors. A Moor is a Moslem of mixed Berber and Arab ancestry, especially one of the Saracen invaders of Spain in the eighth century or a descendant of the Saracens. For centuries before Texas was discovered, the Spaniards and Moors had warred, with captives being enslaved by both sides. The Spanish explorers brought Moorish slaves with them to the area we now know as Texas, and many of them stayed. Some became freedmen and won acceptance in the Spanish outposts. Victor Blanco, a man of color, was second *alcalde* of San Antonio in 1809.

Estevan

In 1528 the first man of color in Texas was Estevan, a Moor from North Africa, captured and enslaved by the Spanish. He came as a slave of Captain Dorantes of the Narvaez expedition and was one of the four survivors who, led by Cabeza de Vaca, finally made

*Estevan with
Alvar Nuñez Cabeza de Vaca.*
— Institute of Texan Cultures,
San Antonio, Texas

their way across Texas to Mexico, giving first accounts which led to Spanish exploration. Affectionately called Estabenico (Stevie) by his companions, he was adept at making friends with the Indians and speaking their dialects. Estevan played an important role in the first exploration in Texas.

In 1539 Estevan was the only survivor who returned to Texas. He was chosen by the Spanish viceroy to guide an expedition under Friar Marcos de Niza to seek the Seven Cities of Gold. He outstripped the expedition and, with Indian guides, crossed the southwest corner of Texas into New Mexico, where he discovered the Zuni Pueblos. Miscalculating his influence as a medicine man, he was captured and killed by the Indians.

The Pueblo of Zuni, one of the "Seven Cities" discovered by Estevan.
— Associated Publishers Archives, Washington, D.C.

Estevan (far right) and the three other remaining members of the Narváez expedition of 1528 used beads and some knowledge of medicine to gain the aid of Indians.

— The Granger Collection

Coronado's Expedition

An expedition in 1540 led by Francisco Vásquez de Coronado, accompanied by several people of African descent, swept across New Mexico and western Texas. Later Spanish expeditions found people of African ancestry among the Indians at the mouth of the Rio Grande. They apparently had descended either from Moors from North Africa or from survivors of other ill-fated vessels along the Gulf Coast.

According to Alwyn Barr and others, in 1691 a black bugler accompanied Domingo Teran on the second Spanish missionary expedition to the Indians of East Texas.

With the French

Two men of African ancestry accompanied the Frenchman Blancpain and helped him establish an Indian trading post on the Trinity River in East Central Texas in 1751.

Early Census

Friar Juan Augustin Morfi's census of San Antonio, recorded in 1777, showed a total of 2,060 persons, including 151 of African ancestry. This included the population of the military post in the area under Spanish control, the adjoining village, and the five missions.

Baron de Bastrop

In 1805, a man known to the Spaniards as Baron de Bastrop came to Texas seeking a land grant so he could bring in colonists. The Baron, whose real name was Philip Henrick Nering Boegel, was Dutch. He brought three men of color as servants with him and established his residence in San Antonio. A few years later he paved the way for the Austin Colony, "the Old Three Hundred." Bastrop and Stephen F. Austin convinced Martinez, the Mexican governor, that the colonization plan was a good idea. Martinez agreed to recommend to the Mexican government that Austin's plan be approved.

Louisiana Purchase

When the United States bought Louisiana in 1803, the Spanish declared any slave who escaped across the Sabine River into Texas automatically free. The border became a sieve. Escaped slaves settled in the forests of East Texas, and many joined friendly Indian tribes.

Kian Long

In 1819 Kian (or Kiamata) Long, a twelve-year-old slave girl, came to Texas as the personal maid of Jane Long, wife of Maj. James Long of Natchez, Mississippi. Major Long tried unsuccessfully to free Texas from Spanish domination. He was defeated by Mexican troops, captured and carried to Mexico City, where he was shot and killed by a guard.

Kian and Jane Long remained alone on Bolivar Peninsula,

*Kiamata and Jane Long
at Bolivar Point.*
— Institute of Texan Cultures,
San Antonio, Texas

where Kian helped the widow Long give birth to a baby daughter. Kian discovered Indians nearby, and Mrs. Long fired a cannon to frighten them away. Kian later went with Jane Long and her infant daughter to Richmond and remained closely associated with her until her death. The descendants of Kian Long, now in the seventh generation, live in Houston, Galveston, and other Texas cities. Her grandson, Henry C. Breed, became a veteran policeman on the Houston police force.

Increased Migrations

Anglo-American settlement in 1820 brought a big influx of people of color. Many were slaves of the Anglo planters. The Texas economy was plantation-based with cotton, sugar cane, and other crops raised by slave labor. At the same time, many free African Americans from the United States flocked to Texas, where there were opportunities to acquire free land.

Moses Austin

In 1820, Moses Austin rode into San Antonio with all of the

Moses Austin received a Spanish land grant and permission to bring colonists to Texas.
— University of Texas at Austin, Center for American History

capital he possessed, including the gray horse he was riding, an African slave astride a mule, and $50 in cash. The male slave was the most valuable capital asset, being worth an estimated $600 on the open market. Austin was seeking a Spanish land grant and permission to bring in colonists.

By May 1821, Austin was informed that the Spanish had approved his request to bring settlers to Spanish Texas. Before Moses Austin could carry out his plan, however, he became critically ill with pneumonia. The long, difficult journey to Texas and his work in preparing for colonization had exhausted him. On June 10, 1821, Moses Austin died at the home of his daughter, Mrs. James Bryan. His dying request was that his son, Stephen, carry out the plans for colonizing Texas.

Austin Colony

When Stephen F. Austin carried out his father's plan to colonize Texas, he allowed the settlers fifty acres of land for each slave. The 1825 census of Austin Colony showed 1,347 Anglo Americans and 443 settlers of African ancestry. Most of the non-Anglo colonists were slaves, but some were free African Americans.

Stephen F. Austin led the "Old Three Hundred" to Texas. Several free African Americans traveled with them.
— Texas Memorial Museum, Austin, Texas

Free African Americans in Colonial Texas

Under Mexican law freedmen had all of the legal and political rights of citizenship. They could own land, accumulate wealth, hold office, and marry whom they pleased. The frontier society of prerevolutionary Texas generally accepted any individual on his personal merit, without relation to race or skin color.

The historical records show there were no strong social bars against intermarriage. This was true even for the Native Americans, who were in this period the low group on the social totem pole.

Hendrick Arnold

One of the first African-American freedmen in Texas was Hendrick Arnold, whose father was a member of Stephen F. Austin's "Old Three Hundred." Hendrick Arnold was a hunting companion and close friend of the two famous colonial scouts, Erastus (Deaf) Smith and Henry Wax Karnes.

According to J. Marvin Hunter, Hendrick Arnold was a true patriot during the Texas Revolution. Who was Hendrick Arnold?

*Hendrick Arnold, hero at the
Battle of San Antonio and
San Jacinto.*
— TAAHO Collections,
Austin, Texas

Where did he come from? How did he contribute to the early history of Texas?

In the winter of 1826, one of the families immigrating to Texas from Mississippi was the family of the matriarch Catherine Arnold. The Arnold family joined Austin's colony on the Brazos River at San Felipe. Accompanying Catherine was her son, Daniel Arnold, and his wife, Rachel. Daniel and Rachel had two sons, two daughters, and five slaves. One of Daniel's sons was a free black male named Hendrick Arnold. The Arnold boys' mother was a black woman. There was no need to conceal the Arnold boys' relationship to the Arnold family because under Mexican law there was no difference made in the treatment of persons due to their color or birth. Anyone could own land, accumulate wealth, or hold office, and intermarriage was permissible. All persons had the same legal and political rights. As far as can be determined, the Arnold boys were among the first free persons of color to come to Texas from the United States.

Very little is known about Hendrick Arnold's life and activities from 1826 to 1835. We do know that Arnold became a fine hunter, guide, and scout. He explored many of the trails of early Texas and spent considerable time learning the lore of the Indians of Central and East Texas.

When Texan volunteers prepared to drive Mexican troops from San Antonio in December 1835, the attacking forces were organized into two divisions—one commanded by Col. Francis W. Johnson, and the other by Col. Ben Milam. The guide for Johnson's group was the noted scout Erastus "Deaf" Smith, and the guide for Milam's group was Hendrick Arnold.

According to Houston Wade's account, the records show that: "During the Texas Revolution Hendrick Arnold, described as one of the boldest and oldest pioneers of the west, joined the Army and fought valiantly for his adopted country."

Sometime before January 4, 1836, Hendrick Arnold married the stepdaughter of his friend "Deaf" Smith. She was from San Antonio and was of Anglo-Mexican ancestry.

In the siege and capture of Bexar, December 3–10, 1835, Hendrick Arnold distinguished himself for bravery and fighting ability, as the following account of that desperate undertaking shows:

> The siege was continued until December 3, when it appeared to be about to end in disorder. On that morning three prisoners, who had been detained under surveillance since the beginning of hostilities, made their escape from the city and reached the Texan camp.
>
> On the basis of information given by them as to the strength of the city, a call was made for volunteers. The original plan of assault proposed that three hundred troops should be led into town in three divisions (the plan was changed to two divisions). "Deaf" Smith, J. W. Smith, and Hendrick Arnold were to act as guides to the three divisions.
>
> During the day and night, preparations were made for the assault, and the men waited impatiently for the hour to advance. General Burleson, who replaced Austin as Commander-in-Chief, called a council of officers, and this council decided to postpone the attack. The value of Arnold may be judged by the fact that his absence was given as the reason for postponing the assault, the officers of one of the divisions refusing to march without him.
>
> On the morning of December 5th the assault was made. Arnold, according to the plan, acted as pilot to Colonel Milam in conducting his troops in the town and they began fighting their way in from house to house with great courage and determination, finally forcing General Coz *[sic]* to capitulate five days later. Hendrick Arnold performed his service well.
>
> Colonel F. W. Johnson, who was left in command upon

Milam's death on the third day, in his official report of the battle said:

". . . All (of the men) behaved with the bravery peculiar to freemen, and with decision becoming the sacred cause of liberty. To singalize every individual act of gallantry, where no individual was found wanting to himself or to his country, would be a useless and endless effort. Every man has merited my warmest approbation, and deserves his country's gratitude."

Yet, Johnson did not end his report without giving a special citation to Hendrick Arnold, who, he said, performed important service.

Then, on April 21, 1836, at the Battle of San Jacinto, which won the independence of Texas and sent the Mexican hordes fleeing before the wrath of Texas patriots, Hendrick Arnold again distinguished himself.

Although Texas law, following the Texas Revolution, prohibited free persons of color from remaining in the Republic without congressional consent and denied those who remained the right to own land, Hendrick Arnold stayed on. There is no record that he ever asked or received permission to remain in the country that he helped to free. It is recorded, however, that he was granted 640 acres of land for his invaluable service at the siege of Bexar. Arnold made his home in San Antonio, where he operated a gristmill. A portion of that mill stands today near the mission San Juan Capistrano.

Hendrick Arnold, a free African American, faithfully served the struggling Republic, and for his services was given a vast amount of land. Old maps of Bandera County, Texas, show six land surveys, numbers 59, 60, 61, 62, 69, and 70 respectively. These surveys all touch the Medina River and lay a few miles north and northwest of the town of Bandera, and today the land embraced in the surveys is considered about the most valuable farming and grazing land in the county. Prosperous ranches and farms cover the tracts, which are well watered by running creeks and the Medina River, and there is an abundance of timber of various kinds. The land is fairly level, being broken only by small hills. Arnold received from the Republic and the State of Texas something like 1,920 acres for his services as a soldier.

Hendrick Arnold became a victim of the cholera epidemic, which swept the area in 1849, and he is buried on the banks of the Medina River southwest of San Antonio. He was a tower of inspiration to both slave and free persons of African descent. No mention

Greenbury Logan, a free African American who fought for Texas independence.
— TAAHO Collections, Austin, Texas

was made of his color or race; that fact paled in the face of his accomplishments.

Greenbury Logan

A free African American of color who fought for Texas independence was Greenbury Logan, a soldier under Fannin at the Battle of Concepcion. Logan was one of those who accompanied Ben Milam into San Antonio in December of 1835 when the Texas army defeated General Cos. He was wounded during the fighting in the vicinity of the main plaza in the heart of San Antonio, when a bullet passed through his right arm, permanently disabling him.

Logan immigrated to Texas from Missouri in 1831. He was granted a quarter league of land from Stephen F. Austin, located on the Chocolate Bayou in Brazoria County. His wounds made it impossible for him to continue in the blacksmith trade; therefore, he and his wife, Caroline, operated a boardinghouse at Brazoria.

According to Wharton's *History of Fort Bend County*:

The provisional government and the Republic were very antagonistic to free African Americans and they were denied residence here. Logan and others, including James Richardson (Handy's Jim) petitioned the Congress for permission to remain in Texas, and it was grudgingly given, but they were refused any muneration for their services, were not granted land as white soldiers were granted.

According to the late F. M. O. Fenn of Richmond, for many years an authority on Fort Bend County history:

> Greenbury Logan married a German woman. In later years a daughter of this union married a white man after Logan had died and settled in West Texas. They had a son, who grew up in ignorance of his grandfather's color. His mother told him that her father had left some land and that the grandson journeyed to Richmond to see about getting title to the land. He learned for the first time that his grandfather was of African descent.

Fifteen years after the Texas War for Independence, Greenbury and Caroline were living on a little farm on Big Creek valued at $600 and he was hammering his forge with an arm withered and crippled in the defense of his country. Logan was well-liked in Fort Bend County, and at each annual veterans' reunion in Richmond, he sat at the table with the white men. Slaves and free African Americans who knew him thought of him as being a hero, and he was an inspiration to them.

William E. (Bill) Goyens

The Texas Congress awarded a tract of land to William Goyens for his service to the Army of Texas in 1836. Goyens already was a wealthy man who operated a blacksmith shop and bought and sold land and racehorses at Nacogdoches. The first recorded mention of Goyens was in 1832, when a visitor to Texas named Benjamin Lundy wrote that Goyens' two white brothers-in-law from Georgia had come to visit him and their sister. Gen. Sam Houston appointed Goyens as agent to deal with the Cherokee Indians, and a successful treaty was negotiated. Goyens spoke Spanish and several Indian dialects, as well as English. He had freed himself, having run away from a life of slavery in South Carolina in 1821. He came to Texas via Galveston Island. Goyens later operated a sawmill on a 2,000-acre tract west of Nacogdoches on what is still known as "Goyens Hill," and also raised cattle and horses.

Historical records show that in 1834 he owned 4,160 acres of

William E. Goyens, born a slave in South Carolina and escaped to Texas in 1821. Became one of the wealthiest men in early Texas and rendered valuable service to the Texas Army in 1836.
— TAAHO Collections, Austin, Texas

improved land worth $20,600, two town lots, fifty head of cattle, two work horses, and other property. A State of Texas Centennial marker was placed at the Goyens Cemetery near Nacogdoches, and the inscription read:

William (Bill) Goyens, born a slave in South Carolina, 1794. Escaped to Texas in 1821. Rendered valuable assistance to the Army of Texas, 1836. Acquired wealth and was noted for his charity. Died at his home on Goyens Hill, 1856. His skin was black, his heart, true blue.

Goyens and his wife both died in 1856.

Samuel McCullough, Jr.

One of the first soldiers to shed blood during the Texas Revolution was Samuel McCullough, Jr. Samuel McCullough, Sr., a white man, came to Jackson County, Texas, in 1835, bringing with him two women of African descent (Peggy and Rose); his three daughters (Harriet, Jane, and Mahaly); a son, Samuel McCullough, Jr.; and a free African-American girl named Ulde. According to the *Southwestern Historical Quarterly,* no mention was made of the mother of this family, unless it was either Peggy or Rose.

Samuel McCullough, Jr., was born in South Carolina in 1810. His father was white and his mother was African American. Therefore, he was referred to as being a mulatto.

Samuel McCullough, Jr., was one of the first soldiers to shed blood during the Texas Revolution.
— TAAHO Collections, Austin, Texas

When a volunteer company was hastily organized near Matagorda early in October 1835 for the purpose of driving away some Mexicans alleged to be committing outrages at Victoria, Samuel McCullough, Jr., a free African American, was among them. The company under Capt. James Collinsworth did not rest at Victoria, but continued on to Goliad. Collinsworth estimated that there were 60 to 100 troops at Goliad, and he believed his "47 Good and Effective men," of whom McCullough was one, "all sufficient to take the place."

On October 9, the company stormed the fort. In a letter urging Capt. Benjamin Smith to reinforce him, Collinsworth explained his position and reported the battle in which one Mexican was killed, three wounded and captured, and three officers and twenty-one soldiers surrendered. He wrote, "I had one of my men wounded in the shoulder." This man was McCullough. He was the only one of the Texas troops wounded in that battle, and claimed to be "the first whose blood was shed in the war for independence."

McCullough paid dearly for this unique distinction, as his shattered shoulder left him a helpless invalid for nearly a year and handicapped for life. The wound in his right shoulder entitled McCullough to a bounty grant of one league of land in 1838. In 1840, he and his sisters were exempted from the order compelling free African Americans to leave Texas.

Despite his crippled shoulder, McCullough participated in the Plum Creek Fight in 1840 and was sent as a spy into San Antonio after its capture by Mexican General Adrian Woll in 1842. In 1852, he and his family moved to Bexar County, near Van Ormy, and he became an active member of the Texas Veterans Association. He died in 1893 and is buried in McCullough Cemetery near Macdona in Bexar County. He came to Texas, and now it will always be his home.

Peter Allen died with his fellow Texan soldiers on Palm Sunday at the Goliad Massacre.
— TAAHO Collections, Austin, Texas

Peter Allen

An African-American musician named Peter Allen was with Col. James W. Fannin at the Goliad Massacre; he played a flute and the banjo. He died on Palm Sunday, with his white comrades.

When Col. James Fannin called for volunteers to form an army to go to Matamoros and face the Mexicans, Peter Allen, a free African American, answered the call. Allen came to Texas from Pennsylvania. He operated a blacksmith shop at Huntsville. Allen volunteered for Captain Wyatt's company at Huntsville in 1835 and was designated the company musician.

The Mexicans were invading Texas in force, and Fannin decided to wait for them at Goliad instead of going on to Matamoros. The main forces of the Mexican army stormed the Alamo from February 23 to March 6; they finally took it in a final attack without quarter.

About the middle of March, Fannin received orders from Houston to retreat to Victoria; on March 19 he started to fall back.

He had gone but a few miles when his force was surrounded by Mexicans, and a fight ensued which ended at nightfall. The following morning, finding himself in a hopeless situation, Fannin surrendered. A week later, on Palm Sunday, the prisoners were marched out under guard and shot without warning. Peter Allen was among the 300 Texan soldiers who were slaughtered. The bodies of the murdered soldiers were piled in a heap, covered with brush, and burned. Allen gave his life trying to make Texas his home.

Dick the Drummer was a soldier in the Texas Army during the Texas Revolution.
— TAAHO Collections, Austin, Texas

Dick the Drummer

Several African Americans participated in the Battle of San Jacinto in various capacities. Their patriotic spirit is personified by a gray-haired free man of African descent known as "Dick the Drummer." In addition to being at San Jacinto, Dick went on to serve as a drummer with the U.S. Army in the Mexican war at Monterrey and Buena Vista.

Kilman refers to an article in the *Texas Gazette*, May 21, 1850, which tells of an African American named Dick at San Jacinto, saying, "By the effective beating of his drum, this gray-headed descendant of Ham carried consternation into the ranks of Santa Anna's myrmidons." The article does not give the man's last name nor is it found elsewhere. Reference is made to a dinner given for San Jacinto veterans in May 1850, "the venerable drummer" was present "and seemed to live his early days over again when witnessing the ceremonies of the joyous occasion." The *State Gazette* gave "Honor to the patriotic old man" and predicted that "his name will be handed down to posterity associated with those immortal heroes who wear the well earned laurels plucked upon the deathless plains of San Jacinto."

Joe Travis fought heroically beside his owner, William B. Travis, at the Alamo in 1836.

— TAAHO Collections, Austin, Texas

At the Alamo

When the Mexican army captured the Alamo and killed Col. William B. Travis and all of his soldiers, they spared his slave, Joe Travis, who was considered a combatant. Joe went to Washington-on-the-Brazos and gave one of the first eyewitness accounts of the fall of the Alamo to members of the provisional Texas government. Joe described the deaths of Crockett, Bowie, and Travis. He told how he was taken to Gen. Antonio López de Santa Anna, who questioned him about the Texas army. Joe said he was detained in San Antonio long enough to watch a review of the Mexican troops and was told that they numbered 8,000. He was then permitted to go.

The battle at the Alamo is much more significant when we include African Americans who fought, bled, and died there.

John, a male slave, who belonged to Francis De Sauque, was left at the Alamo by his master. John armed himself and fought to the death alongside the other heroes in the Alamo, and lies buried with them in a common, unmarked grave. He was willing to fight and die for a freedom he never had.

Other persons of African descent who were at the Alamo include a man called Charlie and a woman who was a cook named Betty, who had been a cook for James Bowie.

Sam, the slave of Jim Bowie, fought at Bowie's side at the Alamo, and was questioned and released by Santa Anna when the battle ended.

Emily Morgan, called the "Yellow Rose of Texas." This beautiful slave girl sacrificed much for the freedom of Texas from Mexico.
— TAAHO Collections, Austin, Texas

Emily Morgan

Much is known about Emily Morgan, "The Yellow Rose of Texas." Emily was named Emily D. West at birth, but she took the name of her slave master and was known as Emily Morgan. Col. James K. Morgan brought Emily to Texas from New York in 1835. Martha Anne Turner describes Emily as "a golden-skinned girl resembling a Latin goddess."

According to Andrew F. Muir's account in his "The Free Negro in Harris County, Texas," Emily was not only breathtakingly beautiful, she was exceptionally intelligent. It is puzzling to note how Texas historians, time and time again, have ignored the gigantic contribution made by Emily to our victory at San Jacinto. When Santa Anna led his 1,000 infantrymen into New Washington (present day La Porte) on April 18, 1836, the colony was deserted. Mexican soldiers looted provisions from the home of Colonel Morgan. A few of Morgan's slaves still remained at the house. Emily Morgan was one of the slaves who had stayed. According to Turner, "legend asserts that the Mexican General first observed the graceful movement of the beautiful slave girl Emily, at the boat landing as she was helping others to load a flatboat with supplies . . . . When Santa Anna saw this bronze beauty it did not take him long to decide that Emily would be an integral part of the loot."

Santa Anna and his troops left New Washington on April 19. The soldiers burned the town and took all of the animals and provisions they could find. Santa Anna took the beautiful slave girl and a light-skinned, young slave boy called Turner. According to reliable sources, Santa Anna tried to bribe Turner, a printer's apprentice of above-average intelligence, to obtain information about the location of Houston and his army. Emily told Turner where Houston was garrisoned and he escaped the Mexicans and went directly to Houston to warn him of the approach of General Santa Anna and his army. Thus, Emily Morgan, loyal to the Texans, conveyed her warning indirectly to Houston before she reached the battle area herself, according to Turner and others.

Reports in the *Texas Almanac* reveal that the Mexicans were ready to advance on the morning of April 20. Santa Anna learned of Houston's position. Turner had returned to the Mexican forces. In an effort to delay the Mexicans, the slave boy, Turner, misled Santa Anna into thinking that Houston was on the Trinity River with his army. The claim, after causing brief confusion, was found to be false.

Again, according to Martha Anne Turner, when Santa Anna found Emily at Morgan's plantation, he had been deprived of feminine companionship for two weeks. Emily was a replacement for the "bride" of his mock marriage in San Antonio before the final assault on the Alamo. Due to an accumulation of circumstances, Melchora Iniega Barrera, the seventeen-year-old common-law bride of Santa Anna, was sent to Mexico City, never to return to Texas and Santa Anna.

When Santa Anna reached the area of San Jacinto Bay, perhaps preoccupied with the impending stay with the beautiful slave girl, Emily, he chose a very poor location for his camp. He ordered his fancy red-and-white-striped tent to be set up and he proceeded to commit several foolish and unmilitary antics designed to impress his copper-toned female guest. Emily's presence with Santa Anna must have impaired his judgment to the extent that he was ineffective as a commanding general on the afternoon of April 21, 1836. If this is true, as it seems to be, Emily Morgan deserves as much credit for the Texas victory at San Jacinto as do Houston, "Deaf" Smith, Arnold, and all the others. After the Battle of San Jacinto, Emily returned to the Morgan plantation.

Emily was a slave who was transported from the east by her master, Col. James K. Morgan. She seemed to have possessed exceptional intelligence and wisdom. She was also acquainted with "Deaf" Smith, Hendrick Arnold, and other Texas spies. These spies from time to time received valuable information from Emily and from the Morgan plantation.

On the night of April 23, Emily supposedly told Colonel Morgan and others, in detail, about her experiences with General Santa Anna of the Mexican army.

When it was all over, Emily was given her freedom and was allowed to return to her home in New York. William Bollaert said on July 7, 1842, that:

> The Battle of San Jacinto was probably lost by the Mexicans owing to the influence of a mulatto girl, Emily, belonging to Colonel James Morgan. She was closeted in the tent with General Santana at the time the cry was made: "The enemy! They come! They come!" She detained Santana so long that order could not be restored readily.

There should be no doubt that Emily Morgan's actions at San Jacinto have earned for her a rightful place in Texas history as a loyal heroine of the first order.

Not only did she help win Texas independence, Emily inspired a song, written from a poem by an African slave admirer: "The Yellow Rose of Texas."

Other Freedom Fighters

James Richardson

The question is often asked: Why did slaves and freedmen choose to aid in the Texans' fight for independence? It was perhaps because they were perceptive and knew what the Mexican government was and had been under despotic leadership, and what the potential could be in a true democratic evolutionary situation in Texas. It was the potential lesser of two evils.

James Richardson came to Texas in 1836 as an indentured servant. When his indenture was over, he refused a pass to return home a free man. Richardson sold oysters and refreshments between Velasco and San Luis on the coast near Galveston. He was also an innkeeper. Richardson joined the Texas army when he was sixty years old in 1836. He enrolled in Capt. Thomas Bell's garrison at Velasco. He was present at San Jacinto but was not permitted to see action; he worked with a supply unit.

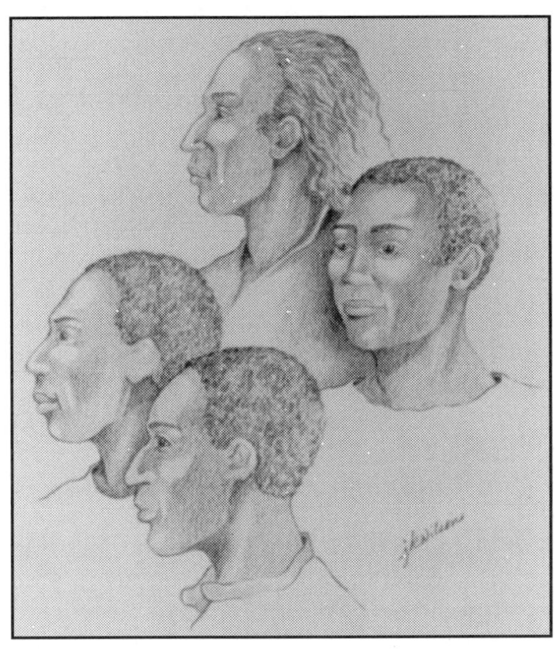

The Ashworth family.
— TAAHO Collections,
Austin, Texas

The Ashworth Family

Free African Americans comprised a very small population in the Texas colony in the early 1800s. In one small area they did constitute a fairly numerous minority. They could vote, hold office, and serve on juries. They were able to own property and to accumulate wealth.

In the 1830s, several mixed couples named Ashworth moved from Calcasieu Parish, Louisiana, across the Sabine River into Jefferson County, Texas. The forefathers of the Ashworth clan were four men who appear to have been brothers.

William Ashworth moved to Lorenzo de Zavala's colony in East Texas in 1831, Aaron migrated in 1833, Abner in 1834, and Moses in 1833. Abner gave money and supplies generously to the Texas army during the Texas Revolution. William contributed to the war effort and furnished both supplies and money; he also served in the Texas army during the summer after Santa Anna's surrender. Two other Ashworths, Luke and Tapter, enlisted in Captain Hargrove's army. There is no evidence of any of the Ashworths fighting with the army during the Texas Revolution; their participation at that time was limited to providing aid such as money and supplies.

James Robinson
— TAAHO Collections,
Austin, Texas

James Robinson

Most African Americans who migrated to Texas were slaves, very few were free, and there were others who were indentured servants. James Robinson was an indentured servant of Robert E. Handy. Robinson came to Texas in 1836. He was offered a pass home; instead he enlisted in the Texas army with Handy. He expected to fight with the Texas army, but was ordered to remain in a rear area at the Battle of San Jacinto.

Thomas Stevens
— TAAHO Collections,
Austin, Texas

Thomas Stevens

From various fragments of historical documents we do know that there were an undetermined number of free and slave persons of African descent who took part in the Texas Revolution. Thomas Stevens was a slave. He fought with the Texan army in the siege of Bexar at San Antonio, December 1835. Stevens was reported to have also fought in Somervell's campaign in 1842.

Mack Smith
— TAAHO Collections,
Austin, Texas

Mack Smith

Although African slaves played a significant role in the Texas Revolution, their contributions have been ignored by historians. Mack Smith was a slave of Ben Fort Smith. Mack fought in the Battle of San Jacinto. Mack came to Texas in 1832. He was a soldier in the Texas army throughout the War for Independence. He was primarily employed transporting messages and goods for McKinney and Williams.

Cary McKinney
— TAAHO Collections,
Austin, Texas

Cary McKinney

Cary was a slave of Thomas F. McKinney. Cary served as a messenger during the Texas Revolutionary War. Because of his faithful, efficient service, he was given his freedom after the war. He operated a livery stable in Galveston.

Robert Thompson
— TAAHO Collections,
Austin, Texas

Robert Thompson

Robert Thompson was a free African American. He became a rancher in Montgomery County in 1831. Thompson sought to volunteer his services as a soldier in the Texas army; he was not accepted. Thompson did, however, find a way to serve his beloved state. He gave an expensive mare horse and a rifle to the army. He neither expected nor received compensation.

Peter Martin
— TAAHO Collections,
Austin, Texas

Peter Martin

African Americans volunteered to be of service to their home state in whatever way they could. Peter Martin was a slave of Wyly Martin. During the Texas Revolution, he hired out his own time and his own wagon and team. He carried supplies and provisions to the Texas army in the field. Because of his faithful and valuable service, he was given his freedom after the war ended.

Joseph Sovereign
— TAAHO Collections,
Austin, Texas

Joseph Sovereign

Joseph Sovereign fought at San Jacinto. He gave his birthplace as Portugal, and came to Texas in 1835. After the Battle of San Jacinto, he re-enlisted in the Texas army for three months. He was captain of a company of volunteers. Sovereign lived in Houston afterward, and when he died in 1877, the health department listed him as "colored."

Joseph Tate
— TAAHO Collections,
Austin, Texas

Joseph Tate

Tate was a free African American. He was listed in the army rolls as a member of Capt. James Shessire's company of Jasper volunteers, March 23, 1836.

President Lamar approved an act of the Texas Congress in 1839 for Tate's relief. It recited that Tate, then residing in Jasper, "is hereby authorized to continue as a resident of the Republic, subject to such laws and regulations as the Congress may from time to time pass in reference to such persons of color as were residents of Texas prior to the Declaration of Independence."

The act further recited that "whereas the said Joseph Tate did faithfully serve a term of four months military service in Captain James Shessire's company in the campaign of 1836, the auditor is hereby authorized and required to admit to audit and the treasurer to pay $213.50 in the treasury notes of the Republic, in lieu of bounty lands of account of said military service."

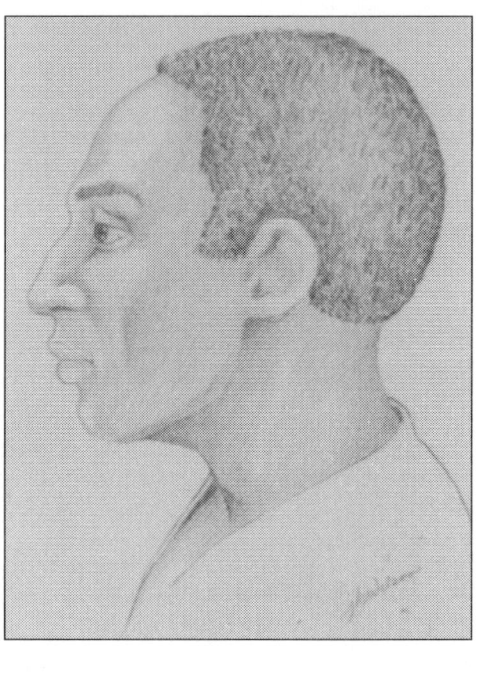

Joe Griffin
— TAAHO Collections,
Austin, Texas

Joe Griffin

Six years after the revolution had ended at San Jacinto, Joe Griffin got caught up in its aftermath. The fighting was still going on at various places. In September 1842, Gen. Adrian Woll led 1,000 Mexican troops into San Antonio. Judges, city and county officials, and city merchants were all taken prisoners.

Samuel Augustine Maverick, Joe's master, was captured and put in prison. Griffin told Mary Maverick about her husband's capture. Mary promised Joe his freedom if he could help her husband escape. Joe died in the defeat and capture of William Dawson's command by Mexican troops near San Antonio in September 1842.

African Americans in the Republic of Texas

The status of African Americans changed drastically when the Republic became a living, functioning organism. They could not re-

Free African Americans were no longer welcome in the Republic of Texas after the revolution.

— Painting by Bruce Marshall.
Courtesy Institute of Texan Cultures,
San Antonio, Texas

main in Texas and own land without special permission from Congress. This permission was granted in a number of cases to freedmen who had played important roles in the Revolution. Others remained illegally, but social attitudes changed more slowly than laws, and they were unmolested for a period of time.

Free African Americans in the Republic of Texas

The laws under the Republic of Texas mandated that free persons of color who were determined to have one-eighth African or mixed blood could not vote, own property, testify in court against Anglos, or engage in interracial marriages.

The free African-American policy of the Republic of Texas, crystallized in the passage of the definitive act of February 5, 1840, which remained in effect until emancipation, was to prove more effectual in theory than in practice. By the terms of the law, immigration of free African Americans was prohibited, and they were required to remove themselves from Texas within two years on penalty of sale into slavery.

The 1836 constitution mandated an appeal to Congress by freedmen who wished to reside in Texas. In 1837, Congress voted to allow all freedpersons of color in Texas at independence to remain if they continued to abide by the laws of the Republic. Several prewar African-American settlers then entreated Congress for property rights, and postwar immigrants sought approval of residence. Despite Anglo-supporting signatures on many of the petitions, Congress refused to pass any of the requests in 1838 and 1839.

In December 1840, Congress again granted prerevolutionary free persons of African ancestry who were Texas residents the right to remain in Texas along with some relatives who came after the war. In 1843, Congress granted property rights to several African-American petitioners. It refused similar petitions from others. Most seem to have continued in control of their property despite local disputes and harassment.

Freedmen in Jefferson and Orange Counties

Many of the freed persons in the area of Jefferson and Orange counties were members of one large family named Ashworth. The progenitors of the clan in southeast Texas were four men who appear to have been brothers. This family has been mentioned earlier in this chapter as supporters of the Texas Revolution. Within two years of the founding of the Republic of Texas the Ashworths had established themselves a place in the community, for in 1838 William Ashworth obtained from the Jefferson County Board of Roads and Revenues a franchise to operate a ferry across Lake Sabine and up the Neches River to Beaumont. The esteem in which their neighbors held them placed them in good stead a short while later. In 1840, the Texas Congress ordered all free African Americans within the Republic to remove themselves from the national limits within two years, upon pain of being sold into slavery. The Ashworths' friends immediately came to their rescue.

One prominent man in the county, G. A. Pattillo, wrote to President Mirabeau B. Lamar enclosing and endorsing the memorial of Jesse Ashworth for permission to remain within the Republic until the next meeting of Congress, when, apparently, he proposed to petition for a relief act. In this letter Pattillo confessed having known Ashworth in the United States and Texas for fifteen years, during which time he had always maintained a reputation for good character and for being "a quiet and unassuming good citizen." In addition, Ashworth was described as "a man of some property" and therefore "of some benefit to the government."

At the ensuing session of Congress, three petitions were presented on behalf of Jefferson County free African Americans. Each of the three was signed by virtually all of the prominent office holders and electors of the community. One petition represented that Abner and William Ashworth had lived in Texas for six years and had "contributed generously to the advancement of the Revolution." A second showed that Aaron, David, Joshua, and William Ashworth, who were mistakenly identified as brothers, had resided within the county for two years and were "peaceable and Respectable Citizens." The third described Elisha Thomas in similar language and identified him as having been a resident at the time of the Declaration of Independence. All three petitions requested Congress to pass relief acts permitting the several free African Americans to remain unmolested within Texas.

Upon the many similar petitions presented to it, Congress acted favorably in only a few cases, but these included the free African Americans in Jefferson County. The select committee of the House of Representatives to whom their petitions were submitted reported that free African Americans as a general rule should not be encouraged but these were exceptions, for they had contributed both their substance and their personal service to the achievement of independence and, in addition, had "at all times conducted themselves well" and had proved themselves "men of good Credit wherever they are known [,] having been at all times punctual to their engagements [,] upright in their dealings and peaceable in their disposition." The attached bill, exempting Aaron, Abner, David, and William Ashworth and Elisha Thomas, together with their families, from the operation of the law of February 5, 1840, passed both houses with hardly a dissent and was approved by the president on December 12, 1840. By this act, the Ashworths and Thomas were permitted to remain in Texas, but a short while later they and others were obliged to seek further relief.

In 1842, a traveling land board charged with detecting fraudulent land certificates refused to certify for patents the headrights and bounty certificates which the board of land commissioners of Jefferson County had issued to Aaron, Moses, and William Ashworth, Henry and John Bird, Aaron Nelson, and Elijah and Elisha Thomas, all free Negroes, on the ground that the law did not cover persons of their color. Nevertheless, all three members of the traveling board, as well as three members of the Jefferson board and some seventy-odd citizens, petitioned Congress that these "good and worthy members of the Community" labored "by reason of their being people of colour under great and embarrassing inconvenience" and requested Congress to direct issuance of the patents. Again, with little disagreement, both houses passed, and the president signed the suggested bill, instructing the commissioner of the General Land Office to issue the required patents "in the same manner, as though the same had been recommended by the Board of Commissioners to detect fraudulent Land Claims for patent."

Except for the two decennial censuses of 1850 and 1860, there are no records showing the exact number of free African Americans in Jefferson and Orange counties at any given time. In 1850, there were sixty-three free African Americans in Jefferson County, of whom thirty-eight were named Ashworth. Three of the original Ashworth brothers were then alive, each with a family.

> Aaron Ashworth, 47 years, born in South Carolina
> Mary Ashworth, 40 years, born in Kentucky
> Samuel Ashworth, 13 years, born in Texas
> Nancy Ashworth, 10 years, born in Texas
> Sublett Ashworth, 9 years, born in Louisiana
> William Ashworth, 7 years, born in Texas
> Mary Ashworth, 4 years, born in Texas
> Aaron Ashworth, Jr., 2 years, born in Louisiana

At this time Aaron was a farmer and estimated his real property at $3,764. He had the unique distinction in the county of having in his house a schoolmaster, a white man named John A. Woods, presumably employed to tutor his four children of school age, who certainly attended school during the year.

> Abner Ashworth, 41 years, born in Louisiana
> Sidney Jane Ashworth, 5 years, born in Texas
> Lydia Ann Ashworth, 2 years, born in Texas

Abner was a farmer with real estate valued at $400. His wife, Rosalia, aged thirty-six, a native of Louisiana, was white.

> William Ashworth, Sr., 57 years, born in South Carolina
> Clark Ashworth, 18 years, born in Texas
> Emily Ashworth, 14 years, born in Texas
> Nancy Ashworth, 13 years, born in Texas
> Melissa Ashworth, 9 years, born in Texas
> Jane Ashworth, 7 years, born in Texas
> Louisa Ashworth, 4 years, born in Texas
> David Ashworth, 2 years, born in Texas

William's wife, Leide or Delaide, aged forty-six, a native of Louisiana, was white. William described himself as a farmer, with holdings to the value of $7,205, and Clark as a stock raiser.

There were also five families of second-generation Ashworths.

> Aaron Ashworth, Jr., 29 years, born in Louisiana
> Serena Ashworth, 22 years, born in Louisiana
> Sarah Jane Ashworth, 3 years, born in Texas
> Martha Ann Ashworth, 1 year, born in Texas
> Jordan Ashworth, 20 years, born in Louisiana

Aaron, Jr. was a farmer and Jordan a stock raiser.

> David Ashworth, 29 years, born in Louisiana
> Anna Ashworth, 18 years, born in Louisiana
> Valentine Ashworth, 1 year, born in Texas

David was also a stock raiser.

> Henderson Ashworth, 23 years, born in Louisiana
> Mary J. Ashworth, 1 year, born in Texas

Henderson's wife, Letitia, aged seventeen, a native of Texas, was white. Henderson was a stock raiser.

> Joshua Ashworth, 34 years, born in Louisiana
> Sarah Ashworth, 20 years, born in Louisiana
> Allen Ashworth, 3 years, born in Texas
> Eli Ashworth, 1 year, born in Texas

Joshua was a farmer.

> Luke Ashworth, 26 years, born in Louisiana
> Lucinda Ashworth, 27 years, born in Louisiana
> Luke Ashworth, Jr., 4 years, born in Texas
> Rebecca Ashworth, 3 years, born in Texas
> Elijah Ashworth, 1 year, born in Texas

Luke was a stock raiser with property valued at $800.

There were five other free African-American families in the county with surnames other than Ashworth. Sarah Burwick, aged sixteen, a native of Texas, was the wife of William Burwick, an illiterate white laborer, aged twenty-one, also a native of Texas. They had no children.

> Eliza Bunch, 38 years, born in Louisiana
> Hiram Bunch, 14 years, born in Texas
> Jackson Bunch, 12 years, born in Texas
> Elijah Bunch, 7 years, born in Texas
> Elisha Bunch, 5 years, born in Texas
> Washington Bunch, 3 years, born in Texas
> Ephraim Bunch, 3 years, born in Texas

Eliza was either a widow or the wife of a slave, freedman or white man who maintained his residence elsewhere.

> Elvina Carter, 25 years, born in Louisiana
> Sidney J. Carter, 8 years, born in Louisiana
> Virgil S. Carter, 6 years, born in Louisiana
> Henry P. Carter, 4 years, born in Louisiana
> Jonathan M. Carter, 2 years, born in Louisiana
> Rebecca Ann Carter, 1 year, born in Louisiana

Elvina was the wife of a white farmer, J. M. Carter, aged thirty-four, a native of Illinois.

> Robert Nelson, 25 years, born in Louisiana
> Mary Ann Nelson, 20 years, born in Louisiana
> Uriah Nelson, 1 year, born in Texas
> Josiah Nelson, 1 year, born in Texas
> Easter Gains, 19 years, born in Louisiana

Robert was a farmer.

> William Nelson, 36 years, born in Louisiana
> Ellen Nelson, 9 years, born in Louisiana
> Elizabeth Nelson, 5 years, born in Louisiana
> Cynthia Nelson, 2 years, born in Texas
> Moses Nelson, 30 years, born in Louisiana

William's wife was an illiterate white woman, named Sarah, aged twenty-seven. William was a farmer and Moses a laborer.

Not the least interesting content of these records is the evidence of miscegenation. Three African-American men had white wives, and two African-American women had white husbands. Of the ten adult males listed, one was a laborer, four were stock raisers, and five farmers.

Ten years later there were only two free African Americans in

Jefferson County and but twenty-nine in Orange. The principal cause of this decrease will be hereinafter discussed. The elder Aaron and his wife were listed in 1860 with six children, four of whom — Sublett, William, Mary, and Aaron — had been listed the previous decade and two of whom had been born subsequent to the 1850 census: Harriet, aged ten, and Abner, aged six, both natives of Texas. The whereabouts of Samuel and Mary, listed in 1850, was not made evident. Five of the children had attended school within the year. Aaron was still listed as a farmer, with real and personal property valued at $4,870, and Sublett as a stock raiser.

Abner apparently had died during the decade, but his widow and three children — Sidney, Lidda A., and Phillipa, aged five, a native of Texas — were listed. Rozella's property was valued at $11,444. William and his wife had survived, and they were listed together with their children: Melissa, Jane, Louisa, David, and a second Louisa, aged two, a native of Texas. William was described as a laborer, with property valued at $4,000.

Luke and Lucinda had seven children. In addition to the three listed in 1850 were Delilah, aged eight; Sarah, six; Melissa, five; and Clark, three, all born in Texas. Luke was also a laborer, with property valued at $1,160.

Eliza Bunch had disappeared, but three of her sons — Hiram, Elijah, and Washington — were all listed as laborers.

These data are not sufficiently numerous to serve as the basis for any generalizations, but it is interesting to note that during the decade 1850–1859 William's occupation changed from farmer to laborer and Luke's from stock raiser to laborer. During the same period, the value of William's real estate dropped from $7,205 to $4,000 and Luke's from $800 to $160. These reductions, however, were probably the result of sales rather than of depreciation.

That the free African Americans in the area were no worse off than the bulk of their white neighbors and indeed better off than most is evident from their real estate holdings. Thirteen members of the family acquired land within Jefferson and Orange counties, which they used principally for grazing large herds of cattle. In 1850, six of them were listed in the agricultural census. One of the two Aaron Ashworths there listed, probably the younger, was the largest cattle raiser in the entire county, with 2,570 head, 220 head more than the runner-up.

Not only did the free African Americans own land and cattle, but they also owned slaves. This was more unusual in Texas than in Louisiana, where many free African Americans had large slaveholdings. In 1839, William Ashworth sold Lucy, aged about twenty, and her child, Sarah, about two, for $1,200, probably Texas money, and a short while later he purchased for $1,150 an eighteen- or nineteen-year-old slave, Thornton, whom he sold three years later for $1,000. In 1846, Abner Ashworth bought Moses, aged twenty-two, and in 1863, Mary Ashworth bequeathed a slave, Peter, to one of her sons. At least one slave held by the Ashworths interpreted his ownership by a freedman to be loss of caste, as reported by a Northern traveler:

> At another house where we stopped . . . we heard some conversation upon a slave of the neighborhood, who had been sold to a free African American who refused to live with him, saying he wouldn't be a servant to a nigger. All agreed that he was right, although the man was well known to be kind to his slaves, and would always sell any of them who wished it. The slave had been sold because he wouldn't mind.

Despite this attitude on the part of some slaves, in 1850, Aaron owned six slaves, Abner three, Joshua one, and William two. Ten years later Aaron, the white widow of Abner, and the white wife of William each owned four.

Free African Americans in southeastern Texas, we have seen, acquired both land and slaves. Their equality was not, however, merely economic. As hereinbefore mentioned, some of them intermarried, at least by common law, with whites, and their social equality is nowhere better demonstrated than in the titles of respect given to both their men and women. As early as 1844 and as late as 1861, Ashworth men and the women, both white and black, they married were given the titles of Mr. and Miss by county clerks when filling out marriage licenses.

Summary

Finally, we can say that several hundred African Americans lived in Texas from 1836 to 1863. Several had made Texas their home prior to the Revolution. Men of African ancestry served with Texas armies during the Revolution and a few were granted land for their services. Some African-American women such as Emily Morgan also found ways to be a part of the war at the Alamo and at San Jacinto.

A few free African Americans lived in the towns; however, most were farmers in rural areas. In 1840, the Congress of the Republic passed a law allowing free African Americans to petition for the right to remain in Texas. Most petitions were denied, but free people stayed, and for the most part were unmolested.

Chapter 2

Statehood to Civil War

1845–1863

From statehood to the Civil War, the situation of African Americans in Texas deteriorated rapidly. In 1845 a major part of the population of Texas comprised a significant number of African Americans. Some were free, but many were slaves. In West, North, Central, and South Central Texas the slave population was small.

The situation was different, however, throughout East Texas, Southeast Texas, and the Brazos River Valley between 1836 and 1860. In these areas, African descendants made up the second-largest group of people in the state. Anglo Americans were the largest group.

In Chapter 1 it was mentioned how some African Americans like William Goyens, Greenbury Logan, and Hendrick Arnold came to Texas before 1836 as free persons. And there were others like them. Emanuel J. Hardin came to Texas in 1822, settled in the Brazoria area, and became a prosperous farmer. He married Tomas Morgan, who came to Texas in 1832 as a slave. She managed to save enough money to buy her freedom before marrying Hardin. An-

Field slaves in the Republic of Texas.
— Institute of Texan Cultures, San Antonio, Texas

other well-known free African American was Robert Thompson of Montgomery County. He arrived in Texas in 1831 and soon had a successful ranch.

During the days of the Republic, the legislature approved a law which threatened all free African Americans in Texas. In 1840 the Texas Congress passed a law that forbade the immigration of any more free African Americans and ordered all free African Americans then living in Texas to leave. Those who did not leave were to be made slaves. The law was never seriously enforced.

There were several reasons such a harsh law was passed. Some Anglos feared that the free African Americans would lead the slaves in a revolt for their freedom, a revolt sure to be bloody. Others were probably jealous of the progress made by men like Goyens, Hardin, and Thompson.

Anglo Texans feared more than individual violence or escapes. They were concerned about the threat of a slave revolt, which the legislature defined as "an assemblage of three or more, with arms, with intent to obtain their liberty by force." In September 1856, Anglos in Colorado County announced the discovery of an insurrection plan which involved over two hundred slaves armed with pistols and knives. They apparently intended to kill anyone who opposed them, seize supplies, and escape into Mexico.

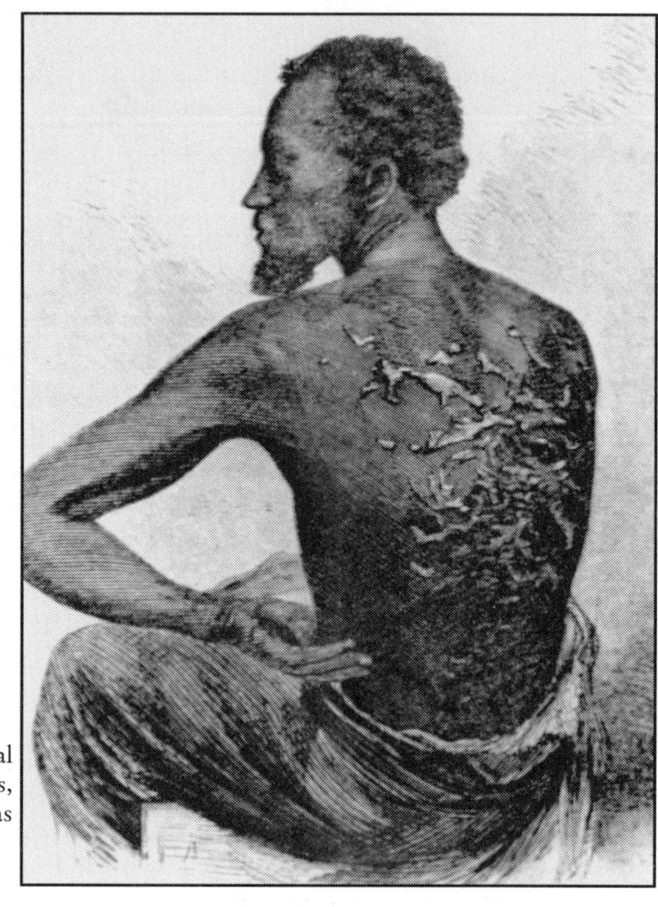

Many slaves were whipped for even the slightest provocation.
— Texas Historical Commission files, Austin, Texas

In 1850 the United States census showed that there were 58,161 slaves in Texas. In 1860 the number had more than tripled to 182,566. Three of every ten Texans were enslaved Africans.

Farmers who wanted to increase their earnings in the 1850s turned to slavery to have more laborers to clear the fields, plant the seeds, and harvest the crops. Infants were taken from their parents and sold like dumb animals for around $100. Field hands were sold for $1,200 to $2,000 each. Slaves with special skills such as carpentry, blacksmithing, metallurgy, and cooking brought higher prices. This investment in enslaved human beings brought profits, and unfortunately, the state's economy came to depend on slavery.

The treatment of slaves varied from slaveholder to slaveholder. Some probably cared for their slaves and provided them with ad-

This slave ran away from his slave-home to live in the Florida Everglades.
— William Loren Katz Collection, New York City

equate food and clothing. Other slaveholders were cruel. They overworked their slaves, seldom provided them with sufficient food or clothing, and often whipped them for even the slightest provocation.

Even under the gentlest slaveholders, slavery was horrible and inhuman. Within the peculiar system of slavery in Texas, one human being was totally at the mercy of the other. One group had full protection and support of the legal system from the courthouse to the statehouse, while the other group was totally void of legal recourse of any sort. A slave in Texas was not allowed basic human rights. Families often were separated when a wife or children were sold.

Like any other human beings, most slaves longed for freedom and a better way of life. The number who ran away during 1850, just five short years after statehood, rose sharply. A large percentage of runaway slaves were recaptured. Those slaves who did escape often found life difficult in frontier society. Many Anglo settlers did not welcome them. Runaway slaves always had to be alert. At any time

Chief John Horse, leader of the Black-Seminole Indians.
— William Loren Katz Collection, New York City

they might be seized and returned to their owners. Nevertheless, some slaves were able to escape to Mexico or to Indian Territory.

For a number of years, runaway slaves fled to Florida and lived among the Seminole Indians. Eventually, they intermarried. When the federal government moved these Black-Seminole Indians to the reservation near Fort Sill, Oklahoma, in 1848, they experienced prejudices. Some of them were kidnapped and sold into slavery. In 1849, Chief John Horse led a group of Black-Seminoles across Texas. They settled on both sides of the Rio Grande, living in Mexico at times and living in Texas at other times between 1850 and 1875. In the early period of migration, they lived in the vicinity of Eagle Pass, Texas, as well as Piedras Negras, Nacimiento, Matamoros and Guerro in Mexico.

Descendants of Chief John Horse and his tribe still live in South Texas, primarily near Brackettville. The chief's grandson, Robert Jefferson, attended public school in Del Rio, Texas. Robert is the son of the late John Jefferson, grandson of Chief John Horse, a Black-Seminole Indian scout with the 10th United States Cavalry. Chief Horse is described as a large, tall, handsome and bold brown-skinned man who wore a turban, bracelets, skirts and leggings. He was said to be a daring horseman. He died in Eagle Pass in 1877.

The period from 1845 to 1863 was a bleak period for African

Americans in Texas. It was slavery and the slave trade that provided the initial thrust to the Texan economy. It was slavery that built Galveston and Houston. Slavery shaped the Constitutions of 1836, 1845 and January 28, 1861. Slavery was a major formative influence in the overall development of Texas, and it is difficult if not impossible to understand the African American or the Anglo American or Texas without previous comprehension of that peculiar institution. It is necessary that slavery in Texas be understood from the inside out; in other words, from the standpoint of the slave. Slavery in Texas was a total system of social, economic, political and sexual exploitation based on force and violence and an ideology of racism.

At its heyday, in the period before the Civil War, this system of forced labor claimed the collective energies of nearly 200,000 slaves, most of whom labored to raise stable crops on plantation-sized units in the Brazos Valley area and the piney woods areas of East Texas. Smaller plantations and farms existed in Central and North Texas, where some slave labor was used to a much lesser degree. Slavery in Texas had foreboding political and psychological incriminations. Slavery in Texas not only stole the labor of the slaves, it also stole the meaning of their lives and subtly distorted the lives of their tormentors. It has been rightly suggested that slavery in Texas was designed to turn human beings into human machines. The disgraceful slave codes enacted by the state legislature of Texas outlawed the humanity of the slave by investing slavemasters with absolute power.

It was a crime under these laws for a slave to read and write. It was a crime, punishable by a brutal lashing, for slaves to stand upright and look a white man in the eye. It was a crime for slaves to hold meetings or religious services without white supervision or witnesses. In Texas, slaves could not congregate in groups of more than two or three away from the home plantations. Normally, they could not beat drums, wear fine clothes, or carry sticks or weapons. They could not legally marry, nor protect their children or their mates.

The power of the Texas Legislature stood behind these oppressive laws. An immense police force was created by the state to overwhelm the slaves and to beat them into submission. Slave patrols, authorized by state laws, policed plantation areas and made regular searches of slave cabins looking for weapons or evidence of escape plans. Violence was not an accidental by-product of the slave system in Texas; the system itself was violent.

Slavery in Texas was characterized by systematic brainwashing. Slaves were taught to hate themselves and to stand in fear of every white man. There was military-type regimentation on the plantations. For males and females, for young and old, life on the plantations and farms in Texas was a round of toil, whips, bells, and military-type formations.

Despite the terror of bells, despite the regimentation and brainwashing, despite the whips and guns and chains, these involuntary servants kept a sense of expectancy and an unbelievable optimism. The slaves on Texas farms and plantations and elsewhere believed that their suffering had a meaning and that someday it would come to an end. As Ralph Ellison has said: "Any people who could endure all of that brutalization and keep together, who could undergo such dismemberment and resuscitate itself, and endure until it could take the initiative in achieving its own freedom is obviously more than the sum of its brutalization. Seen in this perspective, theirs has been one of the great human experiences and one of the great triumphs of the human spirit in modern times, in fact, in the history of the world."

The attitude of the church in Texas toward slavery and the slave system was inconsistent with Christian principles. The Anglo church actually approved of the system. Little relief from such malevolent conditions could then be expected when almost all institutions of the state, including the Christian church, approved slavery. The legal establishment of an organized church for blacks was not allowed in Texas from 1845 to 1865. Slaves and freedmen were forced to accept what accommodations were given them in white churches. They gradually yielded room, then, to the increasing membership of the whites until the people of color were forced to the galleries or compelled to hold special services following those of the whites.

Often efforts were made to establish separate churches for slaves. These segregated churches were placed in charge of white ministers. In many situations the African slave was left in a heathen state. The awful condition of the slave became more pronounced as churches which were supposed to speak in behalf of the African descendants tended to have little to say against slavery. The Methodist church in Texas, which attacked slavery during early statehood, later took the position of saying nothing at all about it. The Baptists had practically the same attitude.

There were, moreover, white churchmen who were busy writing articles on the wisdom of Providence in bringing the Africans into such servitude. Africans, they said, had been cursed of God. When these ministers preached to the slaves, they explained the ancient proclamation: "Japheth shall dwell in the land of Shem and Ham shall be his servant. Servants, therefore, obey your masters." They were faithfully supported in this preaching by writers who were then regarded as scholars. Such authors were producing numerous books, explaining in detail the various ways in which the inferior "wooly-headed, flat-nosed, prognathous race" differed from the Caucasian. Such nonsense, however, should not hold back the student of history except so far as it is necessary to note how near people sometimes approach insanity. It is fortunate that not many scholars now accept any such theory as the inferiority or superiority of races. One race makes more progress than another because it has more opportunities, but this does not mean that the one is inherently superior to the other.

According to Robert A. Calvert and Arnoldo De Leon, "Many slaves in Texas did not resign themselves to complete submissions to slavery. They expressed their disapproval of the system by running away to Mexico, and they sabotaged the institution by breaking tools, burning barns, stealing farm animals, and slowing down on the job." Further, Calvert and De Leon stated that: "Although there is no record of major slave rebellions in Antebellum Texas, a wave of insurrection hysteria is known to have passed over the state in the 1850's, mirroring similar paranoia prevalent in the rest of the South as the country neared the Civil War. Suspected instigators were swiftly executed by vigilantes."

Anthony Bewley, a white minister of the Northern Methodist Church, was accused of being a participant in a widespread abolitionist plot to devastate Texas by fire, poison, and raids through slave insurrection and covert activities.

The decade of the 1860s is the period in which Texas led the nation in the number of vigilante activities. This is because Texas, like other slave states, was smitten with the overwhelming fears concerning the security of the strange institution of involuntary servitude. Some excused the savage lawlessness to other causes like Indian raids or lawless outsiders, but this could never account for the brutality that the vigilantes inflicted upon innocent white Northerners, suspected slaves, and other strangers. Nowhere in the

United States was this tendency more prevalent than in the South, and nowhere in the South more than Texas, which by one scholar's count experienced fifty-two separate vigilante movements in the nineteenth century.

The Civil War ended slavery in Texas, and along with that unhappy and unfortunate institution would pass the necessity of using vigilantes to protect white citizens against alleged abolitionists and slave uprisings. Vigilante groups did not die with the end of war; they merely moved the locust westward, following the frontier. Yet, although vigilante organization passed from the South, the idea behind it — that men can take the law into their own hands to protect the larger community from outside threats — remained as an article for many. It would inspire subsequent generations of Southern racist bigots, using other tactics, to undermine provisional governments during Reconstruction, conduct lynching bees in the late nineteenth and early twentieth centuries, harass African-American communities, and seek to deny them the right to vote and the right to a quality education.

Summary

From statehood to the 1860s, the number of enslaved African Americans in Texas more than tripled. Many whites defended slavery using a variety of arguments. Several free African Americans lived in Texas before the Civil War. Some lived successfully, but their rights as citizens were drastically curtailed. The oppressive institution of slavery was made more horrible by the mass fear of slave insurrections. Vigilantes carried out lawless acts against Northern whites and suspected agitators, black and white. Vigilante groups unfortunately extended beyond the Civil War and appeared in many ways from the late 1860s to the mid-1900s.

Chapter 3

Pioneers, Trailblazers, and Second Class Citizenship

1865–1945

With the end of the Civil War came emancipation and an opportunity for political and economic improvement. Now, however, the majority of the population was a conquered people. During the occupation and reconstruction, some of the growing bitterness toward the conqueror was transferred to the African Americans, and the racial chasm became a gulf.

General Lee's surrender at Appomattox signaled the end of armed conflict. It also signaled the beginning of Union control of the Texas state government. That control was to continue until 1874.

Gen. Gordon Granger and 1,800 Union troops were sent to supervise Reconstruction in Texas. Granger arrived in Galveston and on June 19, 1865, proclaimed that all slaves in Texas were free. His action carried out President Abraham Lincoln's Emancipation Proclamation. In 1863 Lincoln had declared all slaves free who were living in the areas controlled by the Confederacy. Soon after the Civil War, the former slaves were made citizens of the United States by the adoption of the 14th Amendment to the Constitution. The 13th Amendment freed the slaves and the 15th Amendment gave them the right to vote. (Women of all ethnic groups were denied the right to vote in 1865.)

In addition to making sure that all slaves were freed, General Granger and other federal officials had to see that a new state government went into effect. The method used to create a new state government loyal to the Union soon angered many ex-Confederates. Especially unpopular was a law which said that no one who had fought for the Confederacy or who had served as an officer in the Confederate government would be allowed to hold an office in the state or federal government. Since most Anglo Texans had supported the Confederate cause, this meant that they could not become officers in the new state government.

The end of the war created unprecedented confusion and chaos throughout the state and in state government. There was fear and understandable confusion among the newly freed African Americans as well as among the Confederate troops seeking to be reunited with their families.

Andrew J. Hamilton was appointed governor of Texas in June 1865. While he was serving, Governor Hamilton worked for the restoration of local government. He also established a federal agency, the Freedman's Bureau, to aid needy people. The nearly half-million freedmen in Texas were its primary concern.

At this particular time in Texas history, African Americans who were slaves were now free, but they were not equal. Texas historians in the past have been oblivious to the determination of the African-American Texans to serve, protect and defend their state. According to Dale Baum, some Texans strongly believe that "a Republican Party coalition of ex-slaves, scalawags, and Northern adventurers ran Texas in a despotic fashion after the Civil War and that fortunately for the white race the Ku Klux Klan and the Democratic Party 'redeemers' put an end by 1874, at least at the state level, to what they believed was an artificial and illegitimate experiment in granting full civic and political rights to former slaves."

Many have explained the longevity of the carpetbagger fantasy. There is a loftiness in blaming others (strangers, Northerners) for the many discerned wickedness of Reconstruction. In other words, the blame helps to reduce the collective guilt in white Southern culture over slavery. A check of our history tells us that no generation of Texans caused more death, misery, and destruction than the secessionists who took their state out of the American Union in 1861 and started a civil war for the most pitiful cause imaginable: the defense of slavery. The notion of carpetbagger persecution after the war not only reduces guilt about the cause of the war, but because the myth implies that unscrupulous Yankees came into Texas after the war and injected alien and disastrous ideas into the heads of childlike freedmen. It also helps to minimize the accomplishments of African-American Texans during the Reconstruction era.

Former slaves were not passive participants in the Reconstruction process in Texas. Soon after Gen. Gordon Granger's June 19th proclamation, newly freed slaves made known their aspirations: They wanted to learn how to read and write, dreamed of owning property and land, and hoped that in the new order of things they would have basic civil rights. Nowhere did Reconstruction have more radical consequences than in areas of the Brazos, Colorado, and Trinity rivers. All of the fertile countries along the rich fertile soils of the great rivers were important geographic factors. Here, freedmen quickly asserted their independence from Anglos. They began to create autonomous community institutions. They built churches that not only served the spiritual needs of the ex-slaves but also served as centers of community life and training grounds for future leaders.

Anglos were alarmed by this assertiveness and determined to preserve the old ways. Planters often resorted to violence to maintain control over their workforce. Whites also directed their wrath at African Americans' emerging community institutions, on occasion breaking up worship at the new, independent freedmen churches. In the two years following the Civil War, white Texans firmly controlled local government and used it to restrict African-American freedom. Local officials apprenticed African-American children to labor-starved planters, confiscated African Americans' weapons, and used harsh discriminatory vagrancy laws (known as "Black Codes") to compel freedmen to contract with white landowners. Yet, far from being intimidated, African Americans continued to challenge white authority. They repeatedly filed complaints with the Freedman's Bureau against those who abused them. They frustrated planters' efforts to establish a pace of labor reminiscent of slavery by collectively refusing to obey their employers' directives and by using the chronic shortage of labor to force planters to ac-

This is a picture of the lynching of Jesse Washington, Waco, Texas, 1916.
— TAAHO Collections, Austin, Texas

*Groups such as the Ku Klux Klan perpetuated scenes such as this
in Texas and throughout the South.*
— TAAHO Collections, Austin, Texas

cept sharecropping arrangements that afforded greater freedom from white supervision.

White men, with their world already seriously disturbed, found it totally turned upside down when in the spring of 1867 the United States Congress took over the entire process of Reconstruction. In response to widespread violence against ex-slaves throughout the South, Northern Republicans in Congress declared African Americans citizens of the United States, drafted the 14th Amendment to the Constitution (which provided all citizens, and thus African Americans, with equal protection of all laws), and required the former Confederate states to give the ex-slaves the right to vote. Voter registration began in the summer of 1867. African Americans registered to vote eagerly, notwithstanding the efforts of whites to prevent them from exercising this basic constitutional right. Local African-American leaders, mostly self-taught former slaves, were always first to register. They invariably served as federal voter registrars and helped organize Republican Party Union Loyalty Leagues. Principal branches of the league were set up in Austin, Galveston, and San Antonio. African Americans comprised a majority of the elected delegates attending the first state convention held in Houston in the summer of 1867.

White Texans feared the potential political power of African Americans, and this superficial fear caused them to resort to the Ku Klux Klan and other violence-prone organizations of the Texas Democratic Party to isolate their leaders of color and mark them for death. George E. Brooks, a Methodist minister, schoolteacher, federal voter registrar, leader of the local Republican Party Union League, and head of the Milican African-American community, was lynched by the Klan. White terrorism in the Brazos Valley region of the state where African Americans outnumbered whites did not initially achieve its goal. Freedman's political involvement increased.

African-American leaders elected as delegates to the state constitutional convention, which assembled in the summer of 1868, included: Charles W. Bryant, an African Methodist Episcopal Church minister from Houston; Benjamin F. Williams, a Methodist minister, barber, and mechanic from Brazos County; James McWilliams, a farmer from Montgomery County; Benjamin O. Watrous, the president of Brenham Union League; George T. Ruby, Galveston County, a free-born mulatto who came to Galveston after the Civil War and who was one of the few African Americans to serve as a

G. T. Ruby in the Senate, by M. A. Emanuel.
— Institute of Texan Cultures, San Antonio, Texas

Freedman's Bureau agent; Wiley W. Johnson, a farmer, wheelwright, and property owner from Harrison County; Stephen Curtis, a carpenter from Brazos County; Mitchell M. Kendall, a blacksmith, representing Harrison County; Ralph Long, a farmer from Limestone County; and Sheppard Mullins, an ex-slave and blacksmith. Mullins was elected to serve in the second session of the convention when McLennan County chose him as their delegate after the death of the incumbent George Klappenback.

Of the ten delegates elected to the 1868 Constitutional Convention, George T. Ruby was the most capable politician. He was elected to the State Senate in 1869. Joining him in the Senate was Matthew Gaines, a farm laborer and Baptist minister from Washington County. Gaines proved to be the most forceful, charismatic, and militant African-American leader in Texas politics during Reconstruction.

Contrary to the old carpetbagger myth, the so-called "Radical Republicans" were not vindictive individuals trying to humiliate ex-Confederates. There were never any treason trials, mass arrests, confiscations of rebel property, or nullifications of Confederate

Matthew Gaines.
— From J. Mason Brewer,
Negro Legislators of Texas

transactions. The Davis administration, which African-American votes brought to power, was incredibly effective and reasonably honest. Moreover, for a brief moment in Texas history, African Americans received some semblance of justice and equal treatment under the law.

The provisional government under the Republicans seems to have dealt effectively with the problem of lawlessness and disorder by organizing a state militia, establishing a state police force, expanding a district court system, and restricting the carrying of firearms in cities and taverns.

One of the most significant accomplishments of the Davis administration was the inauguration of the financing of a statewide public school system. Genuinely free tax-supported public schools had been previously unknown in Texas. Before or during the Civil

War, no Southern slave state had ever possessed a practical system of public instruction.

All of the African-American legislators in the House and Senate for the 12th Legislative Session vigorously supported the new school system. They simply believed that the public school system would not only insure success of representational institutions and universal suffrage, but also would allow African Americans to have a chance to compete economically with whites. The school law, modeled on reforms that had first been implemented in Massachusetts, required compulsory attendance for four months out of the year for all children, without regard to race or color, between six and eighteen years of age. The schools were segregated. Senator Matthew Gaines argued strongly for the integration of public schools. Integrated or not, most whites criticized the idea of public schools, fearing that their children would be taught that they were no better than the ex-slaves or that the federal government someday in the future would require the public schools to be integrated. This event was not to happen until the 1960s and 1970s.

African Americans in the 12th Legislature strongly supported the initial effort for higher education. They helped to prepare the bill and to see it through the legislative process that would allow Texas to meet a November 1, 1871, deadline for Reconstruction states to benefit from the Morrill Act.

Texas A&M and Prairie View A&M universities are two tangible achievements of the biracial democracy that was briefly brought to power in Texas by African-American political activism in the late 1860s and early 1870s. Subsequently, essentially what happened was that Texas Democrats chose brute force and expediency over statesmanship and fair play by appealing to the baser instincts of the white electorate and condoning violence against African-American voters to acquire control of the state government. Every year after E. J. Davis was elected, Democratic Party threats, intimidations, and violence exacted their toll on the Republican coalition. Ultimately, the problem of violence in Texas was resolved under Democratic leadership by letting the violent have their way.

Once in power the Democrats destroyed most of the Republican achievements, dismantling the state police, the state militia, and the entire public school system. The Democrats replaced the 1869 constitution with a "horse and buggy" constitution which hampered sound and progressive changes. Amendments are still required to permit even the most trivial government action.

The 1876 Texas Constitution was written and adopted by men who took great pride in their Confederate past, advocated principles discredited by the carnage of the Civil War, and were convinced of their racial superiority over Texans of African descent.

It was a tragic impediment of justice and freedom for African Americans, as well as for Texas, that the first effort to reconstruct Texas ultimately failed. But, so far as these soon to be disenfranchised Texans were concerned, the dream, though deferred, lived faintly on.

Coping and Surviving

The story of Meschack (Shack) Roberts is an account of how one African-American man dealt with the challenges and confusion created by the Civil War. Roberts stayed at home and protected the

Meschack (Shack) Roberts —Recon- struction legislator and principal founder of Wiley College.
— Institute of Texan Cultures, San Antonio, Texas

women and children of his plantation owner. He planted and gathered the crops and kept them in food while his master fought with the Confederate forces. When his master returned, Shack was set free. This was near the East Texas town of Gilmer. Shack worked to provide some leadership among the freedmen in the vicinity, and was badly beaten by an early group of the Ku Klux Klan. He left his home with a small grubstake given him by his former master, and moved to Marshall in Harrison County. From his new base, he was elected to the 13th, 14th, and 15th Legislatures as a member of the House of Representatives. In 1873, he founded Wiley College at Marshall, Texas.

Richard Allen, building contractor, public servant, and Reconstruction legislator.
— Institute of Texan Cultures, San Antonio, Texas

Another former slave, Richard Allen, was born in Virginia. He was brought to Texas and was living on a plantation in Brazoria County when the Civil War started. Allen moved to Houston during the Reconstruction period, became a building contractor, and built one of the early bridges in the city, across Buffalo Bayou at Sabine Street. Allen was a public servant at several levels. He was street commissioner of Houston, member of the Board of the Directors of the Gregory Institute, Houston city alderman, state representative, collector of customs for the Port of Houston, and one of the men who organized the Prince Hall Masonic Lodge of Texas.

Many of the slaves, accustomed to the structured and restricted existence on the plantation, found it difficult to adjust to the complex life of the so-called outside world. But a significant number of former slaves exhibited amazing qualities of leadership immediately upon being freed. Among these was Richard Henry Boyd, who had accompanied his master through the battles of the Civil War on the Confederate side. After his master was killed, Boyd returned to Texas and managed the plantation estate until the end of the war. Then he educated himself, became a Baptist minister, and rose to a position of leadership in the Texas Baptist Convention. In 1897, he organized the National Baptist Publishing Board. This enterprise has published many important books and pamphlets over the years.

The Confederacy was crumbling and its paper money was not worth much in Texas in 1865. Gen. Sam Houston was dead, and his widow, Margaret, was experiencing difficult days, rearing a family at Independence. It was during this period that the slave Joshua Houston rode from Huntsville to Independence and laid a pouch contain-

Joshua Houston, former slave of Gen. Sam Houston.
— TAAHO Collections, Austin, Texas

George T. Ruby, first African American elected to public office in Texas, Reconstruction state senator.
— University of Texas at Austin, Center for American History

Right:
Norris Wright Cuney, born near Hempstead, Texas, in 1846. Political giant in Galveston city government.
— Institute of Texan Cultures, San Antonio, Texas

Left:
Matthew Gaines, Baptist minister and state senator, dynamic leader.
— Texas State Collections, Austin, Texas

ing his life's savings at Mrs. Houston's feet. The pouch contained $2,000 in gold and silver. (General Houston had permitted Joshua to keep the money he earned as a blacksmith.) Mrs. Houston refused the generous offer and told Joshua to use the money to educate his children. He followed her advice. One of Joshua's sons, Sam Houston, became president of the Sam Houston Normal Training School for African Americans at Huntsville. The Sam W. Houston Elementary School at Huntsville is named for the pioneer educator.

George T. Ruby was one of the first African Americans elected to public office in Texas. G. T. Ruby came to Galveston from Maine in 1868. He was twenty-seven years old and a schoolteacher, but he went to work in Galveston as an official of the Freedman's Bureau. In 1868, African Americans finally had the vote in Texas. Ruby was elected as a delegate to the Constitutional Convention of 1869, but resigned in protest over the way the Convention was being conducted.

He later became the permanent chairman of the Republican Convention of 1869. Ruby was elected state senator from Galveston, Brazoria, and Matagorda counties to serve in the 12th Legislature in 1870. He was reelected in 1873 to the 13th Legislature.

For a quarter of a century, Norris Wright Cuney was a dominant figure on the Texas political scene. He was a spokesman for the rights of African-American citizens, and a leading Republican Party official. He was appointed collector of customs for the Port of Galveston in 1889, the highest post in Texas at the time. Before that he had served as secretary of the State Republican Executive Committee, in 1874, and as temporary chairman of the State Republican Convention in 1882. He had been a delegate to the National Republican Convention in 1889, and was elected chairman and national committeeman in 1886. He controlled the policies of the Republican Party in Texas for a number of years. Cuney served as sergeant-at-arms for the Texas House of Representatives in 1879, and was appointed a member of the school board in Galveston in 1871. He was appointed an inspector of customs in 1872 through the influence of Governor Edmund J. Davis. Cuney served as the first Grandmaster of the Prince Hall Masonic Lodge of Texas in 1874 (to many he is known as the father of Prince Hall Masonry in Texas). In 1880 he was elected a city alderman in Galveston.

Norris Wright Cuney was in school in Pennsylvania when the Civil War broke out. He left school in 1863 and went to New Orleans, where he met and talked with P. B. S. Pinchback, who later became the political boss of Louisiana. It is commonly believed that this encounter influenced Cuney to enter politics. Cuney returned to Sunnyside Plantation near Hempstead, where he was born in 1846, for a brief visit at the end of the war. Then he went to Galveston, where he entered politics in 1869. He was described as being medium brown-skinned with black hair and a black mustache, and was an eloquent public speaker.

When the 12th Legislature convened in 1870, Matthew Gaines of Washington County was one of the two African Americans who were seated as senators. The other was George T. Ruby of Galveston. Gaines, a former slave who was born on a plantation in 1842 in Louisiana, learned to read and write at an early age with the aid of a young white boy. He lived in Burton, Texas, after he was freed at the end of the Civil War. He was a preacher and became a leader for the freedmen in Washington County. He pastored and lived in Giddings, Texas, after he left the Senate. He reportedly spoke seven languages. He died in 1900. Many of his descendants live in Austin, Giddings, and Houston.

Prior to the Civil War, Benjamin Franklin Williams, who had been set free in Virginia, came to Texas. He started raising cattle in Colorado County and then moved to Kendleton in Fort Bend County, where he purchased land. This land is still in the hands of his descendants (1995). In 1872, he was elected to the legislature, serving in the House of Representatives. He married a schoolteacher from Oberlin, Ohio, who had come to Texas shortly after the Civil War to establish a school for African-American children in Kendleton.

Benjamin F. Williams, former slave, rancher, minister, educator, and state representative.
— Texas State Collections, Austin, Texas

Williams was one of the most active African-American delegates of the Reconstruction Convention. He was born a slave in Brunswick County, Virginia, in 1819. While still a slave he was transported to South Carolina, and later, in 1830, he was carried to Tennessee. In 1859, he was brought to Colorado County, Texas. After emancipation, Williams was licensed to preach and became a traveling Methodist minister. He was the minister-in-charge when Wesley Methodist Chapel (now Wesley United Methodist Church) in Austin was established in 1868. Combining religion with politics, he became a militant spokesman for African Americans in Texas. As early as 1868, he was vice-president of the Union Loyalty League and as such kept the white Unionists abreast of what was happening in the African-American major communities. It was Williams' involvement in politics that won him a seat at the 1868 Constitutional Convention, when he was forty-eight years old.

It would seem that B. F. Williams made a favorable impression on his African Americans while serving in the Convention — he was subsequently elected by Lavaca and Colorado counties to the 12th Legislature. Waller, Fort Bend, and Wharton elected him to the 16th Legislature. Members of the 12th Legislature nominated Williams for Speaker of the House; he lost by only three votes. Williams and several African Americans were collectively responsible for the settlement and development of Kendleton, Texas.

Not long after the Civil War, William E. Kendall (white) offered to sell land to African Americans in an area of Fort Bend County between Turkey Creek and the San Bernard River. Kendall divided a large plantation site into 100-acre tracts and sold the land for 50 cents to $1.50 per acre. One of the first free African Americans to purchase land was Warner Braxton, a former slave from Washington County. His grandson, R. V. Braxton, was postmaster at Kendleton during the decade of the 1960s. In the decade of the 1990s, Kendleton is still basically an African-American community, although a number of white families live in the vicinity. Other predominately African-American communities that still exist are Broad House, which was established in Blanco County in 1870; Pelham in Navarro County, which has a store, church, and one school; and Galilee, ten miles west of Huntsville in Walker County. Borderville, in north Harris County west of Humble, was named for a family which operated a large sawmill prior to the Civil War and which employed the ancestors of many of the present residents, most of whom are African Americans. Fodice is a small African-American community in Houston County. Cologne is another small African-American settlement, located in Goliad County. Neylandville, located on the Cotton Belt Railroad in northeast Texas between Greenville and Commerce in Hunt County, is an African-American

Kendleton, Texas, an African American township in Fort Bend County.
— Institute of Texan Cultures, San Antonio, Texas

Freedman schools such as this were established in Kendleton and many other communities.
— Institute of Texan Cultures, San Antonio, Texas

community formerly known as "Jim Town," which was founded by James "Free Jim" Brigham in the late 1860s. The Saint Paul School District was located in Neylandville from the 1880s until the district merged with the Commerce Independent School District in the 1960s. Easton, an all African-American community, is located in southwest Gregg County about five miles from Longview in deep East Texas.

During a series of Indian raids in Young County, near Fort Belknap, a number of settlers were killed and several women and children were carried away by Comanches and Kiowas. The captives included the wife and children of Brit Johnson, an African-American slave working as a cowhand on the Allen Johnson plantation. This was in 1865, and Brit spent the next two years hunting for his wife and children in West Texas. His former master furnished him a horse and encouraged him to go in search for his family. During this odyssey, Johnson obtained the release of two white families being held by the Indians. Finally, he ransomed his wife and children and took them safely home. In 1871, while he was driving a freight wagon to Weatherford, a band of Kiowas surrounded and killed and mutilated his body. The Indians paid dearly for the revenge — more than 100 spent cartridge shells were found near Brit's body. Trouble with the Comanche and Kiowa, which started when Brit entered the village and freed his family and several white captives, finally led to his death.

David Abner, Sr., was the patriarch of a family which has been prominent in educational and public service work in Texas for more than four generations. Abner, Sr., a former slave, was elected to the House of Representatives of the Texas Legislature from Marshall, Harris

Brit Johnson, "Indian Fighter."
— Institute of Texan Cultures,
San Antonio, Texas

*David Abner, Sr., patriarch
of a prominent educational
family, state representative.*
— TAAHO Collections,
Austin, Texas

County, in 1874. He also was a delegate to the Constitutional Convention of 1875. His son, David Abner, Jr., was the first student to graduate from Wiley College in Marshall, Texas. Young Abner went on to teach at Bishop College, and was the first African American to join the all-white faculty of Bishop College. Later, he became president of Guadalupe College, and in 1905, he was named president of Conroe College. In 1917, he was president of the National Baptist Convention Theological Seminary at Nashville. He also served as District Grand Master of the Odd Fellows of Texas, New Mexico, and Arizona.

The third generation included Mrs. Eulalia Abner Randle of Austin, Texas, who was a music teacher in the Austin Independent School District for many years, and her brother, Ewart Gladstone Abner, a successful businessman. The fourth generation is represented by David Abner III, son of Ewart Gladstone Abner and grandson of David Abner, Jr. Abner III graduated from Texas Southern University at Houston, and earned his Ph.D. from the University of Indiana. He was professor of business administration at TSU.

The last African American to serve as a senator in the Texas Legislature in the nineteenth century was Walter M. Burton, elected from Fort Bend, Waller, and Wharton counties. Burton was a former slave from Mississippi. He was reelected for four terms, and served from 1874 to 1882. His fellow legislators thought so highly of him that they presented him a gold-headed walking stick to show their esteem for his public service. Before serving in the Senate, Burton had served two terms as sheriff of Fort Bend County.

*David Abner, Jr., first student
to graduate from Wiley College.*
— Institute of Texan Cultures,
San Antonio, Texas

David Abner IV
— Texas Southern University,
Houston, Texas

David Abner III
— Texas Southern University,
Houston, Texas

On the West Texas cattle ranges, old-timers said of a man like Daniel Webster Wallace: "He'll do to ride the river with." This meant that he was a steadfast friend and a dependable neighbor who would carry his share of the struggles and sorrows associated with pioneering. He was given the historic name of Daniel Webster Wallace, but he was known as "80 John" to the day of his death. When he helped move a herd of cattle westward for rancher Clay Mann, Wallace was given the name of "80 John" because Mann's cattle were branded with a large "80" which was said to stretch "from their backbone to their belly." Wallace was seventeen years old when he went to work for Mann. He had left the Victoria area with all of his possessions tied on his saddle behind him.

Wallace was born a slave in 1860. Less than a year before his birth, his mother, Mary Wallace, was sold to a family in Victoria for $1,000. Wallace grew up on a ranch and learned how to ride a horse and how to work cattle. It was in 1877 that he struck out for himself. Fourteen years later, he had established his own ranch and bought his own herd of cattle. During the intervening years, he had helped drive a herd of cattle up the Great Western Trail to Dodge City, Kansas, in the early 1880s. When the other cowboys spent their money in the saloons and dance halls, Wallace went back to the cow camp and saved his money. He used the money he saved to buy cattle, which Mann permitted him to pasture on the Mann Ranch. Wallace first branded his cattle with his name, and then with "DW." When his herd became large enough, he moved ten miles west of Colorado City in Mitchell County, and bought two sections (1,280 acres) of land. Later, he owned more than 10,000 acres of land in Mitchell County. The ranch is still operated by his descendants. In the 1890s, he drilled one of the first water wells in West Texas to be pumped by a windmill. This early-day windmill, with wooden tower, cost him $2,500 to put in operation. Wallace contributed toward the establishment of a school for African-American children and two Christian Methodist churches. The school was named Daniel Webster Wallace School in his honor. In the late 1960s the school was desegregated and continues to bear the Wallace name.

Paul Moultry was born a slave in South Carolina in 1853. Moultry became a free "man" at the age of twelve, and decided to go out west. He was accompanied by a white boy his age, the son of an overseer. The white boy decided to live in Rosebud, and Moultry went to Georgetown, where he went to work in a blacksmith shop.

Walter M. Burton, former slave. Elected to four terms in the Texas Senate representing Fort Bend, Waller and Wharton counties.
— TAAHO Collections, Austin, Texas

Above left:
Daniel W. ("80 John") Wallace.
— TAAHO Collections, Austin, Texas

Above right:
Laura Deloach Owen Wallace, wife of "80 John" Wallace.
— TAAHO Collections, Austin, Texas

Right:
Eula W. F. Harris, daughter of "80 John" Wallace.
— TAAHO Collections, Austin, Texas

Nathaniel L. (John) Word.
     — TAAHO Collections,
          Austin, Texas

In 1855, Moultry purchased the shop and made enough money running it to buy two farms. He taught all four of his sons the blacksmith trade. Descendants of Paul Moultry continue to live in Georgetown.

The progress African Americans have made in ranching in Texas is akin to the progress made in other areas of life and work between 1865 to 1965. Texas historians, however, have failed to include these darker ranchers in their accounts of Texas history.

Nathaniel L. (John) Word's accomplishments in ranching are remarkable. Word was born February 7, 1880, fifteen years after emancipation in Texas. He was born in a log cabin in Goliad, about 100 miles south of San Antonio. Word worked as a cowpuncher from his early teens until he was twenty-one years old. In 1902, he moved to Sutton County. He married Willie M. Brown in 1908, and he had one child by a former wife, Ida Walker.

Word left home when he was fifteen years old to work on a farm for $15 a month or about $3.75 per week. The man he worked for wanted to pay him with cattle, and often advised him on how to manage his possessions to get ahead in life. As a boy, Nathaniel drove oxen and cut firewood. When he was a young man, he worked for ranch owner Jim Chittum, who owned 120,000 head of cattle. After working for Chittum, Word went to work for George West at Oakville in Live Oak County.

Word moved to Sonora in 1902 and bought a few head of cattle and ranched on a few acres of land. In 1918 he went to work for D. J. (Joe) Wyatt. In 1927 he bought three sections of land (1,920 acres) from Wyatt in Sutton County.

Nathaniel Word became the first African American to become a successful sheep rancher in West Texas. He was one of the hardest workers in the sheep industry. After Word had been working as an independent rancher for fifteen years, he owned 1,920 acres of fine Sutton County ranch land. He leased another six sections (3,840 acres) for grazing. He ran about 300 goats, 1,800 sheep, and 200 head of cattle.

In 1949, Word leased his ranch to another rancher. He moved to San Angelo in 1950 to retire. He sold the ranch to Walter Fluger.

Nathaniel L. (John) Word died at his home in San Angelo on Saturday, December 1, 1957. He was a valiant pioneer who knew what he wanted and would allow nothing to prevent him from being successful.

An acquaintance of Joseph Cuney remembered him as "a quiet man who spent a great deal of his time reading." Reserved though he may have been, Cuney was a man of strong convictions. The older brother of Norris Wright Cuney, he was born at Sunnyside Plantation in Waller County in 1840. Joseph was given his freedom and sent to a private school in Pittsburgh preparatory to entering an eastern college. He was attending this school in Pittsburgh when the Civil War started, and he immediately joined the 63rd Pennsylvania Volunteers in 1861 and fought as a Union soldier during the entire war. His mother, learning that he was stationed in Virginia, wrote and asked him to go see her mother, Hester Neale Stuart of Centerville, Virginia. Joseph found and "liberated" his grandmother in Virginia in the closing days of the war. His mother, who had not seen her mother for forty years, was overjoyed to find her again. Joseph's grandmother lived to be 100 years old. After the war, Joseph joined his brother, Norris Wright Cuney, in Galveston. Joseph is believed to be the first African-American attorney who was a native Texan to practice law in the state. He and his brother also operated a print shop.

Samuel Johnson Sutton, a native Virginian, came to Texas in 1885 and started teaching school in San Antonio. He was one of the first African-American schoolteachers in Bexar County after Reconstruction and he was the first principal of the Riverside School, the Frederick Douglas School, and the Phyllis Wheatley School, all high schools. He was in the school system for fifty-four years. He and his wife, the former Lillian V. Smith of New Orleans, were the parents of fifteen children. All of their children were born in the house which eventually became the place of the family business, the Sutton and Sutton Mortuary.

Many of the Sutton children have made significant contributions in the fields of public service. John Sutton served as secretary to George Washington Carver, and while on a technical aid program to Russia, he invented a process for the manufacture of rope from rice fiber. After retirement he lived in New York. G. J. Sutton of San Antonio was the first African American in the South to be elected to a public office in the twentieth century. He was a member of the board of trustees of the San Antonio Junior College in 1948. Percy Sutton practiced law with his brother, Oliver Sutton, in New York. He was elected president of Manhattan Borough. Samuel Sutton became well-known in the horseracing circles, and operated concessions at the racetracks in Louisville, Kentucky, New Orleans, Louisiana, and Little Rock, Arkansas. Lillian Sutton Taylor taught school at Booker T. Washington Elementary School in San Antonio. Smithie Sutton Henry taught school in San Francisco. Cora Sutton Jackson and Essie Sutton became supervisors in the San Francisco public school system.

During the latter part of the nineteenth century, many African-American males became cowboys. Al Jones became a cowboy. He wore "high water" boots which reached almost to his knees, a broad-brimmed hat, summer and winter, and a broad-buckled belt around his middle. Jones was as genuine a cowpuncher as ever straddled a horse. He was as real as a blue norther in January.

Monroe Alpheus Majors was born one year before slaves were emancipated in Texas. Majors showed a flair for schol-

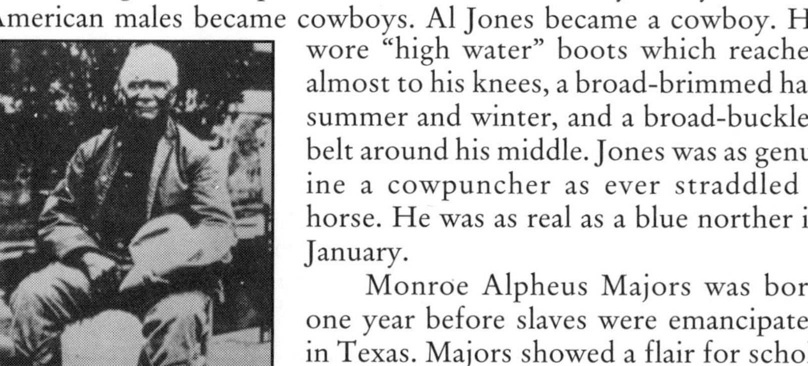

Al Jones, trail boss on cattle drives to Kansas.
— TAAHO Collections, Austin, Texas

arship at the age of fourteen, when he was admitted to Tillotson College in Austin, Texas. He was born in Waco, Texas, in 1864. While attending college in Austin, he served as a page in the House of Representatives. Monroe entered the medical branch of Central Tennessee College (Meharry Medical College) in 1883 and graduated in 1886. When he opened his office in Brenham, Texas, the same year, he became the first native African-American Texan to practice medicine. Soon after he began to practice medicine, he and thirteen others organized the Lone Star Medical, Dental and Pharmaceutical Association in a meeting at Galveston, Texas. Dr. Majors practiced medicine in Calvert and Dallas.

Benjamin Rufus Bluitt was a farm boy from Limestone County. He rose from farm boy to become a doctor, a surgeon, a lodge leader, and a banker. Dr. Bluitt graduated from Meharry Medical College in Tennessee on February 20, 1888, and was admitted to practice in Dallas, Texas, the same year. He was the first African-American surgeon in Texas. He established a hospital for African Americans at the corner of Pearl and Commerce streets in downtown Dallas. Dr. Bluitt served as grand medical director of the Prince Hall Masons. He helped organize the first African-American bank in Dallas, the Penny Savings Bank.

Old-timers remember seeing Marcellus C. Cooper sweeping the floor of the Sanger Brothers Department Store in Dallas, Texas. Cooper was born in the White Rock Community near Dallas. He saved his earnings as a porter at the Sanger store to help pay for his studies at dental school. In 1894, just twenty-nine years after emancipation in Texas, he became the state's first African-American dentist. The M. C. Cooper Dental Society in Dallas was named after Dr. Cooper, a true pioneer.

Robert L. Smith was a free man when he came to Texas. He was intelligent and energetic. He never quit trying to improve the conditions of African Americans. Robert L. Smith was born in South Carolina in 1861, during the Civil War. He graduated from Atlanta University and soon afterward came to Texas. He was elected to the Texas Legislature in 1894 and again in 1896, representing Colorado County. He was the last African American to serve in the Texas Legislature in the nineteenth century. In 1902, he was named a deputy U.S. marshal in the Eastern District of Texas by President Theodore Roosevelt. He held this position for seven years. While Smith was in the legislature, he successfully opposed a bill which

Robert L. Smith, a free African American, was elected to the Texas Legislature in 1894, and served two terms.

— From J. Mason Brewer, *Negro Legislators of Texas*

would have established separate waiting rooms for African Americans and whites in railroad stations. In 1915, he was the first head of the Negro Agricultural Extension Service (NAES), with headquarters at Prairie View A&M. He established the Farmers Improvement Society of Texas, which operated the Farmers Improvement Agricultural College at Ladonia.

M. M. Rogers began his public career by teaching school when he was only sixteen years old. Rogers was born a slave in Wharton County on July 13, 1859. After he received his basic education, he taught a group of African-American students to read and write. He married in 1878 and moved to Schulenburg. It was then that he felt the need for higher education. He enrolled in Prairie View State Normal (now Prairie View A&M University) and graduated with honors in 1881. Rogers moved to La Grange and became principal of the segregated school for African Americans. He also was elected a city alderman. Rogers established the first funeral home for people of color in that area. It was one of the first funeral homes in the state. Active in the Republican Party, Rogers was a delegate to the National Republican Party Conventions of 1888, 1892, 1896, 1900, and 1904. He was appointed deputy collector of Internal Revenue for the Third District of Texas in 1896. In 1906, Rogers was elected secretary of the board of directors of the Knights of Pythias. Eventually, he moved to Dallas and was active in the affairs of the lodge for many years. He was elected auditor of the National Baptist Convention in 1915. His grandson, Louis Bedford, became a Dallas attorney and a corporation court judge.

At the turn of the century in the late 1890s, few African-American Texans were involved in athletic endeavors. Jack Johnson was an exception. This Texan was the first African American to become

Jack Johnson, prize fighter.

heavyweight boxing champion of the world. He won the title in 1908, but there were clamors for "Gentleman Jim" Jeffries (a white man) to return from retirement and win the championship from Johnson. When the two men fought, Johnson knocked Jeffries out in the fifteenth round of the fight on July 4, 1910, at Reno, Nevada, to retain the championship which he held until 1915.

Before he became a professional boxer, Johnson was a longshoreman on the ship docks at Galveston, Texas. He started boxing in his teens. By the time he was twenty, he was a professional. During his professional career, he fought in Cuba, Australia, and Spain. Johnson appeared in the opera *Aida,* made nightclub appearances, and played a role in a movie. Many Americans, mostly whites, objected to Jack Johnson's interracial marriage. Johnson was killed in an automobile accident in 1945.

William M. McDonald was affectionately known as "Gooseneck Bill" during his long political career. William Madison McDonald took over a substantial portion of the Republican Party in the 1890s, about the time that Norris Wright Cuney lost control of the State Committee. It was a significant period in Texas politics. The Republican Party had adopted a "lily white" attitude which was being condemned publicly by Cuney. The Democrats were not seeking African-American support. The Populist Party endeavored to capitalize on this situation by asking African-American support and trying to combine African Americans and small farmers into a new political force. McDonald became the private secretary to a wealthy man, E. H. R. Green, in 1897. He attended many National Republican Conventions and continued to fight for the Republican Party

William M. "Gooseneck" McDonald, politician, civil rights leader, and financial genius.
— University of Texas Center for American History, Austin, Texas

until their prejudiced practices prompted him to leave the party in 1924 to switch to first the Progressives and then to the Democrats. McDonald founded the Fraternal Bank and Trust at Fort Worth in 1911. For thirty years he was Grand Secretary of the Prince Hall Masonic Lodge of Texas. McDonald was born on June 22, 1866, in Kaufman County. He died on July 4, 1950.

Col. West Alexander Hamilton was a professional soldier. When the Mexican bandit Pancho Villa raided Columbus, New Mexico, in 1916, Gen. John J. Pershing was ordered to invade Mexico and eliminate this threat to United States citizens. Members of the 10th Cavalry (Buffalo Soldiers) accompanied Pershing to Mexico. Col. West Alexander Hamilton, who was then a lieutenant, was assigned with a group of troops to protect the Arizona border. Hamilton was sent to France, where he commanded an infantry company in 1918. After World War I, he commanded the 428th Infantry Reserve Regiment. He was promoted to colonel in 1933. Colonel Hamilton served as commanding officer of the 366th Infantry at Fort Deven, Massachusetts, during Word War II, and later served as commander of the ROTC forces at Prairie View A&M University.

Hugh McElroy enlisted in Teddy Roosevelt's Rough Riders at the age of fourteen, having lied about his age. He served in the war of 1898 against Spain and served in the 10th Cavalry (Buffalo Soldiers) after that. McElroy was among the troops who accompanied

Pershing into Mexico in 1916. During World War I, he served with the 317th Engineers, but was temporarily assigned to the French Seventh Army. While with this French outfit, he was awarded the Croix de Guerre for gallantry in action.

There were hardly any positions of employment for young, ambitious African Americans in Texas during the first quarter of the twentieth century, and many, therefore, turned to the military. Gen. Spencer Cornelius Dickerson, a native of Austin, Texas, attended Tillotson College and then went to Rush Medical College, where he graduated in 1901. He practiced medicine for several years and then went overseas as a medical corps officer with the Allied Expeditionary Forces in 1918. He was promoted to colonel in 1929, and later commissioned a brigadier general. He was the first native African-American Texan to have been named a general in the United States Army.

The first two decades of the twentieth century were periods of denial, confusion, hate and violence for the African Americans in Texas. Whites continued to contribute to their miserable and destitute condition in many ways, from the courthouse to the statehouse and beyond. Their faith sustained them, however, and their will to survive and be productive citizens of this state caused them to persevere.

Charles W. Pemberton was a native of Marshall, Texas, where he graduated from high school. Pemberton came home from World War I in 1918 with his future positively planned in detail. He graduated from Wiley College and went on to medical school at Meharry College. He became a medical doctor and opened his office in Houston, Texas, in 1927. He was later named president of the Lone Star Medical Association. Pemberton was the first African-American doctor to serve in the school district's health department. Dr. Pemberton also served as consul for the Republic of Liberia, and was decorated by Liberian President William V. S. Tubman with the Knight Commander of the Humane Order of African Redemption in 1966.

Julius Bledsoe made his first appearance in Waco at the age of five, when he sang at the New Hope Baptist Church. The church had been established by his grandfather, Rev. Steven Cobb.

Born in 1899 and christened Julius, he was also known as "Jules." Bledsoe became world-famous in 1928 when he sang "Old

Julius Bledsoe. Became world famous in 1928 when he sang "Old Man River" in Florenz Ziegfeld's New York production of Showboat.
— Institute of Texan Cultures,
San Antonio, Texas

Man River" in Florenz Ziegfeld's New York production of *Show-boat.* By the time he reached New York, he was able to sing opera in six languages. He went to Columbia University in New York to become a medical doctor; his musical talents exerted too strong an influence, however, and he earned a degree instead at Chicago Musical College. He was studying at Columbia University when Ziegfeld discovered him. Later, he played the lead role in the Eugene O'Neill Broadway play *Emperor Jones.* He went to Europe with *Emperor Jones* and remained to sing opera in England, France, Spain, and the Netherlands. He sang Amonasro in the opera *Aida,* the role of Tonio in *Pagliacci,* and the part of Mephisto in *Faust.* He was denied permission to sing in Nazi Germany, but elsewhere in Europe his richly burnished voice and interpretive insight made him a welcomed and much admired artist.

Bledsoe was forty-five and at the peak of his career when he died unexpectedly in Hollywood in 1943. He is buried in Waco at Greenwood Cemetery. Inscribed on his tombstone is the last stanza of "Old Man River."

Etta Moten was beautiful, ambitious, and talented. She became an early twentieth-century movie star. Etta was born in Weimer, Texas, the daughter of an African Methodist Episcopal Church itinerant minister. Etta Moten appeared in the Warner Brothers movie *The Gold Diggers* in 1933, and sang "The Carioca" in the RKO movie *Flying Down to Rio* in 1940. In private life, she was Mrs. Claude Barnett of Chicago, the widow of an African-American journalist. She retired from the stage and theater after singing the role of Bess in *Porgy and Bess* from 1942 to 1945.

Quest for Empowerment

For many years prior to 1945, African Americans were discouraged from joining the Democratic Party. When the Democrats became the dominant party in the state, African Americans found themselves, in effect, disenfranchised. The National Association for the Advancement of Colored People decided to make a court test case, suing for the right of African Americans to vote in the Democratic primaries. A. Maceo Smith of Dallas was state president of the NAACP, and his fellow executive committee members were John Clouser of Galveston, Rev. A. A. Lucas of Houston, and Lula White, Houston. W. J. Durham, Dallas, was the attorney and advisor. The NAACP officials requested the help of Thurgood Marshall, then attorney for the NAACP and who in 1967 would be appointed to the United States Supreme Court by President Lyndon B. Johnson. The first case was filed in 1927 by Dr. L. A. Nixon, an El Paso dentist. The Supreme Court upheld Dr. Nixon's right to vote, but the Texas Legislature changed the states' voting laws, and Dr. Nixon was forced to return to the higher court in 1932. The final breakthrough came in 1944, when Dr. Lonnie Smith, a Houston dentist, filed suit against an elected official in Harris County, Texas. Since 1944, African Americans have continued to vote in the primaries in ever increasing numbers.

In the past fifty years the situation of African Americans in Texas has improved at a steadily accelerating pace. As we near the year 2000, many long-closed doors of opportunity have opened and a number of Texans of African descent have attained positions in the state and nation. Now, as in the days of the Republic, when the trend was in the reverse, attitudes of people as a whole change slower than the laws. The trend, however, is clear and discernible.

A. Maceo Smith, civil rights leader.
— Institute of Texan Cultures,
San Antonio, Texas

Lawrence A. Nixon, an El Paso dentist, principal in voting rights action in Texas.
— Center for American History,
University of Texas at Austin

Chapter 4

The Progressive Era

1945–1995

The 1930s were very difficult times for African Americans. Jobs were few, Jim Crowism was a cancer that would not heal, and legal segregation was on the throne. Low pay, violence, race-hatred, second-class citizenship — all contributed to the abject hopelessness felt by Texas citizens of African descent.

Most African-American Texans, however, felt that where there was life there was hope, and hope kept them alive in times when it seemed that government, society, and the political system had assigned them to extinction. Nevertheless, the same optimism that had sustained them through the dark years of slavery and Reconstruction, transferred into the dark days of the depression, which were filled with abject racial hatred and segregation. Violence, along with unfair and unequal administering of the law, continued to be major areas of tension and conflict for African Americans in Texas, into the decade of the 1940s.

African-American Texans and the Two World Wars

World War I

During World War I, African Americans made up nearly 25 percent of the soldiers from Texas. For some, the army provided better clothes, food, housing, and pay than they previously had been able to afford. Large numbers of African-American Texans were sent to the stevedore regiments to labor under abusive officers, and their hardships were numerous. White soldiers judged most African Americans in uniform as lazy cowards and illiterates. Racial hatred and segregation was the rule so far as the U.S. military was concerned.

The French received the African-American military servicemen as friends; and the African-American soldiers, in appreciation of the democracy of France as they saw it and felt it, willingly sacrificed their lives to save these beautifully humane people. In Champagne, in the Argonne Forest, and at Metz, it was the history of the African-American military man repeating itself — eagerness to engage in the conflict, unflinching stand before the enemy, and noble endurance in the heat of battle. But these African Americans were not merely victors. Some of them achieved honor and distinction.

Spencer Cornelius Dickerson of Austin served as a doctor with the army in 1918 and later was commissioned brigadier general. Hugh McElroy of Houston, who had served in the Spanish-American War and on the Mexican border with Pershing, won the Croix de Guerre for gallantry in action while temporarily attached to the French Army. Corp. Russell Pollard, Company H, 365th Infantry from Weatherford, Texas, was the recipient of a Distinguished Service Cross Medal #1899 for extraordinary heroism in action at Bois Frehaut, France, on November 10, 1918. First Lt. Charles G. Young, who hailed from Austin, Texas, 366th Infantry, was the recipient of a Distinguished Service Cross Medal #931 for extraordinary heroism in action near Binarville, France, September 27-28, 1918.

On returning from the war, African Americans were warmly welcomed in some of the cities, especially in New York. In the less tolerant areas of our nation, they were given a hostile reception. Whites opposed the presence of African-American troops. Many in uniform were often insulted and beaten. In fact, sometimes before the African-American soldier could return to visit his family at home, he had to take off his uniform. There were cases in remote areas of the state of some nonwhite soldiers being killed.

World War II

When the United States entered World War II, they did so to preserve democracy. Thereupon, African Americans, with more emphasis than ever in the history of the country, demanded that we have some democracy at home before we pay too much attention to democracy abroad. African Americans in the Lone Star State felt that Hitler was merely trying to do to other races and nations exactly what the race-hating elements in Texas and the United States had been doing to African Americans and other minorities for three centuries. African-American newspapers and magazines in this state and throughout the United States took up the refrain. Texans of African descent monitored the situation closely. Walter White of the NAACP, with other African-American leaders including some prominent Texans, sought conferences with the president and members of his cabinet. A. Phillip Randolph undertook to organize a "March on Washington."

At first the Texas Legislature and the Congress of the United States were noncommittal to this question, but in both instances, the bureaucrats in charge had to say something to African Americans who now faced induction into the lower orders of the army and exclusion altogether from the navy. The African-American units known as the 9th and 10th Cavalries and the 24th and 25th Infantries, which served Texas so well during its westward expansion, had been demilitarized to serve mainly in menial capacities for the elite of the army. Would African Americans be drafted thus humiliated? their spokesman inquired. President Roosevelt finally promised that African Americans from all states would be admitted to all branches of the military service, but he did not thereby pledge that the policy of segregation would be abolished.

The local draft boards and induction centers in Texas followed a rigid policy of discrimination, and military bases throughout the state were segregated. African-American military personnel in Texas were expected to conform to the local segregation policies of the white Southern communities. Training camps had separate and inferior facilities for African-American military troops. Nonwhite soldiers at Camp Wolters, near Mineral Wells, constructed their own service club because they were not admitted to white facilities. Recreational facilities had separate movie showings because blacks and whites were not allowed to mix publicly. African-American air force cadets trained at Hondo Field with integrated dining and recreational facilities, but with separate classrooms and barracks.

Glimpse of Evolution

Patriotic African Americans in Texas took some courage from the fact that a growing number of white citizens were becoming disgusted with the hypocrisy chargeable to both state and federal governments, and these advocates (though not loudly enough and often enough) for fairness and equality were speaking out more forcefully than they did a generation before. They wanted to be heard in behalf of a real democracy which would embrace all the people. These awaking voices were rising into a louder chorus as the days passed. The chorus of opposition was loud also in the effort to maintain the status quo where it had been for more than three centuries, but the clamor had grown consistently weaker.

Observing this change in attitude of an increasing number of citizens, the United States Supreme Court had the courage to reverse itself in the recent decision of the white citizens' primary in holding that African Americans should be permitted to participate inasmuch as the officials of the state are thereby elected and the exclusion of African Americans therefrom is a violation of the Constitution of the United States. This mandate, however, was too much for Texas and the other Southern states, thus offending, and they threatened to do almost everything but to secede in order to prevent the exercise of the privileges of full citizenship by African Americans, without whom the war could not be won.

Asset or Liability?

Ever since the dawn of emancipation, many Anglos have felt as kindly toward African Americans as they could, while "enduring" them, and making the most of them as a "necessary evil." As servants and "common" laborers they were useful as long as they were kept in their place. They were never thought of as being citizens of the nation, or of the state. Many saw them as a "burden" or a "liability." The Second World War, however, made the efficient and talented African American an asset. The draft in Texas drew a much larger number of African-American citizens for military service than was the case in the First World War. The reduction of manpower necessitated the employment of white women and children to take the place of men in the military service, and when the demand could not thus be met, African Americans were called to the rescue. Men and women of African descent were placed in many positions which had been regarded as being beyond their traditional range. Racial barriers were maintained despite the fact that in proportion to their population, African Americans supplied more men for the war than any other ethnic group. The drafted African Americans, moreover, were sent mainly to labor battalions as African-American draftees had been during the First World War. The army, however, reluctantly admitted men of color to the air corps on a restricted basis, and the navy in like fashion accepted a limited number for active service in contradistinction to the former policy of using African Americans only in food services or mess. The army admitted African-American women to the Women's Auxiliary Army Corps. Benjamin O. Davis, Sr., who advanced to the grade of brigadier general, was restricted to investigation and adjustment of difficulties arising from racial clashes in military circles.

Yet, in spite of these restrictions, a number of African Americans distinguished themselves by exceptional heroism in hotly contested battles. The most conspicuous Texans of these were Doris Miller at Pearl Harbor and Leonard Roy Harmon on the *San Francisco* in the Solomon Islands.

Doris Miller was twenty-one years old on that infamous day

when the Japanese attacked Pearl Harbor. He was a mess attendant. Miller was below decks when the Japanese dive bombers made their pass at the USS *West Virginia.* He ran topside and found that one of the machine gunners was wounded and unable to fire his weapon. Miller took hold of the

Doris Miller, Navy hero in World War II.
— TAAHO Collections, Austin, Texas

gun and brought four Japanese bombers down. Before this, his principal shooting had consisted of dropping squirrels out of trees with a rifle in the Brazos River bottom near Waco. Adm. Chester W. Nimitz pinned the Navy Cross on Miller in 1942. Unfortunately, Miller's bravery did not earn for him the Medal of Honor. In 1942, Miller toured the United States selling war bonds; then, following a Christmas reunion with his family, he returned to active duty aboard the USS *Liscombe Bay,* an aircraft carrier. On November 24, 1943, the ship was sunk in the Gilbert Islands. Miller was lost at sea.

Leonard Roy Harmon of Cuero, Texas. The U.S. Navy named a warship in his honor in 1943.

— Institute of Texan Cultures, San Antonio, Texas

Naval warships most often bear the names of famous battles, cities, states, and war heroes. Leonard Roy Harmon of Cuero, Texas, in DeWitt County, was the first African American to have a naval warship named in his honor. Harmon was born in 1917. At the age of twenty-two, he joined the navy, and after basic boot-camp training at Norfolk, Virginia, he was assigned to duty aboard the USS *San Francisco.*

Harmon's supreme act of valor occurred in the early morning of November 13, 1942, when the *San Francisco* engaged a Japanese naval force in the Solomon Islands. The American warship disabled an enemy battleship at 3,000 yards, sank a destroyer, and severely damaged two other vessels, but was hard hit during the encounter. Steward First Class Harmon took countless risks that morning, and was killed while evacuating the wounded from the deck. Later, the USS *San Francisco* was presented the Presidential Unit Citation, and Leonard Harmon was posthumously awarded the Navy Cross. He, like many other brave and fearless African Americans, never received the Congressional Medal of Honor, though he gave his life for his country.

In 1943, the U.S. Navy honored the hero by launching the USS *Harmon,* a destroyer escort. The ship was christened by Harmon's mother. The USS *Harmon* served almost a year with the Third Fleet in the South Pacific, then with the Seventh Fleet until 1945, receiving a total of three battle stars for World War II service. For two more years, the USS *Harmon* was used as a training ship; then it joined the Atlantic Fleet. Like her namesake, the ship had served with distinction and valor.

Pending Change

People and their leaders are important in all endeavors. They grow as they cooperate and the results show in their work. Together they discover opportunities. In Texas, however, it was difficult for many African Americans, following World War II, as at earlier periods, to find work for which they were prepared and that they were ready to undertake. Nevertheless, progress was made by them and they too became makers of history, each in their own way.

In the 1940s, a new position for the African American in Texas had developed through the action of several factors: first, the war with its worldwide experience for those in the Armed Forces; second, the organizations of African Americans and non-African Americans who endeavored to make more practical the ideals of the founders of the nation; and third, the courts which issued decisions more favorable to African-American advancement. These changes created a foundation for greater achievement in spite of the remaining handicaps.

Civil Rights in Texas

Legal Separation

If you were African-American and you lived in Texas before the late 1960s, you were not allowed to commingle publicly with white people. From the mid-1800s to the late 1900s, legal segregation created difficult times for African-American Texans. The Constitution of 1876 required separate schools for African-American children. In 1891, a state law mandated separate railroad coaches. Many cities and towns passed local ordinances called Jim Crow Laws, making it a punishable offense for whites and African Americans to mix in public places. Many of these laws stayed on the books and were enforced until 1964. Major hotels, restaurants, and entertainment events were not open to African Americans. Separate water fountains, restrooms, railway cars, buses and waiting rooms were maintained for African Americans. People of African descent were made to sit in the rear seats of streetcars and buses and in the balconies of movie theaters.

Weary of violence and discrimination, African Americans sought legal and nonviolent means to end this painful second-class citizenship status. In 1912, the NAACP organized a chapter in Houston. By 1930, more than thirty other chapters had been organized in the state. Church leaders, fraternal groups, and newspapers such as the *Houston Informer,* the *Dallas Express,* and the *Texas Freedman* spoke out against segregation and discrimination. The NAACP also took steps to end political discrimination and segregation in higher educational institutions.

Two Giant Steps

The protest of segregated higher education in Texas was a significant undertaking in the quest for abolition of separate and unequal public facilities. The movement could appropriately be called the "Jericho of Texas."

"The Legislature shall also, *when deemed practicable,* establish a college or branch university for colored youth . . ." So said the Texas State Constitution of 1876. For too many years, however, lawmakers found it difficult if not impossible to determine just how this constitutional provision was to be implemented. Some felt that the establishment of Prairie View had fulfilled the constitutional requirement. Critics held that Prairie View was only a "normal" school, or, at best, an agricultural and mechanical college. They felt that the Constitutional Convention of 1875 had intended that the African-American youths should have a "classical" university similar to the University of Texas at Austin. There were those who advocated the expansion of Prairie View so as to include a "classical" division, while there were others who insisted that a new separate university be constructed, exactly like the University of Texas at Austin. The resulting controversy over the issue became one of the most heated in Texas educational history.

Time after time, the Texas Legislature failed to act on the university issue. Usually, the appropriation blockade was the extent of their action. African Americans, however, were uncompromising in their efforts to have a university of quality established.

As a stop-gap measure to provide higher educational facilities for African Americans until a segregated university might be established, the legislature in 1945 changed the status, function, and name of Prairie View Normal and Industrial College. It was provided that Prairie View should:

1. Be authorized, in addition to the courses of study then authorized of study in law, medicine, engineering, pharmacy, journalism, and any other generally recognized college course taught at the University of Texas, such courses to be substantially equivalent to those offered at the University of Texas.
2. Remove the obligation to teach in the African-American public free schools for one year in case students of law, medicine, engineering, pharmacy, journalism and any other generally recognized college courses taught at the University of Texas.

Hiding behind the constitutional and practical restrictions on funds for the University of Texas, legislators claimed that these restrictions made it impracticable to establish a respectable branch of the university for African-American Texans.

In 1947, the legislature provided for the establishment of an entirely separate and equivalent university of the first call for Texans of African descent. The provisions of the act were:

Section 1. The Legislature of Texas deems it impracticable to establish and maintain a college or branch of the University of Texas for the instruction of the colored youth of this State without the levy of taxes and the use of the general revenue for the establishment, maintenance and erection of buildings as would be required by Section 14 of Article VII of the Constitution of Texas, if such institution were established as a college or branch of the University of Texas. Further, the Legislature of Texas deems that establishment of a Negro university with such limitations as to funds and operation would be unfair and wholly inadequate for the purpose of providing an equivalent university of the first class for Negroes of this State. Therefore, it is the purpose of this Act to establish an entirely separate and equivalent university of the first class for Negroes with full rights to be the use of tax money and the general revenue for establishment, maintenance, erection of buildings and operation of such institution as provided in Section 48, Article III, of the Constitution of the State of Texas.

Section 2. To provide instruction, training and higher education for colored people, there is hereby established a University of the first class in two dimensions: the first, styled "The Texas State University for Negroes," to be located in Houston . . . , the second, to be styled "The Prairie View Agricultural and Mechanical College of Texas," at Prairie View . . . at the Prairie View Agricultural and Mechanical College shall be offered courses in the mechanical arts, engineering, and the natural sciences connected therewith, together with any other courses authorized at Prairie View at the time of the passage of this Act, all of which shall be equivalent to those offered at the Agricultural and Mechanical College of Texas. The Texas State University for Negroes shall offer all other courses of higher learning . . . all of which shall be equivalent to those offered at the University of Texas. Upon demand being made by a qualified applicant for any present or future courses of instruction offered at the University of Texas, or its branches, such courses shall be established or added to the curriculum of the appropriate division of the schools hereby established in order that the separate universities for Negroes shall at all times offer equal educational opportunities and training as that available to other persons of this State . . .

Section 2 of the act provided for the establishment of an interim School of Law at the Texas State University for Negroes and made an emergency appropriation for that purpose. The emergency clause declared that:

The fact that the people of Texas desire that the State meet its obligation of equal educational opportunities for its Negro citizens from State-supported institutions, and the fact that a separate and equivalent university of the first class for Negroes cannot be established and maintained under the limitations and restrictions contained in Section 14, Article VII, of the Constitution of Texas in such institution were made a college or branch of the University of Texas, and the fact that the only means of establishing an equivalent university of the first class for Negroes with use of tax money and the general revenue is to create a separate university entirely independent of the University of Texas, and the fact that interim courses must be established immediately by establishment and operation of said separate university of the first class for Negroes . . .

It is important to understand that this was a promise made that could not possibly be delivered. Time makes great institutions, not legislation which promotes empty promises of separate but equal.

The disparity between the legal and educational rights of African-American Texans and the actual educational benefits afforded them gave rise to some significant court action in the Lone Star State. *Givens v. Woodward* was the first case, coming on September 30, 1946. The case ended in a dismissal.

The second and perhaps most important case was *Sweatt v. Painter.* Heman Marion Sweatt opened the doors for graduate and professional study at previously all-white institutions with his suit against the University of Texas. It was this particular suit that disturbed legislators, who had previously resisted all appeals, petitions, and prayers to establish two "Universities of the first class" for African-American Texans. The intended maintenance of segregated Jim Crow colleges and universities, however, did not materialize. In the spirit of Heman Sweatt and the NAACP, in their rejection of the "basement law school," African-American Texans insisted that state-supported higher educational institutions in Texas should be color blind; there were not to be any institutions labeled "for Negroes only."

Heman Sweatt applied to the University of Texas School of Law for admission in 1946. He was a graduate of Wiley College and held a master's degree from the University of Michigan. He was qualified for admission in every way except that he was not white but African-American. Sweatt filed a lawsuit against T. S. Painter, president of the

Heman Marion Sweatt. His efforts to be admitted to the University of Texas led the way for the desegregation of higher education in Texas.

— TAAHO Collections,
Austin, Texas

University of Texas, in the 126th District Court. He asked the court to force his admission based on his rights guaranteed in the 14th Amendment of the U.S. Constitution:

> All persons born or naturalized in the United States, and subject to the jurisdiction thereof, are citizens of the United States and of the State wherein they reside. No State shall make or enforce any law which shall abridge the privileges or immunities of citizens of the United States; nor shall any State deprive any person of life, liberty, or property, without due process of law; nor deny to any person within its jurisdiction the equal protection of the law . . .

The court's decision was that because no law school existed for African Americans in the state of Texas, Sweatt's rights for the pursuit of a professional law degree had indeed been denied. The State was required to either create such school or admit Sweatt to the University of Texas.

The State of Texas made a poor attempt to establish such a school, but with the advice and support of the NAACP and the legal counsel of Thurgood Marshall, that attempt was promptly rejected. A second attempt was made following 1947 legislation creating a new university. That school, Texas State University for Negroes, later became known as Texas Southern University. A law school to be built in Austin was included in that legislation and Sweatt was notified, but he refused to attend the makeshift, so-called law school. In 1948, the State Appellate Court denied Sweatt's motion, stating that the State was then in compliance with the "separate but equal" doctrine.

After appealing to the Texas Supreme Court, which refused to overturn the lower court's decision, Sweatt took his case to the United States Supreme Court in 1949. On June 5, 1950, the Supreme Court agreed that "the educational opportunities offered white and African-American law students by the State of Texas were not substantially equal, and that the equal protection clause of the 14th Amendment required that Sweatt be admitted to the University of Texas Law School."

Historians have called Heman Marion Sweatt the father of the integration movement in Texas. This assessment may be seen as accurate in the light of his decision, under counsel of the NAACP, not to attend the separate Texas State University for Negroes Law School created in response to *Sweatt v. Painter*. Prior to this time, the

NAACP had been filing equalization suits all over the country. In 1950, Thurgood Marshall penned an edict, endorsed by the board of directors of the NAACP, to stop filing equalization suits and, on the strength of the Sweatt decision, to sue on the ground that the segregation itself was illegal.

In 1948, Herman A. Barnett, a Samuel Huston College honor graduate, applied to the University of Texas Medical School in Galveston. The NAACP saw this as another opportunity to test segregation and Jim Crowism in Texas through the legal process. More than forty students applied for admission to the graduate, medical, and dental schools of the University of Texas and were denied admission. In April 1949, students from Bishop, Wiley, Jarvis, Texas, Tillotson, and Samuel Huston colleges traveled to Austin to peacefully demonstrate at the Capitol in protest of the State's refusal to admit Herman A. Barnett to the University of Texas graduate medical school. Several white students from the University of Texas joined in the protest. President Joseph J. Rhodes (president, Bishop College), U. Simpson Tate (attorney), Donald Jones (NAACP field representative), W. J. Durham (attorney), Arthur DeWitty (advisor), and Thurgood Marshall (attorney) monitored the activities and gave advice. Student leaders were David A. Williams (Southwest regional president of College NAACP Chapters), Lewis A. Brown (Bishop College NAACP president), Ruth Naomi Banks (secretary), Roland Brown (Bishop College NAACP Chapter vice-president), Ethel McDonald (Bishop College NAACP Chapter treasurer), and Tommy Brown (Bishop College NAACP Chapter chaplain).

Following the students' peaceful protest march and audience with Texas Governor Beauford Jester, Barnett was admitted to the Galveston Medical School, but the legislature attempted to maintain a segregated situation in that they proposed to have Texas Southern issue Barnett's degree rather than have him march with the white students at the graduation ceremonies.

In 1950, after the Supreme Court ruling in the Sweatt case, Barnett was graduated and the University of Texas Medical School accepted African-American students, as did the dental school in 1951.

In 1952, several undergraduate colleges were desegregated, among them Wayland Baptist College, Southern Methodist University, Del Mar College, Amarillo College, Southwest Baptist Theological Seminary, Abilene Christian College, Hardin Simmons University, and San Angelo State College. Many other private and community colleges also opened their doors to students of African descent.

Protest of Segregated, Jim Crow Public Accommodations

Prior to World War II, African-American Texans realized that they were unprotected by the legal system and were therefore inclined to accept the forced segregated public accommodations malady. When the war ended, however, most returning veterans of color went home with a determination to end second-class citizenship in Texas. The National Association for the Advancement of Colored People sought to help African-American Texans end discrimination and segregation. This was to be accomplished through court action, education to change public opinion, cooperation in voter registration, picketing, and selective purchasing. Leaders such as James L. Farmer, Joseph J. Rhodes, E.C. Estell, W. J. Durham, A. A. Lucas, Lula White, Juanita Kraft, C. B. Cash, J. J. Sutton, and A. Maceo Smith strongly advocated bringing equality of opportunity through nonviolent protest to all spheres of life in Texas regardless of race or color. Religious, labor, and church organizations gave cooperation and supported action movements.

Actions were initiated by young African-American Texans when students from Wiley, Bishop, Jarvis, Samuel Huston, Tillotson, Texas, Paul Quinn, and Texas Southern colleges began sit-ins at lunch counters in their respective locations. This kind of participation in demonstrations for freedom gradually brought results. Public opinion manifested change, as some state and local public officials began to make statements favorable to improvement of human relations and the ways in which people live, work, and play.

Many non-African-American Texans refused to support a federal civil rights bill which would end separation or exclusion of African Americans at hotels, motels, theaters, public transportation, and restaurants. President Lyndon B. Johnson and Senator Ralph Yarborough favored the bill as a step toward equal opportunity and treatment for all citizens.

The impact of the Civil Rights Bill of 1964 has been monumental. The plight of African-American Texans has improved legally and socially, at a pace that is satisfactory to some but unsatisfactory to many others. At this point in time many democratic citizenship options once forcibly denied are available and offer positions of economic security, importance, and empowerment. To be sure, there are still many problems without solutions; not all of the hostility and intolerance have disappeared, nor are all opportunities yet equal in our Lone Star State.

Now, as in the years of the Republic, when trends were reversed, attitudes of the people as a whole change slower than constitutional law. The trend, however, seems relatively clear and predictable.

An education was needed for all Texans who have been nurtured, educated, and cultured in the philosophy of superiority and inferiority on the basis of color or ethnic origin. Some Texans have learned to regard persons of darker color as far less capable than themselves. These attitudes were learned consciously and unconsciously. A new eduction during the decades of the '60s, '70s, '80s, and '90s then became a fundamental factor in the achievements in the future of African-American Texans, and in opening the eyes of all Texans and others to accept these achievements.

Although African-American Texans have faced many unfavorable conditions, the progress they have made in many significant areas of endeavor has been commendable. They have become an important factor in industry, agriculture, education, citizenship, the fine arts, literature, housing and health, and the economic and political life of Texas. Interracial and intergroup movements have brought numbers of leaders into a unification of leadership activities which have created goodwill in many communities in the state. From both groups, there have come continuously the makers of history.

Section II

Lt. John L. Bullis led the Seminole Indian scouts in the mid to late 1800s.
—TAAHO Collections, Austin, Texas

Pompey Factor was awarded the Congressional Medal of Honor.
—TAAHO Collections, Austin, Texas

Chapter 5

The Seminole-Negro Indian Scouts in Texas

By Thomas A. Britten

In the spring of 1875, 1st Lt. John Lapham Bullis of the 24th U.S. Infantry and a small detachment of scouts conducted a search for marauding Indians near the Pecos River in the Big Bend region of Southwest Texas. Coming across the trail of their quarry, Bullis and his men pursued the Indians and caught up to them as the warriors were about to cross the Pecos.

Quickly dismounting, Bullis and his scouts opened fire on the Indians and a fierce gun-battle ensued for nearly forty-five minutes. Outnumbered and fearful of being cut off from their horses, Bullis and his scouts scrambled back to their mounts and were in the process of retreating when Bullis' horse threw him, leaving the hapless officer to face the rapidly approaching Indians on foot. Thanks to the courage and loyalty of scout John Ward, however, Bullis "saved his hair" by leaping on the back of his scout's horse which carried the two men to safety. Not surprisingly, Bullis recommended that his scouts, John Ward, Isaac Payne, and Pompey Factor, be recognized for their gallantry and bravery and the men subsequently received the Congressional Medal of Honor for their service.

These scouts belonged to a unique and relatively unknown group of individuals known as the Seminole-Negro Indian scouts. Although their service to the U.S. Army in Texas in the 1870s to 1880s has gone unnoticed compared to the famous "Buffalo Soldiers" of the 9th and 10th Cavalry regiments or the army's widespread use of Native American auxiliaries on the Texas frontier, the Seminole-Negro Indian scouts were instrumental in the ultimate pacification and spread of Anglo civilization in Texas.

A division of Florida's Seminole Nation, the Seminole-Negroes were unique both physically and culturally to other North American peoples. They were known to a few government officials and residents of northern Mexico as the "*Mascogos,*" while Americans commonly referred to them as the Seminole-Negroes or Seminole scouts. As the name implies, the Seminole-Negroes were of mixed Seminole and African-American lineage, although predominately of the latter. During the late seventeenth and eighteenth centuries, black slaves escaped the plantations of the Carolinas, Georgia, and Alabama to freedom in Spanish Florida. Once there, the Seminole Indians welcomed them as allies in the struggle against Anglo expansion into northern Florida. Because of the similar cultural backgrounds of the Seminoles and blacks, many of whom were recent arrivals from Africa, an affinity between the two peoples soon developed. Although the fugitive blacks were technically slaves of the Seminoles as well, they readily adopted Seminole customs in addition to Muskogee, the dominant Seminole language. In sharp contrast to blacks' experiences under Anglo slavery, however, the Seminole-Negroes were allowed to live in separate villages from their Indian masters, and enjoyed a considerable degree of autonomy.

Throughout the Seminole Wars in Florida that lasted from 1811 to 1858, the Seminole-Negroes proved to be faithful and courageous allies to the Seminoles. When the U.S. Army relocated the southeastern tribes to the Indian Territory in the 1820s to the 1850s, the Seminole-Negroes went with the Seminoles, where their unique status as *de facto* continued for a brief period.

Despite assurances by officials of the United States government that they would be happy and well cared for in their new home, many Seminoles and Seminole-Negroes became disillusioned with their lack of food and supplies (although the federal government had promised them these items in the treaties of removal). In addition, the constant threat by slave-catchers to steal the Seminole-

Negroes ultimately undermined the relationship between the Seminoles and Seminole-Negroes. Soon after arrival in Indian Territory, tribal factions developed over the issue of the Seminoles' obligations in protecting their black allies from slave catchers. Consequently, in the latter part of 1849, the Seminole band leader Wild Cat led an exodus of discontented Seminoles, Creeks, Kickapoos, and Seminole-Negroes south to Mexico, where they hoped to live unmolested and free from government interference and slave catchers. The Mexican authorities welcomed the newcomers and granted them large tracts of land in northern Coahuila. In return for the land grants, the Seminoles and Seminole-Negroes enlisted for service in the Mexican army to act as a buffer against bandits and militant Comanche and Apache warriors who raided into Mexico each year.

For the next decade, the Seminoles and Seminole-Negroes performed this duty very effectively. According to Mexican General Alberto Guajardo, the Seminoles and Seminole-Negroes were "always triumphant on their expeditions" against hostile Indians.

By 1860, however, many Seminoles desired to rejoin their brethren in the Indian Territory, and by the middle of 1861 only the Seminole-Negroes remained in Mexico. With slavery still in force in the southern half of the United States, the *Mascogos* had little to gain by following their Seminole allies to the north. After the conclusion of the Civil War in 1865, the federal government moved to concentrate the Western tribes onto reservations in the Indian Territory as well as in the Dakotas. In pursuance of this policy, on June 23, 1870, Maj. Zenis R. Bliss, the commander of Fort Duncan located at Eagle Pass, Texas, invited the Seminole-Negroes to move north to Texas where, ostensibly, they would remain until their eventual removal to Indian Territory. Whether or not army officials committed the invitation and promise of removal to Indian Territory to writing is unknown (although the Seminole-Negroes remained steadfast in their insistence that a written promise existed). A majority of the Seminole-Negroes accepted the invitation, and in July 1870, over 200 moved north to Texas where they awaited removal to Indian Territory. In the meantime, to pay for their food and supplies, a number of Seminole-Negro warriors took employment with the U.S. Army as scouts and soon established a reputation as able and courageous trackers and fighters.

In the fall of 1872, a group of Seminole-Negro scouts transferred from Fort Duncan to Fort Clark near present-day Brackett-

Seminole scout unit. Such units served at Fort Clark at Brackettville, Texas, and Fort Duncan on the Rio Grande River.

—TAAHO Collections, Austin, Texas

ville, Texas, where they met their new commander, then 1st Lt. John Lapham Bullis. When their families joined them at the end of the year, there were some 200 to 300 Seminole-Negroes encamped along Las Moras Creek at Fort Clark. For the next decade, the Seminole-Negro scouts participated in dozens of engagements with hostile Indians, winning praise and commendations from their commanders.

Among the most daring of their exploits was the raid on Remolino, Mexico. In March 1873, Gen. C. C. Augur, commander of the Department of Texas, ordered Col. Ranald Slidell Mackenzie, the young and enterprising commander of the 4th Cavalry regiment, to take charge of

Col. Ranald Slidell Mackenzie led Seminole scouts in raids across the Rio Grande.

— Fort McKavett Archives

Fort Clark. His orders were to halt the raids and depredations committed by Indians, Mexicans, and Anglos along the Rio Grande border region. Thus, throughout March and April 1873, Mackenzie drilled his troops daily in preparation for the task.

During a meeting held in April 1873 between Mackenzie, Secretary of War William W. Belknap, and Gen. Philip Sheridan, the 4th Cavalry received instructions to march into Mexico to destroy an Indian encampment at Remolino, the reported source of raids emanating from northern Mexico. On May 17, 1873, Mackenzie assembled six companies of his regiment, including eighteen Seminole-Negro scouts. Later that day, Bullis joined Mackenzie, bringing an additional sixteen Seminole-Negro scouts and raising the total of Mackenzie's force to just over 400 men.

Early on the morning of May 18, Mackenzie's troops crossed the Rio Grande and headed south to the Indian encampment at Remolino. After marching all night, the American force attacked the Indian stronghold, killing nineteen warriors and capturing forty women and children, sixty-five ponies, and a Lipan Apache chief named Costillietos, who had allegedly been lariated by a Seminole-Negro scout. On the way home, Mackenzie deployed the scouts to guard the flanks and serve as a rear-guard against a surprise attack. Their retreat was completed without incident, however, and Mac-

Seminole scouts at Fort Clark.

— Fort Clark Museum

kenzie's troops arrived safely back at Fort Clark after having covered 140 miles in twenty-seven hours with nothing to eat except hard bread.

The Seminole-Negro scouts distinguished themselves again the following year during the Red River War of 1874–1875. In hopes of forcing militant Comanche, Kiowa, Southern Cheyenne, and Arapaho warriors back onto their reservations in western Indian Territory, the U.S. Army launched a campaign to subdue these formidable warriors of the southern Plains.

In July 1874, Mackenzie received orders to move the 4th Cavalry north from Fort Clark to the Red River Valley. In pursuance of these orders, Mackenzie assembled eight companies of cavalry and five companies of infantry as well as a detachment of scouts that included thirteen Seminole-Negroes. At the Battle of Palo Duro Canyon in September 1874, Mackenzie's troops again performed with deadly precision. Not only were the Indians defeated, but vast caches of supplies and munitions were destroyed as well. To insure that the defeated Native Americans would remain on their reservations in the future, over 1,000 Indian horses were killed to destroy the warriors' mobility. A Seminole-Negro scout named Adam Payne was subsequently awarded the Congressional Medal of Honor for his invaluable service to Mackenzie. In his report of the events associated with Payne's performance at Palo Duro Canyon, Mackenzie asserted that Payne had "more cool daring than any scout he had ever known."

Despite their commendable service to the U.S. Army, the Seminole-Negroes lived in a destitute condition at Fort Clark and Fort Duncan. When they requested permanent land grants or removal to Indian territory, however, officials in the War Department responded by informing them that they should have stayed in Mexico. To exacerbate matters, army officials ordered the Seminole-Negroes' rations reduced, except for the families of scouts. Many families, consequently, were forced to forage for food, grow their own crops, or steal. The citizens of Kinney County complained that the Seminole-Negroes stole their cattle and other livestock and gave shelter to horse thieves. However, the Seminole-Negro scouts continued to serve the army faithfully, no doubt believing that the government would fulfill its obligations made back in 1870.

By 1880, the number of border incidents had greatly diminished. Nonetheless, in December 1879, Lieutenant Bullis and the

Seminole-Negro scouts received orders to accompany a party of railroad surveyors, miners, explorers, and prospectors on an expedition to the Chenati Mountains in Presidio County. Two months prior to this, Victorio and his band of Warm Springs Apaches had slipped away from their reservation at Fort Stanton, New Mexico. For the next year, Victorio's men raided and pillaged throughout southern New Mexico, northern Mexico, and the Big Bend of Texas. It was not surprising, therefore, that army officials turned to Bullis and the Seminole-Negro scouts to protect railroad interests in southwest Texas. For the next four months, therefore, Bullis and his faithful scouts scoured the Big Bend region for signs of Indians or Mexican bandits. After returning home to Fort Clark for a brief rest at the end of April, the Seminole-Negro scouts again set out for the Big Bend in July and occupied a remote outpost at Pena, Colorado. From this vantage point, the scouts could better protect the construction of a road through the region. For the next five years, the Seminole-Negroes served at Camp Pena, Colorado, conducting scouts, protecting prospectors, surveyors, and road builders, and completing the construction of post facilities.

With pacification of the Indians on the Texas frontier completed by the late 1880s, the Seminole-Negroes faced a much more formidable foe. The United States government refused to acknowledge the Seminole-Negroes' claims for land, and, now that their usefulness as scouts had ended, the federal government worked to decrease the number of enlisted scouts and to force the Seminole-Negroes to leave Fort Clark.

On September 1, 1886, Gen. D. S. Stanley, commander of the Department of Texas, reported an increase in the number of robberies along the Rio Grande border. Despite the fact that no United States troops in Texas were killed by Indians in 1886, Fort Clark, because of its strategic location, continued to garrison over 400 men, nearly double the number of any fort in Texas. The number included a detachment of twenty Seminole-Negro scouts. From 1886 to 1892, their number varied from fifteen to twenty individuals. In September of 1892, the scouts were transferred to Fort Ringgold, although their families remained at the settlement on Las Moras Creek at Fort Clark. Contrary to the Army Adjutant General's Office suggestion of September 10, 1894, that all the Seminole-Negro scouts be discharged, army officials decided to keep ten scouts at Fort Clark and ten at Fort Ringgold for two more years.

The Seminole-Negroes, meanwhile, continued their requests for permission to move to the Indian Territory or have land granted them in Texas. With fewer men receiving paychecks for scouting duties, the economic status of Seminole-Negro families was precarious at best. Former scouts assumed new duties as a result of the pacification of Indians and the federal government's decision to reduce their activities in the army. Despite recommendations in 1903 that the Seminole-Negro encampment at Las Moras Creek be disbanded altogether, the fort's commander, Col. Joseph H. Dorst, employed former scouts as clerks, teamsters, officers' servants, firemen, and carpenters. Others farmed, hired themselves out as ranch hands, or in the case of the women, worked as house servants or laundresses. The Seminole-Negro men who were fortunate enough to retain their enlistment served as a service corps, performing duties that the white troops despised. The duties included daily rides along the reservation fence lines to make needed repairs, keeping nonreservation cattle off reservation pastures, and guarding the forests against trespassing woodcutters. In addition, the scouts served as conservation officers by keeping hunters and fishermen off the Fort Clark reservation.

Although some performed useful functions, most of the Seminole-Negroes were unemployed and the military officials at Fort Clark became increasingly concerned with the number of civilian complaints registered concerning them. Among the grievances were charges of theft, drunkenness, domestic violence, and providing sanctuary for black criminals. Colonel Dorst attributed the scouts' unemployment to their "lack of inclination to work steadily, or to work at all when they don't have to." The colonel also described the Seminole-Negro settlement along Las Moras Creek as cluttered with trash piles and manure heaps. In addition, he reported that their cattle, horses, and goats were depleting the grass supply of the cavalry stationed at Fort Clark, and that they were grazing civilian livestock on the reservation for pay. Dorst concluded his report by stating that the dams and fences built by the Seminole-Negroes along Las Moras Creek interfered with military exercises conducted by the soldiers stationed at the fort.

By 1909, many of the Seminole-Negroes at Fort Clark had become a people quite unlike their ancestors of the nineteenth century. Once expert scouts and fighters, they had become, due to circumstances outside their control, servants, laborers, and beggars. As a result of their marriages with Mexicans and African Americans, the Seminole-Negroes exhibited few physical characteristics of Seminole blood. Their skin color varied from black to light brown, although eighteen of the twenty remaining Seminole-Negro scouts continued to insist that they were Indians rather than African Americans.

On November 6, 1909, a Seminole-Negro named Morrell Hall wrote a letter to Secretary of War Luke E. Wright, asking permission for the Seminole-Negroes to stay at Fort Clark. Hall described the condition of his people by stating that:

> . . . some are old and blind, some are old and crippled, we are neither citizens of Mexico, nor can we claim our citizenship in this country, we have no other home, we do not know any other country, and we most earnestly ask that we be allowed to remain in our homes on Ft. Clark reservation.

Hall also claimed that the alleged treaty document made between the United States and the Seminole-Negroes when they came to Texas from Mexico in 1870 was destroyed in a fire ten years earlier. Officials in the War Department, however, claimed neither knowledge of such a promise made to the Seminole-Negroes, nor a copy of a treaty document.

On June 29, 1914, Capt. Sterling Price Adams, the commanding officer at Fort Clark, received the final order to disband the Seminole-Negro Indian scouts. The order called for the detachment of Seminole-Negro scouts to cease to exist as an organization after September 30, 1914, and set a timetable for their removal in three detachments beginning on July 31, 1914. A group of twenty-four elderly blacks and single parents were allowed to remain until the older people died or the War Department saw fit to order their removal. Some of those forced to move traveled to Del Rio, Kerrville, San Antonio, and other communities in South Texas. Most simply moved to Brackettville, where they took what jobs they could find on the nearby cattle and sheep ranches.

Thus ended the existence of the Seminole-Negro Indian scouts after having served the United States Army faithfully for over forty years. During that time the scouts traversed thousands of miles throughout the rugged expanses of the Rio Grande frontier, endured countless hardships, and fought against both hostile Indians and ruthless bandits. Although few in number, the scouts received high praise from their commanders for their tenacious fighting and tracking abilities, endurance, and loyalty. Four Seminole-Negro scouts received the Congressional Medal of Honor. In the long run, however, the fact that they were more Negro than Seminole worked to their detriment. The federal government proved unwilling to provide land grants or funds for the Seminole-Negroes, and invented a number of unconvincing excuses (i.e., the Seminole-Negroes were not officially registered on the Seminole tribal rolls) for their refusal of assistance. Undoubtedly, the ugly hand of racism lay not far beneath the surface in explaining the federal government's reluctance to aid the Seminole-Negroes. Despite their unfortunate demise, however, the Seminole-Negro Indian scouts deserve recognition for their outstanding contribution to the spread of Anglo civilization into Texas and should rightly take their place among the heroes of Texas history.

Chapter 6

They Danced Until Dawn and Other Untold Texas Legends

by Cindy Bland Verheyden

Hollywood has portrayed many lasting impressions of early Texas settlers. The men were rugged, brave, stubborn, fearless, aggressive braggarts dedicated to scratching a life from a territory plagued with violent Indians, harsh weather, rugged terrain and rocky soils. The women were just as tough as the men. Undaunted by others' claims of ownership or territorial rights, these settlers took the land and the turmoil that came with it. They often gave their lives in defense of their actions.

Legends of these fearless adventurers are engraved in Texas' history. But between the lines lie tales of joy and gaiety, parties and dances, concerts and recitals, receptions and celebrations — and an enduring love of fun, dance, and music that spanned the vast territory. The responsibilities of six-shooters, cattle and crops were regularly (although temporarily) displaced by eager anticipations of special social events, temporarily evicting the worries and cares of the hard times and the harsh environment.

One of the first official social events of the new Republic was so magnificent its legend supersedes all others during Texas' early years. The first anniversary celebration of the victory of the Battle of San Jacinto will always be the "greatest ball of the century."

In 1837, the state capital was a mere settlement along the banks of Buffalo Bayou near the Gulf Coast. Named after the Republic's first elected president, Houston consisted of a few one-story buildings, several dirt-floored cabins, and a few tents (Daniels, p. 4). Nevertheless, the local citizens prepared for a grand celebration, including a parade, a formal ball and a midnight dinner (Daniels, p. 4; Ellis).

The parade began about 3:00 P.M. on April 21. "One of the most popular songs during the parade, sung with great enthusiasm and gaiety, was 'Will You Come to the Bower'" (Daniels, p. 4). Later that evening, after donning elegant costumes in one of the few cabin homes in the settlement, a crowd of ladies and gentlemen, including President Sam Houston, proceeded to a large unfinished building which had been prepared for the grand ball. As the walking cavalcade neared the ballroom, the band played "Hail to the Chief" (Ellis).

At midnight the weary dancers strolled one block to the hotel for a dinner of turkey and venison. After a brief respite, they were ready for more:

> Returning to the ballroom, dancing was continued until the prompter's voice failed and the cotillion gave way to the Virginia reel. By the time each dancer had "gone down the middle," as the last figure of the reel was known, it was daylight and time to go home. (Ellis)

In her notes of the event, Mrs. Mary J. Briscoe tells that "Visitors came from Brazoria, Columbus, Harrisburg and from most of the adjacent country . . . [and] from as far away as 60 miles to attend the event" (Ellis).

Other Texans were eager to celebrate the anniversary of Santa Anna's defeat in high style too. Mrs. Mary Austin Holley, a cousin to Stephen F. Austin, wrote of preparations for a ball to be held in Velasco (once the temporary government seat, where the Treaty of Velasco was signed on May 19, 1836, establishing the Rio Grande River as the Texas-Mexico boundary.): "All the world who can move, wind and weather permitting, are to be there" (Ellis). Apparently the new Republic was ill-equipped to outfit the public for such a grand occasion, since Mrs. Holley added, "Everything available for dresses in Texas has been bought up for the occasion" (Ellis). Additional supplies, including men's clothing from New York, were expected on a ship coming from New Orleans.

High society weddings were often occasions for formal balls. The memoirs of Noah Smithwick, a "pretty fair Arkansas fiddler," include descriptions of several weddings he attended after settling in Texas in 1827. Smithwick recalled the wedding and ball of Candice Thompson and David Holderman held in Bastrop — Austin's "Little Colony": "This being an extraordinary occasion, all the elite in the country round were invited, and few regrets were sent." Smithwick placed great emphasis on the "luxury" of a good plank floor having the ability to assure a full attendance (Ellis).

Balls and receptions began an early Texas tradition for all types of special occasions. Presidential inaugurations were the cream of these affairs. Describing the 1838 inaugural ball (Houston was still the capital city in 1838) honoring President Mirabeau Buonaparte Lamar, Dr. Ashbel Smith said, "The elite of the land, its beauty and worth were collected there" (Daniels, p. 18). Balls were held on all patriotic holidays.

Following Texas' union with the states in 1845, Texans celebrated July 4, another special holiday for balls. Later, during the Civil War (1845–61), formal balls and cotillions were held to raise money for the Confederacy (Pugh, p. 66). Dress and masquerade balls were the major entertainment attractions in Houston (Pugh, p. 12).

Although the events are less well documented, Negroes were participating in similar high-society events of their own making. The occasions became so popular and organized that Houston's city leaders feared insurrection and passed an ordinance in 1841 prohibiting Negro-sponsored balls (Pugh, p. 14). In 1862, however, some were allowed under supervision of the marshal. Some white men attended these functions, evoking harsh criticism from the press: "We consider every white man degrades himself to take part in these balls, and none but the lowest class of men would be seen in such places" (Pugh, p. 67).

A box of 1870s invitations belonging to an Austin man reveals that many organizations sponsored balls and that one's social calendar could fill very fast. The collection includes solicitations for balls sponsored by the Austin Star Club (Dress Ball and a Bal Masque), the E. C. C. (honoring a new member), the C. D. C. (managers of the Rail Road Reception Ball given by the Citizens of Austin to celebrate the arrival of the first train in December 1870), Mab's Merrie Men (Mardi Gras Ball), various militia and fraternal organizations, and the Washington Fire Engine Company No. 1 (Hart).

Because there was a shortage of women, early invitations announced: "Only women who receive written invitations admitted." The San Jacinto Anniversary Ball of Houston in 1938 was attended by 300. Sixty girls and married women danced with 240 gentlemen (Pugh, p. 14). The official population for Houston in 1839 listed a total of 2,073, including 453 females (Daniels, p. 22). Texas justly earned her nickname of "The Bachelor Republic" (Casey, p. 31).

During the antebellum period (1846–1865), temperance balls became popular for teetotalers (Pugh). In 1838, however, Houston citizens gave the cold shoulder to announcements of a temperance lecture to honor visiting clergymen. President Houston, who requested permission to preside over the meeting, drew a large crowd with his appearance and delivered a "sermon" warning of the evils of drink — a subject of which he had some personal knowledge and experience, as he admonished listeners to "follow my words and not my example" (Daniels, p. 12).

Around this time *The Nation*, a Boston publication, printed the following summary of the Houston business community: "Houston has a theatre, fifty gambling houses and nearly a hundred grog shops and no house of worship" (Daniels, p. 19), further proof that music and entertainment were held in high esteem by the earliest Texans.

The determination of Texas' elite society to have fun is paralleled by the cleverness and vitality of her poorer classes. Although the dances of the rural folk were less formal, they were no less organized.

Once a dance date was set, a "grapevine telegraph" of riders dispensed invitations to "every person they happened to meet." Unlike the invitation-only gatherings of the urban gentry, cowboy dances were open affairs: "Everybody invited and nobody slighted" (Craddock, p. 183).

Neighbors of a dance's host would drop in early to help with preparations. Most guests arrived around dusk. Men would travel from great distances to attend these affairs. According to J. R. Craddock, the longer the distance a man had to come, the more popular he seemed to be with the ladies (Craddock, p. 185).

When the revelers (or the fiddler) needed a break, coffee was served in the kitchen, where the children were bedded on the floor. The men passed around whiskey, although not openly, and if a cowboy got out of hand, he could expect to get slapped around and locked up away from the dance (Craddock, p. 187).

The XIT Ranch — still one of Texas' largest working ranches — hosted annual dances. A 1939 printed XIT rodeo program describes musician Jess Morris' recollections of some of the early gatherings:

> Everyone within a range of 50 miles attended. Dancing was from sunset to sunup. One dance in Tascosa lasted a week . . . Big "program" dances were extra special events with a grand march led by a prominent ranch couple. The women were especially well turned out for the big dances as they had a whole year to plan their costumes. ("They Came from 50 Miles Around . . . " p. 76)

William Hale (Stone), a working cowboy and ranchman, described his own experience passing through Tascosa on a trip from New York City to Galveston:

> We stopped at a town in the Panhandle of Texas by the name of Tascosa, and took in a ball that night. Tascosa was a Mexican town, and they gave a ball and we all went. Some of my men got to drinking, and we had to lay them out until they got so they could go to camp and to bed. (Hale, p. 136)

Hale's narrative continues, describing a knife and gun scuffle over a Mexican girl with an exciting finish: "The boy shot the house full of holes, and then came to camp and went to bed" (Hale, p. 136).

In 1871, the small town of Lampasas held a dance each night the week before Christmas. The Christmas Eve event was the climax, ending with a "whiskey-drinking and six-shooter-firing orgy in the saloons on the square" (Steelman, pp. 2-3).

An important ingredient for cowboy dances was the fiddler. General opinions of fiddlers held that they were shiftless, lazy men, but once his music started, every dancing man had to pay his due.

Olcutt Sanders says that communities not blessed with a resident fiddler would form impromptu dances whenever a fiddler passed through town. For special celebrations, fiddlers might be hired from as far away as 130 miles (Sanders, p. 78). Fiddlers earned good money for the times. Five dollars for an evening's work was average, and bands could earn $20 for five hours' work. As many dances lasted all night, fiddlers could earn extra pay and tips for their long hours (Sanders, p. 83).

Slaves and black freedmen often provided music for various gatherings. Noah Smithwick recalls a wedding near Columbus when the fiddler never showed up, "so we called in an old darky belonging to Col. Zane Philips, who performed on a clevis as an accompaniment at his singing, while another Negro scrapped on a cotton hoe with a case knife" (Ellis).

Frank Bryan described a scene typical for overnight campouts in East Texas in "On the Jefferson Road":

[Negroes] slept just across the campfires at night. And around the campfires, in the long evenings, they furnished music and entertainment. Banjos, french harps and Jews ("juice") harps were brought out. The ground was floored with tailgates from wagons. This for the benefit of the young bucks with talking feet. (Bryan, p. 16)

Pugh describes an informal dancing party in Houston in February 1838 where "rells" *[sic]* were danced to "two discordant violins and a young Negro slapping his hands and his sides to keep time instead of a banjo" (Pugh, p. 14).

Dancing is deeply rooted in Mexican traditions, but early Texas invaders fought against their Mexican neighbors to establish their own new settlements. This cultural rift between Anglo pioneers and displaced Mexicans was almost impenetrable. Sanders lists "Over the Waves" as one of only a few Mexican tunes used at Texas dances (Sanders, p. 89). A black fiddler named Old Cox "played for many Mexican dances that lasted all night" (Sanders, p. 83). Mexican parties and dances are seldom mentioned in traditional Texas historical chronicles.

Despite the early Texans' reputations as crude, harsh, unsophisticated brutes, a fiddle and a song could melt away their hearts. "We take our Texas history too seriously," wrote Anna Ellis. "The yellowed pages and faded ink of old letters, old diaries and memoirs of Texas life fairly glow though they tell but of such simple things as . . . balls and weddings . . . gay indeed" (Ellis).

And just as the Texas mystique continues to intrigue outsiders, the spirit of early Texas settlers flows freely in the veins of modern Texans.

Grieving for Their Dead:
Mother Nature and Human Neglect Threaten
Austin's Historic Black Cemeteries
by Cindy Bland Verheyden

Rev. A. C. Franklin has been making trips to Williamson Creek Cemetery for as long as he can remember. Like many of South Austin's oldest black families, Franklin's ancestors rest in quiet repose among towering weeds, impetuous cedar trees and heaps of garbage.

Franklin recalls that a dairy gave — or "sold for next to nothing" — the five acres to the black community in 1909 "for a burying ground . . .

"It didn't have a fence around it then and the cows from the dairy grazed to keep the cemetery clean," says Franklin. Today Franklin heads a small group who supervise and maintain this graveyard dating back to 1867 and probably earlier.

Although the tombstones bear more than 200 different family names, Franklin's group consists of only five people who have difficulty raising the money necessary to keep the grounds in order.

Says Edna Satterwhite, the secretary of the Williamson Creek Cemetery Association, "Even if we only ask the families for $5 or $10, we can't even get that. Sometimes we have to use our own money to hire help."

Mowing and trimming aren't the only maintenance required. "We had to pay a man $900 to clean up the trees after a tornado," says Satterwhite. And Franklin recalls paying another man $1,400 to haul off a truckload of tires dumped on the grounds. Vandals have torn down the fence several times and recently stole the gate.

"I just wish we could get some help to keep up the cemetery like we should," says Franklin.

Satterwhite's mother and grandmother were buried at Williamson Creek when she was only four years old. "I come out here and try to do my part," she explains. "But I'm the youngest one [of the association] and I'm 68 years old."

Both Franklin and Satterwhite feel that the younger generations do not care about preserving cemeteries and their valuable history. And according to Dr. Terry Jordan, a geography professor at the University of Texas who has studied cemeteries around the world, this is true.

"We need to be aware that customs are changing," says Jordan. "People don't want what their grandparents wanted. I think it is probably impractical to try to get people to preserve the old way because it's not what they want. They want something new.

"I think Americans are supremely uninterested in history or traditional culture," continues Jordan. "Supremely uninterested."

Murray Owens, an eighty-six-year-old East Austin resident, mows the grass around his parents' plot at the Bethany Cemetery about twice a month. "My grandparents are buried back there somewhere," says Owens. "I lost them. I don't know where they are. We had it marked with some crosses. The crosses are missing."

Ironically, the Owens plot has no grass, an example of a "scraped grave" which Jordan explains is an African custom "embedded in southern traditions." Scraped graves are devoid of any growth and are designed for low maintenance. Owens mows the grass on graves around his family's plot.

Owens and a few others look after their own families' graves at Bethany, also dating back to the 1860s. Although an organized group was once in charge of maintenance at Bethany, it has been defunct for years.

Some concerned citizens and family members have approached the city about taking over the property and maintenance. These efforts to turn the site over to the city fell through when no one could produce a clear title to the property.

Just fifty miles north of Austin, due to the diligent efforts of the Salado Historical Society, the community of Salado recently installed a historical marker at the West Salado Cemetery. The property, which was deeded by plantation owner Elijah Sterling Clack Robertson "for use as church, school and graveyard purposes" was recently purchased at auction by a private individual, clearing the way for the site's historical recognition.

"Thelma Fletcher is the person who kept saying from day one, 'There *is* a black cemetery up there in those weeds. We need to take an interest in it,'" says two-term Historical Society president Jean Davis.

In preparation for the historical marker dedication and since, the property has been mostly cleared and trimmed.

"Mr. [Ernest] Wilkinson is the owner and supervisor," says Thelma Fletcher, "and he's a good one because this is his personal property now and he's very proud of it."

Fletcher, who came to Salado in 1954, first heard stories of the town's slave cemetery from Wilkinson's aunt, Mary Wilkinson Fulbright, who worked for her. "She told about her parents being the Robertsons' slaves and she was very proud of this," Fletcher adds.

The West Salado Cemetery is an example of how citizen interest can make a difference in preserving black cemeteries. "That whole little area was set aside for the colored people," says Fletcher. "I had felt that the Historical Society should do something about it."

Jordan explains that "perpetual care is reeking havoc with all of these old customs." While Jordan says perpetual care is not the problem in itself, perpetual care contractors do not want to offer "traditional" maintenance services. "They want to level the graveyard of mounds and take all the decorations away so that their lawn mowers can go through," he adds.

"Anyone dedicated in this life to wanting to maintain constancy and tradition is in for a frustrating life," says Jordan. "I think we should document the way things were, and that way, everyone will find out sometime. There will be books that we can go to."

In the meantime, there are still those who will do everything they can to preserve Austin's black cemeteries as monuments to the community's history and cultural traditions: people like Murray Owens, Rev. A. C. Franklin, and Edna Satterwhite.

Chapter 7

Black Women and Texas History

by Johnnie M. Armstead

Abstract

"Many Black women were among the noble army of women in Texas who labored so tirelessly in the civilization of this great state. In a period that was plagued by Indians, drought, slavery, outlaws, transitional and unsettled they labored bravely through a time of discouragement, dangers, and life threatening circumstances to free, to support, to encourage and to serve."

Black women had not only the above mentioned difficulties to overcome; they also struggled against racism as well as sexism. They used stumbling blocks as stepping stones as they fought for equal treatment for everyone.

Christi Adair overcame the discriminations against her, both as a female and as a black, as she challenged those discriminatory laws. She believed that those laws violated the United States Constitution, that they were unfair, and unjust. Because of her belief in the equality of *all Americans*, she worked persistently for more than fifty years to gain the victory.

Dr. Mary Branch was only one of the many black women who worked at state and national levels insuring that all eligible children were enrolled in school, and demanding sanitary drinking facilities and equal and quality education for all children.

Larone Bennett wrote: "It is a long past beginning in 1619 a year before the landing of the Pilgrims when a Dutch freighter landed a cargo of 20 Blacks at Jamestown Virginia. Among them there were at least three women."

In Africa the black woman had filled every position from queen to prostitute. In America, as a slave, she was dropped suddenly and completely to the bottom of the social scale in a highly vulnerable position. In spite of her circumstances, she labored with the noble army of women who shone like beacon lights in the establishment of the state of Texas.

"Black women have always understood that education is the richest and safest investment possible to man and they have made sacrifices to ensure educational opportunities for their children," Alwyn Barr noted. They served as teachers beginning in the 1790s, and became school founders and directors in the nineteenth century.

In 1867, Miss L. S. Dickenson organized a public school in Hempstead, and in 1892, Mattie B. White founded the only private school for black girls in Austin, Texas.

Alwyn Barr wrote about a most influential woman in the development of higher education for blacks:

> Dr. Mary Branch, the first Black to serve as College president in Texas, participated in a long tradition of Black women as leaders in State and National education. Born in 1881, when opportunities for Black public education were quite limited, she and her brothers and sisters were among the more fortunate Black children who attended the local elementary school. Her parents actively sought to instill in [her] the [desires] for culture and education. She acquired from her parents not only a desire for education but also an inclination towards initiative and leadership.
>
> Mary Branch was thirteen when she first "attended" college at the state college in Farmville, Virginia. She was there, however, not as a student but as an employee. Working there amid the shelves of books, she was fascinated by the wealth of knowledge at her fingertips and determined that she would somehow secure an education. She received a Bachelor of Philosophy degree in 1922

. . . A Masters of Arts degree in English in 1925 . . . and began studies toward a Doctorate in the field of Education.

In 1930 Mary Branch accepted the job of President of Tillotson College in Austin, Texas . . . a declining institution. Her tenure at the institution was successful, and her contemporaries frequently sought her for advice, and placed her in an elite group of Black women who successfully directed institutions of higher learning . . . Branch had only two comparable contemporaries. One was Mary McLeod Bethune, who founded Bethune-Cookman College in Florida . . . And Ottemissia Bowden, who between 1902 and 1954 served at St. Phillips College in San Antonio as Instructor, Dean, and President. Mary Branch's contributions to Tillotson College however, were equally impressive. She was without question the woman for the time.

Just as Mary Branch was an advocate for higher learning, Texas gained a state representative who advocated the continued tradition. Wilhelmina Ruth Fitzgerald Delco, a member of the Texas House of Representatives, has been instrumental in improving the education system in Texas. She chaired the Texas House of Representatives Higher Education Committee and proposed a constitutional amendment to provide funds for higher education. Although not in the classroom or on the college campus, she actively endorsed equal education as a tool for advancement. She legislated for additional and adequate funding for black colleges and universities.

A fact not so well-known is that black women were pioneers in the field of medicine. Carrie Jane Sutton from San Antonio, Texas, was the first black female doctor to practice medicine in the late '20s in Texas.

Ten years later, two sisters from Austin entered Maharry Medical College in Nashville, Tennessee, and completed their internship in Kansas City, Missouri. They were Drs. Connie Yerwood and Joyce Yerwood Carwin.

Although Connie Yerwood originally planned to take her M.D. and enter private practice, upon finishing medical school she was asked to consider entering the public health care field rather than establishing a private practice. Connie Yerwood was "a first." Up to that point there had been no black physicians in the Texas division of public health services. Dr. Yerwood's appointment as chief of the Bureau of Personal Health Services made her the first woman to advance above a directorship in the health agency. Dr. Yerwood oversaw three operations: Maternal and Health Care, Early Periodic Screening Diagnosis and Treatment, and the Chronic Disease Division.

Dr. Joyce Yerwood Carwin practiced medicine for more than fifty years and devoted her practice to helping low-income women and children. She said that "Texas women have always loved their children — their own and others who needed help or attention. They gave birth and provided for physical needs. They gave love and satisfied emotional needs. They introduced values and acceptable codes of behavior that helped their children achieve success or learn what society expects of them."

Texas women also reached out beyond their own families to help children who were not their own, and who may have differed from them in terms of heritage, race or economic class.

According to Dr. Carwin, "Women saw rundown schools and worked for improvements. They demanded sanitary drinking fountains for schools when they saw children drinking from a common cup and spreading disease. When they saw children of eight or nine working in the fields instead of attending school, they lobbied for school attendance laws. When they realized that some children spent their whole childhood without ever seeing a doctor, they demanded funds for children's clinics."

Grief over lost children was a common experience for Texas women in general and black women in particular. One out of every ten babies born before 1917 died before their first birthday. The death rate for Texas children did not drop before the national average until 1979.

Women have always assisted each other at childbirth. I can remember my grandmother, Mrs. Odoms, who was a midwife who was born in Caldwell County in 1892. She delivered most of her grandchildren and many of their friends. She assisted my mother in my delivery as well as those of my siblings.

When I was growing up, "childbirthing" was an important event. My mother would take to her bed and the neighbor women would either take us to their homes or come to our home to wait for the stork. I always thought the stork was invisible because I never saw him leave the new baby. The birthing day was a time for boiling water, making black pepper tea, making sugar tits, and muffled sounds with an eventual loud baby cry.

Midwife Matilda Boozie Randon of Washington County delivered most of the babies born between 1875 and 1900.

Minnie Thornton of Bryan delivered 2,000 babies since her career as a midwife began in 1915. "Ain't nobody learned me," Minnie says. "I don't hardly know how I got started, but I just love it."

As Aunt Minnie got older she assisted Mrs. Effie Harrison in delivering babies. Both were registered as midwives with the Brazos County Health Unit.

Three of the most active midwives in Austin were Mattie Caperton, Lena Whittington, and Mary Freeman. Hundreds of Austinites were delivered by these women. The wisdom and judgment of these women were trusted and respected. They were looked upon as Angels of Mercy. These women practiced their trade in the mid-'30s. They often served as aids to doctors who delivered babies at home.

Historically, black families had their own built-in child care service. The average family had three or four generations living in the same homestead or in close proximity. There was always someone to look after the baby. Between 1915 and 1921, as Austin became more urbanized, there developed a need for a kindergarten in East Austin, and Bunny Cummins operated a kindergarten in her home. She operated her private kindergarten and primary school until the mid-'50s.

In the 1940s, as more mothers went to work, many children were left without supervision and protection. One woman who saw the need was Mrs. Mary J. Sims. She worked to provide not only protection for these children, but a place to grow and develop educationally.

Naomi Polk of Houston was a believer in the virtue of hard work and instilled this value in her children. Naomi lived in the Fourth Ward for some sixty of her ninety-two years. She only traveled from Houston once, when as an eighteen-year-old babysitter she accompanied her employer on a vacation in Canada. Polk kept a diary of her life in the Fourth Ward, chronicling the remarkable changes that occurred during her tenure there. She always felt that she could have done more for the world if she had been given a better education.

Naomi's second husband, Robert Polk, was killed by a policeman in the early 1920s. She was left with three children and only $36 a month from Aid For Dependent Children.

To supplement her meager government check, Polk devised her own method of survival for her family. She sold cosmetics and plant cuttings and had her "cottage industry" of insect poisons. During that time, Polk approached her writing and art seriously, and considered it to be her life's work.

Polk viewed herself first and foremost as a poet, then an artist. She was a self-taught artist who worked with found materials, mixing oil-based enamel paint with whatever agent was available. Her poem "My Little Ghetto Kitchen" describes her home on Maxroy Street (where at the table she sat composing her poetry), and "Lonely Tears" reflects her deeply personal and individualistic Christian views. Her drawings, *Stick Doll, Baptism, Those Reaching Hands, Lonesome Road,* to name only a few, have been shown in the exhibition "Art and Culture: The Fourth Ward" at Diverse Works Gallery.

Her self-portrait with its inscription "Now Where Do I Go From Here" inspired the title of the 1988 exhibition "Now Where Do I Go From Here: Houston Women (a look at where they've been and a look at where they're going from here)."

Naomi Polk did not live to experience recognition as an artist. Her work was not shown in public until after her death.

Christia Daniels Adair was born in 1893 and grew up in the little town of Edna, Texas. It was general practice that politics be discussed at the family table every evening. Christia found the discussions to be boring, but knew that her father expected her to take a knowledgeable, active role in the family discussions of current political events.

Although Christia's parents had not attended school, they expected their children to get a good education. Her schooling included high school in Austin, and in 1914 she enrolled at Prairie View State Normal and Industrial College (now known as Prairie View A&M). In 1918 Christia married Elbert Adair and moved to Kingsville in South Texas. She found there were few social or cultural activities that a young, educated black woman could attend. But she had too much energy to sit at home. Christia found volunteer work. During this time she got Kingsville's Black and White Women's Club to work together to shut down an illegal gambling house on the edge of town. After their success with that cause, they moved to a new goal: the right for women to vote.

Texas women won the right to vote in the state's party primary elections in 1918. Christia and her friends were delighted. They were eager to cast their first ballot. But when she and her friends got to the polling place they were turned away. Christia and her friends were told they could not vote because they were black. "That just hurt our hearts real bad and we went on. There was nothing we could do about that but just take it as it was," she said.

Discrimination had always been part of Christia Adair's life, but she was not prepared for discriminatory behavior that President Warren G. Harding displayed toward a group of black Sunday school children who had gone to the train depot to greet him as he arrived in Kingsville. To their surprise and dismay Warren G. Harding didn't even look at them, but proceeded to look over their heads and shake hands with a group of white children. Several years later Christia joined a national organization that was involved in seeing that existing laws protected all people. Nearly thirty years after she had worked for women's suffrage in Kingsville, Christia Adair was allowed to vote in a state primary election. Christia experienced a sweet victory.

Because of many and varied injustices that Christia Adair had lodged against herself and other blacks, she became executive secretary of the Houston Chapter of the National Association for the Advancement of Colored People (NAACP) when it was very unpopular to do so. Sometimes she had to worry about keeping herself alive. Christia continued talking and working all through the 1940s and 1950s and finally saw some changes.

As the years went by, all of this work began to take its toll on Christia. Although she retired as executive secretary of the NAACP, she did not stop her work to end discrimination. She watched the courts strike down discriminatory local, state, and federal laws. And she saw the United States Congress enact the landmark Civil Rights Act of 1964.

The Houston Chapter of the National Organization For Women and its Task Force on Minority Women and Women's Rights paid tribute to Christia Adair on the 54th anniversary of women's suffrage in 1974. They cited that "Christia's life is a history of the struggle of women and other minorities in the society."

Dr. Jeffie O. A. Conner of Waco had an enlightening sentiment: "Now each can give something. It may not be a poem, or marble bust, or fragrant flower even, it may not be ours to place our lives on the altar of the country as a living sacrifice, but each can be one of those strong willing helpers." At a time when not many women had important (paying) jobs in Texas, Dr. Conner was employed by the U.S. Department of Agriculture from 1923 to 1948, as the first black home demonstration agent in Texas. She later served as supervisor of McLennan County public schools, where she had McLennan County schoolchildren make drinking cups from tin cans to stop the spread of tuberculosis.

Many of the black women in Texas who fought for equal treatment of all women came from very humble beginnings, as did Azie Taylor Martin of Dale, Texas, a black farm girl who became treasurer of the United States during President Jimmy Carter's administration.

In 1957 Azie B. Taylor, recently graduated from Huston Tillotson College (in Austin), was hired as the first black secretary in downtown Austin (for the Texas AFL-CIO). This served as a test to the fairness of the legislature in its upholding of the desegregation laws that had been handed down by the Supreme Court. As Azie B. reported for work, she was confronted with signs on the restrooms which read, "White Women Only." Azie took the sign in stride and lettered in her own insertion: "And Negro."

There is a large photograph of Azie B. on the wall of the Institute of Texan Cultures showing Texans who have accomplished much.

Another of the widely known personalities in Travis County was Ada DeBlanc Simond, a writer, historian and educator.

Known for her charm, wit, and wealth of historical information, Ada is most remembered for her historical contributions. Her books, her columns and the frequent speeches and lectures she presented took people back to other times and other eras.

Ada worked with the Texas Tuberculosis Association for twenty-five years, before going to work for the Texas Department of Health. She felt that her greatest accomplishments were in the health clinics in East Texas.

"Basically I'm a health educator," Mrs. Simond said. "I work for community development through training the people to recognize and solve their problems with the resources they have. I hope it will pave the way for a better life for their children."

"No one should pass up an opportunity to help somebody," was the lifelong philosophy of Ada DeBlanc Simond.

For after all, the highest gifts are not measured in dollars and cents.

Mrs. Ollie L. Byran, DDS, graduated from Meharry Dental College in Nashville, Tennessee, in 1902. She was the first and only female graduate of Meharry Dental College, and the first black woman practicing in the South.

Dr. Byran began her dental practice in Dallas, Texas, in 1905, at 115 Ball Street. After several moves she purchased property at 2622 Bryan Street, where she set up practice in her home so she could attend her home duties and continue her dentistry.

In 1911, Dr. Byran and seventeen other black women organized the Royal Arts and Charity Club in Dallas. Its purpose was to promote the appreciation of cultural art in the black community. By 1935, Dr. Ollie Byran was no longer listed as a resident of Dallas, but her efforts to obtain an education, practice her profession with diligence, and her efforts to elevate the standard of living for her neighbors and friends were not forgotten.

The black woman is still making inroads. She has learned to capitalize on her adversities by using them to her advantage. She has developed a mechanism for overcoming the abuse of everyday life. She has a sensitivity that no matter of abuse, denial, or hardship can destroy.

Hays County Historical Commission Nomination for the Outstanding Volunteer of the Year Award:

Johnnie Armstead

The Hays County Historical Commission would like to nominate Johnnie Armstead as the outstanding volunteer of the year due to the job she has done with finalizing the restoration of The Calaboose, a Recorded Texas Historic Landmark in San Marcos, Texas. The interior was completed in time for Black History Month.

The second phase of the restoration of The Calaboose began in January 1991. This interior restoration was separate from the restoration of the exterior which came about through a matching preservation grant from the Texas Historical Commission. The building, Hays County's first jailhouse, had been dedicated a Recorded Texas Historic Landmark during December 1990.

Johnnie Armstead spent many hours in order to complete the interior and its furnishings. She worked with the contractor, coordinated with the architect, and recruited volunteers from the adult probation group, from SWTSU fraternities, especially the organization for young black men, enlisted city employees as volunteers as well as her own family.

Meanwhile all this was coordinated with the City of San Marcos administrative staff in order to comply with city ordinances. The many hours spent with workers were to insure they not only followed the blueprint but the result would be a quality job. Hours of volunteer hours were spent on the telephone and on-site visits to insure these details. The remarkable part was how she was able to relate to each and to become a part of the action without being considered a nuisance.

Mrs. Armstead also coordinated the opening when it was completed and furnished. She worked hand-in-glove with those who had obtained the grant from the Heritage Association of San Marcos for the sturdy round tables, upholstered folding chairs, electric stove, refrigerator, lighting fixtures, and blinds to complete the furnishings.

She researched and put together an exhibit which added a very special touch to Black History Month. Additionally she spent many hours writing thank you notes to Calaboose sponsors, benefactors, supporters and friends who had assisted in making the building ready for use.

In May 1991 when the Calaboose was selected as part of the Heritage Association's Tours of Distinction she spent many hours preparing the building for visits by the tourists, again setting up the Black History exhibit, obtaining the docents for duty during the Tour, preparing refreshments for them and working full time herself both days explaining the history of the building and how it was saved and restored.

Earlier Johnnie Armstead had been honored among the Women of the Year for San Marcos.

In August she spent many hours and labor moving furniture from the Calaboose to be used temporarily in the Archives Room of the Courthouse Annex, a room the HCHC had been authorized to use, although shared with another department.

Mrs. Armstead is a supportive and active member whenever an HCHC project is underway. She has helped with the labeling and preparation of the Commission's quarterly newsletter for mailing.

In November she assisted with the area-wide workshop held by the Hays County Historical Commission on how to research and write official Texas historical markers. She arranged the reopening of the Calaboose for this meeting and brought from her own home accessories needed for the coffee hour.

In December as a result of many conversations with prospective do-ers and donors, city and county officials and a landscape architect, a parking lot for the Calaboose was finally underway. She has worked with the Spring Lake Garden Club president repeatedly on their plans for native landscaping the grounds around the building. She spent many hours arranging with the media pictures of the parking lot groundbreaking and the placing of the sign for the building which she had secured as a donation from the sign company. She planned the formal dedication of the building during Black History Month February 1992.

Mrs. Armstead said in doing all she has done the past year:

I did not think about how I was to go about it, I just did it. It is work I believed in, was educated by, and gained friends and know-how I would not have had otherwise. I feel very grateful for all I have reaped from it. This last year has been nothing but fun. I now spend much time answering questions about the history of Calaboose and how it will be used — Believe it or not, the City directs inquiries about it to me!

— Frances Stovall, Hays County Historical Commission

Chapter 8

Freedmantown: The Origins of a Black Neighborhood in Houston, 1865–1880

by Louise Passey Maxwell

In September 1866 Byron Porter, Houston's local agent of the Freedmen's Bureau, reported to Bvt. Col. William H. Sinclair that Houston's freedmen[1] had constructed 125 houses, costing between $50 and $500. He estimated that they had purchased 100 building lots at amounts ranging from $30 to $250 and had leased approximately forty lots with the option to purchase. These accomplishments, Porter asserted, speak "well for the steadiness and industry of the free people" in Houston.[2] Porter's praise for the postwar achievements of Houston's black population both demonstrates that blacks had successfully overcome the hardships they faced upon emancipation — most had little or no capital with which to begin a life of freedom; few had access to credit sources; most were illiterate; and many had been torn from familiar surroundings — and it also confirms how important land ownership was to blacks in the postwar period.[3]

Despite the hostility that many whites felt toward the idea of black land ownership, African Americans struggled against whites' postwar constraints by purchasing land and establishing themselves as homeowners. As Eric Foner explains, blacks' "desire to escape from white supervision . . . inspired the quest for land of their own."[4] Owning land, the freedmen and women believed, would provide them a chance to assert a certain autonomy they had been denied as slaves. Thus eager to purchase land, blacks exercised their right to move about freely, flocking to areas where opportunities for land ownership appeared greatest. For many, this meant moving to southern cities, which not only offered greater chances to acquire real property, but also provided new employment opportunities, the chance to reunite with loved ones, the protection of Union troops, and more simply, a relative degree of freedom and anonymity not found in the countryside.[5]

As a result of this postwar black urbanization, Houston's African-American population soared, more than tripling from a population of 1,069 in 1860 to 3,691 in 1870. And as Porter's report indicates, the newly arriving blacks immediately set themselves to the task of purchasing land.[6] Similar to the residential patterns that emerged after the war in other southern urban centers such as Richmond, Charleston, and New Orleans, blacks in Houston settled across the city but tended to cluster in pockets.[7] The largest number of the city's blacks chose to settle in the Fourth Ward. Yet within this larger "pocket" of the Fourth Ward, there was even greater evidence of "clustering," particularly in a single residential neighborhood called Freedmantown. Freedmantown stood out from other areas in the ward because of its uniquely high proportion of black land and homeowners. Understanding why this neighborhood followed such a different pattern of development provides a window into the emergence of black neighborhoods in Houston, and in a broader perspective, illuminates blacks' efforts to purchase land across the postwar urban South.

Reconstructing the history of Freedmantown holds additional importance because of the symbolic role that the name "Freedmantown" (or "Freedmen's Town") has assumed in Houston's African-American history. The city's blacks use the term today as a general label when referring to all of the original postwar, predominantly black neighborhoods in Houston's Fourth Ward. The symbolic significance of the name "Freedmantown" arises from the way in which the city's blacks use the term to engender a sense of racial pride in the success that the city's early black settlers had in establishing their own autonomous neighborhoods and communities. The term

"Freedmantown" subsequently has taken on highly political and moral overtones and is used by the city's African Americans as a symbol of the black community's strength and resiliency — both past and present.[8]

Precisely when the term assumed this symbolic role is difficult to ascertain because of the lack of such nineteenth-century sources as newspapers, diaries, personal papers, and church records authored by blacks. This dearth of evidence makes it impossible to know how Houston's postwar African-American community felt about the term "Freedmantown," about the neighborhood itself, or about its inhabitants. All we know from written sources is how white Houstonians felt about and used the term "Freedmantown." Therefore, we can only infer the thoughts of the black community from their actions. By determining how the neighborhood of Freedmantown was formed and how many African Americans lived and owned land there, we can begin to piece together the story of how Freedmantown assumed such an important place in Houston's African-American history. While this preliminary investigation cannot hope to answer definitively the question of how and why the name "Freedmantown" assumed such symbolic significance among Houston's blacks in the twentieth century, it hopefully will lay the groundwork for arriving at a fuller understanding of the evolution of this term.

Specifying Freedmantown as a distinct geographic entity, however, is a difficult task because of the myriad ways in which individuals have used the term "Freedmantown" to describe various neighborhoods of Houston's old Fourth Ward. The city's 1840 charter defined the political division of the Fourth Ward — all of the land south of Congress and west of Main streets — to encompass a large section of the city, including many of its western-most neighborhoods such as Freedmantown and a significant portion of the city's central business area. Yet many historic and popular sources use the terms "Fourth Ward" and "Freedmantown" interchangeably when collectively describing only the predominantly black neighborhoods located in the western portion of the old Fourth Ward.[9]

Adding to the confusion over the specific geographic boundaries of Freedmantown, in 1984 the National Register of Historic Places designated a largely black neighborhood in the city's Fourth Ward as "Freedmen's Town Historic District." The report submitted by the Texas Historical Commission to gain historic status for this black neighborhood identifies "Freedmen's Town" as a forty-block residential area west of Houston's downtown. This historic recognition has prompted many Houstonians — black and white — to accept as fact the Commission's broad definition of and nomenclature for this area of black settlement.[10]

However, the name "Freedmantown" originally referred to a more narrowly defined region of the Fourth Ward than this contemporary usage would suggest. According to official Harris County plat map records, in 1875 the name Freedmantown was given specifically to a twenty-eight-block addition situated in the Fourth Ward *directly* on the southern banks of Buffalo Bayou, north of San Felipe Road, and west of the city's center — a neighborhood adjacent to the area recently identified by the National Register as the "Freedmen's Town Historic District." City and county records indicate that the term "Freedmantown" rarely was used during the nineteenth century — as it is in the Texas Historical Commission's report — as a collective title for the largely black, westernmost neighborhoods of the Fourth Ward.[11] Instead, it was used strictly to refer to the Hardcastle Addition, otherwise known as Freedmantown, as designated in the Harris County plat map records. Thus in reconstructing the history of this neighborhood, this essay employs this more narrow, nineteenth-century definition of Freedmantown. Before we can understand how Freedmantown's development differed from other areas of the city, however, we must first establish the patterns of black property ownership within the city at large.

Black Settlement in Houston

In February 1865, the Houston *Tri-Weekly Telegraph* predicted that with the abolition of slavery the black population in the South would decline precipitously. The newspaper assured Houston's white citizens that once blacks were freed and deprived of the guidance and instruction they had received as slaves, blacks "would be utterly lost sight of from the face of society."[12] However, rather than disappear as the *Tri-Weekly Telegraph* predicted, blacks in Houston, like others across the South, demonstrated their determination to claim their newly won freedom and to ensure their community's survival by establishing themselves as property owners.[13]

Several factors prompted Houston's white property owners to

sell property to blacks in the immediate postwar years. The economic collapse that accompanied the Civil War made many white Houstonians desperate for cash. When they began to recognize the profitability of subdividing their property into small lots that they could then sell to blacks, few were willing to forego the anticipated economic profits simply to ease other whites' anxiety about black property ownership. This desire for profit, moreover, was not confined to the ranks of businessmen and real estate agents. Since many Reconstruction governments, that of Texas included, recognized only a small portion of the debt due to creditors of the Confederacy, a large number of Southerners saw their fortunes disappear following the South's defeat.[14] Selling property to blacks in urban areas was one means by which whites could regain at least a portion of their prewar wealth. The nationwide depression that rocked Houston in the early 1870s sustained this capital shortage among the city's whites, aiding blacks in their efforts to purchase land. The combination of economic hard times in Houston and white resistance to black property ownership in rural areas of the state increased the advantage the city's blacks had in acquiring real estate — an advantage shared by urban blacks across the South.[15]

Regardless of urban whites' eagerness to dispose of their property and the blacks' desire to purchase it, blacks still faced the problem of obtaining the funds necessary to enter into real estate transactions. Individual white property owners in Houston frequently facilitated blacks' attempts to purchase property by agreeing to sell land on credit.[16] Blacks also benefited from the fact that much of Houston's undeveloped land was located on the edge of the city, thus reducing its value to whites and presumably its cost to blacks.[17] Without an effective system of mass transportation in operation throughout the early 1870s, this outlying land continued to hold little attraction as a residential site to the city's white population. Blacks hoping to purchase land in Houston thus were aided somewhat by the availability of outlying land and the cash shortage among whites.[18]

Although it is evident that Houston's blacks quickly set themselves to the task of acquiring land, it is less clear why they chose to settle in the particular areas of the city that they did. Blacks' choices were the product of a number of factors — many of which were outside of their control. As in other Southern cities, the patterns of black settlement in Houston during the postwar period illustrated a combination of the deliberate choices made by members of the black community and whites' attitudes toward black property ownership and the development of autonomous black neighborhoods.[19]

Residential development in Houston, however, contradicted the patterns that appeared in many other Southern cities. Some historians have suggested that the size of a city's prewar free black population and its present stage of development determined the development of postwar black residential areas. They assert that in a rapidly rebuilding city such as Atlanta, where city officials and real estate agents could exercise some control over the postwar growth of residential areas, segregation by race appeared almost immediately. In contrast, in an older city like New Orleans, where the antebellum free black population had been quite large, racially mixed neighborhoods persisted.[20] Yet neither of these models characterizes Houston's postwar development.

Houston, like Atlanta, was expanding rapidly in the postwar years and had contained few antebellum free blacks, but residential segregation by race such as that which occurred in Atlanta did not develop in Houston. Postwar residential growth in Houston indicates that there were factors other than previous experience with a free black population or a city's age that were instrumental in determining the extent of residential segregation. Houston's development suggests that less emphasis should be placed on the city's past circumstances and more on the immediate decisions made by both blacks and whites in explaining the shape of postwar housing patterns.[21]

For many blacks, simply trying to locate adequate shelter was a challenge. Postwar newspapers in Houston complained that blacks were moving into the city in such volume and with such rapidity that they were creating a serious shortage of adequate housing. Blacks, they claimed, packed into abandoned warehouses, stables, or any other vacant buildings they could find, causing overcrowding throughout the city. The old Confederate shoe shop located in the Fourth Ward apparently was a popular gathering place among newly arrived blacks. According to the *Tri-Weekly Telegraph*, there was a large "gang" of blacks of all ages and sexes seeking quarters there. In July 1865 the newspaper reported that many citizens were complaining about the "great crowds of negroes" who were using the city's vacant buildings as "sleeping apartments."[22] Many blacks exercised little choice in locating their living quarters; they took what they could find.

One citizen informed the *Tri-Weekly Telegraph* that although a black family of four had rented a house in his neighborhood, there actually were fifteen people sleeping there nightly. According to the newspaper, this sort of living arrangement created a serious health hazard for the city since "negrodom" and "filth" were synonymous. The paper justified its indictment of black living habits by proclaiming that similar complaints concerning the "filth, want, sickness, and wretchedness" of the urban black population had appeared in a Shreveport paper. Whenever blacks crowded into towns and cities, Houston's newspaper concluded, there was a correspondent rise in urban ills.[23]

The *Tri-Weekly Telegraph*'s prejudicial remarks about the presence of blacks in urban areas demonstrates, at best, a complete lack of understanding of the hardships and obstacles that blacks faced as they moved to the city. Nevertheless, the paper's assessment of the living conditions that most blacks confronted is probably fairly accurate. The newspaper's statement, moreover, clearly reflects the perceptions held by Southern whites concerning the growing presence of blacks in urban areas. Across the South, whites decried the establishment of "shantytowns" and "tent cities" on the peripheries of their municipalities. In Houston, the *Tri-Weekly Telegraph* led the city's crusade to ensure that these "negro dens" would be "effectually cleaned out."[24] Early in September 1865 the *Tri-Weekly Telegraph* reported that the military authorities in Houston had "declared war" against the city's black neighborhoods. "If the darkies must keep house," the newspaper proclaimed, "they will have to keep orderly ones and not have them harbors for negro thieves and burglars." In the same year the city also passed a health ordinance expressly to enforce sanitation in the "Negro districts."[25]

The tremendous increase in the number of black inhabitants in Houston immediately following the war probably did produce overcrowding due to the initial shortage of accommodations, but many blacks moving into the city did acquire property and build their own houses — an accomplishment whites rarely recognized. Complaining about the unreliability of black house servants in the postwar months, the Galveston *News* asserted that "nearly all the freemen and women of Houston and Galveston are living by themselves." The paper's statement, however, was not offered in praise of the black community's efforts, but in condemnation of and retaliation for what it saw as a bold assertion of independence by blacks.[26] Houston newspapers, in fact, rarely commented on the state of black housing except to condemn the filthy living conditions of African Americans.

Surveying the building construction in the city since the war, the *Daily Telegraph* in late 1866 remarked that in contrast to the number of respectable houses erected by the city's whites, the remainder were "merely huts built by planking and waste timber. These," it explained, "are occupied by Negroes, of whom there is unfortunately a superfluity in Houston, and there are sometimes twenty or thirty congregated in a little hovel not over 10 square feet. There are, however, a few Negroes who have bought lots and erected some very nice cottages. These negroes," the newspaper claimed, however, were "not numerous."[27] Other than relating the fact that some blacks were living in "hovels" while others occupied "very nice cottages," the paper's account reveals little, and assuredly exaggerates much. Where, for example, were both types of houses located? Were they in the same or different neighborhoods? Who were their owners? Answering these questions is crucial in assessing the emergence of Freedmantown and other black residential neighborhoods in Houston.

While the land available to Houston's blacks generally was located on the edge of town in areas considered undesirable as homesites to the majority of the city's white inhabitants, the resulting pattern of black and white land ownership was not perfectly concentric with whites at the center of town and blacks on the fringe.[28] Houston's newspapers, for example, complained on several occasions about the presence of black "shantytowns" situated within the city's central business area. In October 1868 the *Houston Daily Times* reported a fire in "Hanna's Nest — the miserable nest of wooden shanties fronting on Main Street, and backing its dirty stern into the rear of the Hutchins House, where Hanna & Co. used to run their 'chebang' of a bogus freedmen's bureau . . ." Hutchins House was the preeminent hotel in Houston at this time and was located on one of the major thoroughfares in the town, yet "wooden shanties" surrounded it. In 1869 the paper described another fire among a group of wooden shanties occupied primarily by freedmen and located on Fannin between Preston and Prairie — another neighborhood near the town center in which these shanties, according to the newspaper, were an eyesore.[29] Whites alone clearly did not occupy Houston's central neighborhoods, and not all blacks lived on the outskirts of town.

This variegated housing pattern may be partially explained by the fact that while proximity to the city center was important, it was not whites' only concern when choosing their residences. According to geographer John Kellogg, wealthy whites exhibited a proclivity for living on the large, important streets of the city; they tended to congregate around parks and churches and to shun the areas near jails, cemeteries, railroads, and other such institutions; and they showed a clear distaste for areas that were flood prone. Accordingly, blacks were left with the city's "unfit" property — often but not always located on the outskirts of the city — that whites had rejected.[30] The *Tri-Weekly Telegraph* explained in August 1865 that "*in almost every part of this city, but especially in the suburbs,* there are miserable hovels, or shanties, which are crowded with lazy thriftless negroes . . ."[31]

Wherever blacks settled — on the outskirts of the city or in the heart of the central business area — their presence incited the white community's disdain. Whites, however, seemed less willing — and less able — to mount an assault on the growth of these black residential areas in the years following the war.[32] In June 1865 the Galveston *Daily News* — a paper printed in Houston since the early 1860s — reprimanded Houston's white citizens for their willingness to rent houses to blacks. The newspaper warned whites of the problems that would arise and reminded them that "our past experience has shown that the good order of the city required that negroes, whether free or slaves, should not live separate and apart from their owners or agents or employers . . ."[33]

With the end of the war and the abolition of slavery, however, whites in Houston and elsewhere apparently were shifting their emphasis from maintenance of their legal superiority over blacks to the enforced physical and social separation of the races in order to maintain their privileged status. Whites felt threatened by blacks who began to improve their socioeconomic positions in the postwar period and began to widen the physical distance between themselves and these blacks, thus giving tacit approval to black residential neighborhoods. In turn, blacks accepted the poor living conditions that often accompanied segregated neighborhoods because this spatial separation brought them increased autonomy.[34]

Living close to one's place of employment, to friends and family members, and to social and religious institutions all mattered deeply to blacks migrating to urban centers and perhaps took priority over living in more amenable sections of the city.[35] However, because of Houston's lack of well-developed antebellum black social and religious institutions, proximity to them would have had no bearing on the residential choices made by blacks entering the city in the war's *immediate* aftermath. Instead, already confined to areas where land and housing were cheap, blacks had the opportunity to base their choices more heavily on the availability of unoccupied land within these restricted areas. The postwar patterns of settlement of Houston's blacks thus should provide a fairly direct view of the role that land ownership played in determining the emergence of black neighborhoods.

While blacks undoubtedly could find "cheap" living accommodations scattered throughout Houston, the wide availability of undeveloped land in the Third and Fourth wards, made possible by the liberal provisions of the 1840 supplement to the city charter, which defined the city limits generously enough to accommodate later expansion within the corporate limits, presumably made them more appealing.[36] Determining precisely how many and where blacks settled in the Fourth Ward in the years immediately following the war is difficult since neither the city nor the county kept records that provide a picture of the demographic composition of the wards during this period. The 1870 manuscript census, where the city's inhabitants are grouped by ward, gives the earliest composite picture of the Fourth Ward.[37] An analysis of the census manuscripts for the Fourth Ward reveals that in *almost* all sections of the ward, blacks and whites were living in close proximity, sharing the same streets and residential neighborhoods. In fact, approximately 50 percent of the ward's black inhabitants were living next door to whites.[38]

Although there were, as previously indicated, certain pockets (often single streets, and less frequently whole neighborhoods) that were inhabited almost exclusively by either whites or blacks, this was not the general rule. And whites, given their fears of rebellion and lawlessness among the black population, undoubtedly exaggerated the danger and prevalence of separate black neighborhoods. The few areas of black concentration in the Fourth Ward as indicated by the census of 1870 were an exception, not the norm; most areas were inhabited by blacks and whites. One may only speculate about the level of interaction that occurred between black and white residents of the neighborhoods where racially mixed housing patterns were present. But the way in which the residential blocks in most of the ward's subdivisions were divided — ten to twelve lots directly abutting each other at the rear, with no alleys in between or behind them — meant that blacks and whites living next door to or behind one another shared a lot line. This arrangement mandated a degree of physical interaction between neighboring households. Two people did not have to be next-door neighbors to have direct contact with each other.

Since streetcar service did not reach the outer sections of the Fourth Ward until the late 1870s at the very earliest, black and white residents of a particular residential area had to walk the same streets to work and to market. Even in pockets where there was a nearly complete concentration of whites or blacks, the occupants of these neighborhoods probably had to pass through other racially mixed areas of the ward on a regular basis. Their children also had to share the streets and yards of the neighborhood as their playgrounds. The very fact that whites and blacks were residents and even homeowners in the same neighborhoods of the Fourth Ward marks a clear departure from the prewar restrictions on the presence of free blacks in Houston and from the decidedly rigid and unyielding patterns of segregation that emerged in the late nineteenth and early twentieth centuries.[39]

The decision to settle in areas of the ward that had become racially mixed by 1870, at least by many white occupants, predated the Civil War and emancipation. The Fourth Ward, in fact, always had possessed a majority of white inhabitants.[40] Having established their homes in these neighborhoods of the ward, some white residents may have been reluctant to move, despite the increasing presence of blacks. But as one moves farther away from the central business area and into the westernmost edges of the ward, this explanation for the prevalence of mixed black and white housing loses some of its persuasiveness. Even though most of the outlying residential areas of the Fourth Ward were only "about one mile above the City of Houston" and still "within its corporate limits," they remained largely undeveloped prior to the war. They simply were too far removed from the city's center to attract settlement as long as other inexpensive land that was closer to the central business area could satisfy the city's residential needs. The 1866 map of Houston shows that although some of the land to the west of the city had been surveyed and the streets platted, most of the property remained uninhabited.[41] Mixed settlement by blacks and whites in these outlying areas thus requires further explanation. Assuming that the land located in the outlying areas of the ward was previously uninhabited by whites because it was considered substandard due to its distance from the city's center and its tendency to flood, then economic considerations may have been the basis for the postwar settlement of blacks and whites in these areas. Poverty may have driven poor whites and blacks into the same areas on the edge of town where they could find affordable land. And if the black and white residents of these racially mixed areas were working in similar low-paying semi- or unskilled occupations, they may have been thrown together in the same neighborhoods out of sheer practicality — both may have sought to establish their homes in close proximity to their places of employment.

Data gathered for the ward from the 1870 census manuscript, however, casts some doubt upon this idea.[42] Although most of the black and white residents held unskilled or semi-skilled positions, and probably were attracted by the cheap land available in the ward, they were not working in the same occupations. Although 34 percent of the black heads of household were engaged in service-related jobs, working as porters, washers, cooks, and domestic servants, only 5 percent of the white population held such occupations. Jobs involving manual labor drew 32 percent of the ward's black workers, but they employed only 5 percent of the white working population. By contrast, 25 percent of the white household heads were engaged in such commercial occupations as storekeeping and manufacturing but only 5 percent of the black population found employment in such jobs. And while 14 percent of the white population were employed as tradesmen, only 4 percent of the black population held jobs in this category. The only occupational group ranked above that of unskilled labor in which black and white workers were more nearly balanced was that of craftsmen, including such trades as carpentry, blacksmithing, and masonry trades that required skills many blacks may have learned as slaves. For the most part, blacks and whites in the ward were not heavily employed in the same occupations.[43]

Instead, blacks and whites appear to have held reciprocal occupations — blacks served in occupations that filled the needs of the white community and vice versa. For instance, there were only four black grocers in the entire ward compared to twenty-two white grocers. With a total black population in the ward of well over 1,000, many blacks must have regularly patronized the establishments of white grocers. White individuals also were the primary owners of retail and wholesale shops in the ward, ensuring that blacks would have to depend on them for most of their store-bought goods. Conversely, since blacks comprised the majority of laborers, servants, and draymen in the ward, white residents probably relied upon them for these types of service.[44] In March 1867, the *Daily and Sunday Telegraph* complained that the cold weather had driven the freedmen indoors, leaving the rest of the city without any way to get manual labor performed. It was impossible, the paper lamented, "even to get a dray."[45]

The census also suggests that a number of blacks living in racially mixed neighborhoods of the ward probably had located there in order to be close to white families for whom they worked as domestic servants. While this evidence indicates that black and white workers did not occupy equal economic footing, it does show that there must have been some degree of interdependence among the ward's black and white residents. These findings also dispel the idea that blacks and whites were attracted to the same neighborhoods of the ward because they were similarly employed. If there was an occupational basis to blacks' and whites' attraction to the Fourth Ward, it more likely was founded upon their ability to capitalize upon each other's needs.

The racial intermixture in the ward perhaps can be better explained by social rather than economic similarities among the inhabitants. Approximately 60 percent of the white heads of household in the ward were of foreign birth, compared to only 17 percent for the city as a whole. An overwhelming number of the foreign-born in the ward indicated their place of birth as Prussia or Germany. There were two specific cases in the census manuscripts for the ward where the enumerator apparently first marked the race of the members of a Prussian-born family as "mulatto," and then changed the designation to "white."[46] The census taker may have mistaken the family's race because of their dark skin color — a mistake others also may have made — but the error clearly reveals something about the census enumerator's perceptions of this group of foreigners.

Blacks and foreign whites thus possibly were "driven" to settle in the same sections of the Fourth Ward because of the discrimination — subtle and blatant — they faced from Houston's white community. However, even if blacks and foreign whites shared similar treatment from Houston's other white citizens, it is doubtful that they shared a similar perception of their "social rank." Given foreign whites' competition with blacks for housing and frequently for employment in Houston, there was more likely a growing animosity between the two groups.[47] Nonetheless, during the postwar period both settled in the Fourth Ward's neighborhoods in growing numbers.

Settlement of Freedmantown

As early as 1870, the racial and ethnic composition of Freedmantown differed dramatically from the relatively interracial housing patterns of the larger Fourth Ward of which it was a part. Although Freedmantown was not very densely settled, its population — in contrast to that in surrounding residential areas — contained an extremely high proportion of blacks. While only 43 percent of the residents in the entire ward were black, the percentage in Freedmantown stood at a remarkable 94 percent. Among the 53 separate households in Freedmantown, only four were headed by whites.[48] Of the white heads of household, one was a retail grocer, the only one who was of foreign birth; one a railroad clerk; one a carpenter; and the fourth claimed her occupation as "Easy Virtue," or prostitution. The census indicates that the grocer was not living in Freedmantown out of economic hardship, since he listed $500 worth of real property. As for the other three, the census lists no assets. Property records for Freedmantown, however, show that John Murchison, the white railroad clerk, had purchased a number of lots in the neighborhood.[49] His economic situation hardly could have been desperate. Available evidence suggests that the few whites who had chosen Freedmantown as their home did not do so because of their poverty-stricken status.

Whether or not poverty drove the black inhabitants of Freedmantown to settle there is more difficult to determine.[50] The occupations held by blacks in Freedmantown, however, were similar — if not superior — to those held by blacks in the rest of the ward. Fewer black individuals were engaged in manual labor occupations and a higher percentage worked as craftsmen in Freedmantown than in the surrounding areas of the ward. Only one black individual was employed in a commercial occupation within Freedmantown, but the majority of the neighborhood's black inhabitants held better positions than those held by the rest of the ward's blacks. Blacks in Freedmantown certainly were in no worse economic situation — if not in a better one — than blacks living in the adjacent areas of the ward.[51]

Given this evidence about the economic status of Freedmantown's inhabitants in 1870, it seems unlikely — at least at this point in the neighborhood's development — that they chose to live in Freedmantown over other subdivisions of the Fourth Ward out of economic duress. In fact, a comparison of the size and composition of the households in Freedmantown reveals that its residents actually may have enjoyed better housing conditions than were average for other inhabitants of the ward. Overcrowding was a ubiquitous problem among the households of the larger Fourth Ward. Only one in four households, or 25 percent, were single-family households. The average number of persons in each was five. In Freedmantown, on the other hand, out of 53 households, 95 percent were occupied by single families. The average number of persons per household was only 3.5. The physical living conditions of the inhabitants of Freedmantown, at least on the surface, were not inferior to those in the rest of the ward.[52]

If the patterns of settlement in Freedmantown had been an anomaly among the ward's neighborhoods in 1870, they were less of one by the decade's end. By 1880 the predominantly black population previously unique to Freedmantown had begun to spread to surrounding neighborhoods in the western section of the ward. The entire area south of San Felipe Road and adjacent to Freedmantown was giving way to black settlement. Within the residential areas adjoining Freedmantown — including the Castanie, Baker, Hopson, and Senechal additions and comprising the area that today is popularly referred to as Houston's "Fourth Ward" — the number of black inhabitants having white neighbors had fallen from 50 percent in 1870 to 32 percent in 1880. The racially mixed housing patterns found in the ward in 1870 had all but disappeared, and the census reveals that large areas of the ward now were occupied almost wholly by black residents. An occasional white household — at most four or five in a row — appeared interspersed among the dwellings occupied by blacks, but these occurrences were rare. Blacks comprised 68 percent of the total population in these additions of the ward, and the percentage of households headed by blacks stood at 70 percent. In contrast, the percentage of blacks within the population of the whole Fourth Ward had risen only to 49 percent.[53]

The proportion of whites living in the additions adjacent to Freedmantown who were of foreign birth had increased similarly, rising to 73 percent.[54] While the demographic composition of the entire Fourth Ward had remained fairly static, that of its western additions had undergone a distinct transformation, becoming simultaneously more black and more foreign born. This western area of the Fourth Ward still was not densely populated nor was it inhabited exclusively by blacks, but by 1880 these neighborhoods near Freedmantown were delineated clearly from the more centrally located areas of the ward. It appears that with the passage of time residential separation by race was becoming more widespread and more distinct.[55]

As the black-white composition of these western neighborhoods of the ward underwent a noticeable transformation during the 1870s, so too did the occupational status of their inhabitants. Blacks and whites in these neighborhoods had suffered a reduction in their wage-earning ability. For both, the percentage of household heads engaged in service-related jobs had increased. In addition, the percentage of blacks engaged as tradesmen and as manual laborers had decreased slightly. Among the ward's white inhabitants, there was a slightly higher percentage engaged in manual labor occupations than there had been in 1870. However, the white population appeared to be increasing its participation in commercial occupations, while the percentage of blacks involved remained steady. By and large, both blacks and whites in these western residential areas were engaged in less desirable occupations than they had been in previous years.[56]

The black occupants of Freedmantown in 1880 shared a similar wage-earning fate with the residents of adjacent neighborhoods, witnessing few substantial gains in their occupational positions over the decade. There had been, for example, a significant drop in the percentage working as craftsmen.[57] The most significant change occurred in the number of female household heads who reported their occupations as "at home" or "keeping house." Whereas only one individual identified herself in this way in 1870, seven did in 1880. The meaning of this increase, however, is ambiguous. Perhaps these individuals no longer had to work outside of the home to maintain their economic well-being and had voluntarily withdrawn themselves from the labor market. The reverse explanation, however, is equally convincing — they may have been unable to find gainful employment outside of the home and either were doing odd jobs or were altogether without employment. Deciding which of these explanations is correct would have a decisive impact on the overall assessment of occupational mobility of blacks in Freedmantown, since 10 percent of the blacks living there in 1880 fell into this category, but available evidence provides no answer.[58]

As for the rest of the blacks in the neighborhood, most were in a worse economic position in 1880 than they had been in 1870. White inhabitants in Freedmantown also saw a reduction in their occupational status over the decade. Forty percent of the neighborhood's white inhabitants in 1880 were employed in service-related jobs, a category none had occupied in 1870. However, the whites still comprised only a minute proportion of Freedmantown's total labor force. Both the white and black residents of Freedmantown, like the other black inhabitants of the ward, had suffered somewhat during the depression-ridden '70s, but they did not seem to have suffered more severely. The average number of individuals per household in Freedmantown remained relatively low, and the number of blacks purchasing property remained high, suggesting that economic hard times had not completely disrupted life in the neighborhood.[59]

The most striking difference between the situation of the residents of Freedmantown and those of the surrounding neighborhoods originated not from occupational structure but from Freedmantown's physical development over the decade. Despite the growing concentration of blacks in the neighborhoods adjacent to Freedmantown, the housing patterns within Freedmantown remained distinguishable by the almost total absence of white residents. Only 12 percent of the black households in Freedmantown were situated next door to whites in comparison to 32 percent for the neighboring areas. The gap between Freedmantown and the adjacent neighborhoods was narrowing, but Freedmantown still stood out among them. Even in 1880, 93 percent of Freedmantown's residents were black.[60]

Land Ownership in Freedmantown

Determining why a higher proportion of blacks settled in Freedmantown than in surrounding areas has produced all sorts of speculation. One popular explanation states that "this area, begun right after the Civil War, was land that was formerly a 'truck gardening' region and was sold by white farmers to the former slaves."[61] The deed records for property situated in Freedmantown contradict this explanation, showing that there was only one owner of land in Freedmantown, G. S. Hardcastle, in 1866. Hardcastle was neither a farmer, nor was he selling land to his former slaves. According to the 1860 census, he owned only one slave.[62] There simply is no indication of an organized, collective effort among the city's white residents to establish Freedmantown as a black neighborhood.

Others have assumed as fact popular myths about the neighborhood's development. Some trace the history of Freedmantown to a story told by the compilers of the Works Projects Administration's *Houston: A History and Guide*. The guide recounts the legend that one of the city's slaveowners and a resident of the Second Ward, Charles S. Longcope, called his slaves together in June 1865, "and, as he stood in his front door, read to them the proclamation that gave them their freedom. He then offered *each* of his former slaves a building lot in the Fourth Ward." The WPA states that Longcope owned a "dozen Negroes who had long been a part of the household." According to the 1860 census, however, Longcope was the owner of only three slaves, two females ages forty and eighteen employed as domestic servants, and one male, age eight. Even if Longcope provided each of these three with property in the Fourth Ward, his actions hardly could be credited with starting a settlement boom in the ward.[63]

It also is tempting to seize upon the connotations of the name "Freedmantown" to explain the growth of this area as a black neighborhood. In many Southern cities, for example, black neighborhoods emerged in locations where Union army and Freedmen's Bureau camps had been established during and just after the war. Former slaves flocked to these areas in hopes of receiving protection. When the government hastily closed these camps in the war's aftermath, blacks who had moved into their vicinity often decided to remain rather than to return to their previous homes. In this manner, a number of black neighborhoods, or so-called "freedmen's towns," were established on the fringes of cities across the South.[64] This scenario, however, does not explain the establishment of Houston's Freedmantown. Official records of the War Department indicate that federal troops were stationed in Houston for a time, but they were actually housed in former Confederate camps located in Harrisburg, a town situated eight miles east of Houston on Buffalo Bayou. In addition, the local office of the Freedmen's Bureau, when it finally was established in Houston in November 1865, was located on Commerce Street between Main and Fannin, in the city's central business area.[65] Apparently, there was no connection between the blacks' choice of Freedmantown as a residential area and their access to the local office of the Freedmen's Bureau or to federal encampments.

Explanations that emphasize the geographic features of Houston's Fourth Ward seem more plausible in explaining the predominance of black residents in Freedmantown. Some have suggested that since many blacks entered Houston from plantations on the Brazos River "by way of the old San Felipe Road" — a major thoroughfare for the city — some probably stopped at the first vacant areas they encountered within a short distance of the town center. Freedmantown would have been one such area.[66] And the most obvious explanation for Freedmantown's growth as a black neighborhood was its location. Situated directly on Buffalo Bayou, the property in Freedmantown likely was subject to regular flooding, and due to poor drainage, probably fostered a high rate of disease.[67] The neighborhood also abutted two cemeteries and land that had been set aside for a city hospital. On several occasions in 1871, the newspapers decried the "most neglected and dilapidated" condition of the cemetery adjacent to Freedmantown. These geographic disincentives to settlement — called "locational mechanisms" by Kellogg — help explain the patterns of Freedmantown's growth.[68]

Blacks, however, may not simply have been *forced* to settle in Freedmantown; they may have *chosen* Freedmantown as a residential site — despite Freedmantown's physical shortcomings — because they found improved opportunities for land and home ownership there. As indicated previously, blacks across the South longed to become property owners, and in Houston during the postwar years blacks' desire for land ownership probably was fueled by the exorbitant rents being charged in the city. A local agent of the Freedmen's Bureau reported that most blacks were trying to buy their own property because rents were so high. It cost as much, the agent's report stated, to rent lodging for a year as it did to buy a lot and build a house.[69] The prospect of having to pay what probably amounted to a significant portion of their salaries to a landlord — the common laborer reportedly made only $1 a day — assuredly made less wealthy blacks and whites more intent upon purchasing their own lots of land and constructing their own dwellings.[70]

Records of land ownership support the assumption that blacks were drawn to Freedmantown because it offered them greater opportunities to purchase land. Compared to the adjacent Baker, Castanie, Senechal, and Hopson additions, all of which attracted a substantial number of black residents, property ownership by blacks was highest — in both absolute and relative terms — in Freedmantown.[71]

In the first months following the war, Freedmantown itself had not yet been platted by its owner, Garrett S. Hardcastle. When Hardcastle purchased the land from William R. Baker in 1855, the area that later would be known as Freedmantown had developed no specific identity or association with any particular group — racial or ethnic — of the city's residents, nor had it become recognizable by its relative location to any of the city's landmarks. The deed of sale executed on July 14, 1855, transferring ownership to Hardcastle, merely identified the purchased land as being "more or less bounded West by said Hardcastle lands, South by J. Castanie, East by the Hopson Place and North by Buffalo Bayou."[72] This loose wording and the fact that the surrounding property, recognized only by its property owners, also had no readily identifiable landmarks suggests that the entire area around Freedmantown was largely undeveloped prior to the Civil War.

In 1866, even though he had not completed his payments on the property nor had he removed Baker's lien on it, Hardcastle began to subdivide the land and sell small plots. By the time that the official plat map for this neighborhood was filed in 1875, the neighborhood had assumed a distinct identity. Upon the official copy of the plat map, the county clerk wrote, "Known as Freedmantown," even though the formal identification for the property was the "Hardcastle Addition."[73]

Blacks seem to have been attracted to Freedmantown because they were better able to purchase land there, indicating that land ownership was a primary motivation behind the blacks' choices of residential neighborhoods within the city. Since the Hardcastle subdivision — in contrast to the four adjacent additions, the Castanie, Baker, Senechal, and Hopson — had not been developed before 1865, blacks moving to the city after emancipation had no previous residents to contend with in attempting to purchase property in this neighborhood. Property sales did not begin in the subdivision until 1866, but they stayed fairly constant for the remainder of the decade and through the next. Although there was not a single black proprietor in Freedmantown prior to 1865, blacks were quite successful in purchasing property over the subsequent fifteen-year period. Freedmantown's flood-prone location near the bayou, the hospital lands, and the cemeteries thus seem to have facilitated its later development as a black neighborhood.[74]

Even Freedmantown's proximity to one of the major thoroughfares of the city, San Felipe Road, did not alter the racial composition of the addition. Although some of the property in Freedmantown would have been ideally situated for commercial development and lodging establishments, most white Houstonians found this incentive insufficient to attract them to the area.[75] Only 24 percent of the individuals purchasing property in Freedmantown from 1865 to 1880 were white — a total of 32 individuals. In contrast, 65 percent were black — representing 88 purchasers — a noticeable deviance from the percentages found in the surrounding subdivisions of the ward.[76]

Purchasing property and settling in Freedmantown also may have appealed to Houston's African Americans because it allowed them, in contrast to other areas of the ward, to reside in a predominantly black neighborhood. The desire to establish independent black communities probably increased in the 1870s with the "redemption" of Texas state and local government from Republican rule. Without the protection of a Republican government, blacks may have tried to insulate themselves from white persecution by separating themselves into autonomous residential neighborhoods.[77] Likewise, Houston whites may have felt more secure about allowing black residential areas to develop now that they had resumed control over their state and local governments. The high number of black property owners and black residents in Freedmantown in the 1870s lends support to this explanation. The desire to live among other blacks, free from white surveillance, thus may have prompted blacks to settle in Freedmantown.

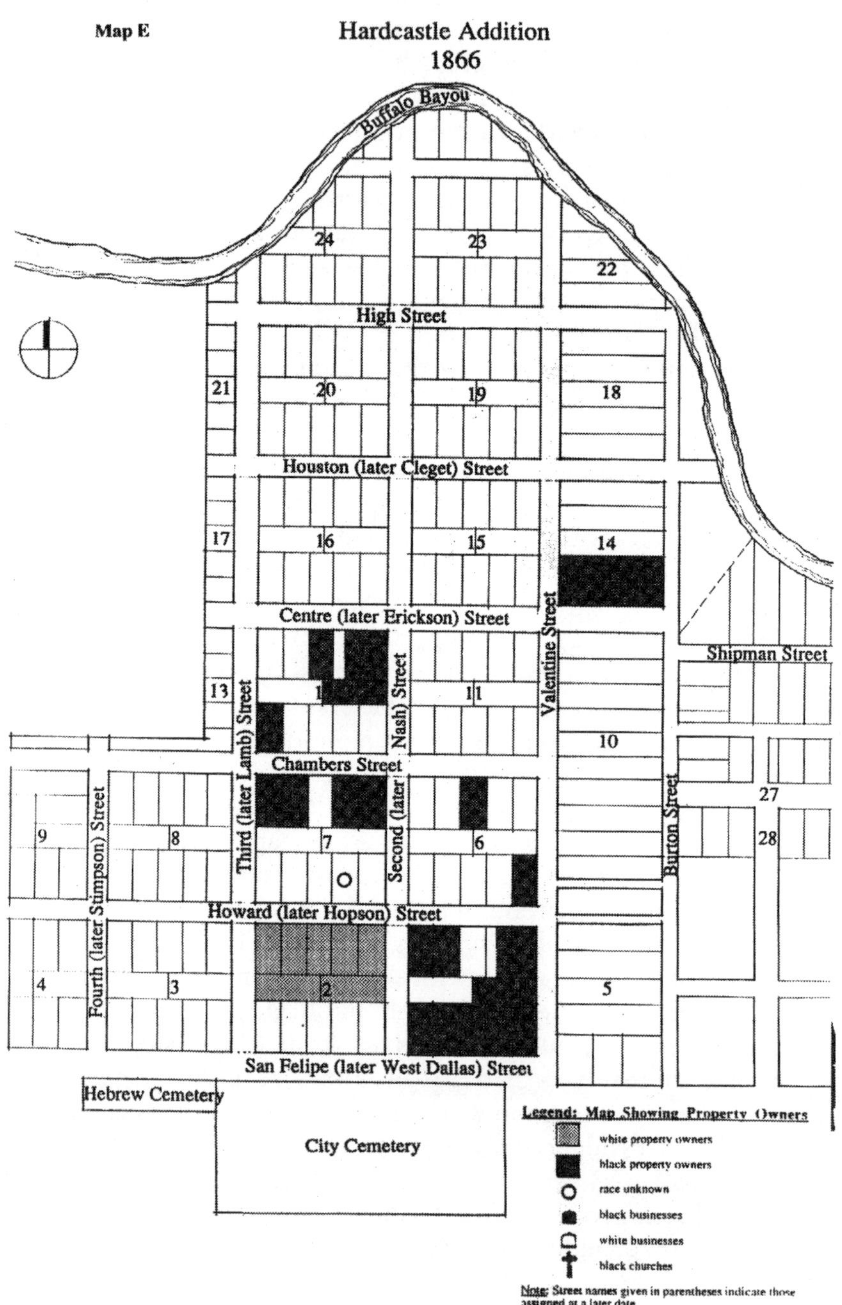

Map E
Hardcastle Addition
1866
Buffalo Bayou
High Street
Houston (later Cleget) Street
Centre (later Erickson) Street
Chambers Street
Howard (later Hopson) Street
San Felipe (later West Dallas) Street
Shipman Street
Third (later Lamb) Street
Second (later Nash) Street
Fourth (later Stimpson) Street
Valentine Street
Burton Street
Hebrew Cemetery
City Cemetery
Legend: Map Showing Property Owners
white property owners
black property owners
race unknown
black businesses
white businesses
black churches
Note: Street names given in parentheses indicate those
assigned at a later date.

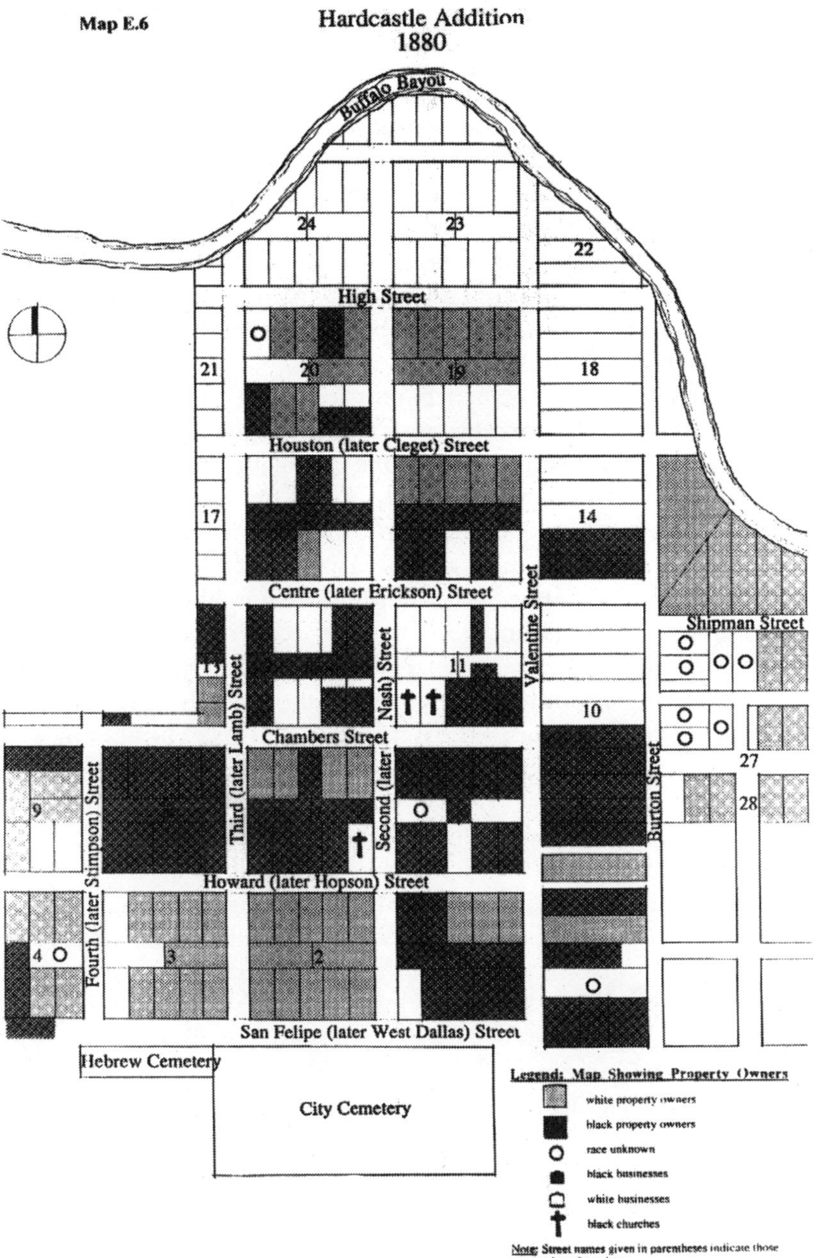
Map E.6
Hardcastle Addition
1880
Buffalo Bayou
24
23
22
High Street
21
20
19
18
Houston (later Cleget) Street
17
14
Centre (later Erickson) Street
Valentine Street
Shipman Street
15
11
10
Nash) Street
Chambers Street
Burton Street
27
28
Third (later Lamb) Street
Second (later
9
Fourth (later Stimpson) Street
Howard (later Hopson) Street
4
3
2
San Felipe (later West Dallas) Street
Hebrew Cemetery
City Cemetery
Legend: Map Showing Property Owners
white property owners
black property owners
race unknown
black businesses
white businesses
black churches
Note: Street names given in parentheses indicate those
assigned at a later date.

Neither the deed nor the census records taken alone, however, clearly indicate whether or not those owning property within Freedmantown also were residents there. Determining how many individuals also lived on the property they owned in Freedmantown is essential for assessing the degree to which blacks were actively attempting to construct autonomous neighborhoods in the ward and how successful they were in doing so. Moreover, considering how important property ownership was to blacks in the postwar years, a high degree of black land ownership in this neighborhood may provide a clue in understanding why the name "Freedmantown" today stands as a symbol of black achievement among Houston's African Americans.[78]

Available evidence is insufficient to obtain a complete count of the resident-property owners in Freedmantown, but the greatest number within the Fourth Ward appear to have resided in this addition.[79] Settlement in the Hardcastle Addition proceeded in a most unusual manner when compared to other additions in the ward. In the first five years after the war, only two white individuals — compared to 34 blacks — purchased land in the neighborhood, and neither amassed holdings on the scale that occurred elsewhere in the ward. John Murchison was the largest landholder in Freedmantown in 1870, owning seven lots of property all of which were located in the same block. As indicated by the 1870 census, Murchison was a resident of the neighborhood, not an absentee owner. The other white owner of property, J. Coryell, owned only half a lot, and although he was not listed in the 1870 census as a resident of the area, the 1869 map indicated his ownership of a dwelling on the property. Thus, either he lived on the property himself and simply was omitted by the census taker in 1870, or he was renting to a third party.[80]

John Murchison's reason for choosing Freedmantown as his residence — possibly the only white individual living there at this time — is suggested by the 1870 and 1880 census records. While Murchison and his entire family were identified as "white" in the 1870 census, in 1880 although *his* race still was identified as "white," his children's race was indicated as "mulatto" (his wife apparently had died or divorced him). In addition, in the 1879–80 city directory for Houston, Murchison was identified as "col'd" — the usual designation given to Houston's blacks. It is likely that Murchison actually was black but had been able to "pass" as white. Even if Murchison were white, however, the ostracism he probably felt from the white community because of his children's mixed race may have led him to choose a residential location removed from areas of largely white settlement. Whatever Murchison's reason for living in Freedmantown, he clearly had chosen to locate in an almost exclusively black neighborhood and continued to live there throughout the decade.[81]

Development in Freedmantown may have remained concentrated in a small radius, but nearly every lot within the area of settlement was held by a black owner who also resided on his or her property. This trend toward blacks purchasing property and settling upon it continued throughout the 1870s, firmly establishing Freedmantown as a neighborhood in which black property owners comprised the majority of the residents. On the other hand, there also was a marked increase during the 1870s in the degree of concentrated land ownership — particularly within the less developed sections of the addition — by white absentee proprietors. Several of these individuals acquired their property in Freedmantown due to Hardcastle's default on notes due them. As for the others, perhaps they viewed this neighborhood as an expanding and vital part of Houston's black community and hoped to "cash in" on its development.[82]

What these absentee owners intended to do or did with their land during this period is difficult to ascertain. The census records indicate a number of black individuals as residents of Freedmantown who were not identified as landowners in the deed records. Most of these residents probably were renting their land from someone in the neighborhood — more than likely one of the white absentee proprietors, since most blacks owned only a single lot of land. The 1869 map also indicates that few of the blacks owning property had subdivided their land further — though some clearly did — to allow for extra tenants.[83]

Although the number of absentee owners and the number of residents in Freedmantown who were renting their houses increased, Freedmantown remained by and large a neighborhood of black property owners — a pattern not duplicated elsewhere in the western additions of the ward. The establishment of the Freedmantown neighborhood marked a tremendous accomplishment on the part of the black community in Houston. Given the fact that the Freedmen's Bureau rarely if ever involved itself in the attainment of personal property or the construction of private dwellings among members of the black community, the blacks in Freedmantown demonstrated an exceptional degree of self-determination in achieving the degree of property ownership that they did. They had limited or no access to credit sources — save the willingness of individual owners to sell property to them on credit — and many had to overcome the destitute economic positions in which slavery had left them. To create in Freedmantown, as they did, an independent black neighborhood in so short a time was a remarkable feat.[84]

Freedmantown's creation suggests that blacks engaged actively in the creation of autonomous black residential areas, for the patterns of development that emerged in Freedmantown differed markedly from those found in the surrounding additions of the Fourth Ward. In the Baker, Senechal, Hopson, and to a lesser extent in the Castanie additions, blacks remained a minority of the property owners. Several blacks frequently purchased property in the same or adjacent blocks in these additions, but these "enclaves" of black residents remained scattered. Blacks then may have chosen to live in Freedmantown over these surrounding areas because the neighborhood offered them an unparalleled opportunity to purchase property and live among blacks. As blacks began to lose their political power and protection from Northern officials during the 1870s, the role of black residential neighborhoods such as Freedmantown probably became increasingly important.

While this conclusion about the degree of agency involved in blacks' settlement in Freedmantown is only tentative, the fact that such a high degree of black property ownership existed there does suggest a possible explanation for the symbolic place that "Freedmen's Town" holds within Houston's black community today. The creation of a nearly all-black neighborhood in Freedmantown makes it a potent symbol of the postwar accomplishments of Houston's African-American population. How and when blacks invested Freedmantown with this symbolic importance, however, remains uncertain. But the facts behind the construction of Antioch Baptist Church, one of Houston's most prestigious black churches, suggests that at least prior to 1880, blacks in Houston did not accord the same symbolic significance to Freedmantown that it holds today.

When Antioch Baptist Church, formed in Houston in January 1866, was given the opportunity to establish itself in Freedmantown in the 1870s, it declined. Initially the congregation had met at a brush arbor on the banks of Buffalo Bayou and then had conducted services in neighboring white churches while their own church building was being constructed. In 1868 they moved to a new building on the corner of Rusk and Bagby streets in the Fourth Ward.[85] Three years later Garrett Hardcastle offered Antioch two lots of land in the Freedmantown addition free of charge. Perhaps because the church had just moved to its present location on Rusk Street, the trustees took no immediate action to use the land given them. However, less than a year later Antioch purchased two lots for the consideration of $400 for the construction of a new church in the Senechal Addition located in the Fourth Ward to the south and east of Freedmantown.[86]

There are several possible explanations for the trustees' decision not to build on the land Hardcastle had given them. Since churches were symbols of both the black community's religious faith and its material progress, relocating Antioch on Robin Street in the Senechal Addition — a more "prestigious" location than Freedmantown because of its proximity to the town center and its greater distance from the flood-prone banks of the bayou — may have been a means for the black parish to assert its progress and to articulate its aspirations.[87] Whatever the reason, the actions of the church trustees demonstrated their feeling that the plot of land given them in Freedmantown was an unsuitable site for their church's location. The church's history indicates, moreover, that in the early 1870s Freedmantown held no symbolic place in the black community's self-perception.

Later events further suggest that the present-day significance of Freedmantown to Houston's African-American community was not shared by earlier black residents of the city. In 1907, the city government established a legally sanctioned red light district, called the "Reservation," in Freedmantown, forcing many black families to abandon the homes that they had built there. The subsequent association of the neighborhood with prostitution probably dashed any significance Freedmantown may have held within the black community.[88] This evidence implies that if Freedmantown held any special place within the African-American community prior to the mid-twentieth century, it suffered periodic or episodic declines.

In fact, the contemporary attachment to "Freedmen's Town" among Houston's blacks may prove to be a very recent phenomenon, and one cannot dismiss the possibility that the contemporary symbolic position of "Freedmen's Town" may be the product of "myth making" or "hero building," as described by Nathan Huggins, within Houston's African-American community.[89] Admitting this possibility does not in any way deny the importance of Freedmantown either in historical fact or in its contemporary context as a symbol of racial pride. Whatever the genesis of Freedmantown's symbolic importance, the popular perception of the neighborhood exercises a powerful hold over the Fourth Ward's black community today. However, given the misperceptions concerning the neighborhood's origins, the significance of the original Freedmantown addition and its history of black property ownership — something that truly does warrant recognition and celebration — remains obscured. Thus this preliminary research exposing the origins and initial physical development of Freedmantown and making the important distinction between it and the other adjacent additions of the Fourth Ward marks a critical first step in understanding how Freedmantown assumed such a symbolic position among Houston's blacks. But further research concerning the black community's changing perceptions of Freedmantown remains to be done, and only when this story is unraveled will the neighborhood's full significance and its role within the historical consciousness of Houston's larger black community be accurately understood.

Chapter 9

The Civil Rights March on Austin, Texas, 1963

by Martin Kuhlman

In all America, true things are happening,
To make the white man try to see,
That we are human, and we are equal,
And that we shall, we shall be free.

In all America, true things are happening,
To make the black man try to see,
That we must fight here, that we must fight here,
If we are ever to be free.

— Freedom song at the Austin rally
August 28, 1963

The summer of 1963 represented a dramatic period in the arena of the civil rights movement. Segregationist governors, a proposed civil rights bill, and a march on Washington made national headlines. Texas shared in the drama of the times with a governor opposed to the civil rights bill and a march on the state capital. As on the national scene a move to change the political climate occurred in Texas. Liberals joined forces to attack the status quo.

Three hundred liberal Democrats opposed to the conservatism

of Democratic Governor John Connally met in Dallas on July 13, 1963. The liberals formed a group known as the Democratic Coalition. The coalition consisted of supporters of civil rights, labor, and other liberal causes. The four co-chairmen of the organization included W. J. Durham, the Dallas attorney for the National Association for the Advancement of Colored People (NAACP) and president of the Texas Council of Voters; Hank Brown, president of the Texas AFL-CIO; Albert Pena, president of the Political Association of Spanish-speaking Organizations (PASO); and Franklin Jones, Sr., spokesman for a group known as the liberal loyalist Democrats. The group identified its immediate intention as bringing about "maximum voter participation in the Nov. 9 election to repeal the poll tax." The coalition also planned to organize a grass-roots movement in an attempt to increase the number of qualified voters in the 1964 election. The focus of such a movement would be on "selected precincts and counties" where liberal support could be garnered.

The black representatives in the coalition asked for an amendment assuring them of an equal share of control in the coalition. Durham stated that similar coalitions had cheated African Americans out of their deserved benefits before. Another section of the amendment denied the coalition's support to candidates who practiced, accepted, or defended gradualism "as symbolized by the voluntary approach to these problems [segregation] as advocated by the conservative element because of social pressures."

Black leaders who had aided in the creation of the coalition sent Governor Connally a petition calling on the officials of Texas to use every means available to bring about equality in all parts of the state. They asked Connally to speed up desegregation by issuing a broad executive order ending segregation in all state facilities, such as pools and parks, and in businesses requiring state licenses. The proposed executive order would be similar to those already enacted by governors in the southern states of Kentucky and North Carolina. Ten members of the subcommittee of the Texas Council of Voters Executive Committee signed the petition. They included Erma and Moses LeRoy and Francis L. Williams of Houston, Rev. C. William Black, Jr., and G. J. Sutton of San Antonio, W. J. Durham of Dallas, Marion J. Brooks of Fort Worth, Willie Melton of Kendleton, and Booker T. Bonner of Austin.

Connally gave his indirect answer to the petition in a thirty-minute televised speech on July 19. The speech directly attacked a proposed federal civil rights bill, especially the public accommodations section of the bill. The speech epitomized the governor's reliance on the private sector to make progress in desegregation. Connally announced that although he supported equality under the law while pledging to continue efforts in that area and advocated the integration of tax-supported institutions, he opposed federal legislation that would ban racial discrimination in privately owned public accommodations. He feared that such legislation would attack the freedom to own and manage private property. The federal law "would deprive the owners of private businesses of the right to decide whom they serve." The governor also objected to the broad powers given to the attorney general of the United States. The attorney general would be allowed to file, under certain circumstances, injunctions on behalf of individuals to force desegregation of schools and public facilities. Connally argued that he could not support "the proposition of violating one person's rights to bestow privilege on another person, regardless of the color or race of either."

He urged Texans to continue to listen to the reasonable voices which had allowed their state to "avoid the cold, arbitrary tool of government edict." He maintained that the civil rights issue remained a question that could be solved locally and was an area in which Texas had already made "tremendous" progress. Texans could be led but did not like to be pushed, and Connally felt federal legislation would be pushing.

Although Connally opposed the legislation, he did promise to uphold the law if it passed. But he believed that what came out of Washington would "not change the character of the problem, nor provide the real answer." Connally, however, did identify voluntary desegregation as strides forward, unlike other Southern governors who strongly opposed desegregation. Of course, the large number of black voters in Texas, as compared with other Southern states, may have influenced Connally's stand on segregation.

A number of Texans supported the governor's speech on civil rights. United States Senator John Tower, a Republican, also opposed the public accommodations section of the civil rights bill. He agreed that desegregation should be on a voluntary rather than a compulsory basis. Other state officials seconded Connally's speech. Dallas Mayor Earle Cabell, a Democrat, said, "In my opinion Governor Connally expressed the views and objectives of a vast majority of the people of Texas — of all races." Republican state legislator Henry Stollenwreck agreed with the governor's opposition to the public accommodations section of the bill but stressed his disappointment that Connally did not attack the employment practices section of the bill. The majority of telegrams to the governor's office supported Connally's stand.

A. B. Beddow, president of the Texas Real Estate Association, praised the governor's defense of the right of private property owners. Support also appeared from segments of the African-American community. A member of the Midland Negro Chamber of Commerce sent a telegram to Connally's office calling it the "best and most outstanding speech by any Governor in the nation today." Rev. A. H. Forbes, Jr., minister of the Metropolitan Church in Fort Worth, wrote, "You have our unquestionable support and confidence in all your endeavors." Disagreeing telegrams covered the political spectrum from civil rights supporters accusing Connally of being "anti-Kennedy" to segregationists labeling the governor a "nigger-lover." A poll of Anglo Texans reported that 75 percent of the Texas population opposed the public accommodations section of the bill.

Opposition to Connally's speech, however, appeared in many sections of the black community. *The Informer*, an African-American newspaper in Houston, marveled at the high percentage of hotels, theaters, and restaurants Connally quoted as being integrated. The paper hoped that "Negroes in East Texas don't take the governor at his word and show up for such public accommodations, [because] it is likely that some one will go to jail." Most privately owned public accommodations in West Texas had desegregated, but East Texas, a region where racial tolerance often mirrored that in the Deep South, followed a strict policy of segregation. Although Connally had pledged to do everything in his power to desegregate tax-supported facilities, *The Informer* noted the slow rate of integration in state parks which the governor could have directly influenced. Other than Bastrop State Park, all of the numerous state parks in East Texas remained segregated. Segregation still continued at the swimming pool in Bastrop Park. The editorial also accused Connally of playing "a Cat and Mouse game" with his black supporters, promising them a lot but delivering little. Although he had appointed some black Texans to state agencies, such as the prison board, few blacks were involved in high policy making. Attorney

General Waggoner Carr had appointed J. Phillip Crawford assistant attorney general in the summer of 1963.

Clarence Laws, the Dallas regional secretary of the NAACP, said Connally had forgotten history when he implied that Texas had extended rights without the precedence of law. The winning of the right to vote in the Democratic primary, to attend institutions of higher learning with whites, and to travel in desegregated carriers had only come about as a result of legislation. Albert Pena said if the governor believed so much in the voluntary approach, he should voluntarily sign an executive order to desegregate state parks and public schools.

Booker T. Bonner denounced the governor's speech as "an affront to all Texans, Negroes and whites." Bonner had watched most of Connally's speech at the Caravan Club, where Bonner worked as a waiter. The speech increased his opposition to the governor's policies. Bonner had worked in Don Yarborough's 1962 gubernatorial campaign against Connally. Although Bonner had not totally agreed with Yarborough's policies relating to black Texans, Bonner totally objected to Connally's paying attention to a select group of African-American leaders. The United Political Organization (UPO), a pro-Connally group consisting of approximately 150 wealthy conservative black businessmen, had formed in 1962. The UPO emphasized employment and voting rights. The group did not speak out against civil rights demonstrations but believed economic and political advances, which the white establishment respected, represented the best way to gain rights. The UPO's endorsement helped Connally win a number of black votes in 1962. Bonner had chastised the UPO for selling out its community and for being "Uncle Toms." *The Informer* had accused the leaders of the UPO of trading political and constitutional rights for a few jobs and political appointments.

Connally's speech also had an impact on the national scene. A few days after the speech Vice-president Lyndon Baines Johnson received a staff memorandum concerning his fellow Texan's speech. The memo pointed out the irony of the state having segregation legislation on its lawbooks which affected private property, and Connally denouncing the interference of legislation in desegregating private property. Hobart Taylor, Jr., a Houston resident and vice-chairman of the national Equal Employment Opportunity Committee, wrote Johnson a letter expressing concern over the controversy caused in Texas by Connally's speech. Although the turmoil gained some national attention, Texans led the struggle.

The state's civil rights supporters believed that Connally had misrepresented himself to black Texans and that the speech represented the true stance of the governor on racial matters. E. Brice Cunningham, a spokesperson for the Texas Council of Voters, stated that Connally's stand on civil rights had aligned "Texas with the Old South (particularly Alabama and Mississippi) and others dedicated to blocking progress." Bonner, Houston Wade, a civil rights activist Bonner had met at the University of Texas (UT), and five other supporters met at the YMCA of UT in the following days. There they decided on an act that would spotlight the governor's civil rights policies. Connally's stand on the desegregation of public accommodations led to direct action.

Bonner sent Connally a registered letter asking for a meeting to discuss their disagreements over the public accommodations section of the civil rights bill. When Connally left Austin without replying, Bonner went to Connally's office in the Governor's Mansion on July 29 to demand an appointment for a meeting. He refused to leave until receiving an appointment. Bonner criticized Connally for allowing segregation to continue. Howard Rose, the governor's executive assistant, argued that Connally had a better civil rights record than most Southern governors. Bonner replied that any segregation represented too much. He stated that the humiliation of being segregated from a few accommodations equaled that of being barred from all. Bonner staged a one man sit-in as he spent the day in the waiting room and moved to the hall when the waiting room closed for the evening. That night he temporarily broke his vigil to lead forty biracial picketers, the majority students from UT, in a one-hour march around the Governor's Mansion. Protesters carried leaflets labeling Connally "a Jim Crow governor of the worst kind" who had "exploited the trust and hopes of Negroes." Bonner announced that he and other civil rights activists planned large scale demonstrations in Texas on August 28 to coincide with the march on Washington. Bonner returned to the hall for the rest of the night and waited in the governor's office the next day. The twenty-six-hour one man sit-in ended when Governor Connally announced from Houston that he would meet with Bonner, although Connally did not believe anything needed to be discussed concerning his position on civil rights. A source of conflict appeared when Bonner stated that he would be accompanied to the meeting by at least four supporters. Rose insisted that only Bonner would attend the meeting.

Reaction to the sit-in came quickly. The private Club Caravan in Austin fired Bonner from his position as waiter the following day. The owners said Bonner was "laid off" because his private affairs interfered with his job and because of an accusation of theft. Bonner, however, did not accept this reasoning. He told reporters that he had been blacklisted by Austin employers and that state and federal police had been investigating him. Bonner stated his anger at the lack of rights for African Americans and labeled the NAACP as "too tame" for him. Bonner had served in Korea and felt disturbed about fighting for the United States and finding out he still had few rights at home.

Bonner continued to lead marches around the Governor's Mansion until the scheduled meeting. He hoped marchers would maintain interest in integration activities and inspire others to join future demonstrations. On August 1 seven civil rights supporters marched and a group of ten segregationists, consisting of youths aged twelve to twenty and calling themselves the Children of the Confederacy, countermarched. Edmond Jackson, a student of the University of Mississippi and a member of the White Citizen's Council, led the segregationists. No confrontation occurred as they left ten minutes after the integrationists arrived. Bonner also planned a parade of pickets around the mansion for the night before the scheduled meeting with Connally. He hoped for a large crowd in order "to prove to the governor on Tuesday that we mean business."

Upon reading about the sit-in, Francis Williams, a lawyer from Houston, searched for other leaders to attend the meeting with Bonner. At 11:30 A.M. on August 6, Bonner arrived in Connally's waiting room flanked by six other minority leaders: four blacks, Dr. Ruth Bellinger and Sutton of San Antonio, E. Brice Cunningham of Dallas, James McCoy of the University of Texas, and two Hispanic leaders, Henry Munoz and Lalo Solis of San Antonio. When told the governor would see him, Bonner asked that the other leaders be allowed to attend. After a short, private consultation with Bonner, Sutton, and Cunningham, the governor canceled the meeting. Connally balked at the presence of the other leaders. Sutton wondered if it was the policy of the governor to meet with African Americans "one at a time." Bellinger became extremely agitated at the cancelation of the meeting since she had served as the co-chairman of Connally's 1962 gubernatorial campaign in Bexar County. The minority leaders left behind a petition once again asking Connally to issue an executive order banning segregation in state-owned facilities. The petition also asked for the enactment of at least a $1.25 minimum hourly wage law, the repeal of all Jim Crow laws in Texas, the immediate integration of all public schools, and the availability of college and university facilities to all races.

Sam Wood, the state capital correspondent of *The Austin American*, wrote that Bonner's sit-in at the Governor's Mansion was "obviously politically inspired to embarrass Connally." Wood said the liberal Democratic Coalition wanted to fan the flames for "liberal opposition to Gov. Connally in the 1964 election." The sit-in represented a planned strategy to revive the minority coalition, Wood stated. But the Democratic Coalition did not join in the sit-in or the planning of further demonstrations. Although members of the coalition, including Bonner and Williams, joined the civil rights activities, the coalition never became officially involved.

After hearing news of the cancelation of the meeting, close to fifty civil rights supporters renewed picketing of the mansion. Bonner said that he had given up on the possibility of a personal conference with the governor and that the picketers would switch their emphasis to the State Capitol. Bonner told reporters that "every Negro man in Texas will know the governor definitely is not his friend. . . . The Negro must know his rights are legal or he will never get them."

Another black leader in Austin, however, did not support the activities at the Governor's Mansion. Dr. J. J. Seabrook, president of Huston-Tillotson College, accused Bonner of attempting to create a sensation. Seabrook said, "We don't want outside people coming in and telling us what must be done in Austin. They do not know how much already has been done in this city." The fact that Huston-Tillotson depended on at least some support of the white establishment may have influenced Seabrook's statement. Opposition to Bonner also appeared from other areas of the state. Rev. C. A. Holliday of Fort Worth, the first African American appointed to the State Board of Corrections, believed Bonner's actions to be "uncalled for at this time." He praised Connally as a progressive in the area of civil rights. Connally had appointed Holliday in March of 1963.

Civil rights supporters planned a march on Washington, D.C.

for August 28 to protest against segregation. Activists in Texas scheduled marches for the same date to correspond with the Washington march. Harry V. Burns, president of the San Antonio chapter of the NAACP, planned a march to the city hall to demonstrate for civil rights and job opportunities. Bonner announced plans to organize a march in Austin to the Capitol and the Governor's Mansion. Civil rights leaders recognized that some black Texans would not be able to make the trip to Washington, but still needed an opportunity to vent their frustration. Although Bonner announced the march, Francis Williams did much of the organizing.

Bonner, Williams, and other civil rights leaders met at a YMCA in Houston to discuss strategy for the march. Civil rights supporters sent out over 1,200 mailings to urge groups and individuals across the state to attend the march. For example, Erma Leroy sent propaganda sheets to various organizations describing the stance of the governor. She accused Connally of aiding the segregationist argument. Leroy urged the organizations to "Make it clear that he [Connally] can't be a hero to the East Texas segregationists and Negro citizens at the same time!"

Williams worked with groups in cities including Dallas and Houston. A few days before the march, Bonner and others handed out leaflets in the Austin African-American community soliciting participants. Clarence Laws urged African Americans to attend the national march but stated that the Austin march would be a good alternative for those who could not afford the trip to Washington. The organizers expected 4,000 civil rights supporters to join the two-mile "March For Jobs and Freedom" through downtown Austin. Along the route a committee of five planned to deliver a petition calling for integration of all state-owned facilities to Connally. The Freedom Now Committee received permission for the August 28 march from the Austin City Council.

Dallas organizations including the NAACP, the Catholic Inter-Racial Council, the Texas Council of Voters, and the Dallas Full Citizenship Committee planned car pools and buses to Austin and Washington. Other Texas cities planned to do the same. *The Informer* announced that air-conditioned buses would leave Houston for Washington and Austin. Approximately seventy Houstonians participated in the march on Austin.

Labor supported both civil rights marches. The AFL-CIO of Houston announced its "whole-hearted support" for the demonstrations in Washington and Austin. Labor called on the state to abolish the use of race, creed, or color as a basis for employment by the state. The AFL-CIO injected some of its own agenda into the civil rights controversy such as the repeal of the right to work laws and the passage of a minimum wage law.

D. B. Mason, attorney and head of the Dallas County Democratic Progressive Voters League, announced his opposition to the march. He said none of his group would join the march "because we feel that Gov. Connally has done well and advanced our cause as well as could be expected in Texas at this time." He pointed to the appointment of two African Americans to state boards as steps in the right direction. Connally's appointments to previously all-white state boards included Holliday and Charles Jackson Clark to the State Board of Morticians. Mason added, "In Texas we must take things slowly and cannot advance as rapidly as in the East or North." Harsher opposition appeared from segments of the white community.

Governor Connally had offers of "protection" against Bonner's group. The Indignant White Citizens Council (IWCC), led by Bob Joiner of Grand View, also asked for a permit to march on the 28th. Connally, however, urged the group to postpone the march saying he feared violence if the two groups confronted. Joiner expressed unhappiness over Connally allowing the integrationists to march while asking the segregationists to stay away. Joiner stated, "We are not barbarians; we know right from wrong" and added his organization would march if the civil rights supporters did. Bonner also disagreed with the governor on censorship of the march. Bonner said, "He's [Connally] asking those people not to express their constitutional right." The IWCC received a permit to march in the streets of Austin on the 28th. They planned their march to begin three hours before the Freedom Now march. Joiner expected to lead at least 3,000 segregationists in the IWCC march.

A fear of confrontation between the rival demonstrations increased the anxiety looming over the state capital. A large number of state and local police organized in Austin to prevent instances of violence and abusive heckling. Police Chief R. A. Miles called every available police officer to duty for the day of the march. He assigned 200 uniformed and plain-clothes police to monitor the protests. The officers received riot equipment including batons and helmets. Even before the marches had been announced, the Austin police initiated a stepped-up program in riot control. State police planned to encircle the Capitol to aid local police.

The IWCC parade started out from Congress Avenue at 11:00 A.M. Eleven marchers swelled the ranks of the segregationists, most of them carrying Goldwater or pro-segregation signs. Joiner told reporters, "One of our aims is to support and protect the governor." When reminded the governor did not seem to want the IWCC's help, Joiner accused Connally of having been in Washington and around "the Kennedy brothers too long." From his red pick-up, which led the marchers, Joiner shouted, "You are either a Communist and a nigger lover, or you will join us. You can't be in the middle." After the march Joiner expressed his disappointment that "so many gutless Texans have refused to stand up and say they are for segregation."

Gen. Edwin A. Walker, who had traveled to Oxford, Mississippi, in 1962 and rallied segregationists in an effort to stop the integration of the University of Mississippi, went to Austin as an observer. In a press conference held after the first march the ex-general stated, "Joiner's group represents, in spirit, millions more Americans over the nation than those [Freedom Now] to parade this afternoon." Walker added, "I came to see how much interest and support the pro-Kennedy, pro-Communist, pro-social rights program could get in Texas. It will be an obvious, political flop." Walker accused the Kennedy administration of supporting the marches "to take the spotlight off their biggest flop — Cuba."

A crowd of participants in the Freedom Now march gathered in the Doris Miller auditorium in east Austin for a pre-march rally early that afternoon. Seven black youths led the crowd in freedom chants and songs. Approximately 600 civil rights supporters, including fifty whites, began the two-mile trek at 2:00 P.M. in 102-degree weather. High school and college students made up the majority of marchers. Other marchers included members of the clergy, representatives of liberal groups, including an official delegate of the state AFL-CIO, and professionals. They streamed past the Capitol as some marchers chanted and spelled "freedom" while others sang "I want to be a free, free man" and "Tell John Connally we shall not be moved." Some of the slogans on the sea of signs included "Jim Crow Must Go," "Gradualism, Tokenism, Connallyism," "Faubus — Wallace — Barnett — Connally," "Total Freedom Is What We Want,"

"If Not Now, When?" and "No more 50¢ per hour." The marchers continued on to a rally in Wooldridge Park.

Opposing forces made their presence known during the civil rights march. Joiner and a few of his followers heckled the marchers along the way, and the segregationists followed the demonstrators to the park. Joiner's group created a disturbance during the opening prayer of the rally and a number of African Americans rose to confront them. Austin police formed a line between the groups, and the racists retreated. Another segregationist had watched the parade from the steps of the Capitol and, commenting on the size of the march, told reporters, "If that's all the supporters Kennedy has here, he's sure flopped."

At the rally Williams introduced eight speakers. Although Bonner had argued for and won the right to speak to the crowd before Durham, he surrendered the platform. Williams introduced Bonner as "the man who started it off." After telling the crowd to applaud themselves for their effort, he said that he had been speaking for the last month and wanted to give other speakers a chance. Bonner hoped to gain the trust of the other civil rights leaders with that move.

A major difference between the national and the state march appeared when President John Kennedy met leaders of the march on Washington, while Connally did not meet with leaders of the Austin march. Although organizers had announced their intention to deliver a petition to Connally, Durham told the cheering crowd that "I didn't want to see the governor. I wanted the governor to see us go by." Connally worked in his office as the marchers passed and commented on being pleased that no serious incidents had occurred during the demonstration. But Connally suffered numerous verbal attacks for his stand on integration during the rally.

Civil rights supporters saw their chance to change the political leadership of the state. Dr. Marion Brooks, a Fort Worth physician, told the crowd that the 625,000 eligible black voters, the 800,000 eligible Hispanic voters, together with the two million liberals and the 500,000 labor supporters, would "sweep the statehouse clean." Rev. Claude Black of San Antonio said, "We are tired of humiliation. We come here to warn Connally and all other segregationists that their days are numbered." Durham stated, "I've got news for Governor Connally. Tell him that each of us Negro voters will remember him on election day." Dr. Bellinger declared that the governor had "let us down."

Durham also attacked the UPO because of the group's support of Connally. But the organization did not give unconditional support to the governor. Although the UPO had called Connally's civil rights speech the "most significant and positive statement on civil rights by a public official in the history of this state," the group did express some disagreement with the speech. Many members remained upset over the speech and resigned from the organization. Rev. H. Rhett James, the UPO executive secretary and a sit-in leader from Dallas, sent a telegram to Don Yarborough, a supporter of the proposed civil rights bill, hinting that he might be asked to run for governor against Connally in 1964. Other members urged Connally to establish a board to recommend state civil rights legislation, which would include the establishment of a human relations committee.

The rally included two clerical speakers from Dallas. Rev. William Oliver of the First Community Church, who had brought a bus load of twenty-eight to Austin, told the crowd that churches should be aware of their responsibility in the area of race relations. Rev. B. L. McCormick of the St. Paul Methodist Church also spoke.

The cooperation between African Americans and Hispanics in the struggle for civil rights became apparent during the march. Durham stated that "They'll never separate Latin Americans and the American Negro any more in politics." Henry Munoz, a representative for PASO, read a statement from Albert Pena ending with the sentence: "Until justice is blind to color, until education is unaware of race, until opportunity is unconcerned with the color of men's skins, we have fallen short of assuring freedom of the free." The rally ended at 5:00 P.M. with Durham stating that the civil rights supporters could unseat Connally in 1964.

The liberal groups of Texas had worked together to change the political scene of Texas. The cause of equality was broad enough to encompass many liberal causes. As in other states, labor unions and other liberals joined in the struggle for civil rights. The size of the alliance between African Americans and Hispanics in the struggle, however, represented a unique element in Texas' civil rights movement. Texas had the largest Hispanic population of Southern states. A split occurred in the Hispanic community, as in the black community, on the best way to win civil rights. A few days before the march the president of the League of United Latin American Citizens, Paul Andow, denounced public demonstrations as casting "aspersions on our government in the eyes of the rest of the world" and identified "education and self-improvement" as the best means to fight discrimination. Although some activists criticized Hispanics for not joining the movement, many members of the two minorities could agree to fight discrimination since both groups had suffered under it. Together with labor unions and other liberals, the coalition would be a force to be reckoned with.

Civil rights activities increased during the summer of 1963. A march on the national capitol, opposition to segregationist governors, and support for a national civil rights law appeared. Texas mirrored many of these civil rights activities on the state level. A march on the state capital, opposition to a gradualist governor, and demands for a state civil rights law occurred that summer. Civil rights supporters, including Booker T. Bonner, understood the utility of direct action. Bonner did not believe that desegregation should occur as a moral obligation but because taxpaying citizens deserved equal access to all public accommodations. He first utilized the tactic of a one-man vigil when he demonstrated in front of the segregated Texas Theater foregoing food and sleep for sixty and one-half hours in 1961. After the march he joined the struggle for a municipal civil rights ordinance in Austin, and became the Texas field representative for the Southern Christian Leadership Conference (SCLC) in 1965. John Connally said that Bonner "apparently believes that progress on civil rights comes through demonstration. I do not." Direct action, however, placed a public spotlight on segregation and aided in bringing about the Civil Rights Act of 1964.

Because of moderate civil rights advances, such as the relatively large number of eligible African-American voters in Texas, national civil rights organizations did not establish many chapters in the state during the early 1960s. But civil rights violations still occurred, especially in East Texas. Although obviously influenced by national events, local groups and activists directed the civil rights movement in the state. The civil rights march on Austin represented an action totally planned and implemented by Texas civil rights supporters.

Chapter 10

Ain't in Vain: Essays for Peace and Integration

by Greg Moses

Welcome to Texas, President Berdahl

Thank you for helping us get acquainted with newly-named president of the University of Texas at Austin Robert Berdahl (*Austin American-Statesman*). His comments on race relations deserve special note.

As reported, Berdahl says racial tensions on campus are "the price of progress." Meanwhile, he opposes mandatory undergraduate course work that would systematically address the chronic problem of racism.

Indeed, integrating our campus environment is the necessary price we must pay for progress. Racial tensions, however, need not be left to fester in a milieu of benign neglect.

White males, especially, have a lot to learn about the concerns of the five affirmative action populations: women, Hispanic Americans, African Americans, Asian Americans, and Native Americans. In the process of becoming educated about these populations, we all — white men included — learn a lot about ourselves and the future we have in common.

"Racial tensions" have traditionally resulted from ignorance about such populations, and "racial tensions" can thus be eased, if not completely solved, by systematic education in this area. As Martin Luther King, Jr., observed twenty-five years ago, African Americans have been working diligently toward a "new appreciation of culture." In the meantime, we might add, so have women, Hispanic Americans, Asian Americans, and Native Americans.

"Whites, it must be frankly said, are not putting in a similar mass effort to reeducate themselves out of their racial ignorance," observed King. "It is an aspect of their sense of superiority that the white people of America believe they have so little to learn."

Twenty-five years after these observations were published, we find them still too true. Is it not high time for educational leaders to rethink their responsibility? If education and integration are indeed necessary to our social health, then why not embrace the challenge wholeheartedly?

Berdahl makes a good point when he observes that we cannot breech the first amendment right to free speech. But he sends a disappointing message when he closes the door to curriculum reform that would overcome a couple of centuries of "racial tension" in Texas.

It remains one of America's peculiar hypocrisies that we advocate education as a tool of progress, yet systematically fail to implement educational programs to address our most chronic social ills.

As Berdahl hails to us from the "Land of Lincoln" let us reply from the "Heart of Texas" that a new emancipation is needed. We desperately need a path that leads us out of age-old ignorance into a future of mutual appreciation. This is the necessary requirement for the future and its leaders, whether those leaders come from the University of Texas or not, whether they learn their lessons in spite of — or because of — the University's required curriculum.

In closing, please do not be misled. The only pressure for "political correctness" on campus is the centuries-old pressure to perpetuate racism and to forestall integration. Such "political correctness" cannot be sustained forever, so we may as well ask Berdahl to get busy and produce leadership for an emancipated, integrated Texas.

Welcome to Texas, President Berdahl. As the Boy Scouts would say, we ask that you leave it in better shape than you find it.

Integration Now!:
Manifesto for a Budget Year

Aw darn it, they say, the state's broke, can't afford to integrate this year, but we say, can't afford not to — integrate now!

Once again, the winds of Texas gather for a political storm in Austin, and austerity is the word we are supposed to hear wooing us into the next biennial cycle. No new programs. No new teachers. Only new students, paying more and more for less and less.

Careerist politicians once again encourage everyone to wait for change. Time's not right, they would have us believe. Can't do the income tax. More gambling is what we need: more fruitless hope that somehow each and every one of us will cash in and rise above the infuriating rat race. Will I be one of the luckiest dozen denizens? Will you be my ecstatic banker?

So it's time to send the signal that we do not elect our representatives for the sake of their own careers. We will not be mollified by the slim odds that one of us will soon be a millionaire. What we want is direct action on issues that will surely kill us if they are not soon recast.

Integration, for instance, has been waiting too long in the wings. There is no question that our governor has been integrating the elite directorships which steer our state agencies. But how long do we wait for integration to trickle down?

Take the classroom for example. Please take the classroom. Yes, the boards of regents who supervise our universities have recently become integrated as never before. But at the same time academic policies have become retrenched against integration as never before.

Integration of the classroom begins when we notice how our cultural habits of education have been systematically exclusionary. Our habits of research and teaching have perpetuated a system of white power. Not necessarily because we — or our regents — are bigots anymore, but because we — and our regents — are too busy with ourselves, we fail to include others. Thus, we have failed to integrate the classroom.

Our failure to integrate the classroom must be seen against a background of centuries of discrimination. If we have worked our way out of segregation, we have only barely begun to integrate. Desegregation is a grudging willingness to tolerate the existence of others. Integration is a wholehearted effort to produce diversity.

Integration means more than declaring that we are not bigots. When we integrate, we care enough about diversity to make it happen. We force new habits upon ourselves. We end our passive complicity, and we actively reconstruct the many ways that we routinely perpetuate a system of white power.

Desegregation was the cry of the fifties and sixties. Stagnation was the cry of the seventies and eighties. Integration will be the cry of the nineties. Don't wait, integrate!

There are many good people working to integrate the classroom. Unfortunately, there are powerful interests working to disrupt integration. The University of Texas at Austin was recently rocked by a display of ugly bigotry. The forces of integration marched and cried out for action. When it was noticed that the English Department had already begun working on a plan to integrate the classroom, the forces opposed to integration proved they were still the most powerful faction on campus. With the voices of integration still ringing in the air, the forces of *dis*-integration slammed down their sledgehammer. The English Department's plans were canceled, but not by the English Department.

Last year at this same university, the faculty voted two to one not to integrate the required curriculum. Perhaps the faculty is not full of bigots anymore, but they have conveniently deferred to the perpetuation of white power. They have, as white power has always, served themselves. Hiding behind the facade of an election, they *dis*-served everyone else.

It is no big secret that multiculturalism is a code word for integration. It takes no complicated calculation to see that the forces arrayed against multiculturalism are at the same time disrupting integration. Any effort toward integration is labeled "politically correct" in an effort to make us think that integrationists are the new storm troopers of the public mind. Of course, we can see who behaves like real storm troopers as they swarm against the English Department and cancel plans to integrate the classroom.

The fact is, some of the most qualified intellects on campus are in need of remedial education. As last year's vote proved, most of our faculty remain culturally illiterate. They are not able to read all the signs that say "white only." They are not able to write a creative response to the simple question: How do we integrate the classroom?

The campaigns of the past two years have left too many people cynical. This cynicism, too, is self-serving. The longer we delay integration, the longer we profit from white power. If nothing can be done about it this year, then we all get another full year's pay unchallenged. Don't wait, integrate!

During the past two years, while anti-integrationists in Texas have refused to be moved into the future, the great white universities of Texas have stagnated. Integration has stalled. The University of Texas at Austin and Texas A&M University have nothing to boast about. Both are poor examples of integration, despite the handful of new faces which have recently appeared on the boards of regents.

Integration means more than living together in spite of our differences. Integration means getting off, because of our differences. Can't wait, integrate!

Shame on the educators! Nearly forty years after the Montgomery bus boycott, integration is still feared. What is being done in the classroom to ensure that the lessons of Montgomery are not lost? We need more civil rights history, more attention to African-American artists, more appreciation for our cultural narrowness.

Why are university educators afraid of integration? Why do they refuse to require integration as policy? Why do they stand in the way of multicultural programs? Why do they disparage integration as "politically correct"? Let them answer these questions, but while they talk, let's not stop moving. Don't wait, integrate!

Yes, there are many things we may do as individual educators at the University of Texas and Texas A&M, but there are some things we might do together. We might, for instance, follow the example of the English Department and undertake wholesale revisions of our curriculum. We might ask the legislature to make six hours of integrationist studies mandatory for all degrees conferred at great white campuses.

How do we know integration when we see it? Integration works to reverse a few centuries worth of exclusionary habits. Thus, a course in African-American philosophy integrates the classroom. A course in Anglo American philosophy at least carries an honest name, but it does not integrate the classroom.

Why is integration a good thing? Do we really have to argue this? I mean if someone asks us what's so great about integration, do we have to answer? Can't we just take our clue from *Wayne's World* and reply, "assphinctersaywhy?"

Assume we are standing on one of the great white campuses, talking to some great scholar, and he asks us why integration is all that hot a thing. Would it be okay if we were a little puzzled by the question? Would it be all right if we were stunned that a great scholar would ask such a question, as if he didn't understand why integration should be the new hot thing?

And yet, there are great scholars on campus who go further than questioning integration. In fact, as we know, the great scholars on campus are likely to oppose integration by a margin of two to one. Is it any surprise that we are stunned at their behavior? We simply don't know how to answer, so we answer with Wayne, "assphinctersaywhat?"

While we have been stunned at the ignorance of our faculty, and while we have been disappointed by the timidity of our new regents, we cannot afford to sit dumbfounded for another full year, especially not this year, when the legislature will be called into session. If great scholars don't understand integration, perhaps the legislature will. More than this, perhaps the legislature will understand how much education is still needed among some well-known scholars.

Six hours of state-mandated integration studies is a very reasonable place to begin to educate future scholars about issues that present scholars do not understand. Three hours at the remedial level, three hours of advanced study. We simply can't afford another two-to-one vote against integration on campus. Very soon, the re-education must begin.

Great scholars must be challenged to meet the need for integration. Evasion is no longer tolerable. Great white campuses are stagnating along the integration front. They lurch from side to side, bounce up and down, yammer and yaw about quackademics, but they evade the necessary step forward.

Integration is the new hot thing on campus this year. And if you don't know why that is, then get smart, enroll in remedial integrationist studies — soon to be required — and bring a stop to academic bigotry once and for all. We say advance!

Racism and *The New Republic*

Divide and conquer is a time-honored, great and therefore, sometimes, nonviolent notion. But on the black-vs.-white cover of *The New Republic* (see the special issue: Race on Campus, February 18, 1991), divide and conquer is a misguided ploy to reinforce racist backlash at predominately white campuses of the U.S.A. The cover says: them or us, white or black, we're clenched in the grip of a win-or-lose contest. The white backhand, straining against a black forearm, drips ice-colored sweat. A school ring with a blue-eyed gem shines on the white youth's pinkie finger, its golden lustre contrasted against shadowy, black flesh. The white arm has been subtly emasculated in a pink sweater, while the black hand has been effeminized with a blue sweatshirt. In complicity with a willing illustrator, the editors have successfully depicted the abiding fear of white racism that a black hand is about to come down on top.

The New Republic, being a magazine of pure thought, seems sincerely concerned that the white hand of "free subversive thought" is about to be overcome by a black-skinned "orthodoxy." What the editors mean by orthodoxy is cleverly ambiguous, encompassing Gibbons and Bloom in one instance, multiculturalism in another. What the editors mean by "free, subversive thought" is equally treacherous.

"Free, subversive thought" is a term loosely applied by the editors to the habits of our mostly white, European-American campuses, from Plato's Academy to Harvard Square. "The most subversive force in our society is the idea of the university," say the editors. And because multiculturalism is, presumably, a threat to the subversive force of the university, the editors of *The New Republic* are compelled to propose a "radical defense of traditional learning."

The assumption of the editors — lest it be lost for its up-frontery — is that multiculturalism is racism. "Scarcely a generation goes by without a 'crisis' in the universities," lament the editors. The "crisis" this time is multiculturalism. Because the editors introduce the word "crisis" in quotes, one imagines they know the difference between "crisis" and the real thing. As they dash off to do battle with multiculturalism, one hopes they mean to mock themselves in combat with a windmill.

Surely the editors don't intend to make good on the promises declared in white type that Irving Howe will defend "the canon," that Fred Siegel will analyze a "multicultural cult," or that Dinesh D'Souza will report on "damaging admissions." These folks are surely aware how neatly they fit the pattern of what James Baldwin called "friends like these."

Please review the cover in question. The white arm on the left supports snide headlines, while the black arm on the right supports the only truth admitted by the editors — "learning is a subversive activity." Surely, these editors mean to jest. The editors are no less clever in the choice of title for their introductory essay, "The Derisory Tower." Please say this is decadent self-parody at its best: "It is tempting to believe that if these crises did not exist, it would be necessary for social critics to invent them." There are no Blooms nor Gibbonses this month; and so there is "the orthodoxy of multiculturalism." Is this a crisis or a "crisis"?

Unfortunately, the editors never get any further than this. The sympathetic reader is left hanging in ambivalent snickers about that black thing which is forcing its hand upon the white campus.

Do the editors of *The New Republic* really mean to suggest that Gibbons and Bloom are to be compared to the multiculturalists? Is multiculturalism already an orthodoxy of familiar and self-interested sentiments about the passing of a golden age? The editors allege that multiculturalism is "based on a familiar rejection of genuinely pluralist thought." Multiculturalism is, "one of the most destructive and demeaning orthodoxies of our time." Furthermore, "the core of the 'multiculturalists' argument is that race is the determinant of a human being's mind, that the mind cannot, and should not, try to wrest itself from its biological or sociological origins."

For anyone involved in multiculturalism on today's white campus, these are perplexing charges. Multiculturalism is founded upon the assumption that our white campuses are still enmeshed in the racist habits of culture which set them up in the first place. Multiculturalism means to subvert European-American racism in all its subtle forms, including the strange thinking practiced by the editors of *The New Republic*.

Perhaps the editors really believe that our white campuses long ago purged themselves of racism. The proposition is not startling. One hears it set forth with frequency. The editors of *The New Republic*, however, should know better. Evidence suggests that the struggle against racism in the U.S.A. has not overcome recalcitrance at white college campuses nor within white intellectual elites. The editors of *The New Republic* reinforce a racist backlash to the limited progress which has nevertheless been made.

A scholarly tradition is emerging into prominence which is able to demonstrate beyond a reasonable doubt that the cultural approach of our white academies has been whitewashed in a centuries-long effort to purify the idea of a university as the idea of white folks.

Dr. Martin Luther King pointed out that the founder of the American Historical Association advocated a popular theory of late-nineteenth-century elites that civilization was born of a Teutonic breed.

Martin Bernal accumulates convincing evidence to show how historians have long been deliberately suppressing or ignoring African contributions to classical Western cultures. Although Plato often acknowledges African sources, and although Herodotus clearly assumes African impositions, our working sense of intellectual progress has been systematically engineered into impressions of Western homogeneity wherein the heroes of advancement seem inherently destined to have been white.

Edward Said issues a compelling indictment against our cultural habits of approach to Arab quarters. It was Arab scholars who kept Aristotle's work alive for a millennium so that when European mercenaries sacked Istanbul they could bring home the seeds for a Renaissance. And yet we still dare to tolerate the commonplace analysis that by comparison to Western standards, the Arab world is brutal and dark. Given the dramatic image on the cover of *The New Republic*, one presumes the editors mean to imply that the value of our white and Western tradition is indeed threatened by the arm of someone black.

As the editors of *The New Republic* fail to know themselves, they also fail to understand what it means to argue that certain traditions of the academy are racist. Multiculturalism does not allege what the editors report: "that Plato and Heidegger, Proust and Thucydides, Hegel and Freud are somehow intellectual equivalents because of their sex, race, and class." To the extent these pairings are relevant to multicultural criticism, they are chosen because of some likeness in thought which may then be correlated to some class interest, whether it be gendered, racial, or of economic interest. This is why white males such as Derrida, Foucault, Nietzsche, and Gramsci may at the same time "get away unscathed."

If multiculturalists celebrate the works of some white male authors, it is because there is something promising in the quality of thought represented. It is perfectly possible that many white thinkers will in turn be judged more worthy than Plato. And one does not have to be black to take exception to some qualities in Plato's thought. One may be white and multicultural at once.

The multiculturalist is aware, as the editors say, that ideas bear traces of "social and sexual biases of their time and place." But the multiculturalist realizes that these constraints may be resisted, nevertheless. John Dewey was white, and there are white scholars who agree with Dewey that Plato and Heidegger have common failings. By accusing the multiculturalists of racism, the editors of *The New Republic* fail to see that multiculturalists help us to understand the term racism in its most precise meaning.

One is not necessarily racist for being a European-American male. One is racist for having persistent habits which accrue to white, male control. The editors of *The New Republic* are not racist because they are white, if they are white. They are racist because they portray multiculturalism as a black thing which has set out to threaten all things white.

When multiculturalists praise some white talent, the editors refuse to reexamine their own presumptions about multiculturalism; instead, they howl that multiculturalists are inconsistent. In this perplexing situation, the editors are adamant in their disappointment that multiculturalism is not racist enough. The editors ignore actual multicultural practice, the better to insist that "racial dogmatists" are bashing like vandals against our gates.

Instead of valuing multiculturalism as a promising, new force against the lingering crisis of racism, the editors of *The New Republic* choose to view multiculturalism as a wasteful misexpenditure: "precious faculty time is spent soothing racial sensitivities or deconstructing the canon on ethnic lines." You see, if a white student challenges material, he's got intellectual sensitivity; whereas a black student's sensitivities are racial and his challenges are along ethnic lines. Efforts responding to the white student are well spent, while energy demanded by the black student is misspent. As the editors say, "our universities, which should strive for an identity in contradistinction to the world at large, have become distillations of our bitterest social divisions." How is it possible to hear the editors speak most truly only by reversing the context of their words?

The editors want to protect a tradition of "free, subversive thought"; therefore, they oppose multiculturalism. They even dare to chastise the multicultural presumption "that the traditional idea of free thought is an illusion propagated by the spoilers of freedom, by the relations of power that obtain in any given society." By using the jargon of freedom to oppose multiculturalism, the editors of *The*

New Republic furnish new evidence to support multicultural suspicions about the role played by the jargon of freedom.

As the editors incredulously observe, at the bottom of the multicultural experience there is a specific suspicion: "that the old liberal notion of freedom is only a sentimental mask of a power structure that is definitionally oppressive of those who are not white males." Although multiculturalism would insist that an understanding of power structures is better developed through practical categories than definitional ones, it has become a very safe wager to anticipate that the liberal tradition of freedom talk is still very much the one exemplified by its historic fathers, John Locke and Thomas Jefferson.

The freedom jargon worked curiously well for the slaveholder, not to mention those who chartered slave territories in the name of their queen. If multiculturalism indeed alleges to find in this kind of hypocrisy, "the very meaning of — the deepest truth about — those texts" established by Western civilization, the editors of *The New Republic* do a poor job of dismissing the charge. In the hands of the editors of *The New Republic*, the jargon of freedom continues to work curiously well in behalf of racist backlash today.

When the reader hears what multiculturalism would have us do to "the established texts of Western civilization," she will not likely share the editors' sense of alarm: "The university should therefore be devoted to blowing the whistle on those texts, to replacing them with those that identify and transcend this white male oppression, and indeed go beyond the mere study to the actual defeat of the racial and sexual structure of society at large." Remember, the university is definitionally free and subversive. Only the orthodoxy of multiculturalism is to be feared.

If the reader is weary of the vertigo imposed upon her by the topsy-turvy world of *The New Republic*, there will be no easy relief: "The furor over affirmative action in admissions and hiring in our universities and over a 'multicultural' curriculum is, in fact, a bitterly ironic distraction from the battle against racial injustice in our society at large." Indeed the furor over these things is distracting. May the editors of *The New Republic*, and all neo-liberals of their kind, someday stop their cacophony, confusion, and complicity to instead join "the battle against racial injustice" and in consequence contribute to the so-called crisis of multicultural reform.

Manhattan that Time

The letters are red and capitalized, but three letters only are lit. From across the avenue, the sign taunts us to take a meaning from this. But nothing comes together. The sign says Key Food. That's all.

If it gets too busy at Key Food, they have a person who stops you at the door. Thus, we find two people waiting under a half-lit sign until one person lets the other person in.

These East-Village nights are filled with the puzzles of such certainties. From an eleventh-floor window, we lean out.

On the left, we see the battle for Tompkins Square Park. The city has ordered squatters removed, sending police. For three days running, a young tribe has gathered to protest.

On the night of June seventh at eleven o'clock the Tompkins Square Park tribe marches East along Fourth Street then turns North at Avenue A. Two blocks further, the tribe gathers its spirit against the police line, pounds drums, and chants, "no more police state."

Then, from the right, come fireworks. A meaty youth bowls cherry bombs along the avenue. Alarms wail. All through the night, there is chanting on the left, cherry bombing to the right. The police stay busy on the left; not to bother the right.

Three nights later, again we lean out. From the right comes a fireworks extravaganza. Stupefied pedestrians cannot walk and watch at the same time. Their shadows along the avenue fall as from pillars of salt. Meanwhile, leftward, the police line stands unchallenged.

Between one night's protest against the state and another night's celebration of it comes the night of the Puerto Rican caravan: thirty-three cars long, snake dancing through the intersection of Fourth Street and Avenue A, turning the corner at Key Food, flags clapping, Salsa slapping.

But, "they're all so nasty," reports an old man. "Used to be we had nice Polish people, Germans, and Ukrainians. Now the blacks and the Puerto Ricans come, and they don't like white people, and they have so many children."

By the time we get to Harlem we are unnerved. The white bus driver jerks the bus in panic from stop to stop, leaving an old man stabbing air with his cane: "F——— white drivers!" We are supposed to place a call as soon as we make it this far.

Returning downtown, we ride thigh-to-thigh in the three-sided square at the back of the bus. The engine dies from overwork, and we share a sigh of hope.

The white driver advises us to open a vent overhead as he turns off the air conditioner. Amid hesitations and encouragements someone pushes open the vent, and we proceed.

Then, POW! A cherry bomb. Right outside the bus. We spasm in unison. An alarm wails.

From under the bill of his cap, the angry eyes of a young man emerge into view. "That's why niggers are always getting themselves shot. If I was out there I'd shoot that nigger myself. Reagan let this stuff out on us, and Bush keeps pumping it on. What if it had landed in some woman's lap? What if she was holding a baby?" He stands up with his brown-wrapped, fish sandwich delicacy, the reason for his Harlem foray, and gets off, steaming, at the next stop. We should have called him brother. We should have said, "It's got nothing to do with niggers." We should have said, "But you're right about Reagan and Bush."

Talking to an old woman, we tell her that we located her name at Ellis Island, commemorating her as one of nineteen million persons there processed for delivery to the United States of America. "But so what?" she says with a slight squint in both eyes. "I have never been happy here. I never wanted to come here. I thought, one or two years and then I could go back. Instead I end up working for twenty-five cents an hour. At the end of the week I get fourteen dollars. With fourteen dollars, what can you do?" Back in the Ukraine she remembers bad summers that ruined crops. Or she remembers soldiers. "They destroyed everything." And yet, "somehow everybody survives." For the past seventy years in America she has been sustained by the memory of distant land. She refuses to shop at Key Food.

So we return to the sign that says Key Food. We look to the left where the police line stands. We look to the right where powder burns stain the air. We think of four days in New York City and hear someone say in rebuttal to the old woman, "but New York is not America." And with desperation we check to see if the lit letters or the unlit letters alone might add up to a clue.

Racism at A&M?

What is racism? The question is still asked with frequency in our community, because there is no simple answer. In spite of the fact that we attend a university where racism has been a pervasive tradition, there has been surprisingly little genuine effort to understand this lingering challenge.

"There is no question about whether racism exists within the university," writes a retired African-American professional who has long experience with the Texas A&M campus. We have sipped coffee and tea one afternoon, and he writes to continue the conversation.

"Racism exists at different levels of intensity within the attitudes of individual members of the staff and student body," continues my correspondent. "This is not to say that all members of the university or student body have this problem. The question is whether it exists within the policies and procedures that guide the decision-making framework."

What my correspondent suggests about racism is important. First of all, it is a pervasive feature of our university, varying in intensity from time to time, place to place, person to person. Indeed, there are some folks who have virtually no problem in this regard, but mostly, we still have a long way to go.

Furthermore, from the point of view of people who have a direct interest in decreasing the amount of racism in the university, the important question about racism revolves around its relevance to a "decision-making framework."

This perspective recognizes that most people who grow up in the South are raised within a milieu of racial tension that affects their personal thoughts in an intimate way. Racial bias, then, is a fact of life, no matter how well-meaning our upbringing was.

But again, the important question is how far we allow our racial bias to characterize the policies and procedures of our university community. When an undergraduate party, for instance, encourages the perpetuation of a racial stereotype, we send a signal that the "framework" of our community is still enmeshed in "procedures" which produce racist results.

Please note that we do not need to characterize anyone as a racist in order to point out that a group of people is perpetuating a racist stereotype. We do not have to claim that the students who painted themselves in blackface, put on grass skirts, and carried bamboo poles are themselves racist. We merely have to point out that their "procedures" perpetuate a "framework" in which racist results are likely outcomes.

As members of a university community which has long specialized in technical vocations and technologies, we have not, as a community, placed much of a priority on understanding the historical context of our day-to-day habits. As a result, we are continually perpetuating cultural traditions, "practices and procedures," which have not been examined for their racist consequences.

From the point of view of a teacher, it is quite understandable to me why the undergraduates at our university can be so busy about embarrassing themselves, since they get so little help in this area. A few years in the classroom here yields enough experience to demonstrate that our undergraduates do not know what racism is, nor do they understand the pervasive ways in which our cultural habits perpetuate a long tradition of racism at Texas A&M.

Those of us who are responsible for curricular and extracurricular development at Texas A&M thus have ourselves to blame whenever large groups of undergraduates plan and organize activities that they cannot recognize as offensive from a racially sensitive point of view.

"In fact, the term racism frightens people and makes it hard to develop a dialogue," writes my correspondent. "The question I keep asking myself is how does one define racism in an operative way, especially in the academic community?"

Immersed as all of us are in a mass culture which is pervaded with stereotypes and traditional antagonisms, it hardly seems "operative" to define racism in such a way that we can only point fingers at "racists" and blame them for everything that's wrong with our world.

Pointing fingers at "racist frats" may have its momentary satisfaction for some, but such accusations actually help perpetuate racism, because they fail to take into account the pervasive character of racist "procedures" among the vast majority of our university community.

The "scapegoat" is such a common mechanism of racism that it is surprising to see "anti-racists" who do not understand its inner workings. Just as media images and political rhetoric in the South have a long tradition of making black citizens the "scapegoat" for hard times, poverty, crime, and deficit spending, it is tempting to believe that "racist frats" are the "scapegoat" for racial friction this year.

Just as some "scapegoats" prevent us from addressing the pervasive nature of our shared social ills, other "scapegoats" will prevent us from addressing the pervasive nature of racism at Texas A&M.

Whatever racism may be, we must continue to search for an "operative definition" that will allow us to treat racist "procedures" as symptoms of a neglected problem. And we must not isolate our response in such a way that "scapegoats" prevent serious analysis and action.

In a university community where we strive to be "true to each other as Aggies will be," it is high time we came together to prove that we are all determined to work our way out of a segregated university system.

Only by means of great intelligence, determination, and financial commitment will we be able to transform hundreds of years of Southern habit into "practices and procedures" worthy of a world-class university. In the meantime, it might be helpful if we kept in mind how much we all have to learn yet.

Speech for a Gulf War Peace Rally

Somewhere, it seems, Saddam Hussein got the wrong idea about greatness. Somewhere along the line he got the idea that to be great, a nation must have a mighty army, and a leader must lead a mighty war. Where do you suppose Saddam Hussein got this strange idea?

There are people who call themselves enemies of Saddam Hussein who share these strange beliefs. Perhaps you've heard the argument that America is proving her greatness, again — that America's president is proving his greatness, at last — because we are wielding a mighty army in a mighty war.

In fact, this war is already the mightiest in history, but if there is anything great about these events or these leaders or ourselves or our nations, that greatness has nothing to do with this war. For this war belittles all of us and prevents true greatness from emerging.

True greatness is born of compassion, understanding, communication, humility, and willingness to share another's burdens. For many long years our nation's involvement in the affairs of the Middle East has been nothing great. Instead of compassion we have brought suspicion, instead of understanding we have brought bigotry, instead of communication we have issued commands, instead of humility we have furnished arrogance, and we have never been slightly interested in taking up any burdens from the so-called Arab world. Perhaps Saddam Hussein got his notions of greatness from us.

In order to liberate the people of Kuwait from their suffering, we are dropping the mightiest bombardment in history on Kuwaiti soil. In order to show our commitment to freedom, we are throwing the whole world into war. In order to show our commitment to peace we continue to scoff at the prospect of talking to Hussein so long as he insists on talking terms of peace broader than the current war.

I am well aware how it is popular today to see this war for greatness. But by the lights of the wisdom of the ages, I cannot see anything but madness here. In another forum we might rehearse the innumerable bungles of American foreign policy which led us to our current disaster. For the moment I will concentrate on three events.

> In 1953 our agents helped overthrow the democratically elected government of Iran so that we might have a more secure surrogate leader in the Shah.
>
> When the Shah was toppled by the people of Iran in 1977, we rushed to demonize their new leader the Ayatollah and thus lent all kinds of support to our good buddy Saddam Hussein, even as he was unleashing chemical weapons.
>
> Finally, having strapped Hussein to an expensive war machine we completely ignored his complaints that Kuwaitis were illegally draining an Iraqi oilfield of its ability to sustain the domestic economy.

In essence, we ourselves undermined the most promising democracy fashioned by the people of the Middle East, we made Saddam Hussein a hero with his chemical weapons, and we watched Hussein turn his army toward Kuwait while we ignored his pleas for intervention. Then we demonized him in turn and planned a kind of intervention that we could truly call our own.

As Dr. Martin Luther King said about the Vietnam War more than twenty years ago, "Somehow this madness must cease. We must stop now . . . the great initiative in this war is ours. The initiative to stop it must be ours." We can today join the contemporary voices of Coretta Scott King and Andrew Young and say about this war, it is time to cease fire.

Andrew Young talked in Atlanta this year for the national celebration of Dr. King's birthday. He warned that Arab popular opinion would not long be patient with American carpet-bombing of Arabian soil. The longer we punish Hussein with these outrageous tons of destruction, the more it will seem to the Arab world that the punishment has far exceeded the crime. The more restless the Arab people get, the less their governments will be able to stand in support of American efforts. If we must see ourselves as the benevolent bully standing up for the little guy in the Middle East, we must realize that the bully loses respect the more he pounds his victim senselessly into the dirt.

But it is not enough at this point to speak out against the war. It is not enough to demand a cease fire. It is not enough to call madness for what it is where our neighbors and friends see greatness. The larger effort before us is to educate the world in the greatness of nonviolence.

We cannot allow ourselves to be satisfied with the narrow goal of stopping this war. We must encourage a worldwide awakening to the difficult work of peace. Yes, we must work hard to see that the guns stop shooting, the bombs stop bombing, but we can't look forward to resting or celebrating until peaceable power becomes the measure of greatness for Iraqis and Texans alike.

What are the conditions which foster violence, and how can those conditions be transformed to nurture peace? We might start here at home. What are the conditions which foster our military traditions, and how might we transform our culture to nurture nonviolence? Every week in the fall we're kicking ass and beating the hell out of somebody, talking about fighting Texas Aggies and the fighting spirit of Texas A&M. Well, maybe every week in the spring we could talk about plowing, and sowing and growing and feeding the hell out of the hungry and teaching the hell out of the ignorant and helping the hell out of poverty and the righteous Texas Aggies and the nonviolent spirit of Texas A&M. If we can do that here, we'll have true greatness to give the world.

If the war in the Middle East teaches nothing else, it must be clear that war cannot be used much longer. If we survive this crisis without it escalating into a global holocaust, we must swear never to let the risks get this real again. You know how close we are to chemical war, nuclear war, and world war. You know this madness has got to be prevented next time, should we be granted a next time to try. And if we are serious about saving ourselves from holocaust, we have got to outpower madness with greatness. We have got to prove that madness no longer works, not just because we disagree with madness, but because we can also demonstrate that greatness offers a better way. In 1967, Dr. King argued that nonviolence could be deployed in the face of international crisis if we were but willing to undertake the challenge. And here's what he said:

> In a world facing the revolt of the ragged and hungry masses of God's children; in a world torn between the tensions of East and West, white and colored, individualists and collectivists; in a world whose cultural and spiritual power lags so far behind her technological capabilities that we live each day on the verge of nuclear annihilation; in this world, nonviolence is no longer an option for intellectual analysis, it is an imperative for action.

These are great words of a great man. May they point the way to greatness that we may soon begin to serve. Thank you. May you go in peace.

Note: Delivered at the Pax Christi Rally for Peace at College Station.

Sand Flat

SAND FLAT — Speaking from a hand-held amplification system, Smith County Extension Agent Joe Radford welcomes us to this program, cosponsored by Prairie View University. Perhaps forty people have begun this sun-baked tour of a twenty-acre farm owned by Tim Caldwell.

"Welcome back to Tim's farm," says Radford, explaining how Caldwell has been cooperating for three years with a Prairie View program on Low-Input Sustainable Agriculture (LISA).

"As you know, the program is designed to use as much on-farm input as possible," says Radford. "So we took Tim's farm and we changed it up. We rearranged the perimeters . . . to make every acre a paying acre."

Radford, holding a bullhorn at his left side, hands a microphone to Caldwell, who is wearing a cap from his employer, Kelly Tires, and a T-shirt that says, "NEVER underestimate the power of a dad."

"Welcome to the farm," says Caldwell. "I just want to say a word about farm safety." Caldwell hints to the audience that they'd better be wearing hats.

Two hours later, and still mostly hatless, the tour has lost ten people, and everyone is huddled at the edge of an acre of pines. Caldwell is standing nearby, gently shaking a tin can full of some kind of pellets. With a shake and a fling from Caldwell's right arm, all the pellets hit the brown water of a square tank that has been scooped out of a corner of Caldwell's farm. Caldwell gives his audience a look before he turns back to watch the water. Everyone turns with him.

At this point in the program, Associate Professor Garland McIlveen of the Texas Agricultural Extension Service is standing next to me, talking quietly. McIlveen works out of an office at the Entomology Department at Texas A&M University. For nearly twenty-seven years, he has been working the hot afternoons of the Texas summer in service to people like Caldwell. I raise a pen as McIlveen begins to speak.

"This is a good example of what we're trying to do," says McIlveen. "LISA was funded a few years ago by the U.S. Department of Agriculture. But there was one requirement. We had to make our findings available to the small farmer." As a result LISA has literally changed the face of the Caldwell family farm.

Caldwell's son, Timothy, standing near his dad, looks back and forth — from the audience to the tank, from the tank to the audience. Perhaps fifty pellets float upon a flat sheet of brown water. And everyone waits.

"Diversity, that's the key," says McIlveen, still speaking softly. "We want to provide some source of income all year round as well as provide food for the farmer. These catfish, for example, are mostly for Tim's family."

Indeed the catfish have now risen to the bait. The brown water swirls like stirred cream.

"That's floating bait," explains McIlveen. "We used to have bait that just fell to the bottom, and the fish had trouble finding it. This bait is easier for the fish to find. Reduces waste." After a pause, McIlveen points to the pond with an ear of sweet corn which he holds in his right hand.

"Look at those fish." McIlveen smiles as he stoops to unload a box of documents from under his left arm, careful to keep from dropping another ear of sweet corn from his left hand. Prairie View administrators Benny Lockett and Alfred Wade come to the box, open it, and distribute its contents — copies of a report prepared by McIlveen.

"During the average growing season, a farmer will spray his sweetcorn with pesticide anywhere from seven to twenty-one times," says McIlveen. "What we are trying to do is cut down on that pesticide use. That way we save on production cost, it's safer for the environment, and better for everyone. One way we can reduce our need for pesticide is by choosing to plant varieties of sweetcorn that are resistant to the corn ear worm."

"The corn ear worm is a larvae that moths place on the silk of sweetcorn," says McIlveen, holding up a fresh ear of corn with a tangle of golden silk. "The moth stops bothering the sweetcorn as soon as the silk turns brown," he says, holding up the other ear of corn. "The larvae, of course, crawl along the silk to eat the kernels. For the past four years I have examined thirty-nine varieties of sweetcorn to find which are more resistant to the corn ear worm.

"You've heard of integrated pest management," says McIlveen. "Well this is it. Screening for pest resistant varieties. Reducing chemical use. That's integrated pest management." McIlveen presents four charts which summarize the data he has collected in collaboration with the help of Wharton County farmer James Hanka.

With the help of information like this, the Caldwell family has been able to craft a model farm which McIlveen calls a "whole farm." With careful planning and arrangement, Caldwell grows peas, watermelons, sweet corn, grapes, berries, apples, and peaches. He runs fifteen head of cattle, raises chickens and ducks. Don't forget the catfish or the job at Kelly Tires.

"I grew up on a farm," says Caldwell. "For me it's a hobby. You know, some guys play softball. This is what I do for a hobby."

Part-time farmers like Caldwell represent a promising resource in American agriculture. And programs like LISA are rare examples of how the state is helping small farms conserve their small-farm ways. No hard tomatoes here.

"This is a number one peach," says horticulturist Marvin L. "Marty" Baker, grading a fruit which has been plucked from one of Caldwell's trees. "It's large, and it has a beautiful red blush."

"The hardest part for me is picking," says Caldwell. "The fur gets all on me, and it makes me itch."

Today's tour is billed as a precursor to Texas Small Farm and Ranch Week, tentatively scheduled for this fall. Prairie View administrators say it will be the first week of its kind in Texas, designed to celebrate farmers like Caldwell and programs like LISA. They are hoping for a proclamation from the governor.

Of course, there are reasons to celebrate the success of Caldwell's handsome farm. A farm crisis continues at a steady rate to expel farmers from their craft. Yet Tim Caldwell has been able to reclaim a few acres so that his son, too, can grow up on a farm.

At the conclusion of today's tour, McIlveen's gentle smile betrays no hint of his age or his long years of service. Every other week he is on the road sharing information with audiences across Texas. No doubt he'll receive another note in the mail thanking him for his work today, and he'll place it on top of a thick stack of letters which trace his twenty-seven years of service. As McIlveen's car hits the road home to College Station, it occurs to me that I live in a world ripe with hope.

Note: *The Texas Observer* filed an Open Records Request with the Texas A&M University System in order to gather facts about Garland McIlveen's efforts to seek readmission to the graduate program in entomology. McIlveen, the only black Texan to attempt such a degree at Texas A&M, was dropped from the rolls of the graduate school six years ago after it was alleged that he failed a preliminary oral exam.

Later note, added in August: *The Observer* is working on a lengthy report about McIlveen's experience with the Extension Service, his efforts to secure a doctorate degree, and the ways in which his experience illuminates ongoing discrimination within the Texas A&M University System. On August 8, the Attorney General's Office upheld Texas A&M's decision to withhold a number of documents concerning the McIlveen case. As this issue goes to press, McIlveen is still working the fields in behalf of Texas farmers, and Texas A&M is still opposed to his readmission to graduate school in entomology.

Later note, added in September: McIlveen reports that, because of lack of support, the Prairie View program on small farming is in trouble. The dates have been suspended pending some new commitment from likely sponsors. After *The Observer* ignores the story for seventy days, the author requests that his name be dropped from the masthead. For two months, at the cost of one page of print, *The Observer* had a chance to contribute to racial integration *and* sustainable agriculture in Texas. But no. Certainly Texas journalism is in need of a new, hot blast.

McIlveen Flunks Out

Garland McIlveen, Jr., remembers the day he was flunked out of school. It was the afternoon of February 17, 1986. At the age of forty-five he had graduated from high school and college, and he had earned his master's degree. He was now working on his doctorate as he sat at a table with seven professors from Texas A&M University in Room 414 of the Soil and Crop Sciences Building at the College Station campus.

McIlveen had been working for six years on a doctorate degree in entomology. He was undertaking a ten-year program to earn a Ph.D. in entomology while he continued working full time as an entomology specialist for the headquarters faculty of the Texas Agricultural Extension Service (TAEX) at College Station. For those unacquainted with academic jargon, entomology is the scientific study of insects. As McIlveen will tell you, with a twinkle in his eye, insects are very adaptable.

As was mentioned, McIlveen had signed up for a ten-year program to earn his Ph. D. in entomology. For some reason, however, after five years of classwork and research, the TAEX administration began sending him letters, telling him that he had six months to finish the degree, suggesting that if he didn't comply with the deadline he might lose his job.

So there he sat in Room 414 with everything on the line. And today, without blinking or referring to notes, he can tell you exactly how the exam proceeded.

As with every doctoral student, his education was in the hands of a faculty committee. McIlveen had a committee of six, larger than most other committees. And there was also a faculty observer appointed to oversee the fairness of the day's proceedings. The occasion was solemn, and McIlveen had little reason to feel relaxed.

In order to get this far, he had to pass all required coursework and a lengthy written examination from each of his committee members. Usually, a few committee members waive their examinations, especially if the student is already being tested by someone who is close to the student's field of expertise. But McIlveen's committee gave him no such breaks.

In fact, the first time he took the written exam, he remembers being shuffled from room to room as "things came up." Later he was told that he had flunked the written test, but he challenged the determination, and he found that only one person, his committee chair, was standing in the way of his progress. He asked for another test, was given six more thorough exams, and passed.

McIlveen was used to this sort of treatment. The agricultural establishment at Texas A&M University is virtually all white. McIlveen was the first African American to enter doctoral studies in the Department of Entomology.

McIlveen's entrance into the doctoral program at Texas A&M very nearly coincided with the school's centennial celebration. After one hundred years of virtual segregation, Texas A&M would not be easy on him, and he knew it.

So he was nervous as the oral exams began. If he passed, he would be allowed to continue work on his doctoral dissertation. If he failed, there were threats that he would not only be kicked out of school, but out of work as well.

"The first questioner started," recalls McIlveen. "I knew at least ninety per cent, and he seemed satisfied. Then the second questioner began. The first two or three questions he asked I answered. Then the chairman of the committee spoke up. 'You guys are letting Garland get away with answers to questions that I wouldn't let him get away with.'

"So the second questioner decided to tighten up. He asked a series of questions together at once. So I answered the first two questions. On the third question I wasn't sure. This questioner was a last-minute substitute, not from my department, and he was asking questions that weren't exactly in my field, so I told him I was going to make an educated guess. That's when the chairman interrupted for the second time. 'How about an uneducated guess?', he laughed, and all the other committee members laughed with him, all of them staring me in the face.

"I didn't see any basis for that kind of statement," says McIlveen, recalling more than twenty years of education. "That's when I choked up, because at that point I realized that my committee chairman was not going to be my ally. I asked if I could be excused to get a drink of water, and I tried to compose myself. To this day, I believe that I passed the exam."

The committee, however, put an end to McIlveen's education. It was the first time in the history of the Entomology Department at Texas A&M that anyone had been flunked from school for failing a preliminary oral exam. Sources familiar with the academic process find reasons to wonder out loud about McIlveen's experience. Why didn't the committee chairman simply call the oral exam into recess if he thought things were going so poorly so early in the process?

Four years later, the committee chair would write, "I believe circumstances of Garland's program from its beginning through his failed examinations were greater challenge *(sic)* than most graduate students confront. His failure to overcome this challenge was not only unfortunate for all concerned, but perhaps predictable if viewed severely."

The failure of Garland McIlveen is thus an enigma of intriguing significance. The mystery has not yet been solved from a "severe" point of view, but that's no reason to presume that a crime was not committed.

That afternoon, when McIlveen got home, his children rushed to him with eager faces.

"Did you pass, Daddy? Did you pass?"

With the laughter of the entire committee still ringing in his ears, McIlveen looked at his children.

"I have two boys. They were eleven and twelve years old at the time. They had been rooting for me since they were six or seven. Of course, I had to tell them that I did not pass. And I had to tell them the truth with as little detail as possible, because I didn't want to give them that complex.

"At that age, they would not have understood. I was worried that, at their age, they would take the full truth of my experience and use it in a negative way. They would think that they were born inferior because of their race. And you don't want to do that to a kid.

"Rather than give them that inferiority complex, I refused to say anything about racism. But since that time, I have gradually talked to them about the reality of life, because I know they are subject to the same experiences that I have had. And if you don't prepare them for it, then some day it's going to hit them square in the face."

McIlveen is still a member of the TAEX faculty at College Station. And he is still trying to get another chance at his doctorate. He has been through committees. He has complained to federal agencies. And he has even been to court. After six years and $20,000 in attorney's fees, nothing seemed to work. Texas A&M University remains unmoved.

In January 1992, McIlveen applied for readmission to the graduate program, and he received the endorsement of the graduate admissions committee in entomology. At last, it seemed, there was hope. Not only did he have faculty support for readmission, but several faculty came forward to organize a new doctoral committee. But late in the spring, after months of delay, after being told by the interim director of graduate studies never to call back, McIlveen was again denied the second chance that he believes he deserves.

The department head of entomology called a meeting of the graduate faculty and informed them that, because of telephone calls which were coming from "the upper administration," it would not be possible for McIlveen to reenter the doctoral program.

"But maybe he can go get his doctorate over in education," quipped the department head of entomology in front of a room full of professors. Did he mean to call attention to the fact that the College of Education at Texas A&M is known for rare commitment to the education of black Texans? Did he mean to call attention to the fact that one finds rare minority representation on the education faculty? Did he actually mean to suggest that McIlveen should start over, give up?

But McIlveen is not giving up his dream to become the first black Texan to earn a doctorate in entomology at Texas A&M. He is not giving up his appeal of the fact that he is the only person ever flunked from that doctoral program for failing an oral examination, even though he passed ten written exams lasting ten days given by seven different professors. At the age of fifty-three, however, McIlveen is not mincing words about his prospects with TAEX.

"They ruined my career, is what they did," said McIlveen. "What I earned, they systematically took away."

Twenty years ago, McIlveen was on study leave, earning a master's degree at the University of Florida at Gainesville. As he recalls, his wife advised him not to return to TAEX. But as we know, McIlveen did return. And he should have known better. He should have listened to his wife.

McIlveen should have known better, because the trouble with TAEX had already started. Nevertheless, the civil rights era was fresh in the air, and McIlveen was optimistic that he was in the right place at the right time to make a difference.

The trouble with TAEX began in 1963. McIlveen was coming out of the army after college. He had grown up on a farm. He had been a junior assistant extension agent. He was full of hope and vision. And so, he applied for a position as Negro county agricultural agent.

"Because of the continuous increase in America's population and depletion in its vital soil components," McIlveen wrote on his application, "it is becoming imperative that close assistance be given to those farmers, ranchers, and young boys and girls who strive to meet the needs of this challenging population."

His commanding officer at Fort Hood noted that McIlveen had "recently been elevated to the position of executive officer of this unit primarily because of his leadership and organizational capability. His duties vary from supervision over administration to command of headquarters functions. The sincere application of sound judgment and his dedication to assigned areas of responsibility have helped me immeasurably in the accomplishment of my mission. I would not hesitate to recommend him for employment in a position requiring leadership or the ability to meet and make friends easily."

McIlveen still remembers how he came to TAEX with his abiding respect for the professional contribution that extension service can bring to a community. He also remembers one of the first phone calls he received from a high ranking, white administrator at the extension headquarters staff.

"'We have a big program scheduled with the 4-H kids at the Huntsville camp this summer. The camp is dirty. We want you to take some kids there and clean up,'" McIlveen remembered the caller saying. "Here I was, a college graduate, with experience as a military officer, and an image of myself that was quite professional. I couldn't believe that I was being subjected to the stereotypical role of janitor."

Some years later, McIlveen was promoted into the faculty of extension specialists on the Texas A&M campus at College Station. He still remembers his first statewide faculty meeting. Rachel Carson's important book, *Silent Spring*, which demonstrated the hazards of pesticide use, had been out for a number of years. Extension specialists were looking for ways to cut back on the use of toxic chemicals. The concept that was developed to meet the new age was "integrated pest management."

In its sophisticated form, as developed by pioneers such as Perry Adkisson, former chancellor of the Texas A&M University System, integrated pest management was a system which viewed chemical use as one of many possible tactics which might be deployed to protect crops from pests. The concept was not easy to convey, however, to tradition-bound extension specialists.

"I think I've got it!" McIlveen remembers how one speaker quipped in the middle of the meeting. "I think I finally understand what integrated pest management is — it's a nigger driving a Temik wagon." Temik is a highly toxic pesticide, and McIlveen didn't see how a Temik wagon could have any relevance to integrated pest management. The room, however, exploded in laughter. That laughter still rings loudly in McIlveen's ears.

In 1972, as McIlveen was in Gainesville working on his master's degree, a TAEX administrator wrote him a letter indicating there might be problems disbursing his partial paycheck for "faculty development leave." McIlveen showed the letter to University of Florida administrators. They quickly reclassified him from a teaching assistant to a graduate fellow, and they fired off a snappy letter to Texas A&M.

"We are happy to do this for Garland in order that he may continue his graduate studies under your Faculty Development Leave policy," wrote W. G. Eden, chair of Florida's Entomology Program.

Next came a peculiar job offer from Texas A&M, asking McIlveen to take the job first, and they would tell him the salary later. Attached was an eight-page job description.

"My thanks to you for your descriptive letter," answered McIlveen. "The job description was quite thorough and my thanks extends to [two specialists] for their efforts spent in preparing it.

"It is my understanding from your letter that the entomology position is being offered to me, but a definite salary will be determined after I have indicated a definite interest in the position. Normally, a decision at this point would be very difficult to make. However, in view of the fact that you have provided me with such an extensive job description, I feel it is impossible for me or any one person to accomplish the program as outlined . . .

"Again, thanks to you and all others involved in programming this position. I am not interested."

At this point, McIlveen's wife advised him to stay in Florida. Friends at the University of Florida encouraged him to stay as well. He could get his doctorate and enter upon a career with the Florida extension service. But McIlveen is a native Texan of the true-grit variety. He would take his master's degree back to Texas, start a family, enter doctoral studies, and blaze all kinds of trails for his kids. At least that was the plan.

Back in Texas, black professionals were restless with the administration of TAEX. Since the passage of the Civil Rights Act of 1964, they were no longer referred to racially as Negro extension agents. They were now universally known as associate extension agents. And new job descriptions were typed up.

Preston E. Poole, who worked as an extension agent from 1939 until his retirement in 1974, later recounted his memory of the "transition years" after the Civil Rights Act.

"The status of the new job descriptions put us to work under our white counterparts, with no possible chance of advancement. And there was quite a gap in the money we made compared to our white counterparts. In terms of blatant discrimination, the salary schedule was inexcusable. No effort was made to cover up the fact that the status of the black agents was automatically below whites."

In 1972, Poole "finally got enough courage" to file a class action lawsuit against the Texas A&M University System.

"Plaintiff Poole," the suit alleged, "was denied assignment to County Agricultural Agent of Galveston County solely on the basis of his race. He has longer tenure and higher educational qualifications than the white who was promoted to this position had at the time of his promotion."

Six months after the suit was filed, TAEX eliminated the "associate" classification from the title of its black agents. In 1974, the women of TAEX joined as plaintiffs. In 1976, Texas A&M signed a "consent decree," agreeing to end its "three tier" salary schedule and its discriminatory practices against blacks and women.

Has the discrimination stopped? Another, more recently retired black agent answers flatly, "No sir — there were diversionary tactics and subtleties and all sorts of deceitful ways of projecting discrimination. Right up to the time I retired, separation has been extended all these years."

David McGregor works as county extension agent in Waller County. He was the first African American to be promoted to county coordinator. He still holds that position in Waller County.

"Preston Poole paved the way for the black agents in this state," says McGregor. "But we still have a long way to go. I know I'm as high up as I'll ever get. I'm on the highest plateau, and I'll never get higher. I know I'm a labeled man."

McGregor ran afoul of the TAEX establishment for two reasons. He fought for his promotion, and he talked to the press.

"I watched them move two people in over my head," recalls McGregor. "The second time they moved in somebody just out of school. So I said, the next time around they are going to do the right thing. By then I had seven years of experience and a master's degree.

"The next time the county coordinator position came open, I worked here by myself for over a year while they decided what to do. Sometimes I worked all night long, because I didn't want anybody to say that I couldn't do the job. Sometimes I was going to quit, but the people kept me here. They encouraged me to stay.

"After I got the promotion from the state office, the local commissioners court (which pays the salary) wouldn't give me the raise. And it was white farmers that came to my rescue. You know I have lots of white friends, and they don't feel that discrimination is right."

Even with the help of white farmers, however, the county commissioners court was no easy mark. Since commissioners refused to place the matter on the agenda, one white farmer had to trick them into it. He petitioned for an unrelated agenda item, and when his turn came up, he raised the issue of McGregor's salary. By McGregor's count, there were twenty white farmers in attendance ready to back him up.

"So the white farmers came to court and told them that I was a good county agent and deserved the raise. That was in 1983, and a reporter from *The Houston Chronicle* happened to be in the room, so I told him exactly how I felt."

A TAEX administrator called McGregor to College Station to advise him that it was "not smart" to talk to the press. McGregor told her that if he had to do it all over again, he'd do just the same thing. McGregor was fuming as he left the state headquarters and drove to a retirement reception for a fellow county agent. His fume turned to steam, however, as the state administrator passed him on the highway, en route to the same retirement reception.

"And I thought," recalls McGregor, "if they knew they were going to be in my area in the first place, why didn't they arrange to meet me a little closer to my office. But no, they had to waste all my time."

Back in College Station, McIlveen also thinks about wasted time. It's been twenty years since he left Florida. He, too, feels like a marked man, dispatched into a dead end career.

"What these people don't realize is that denying a person a doctorate degree is a real blow in terms of time and sacrifice. And with a family, you are not the only one who sacrifices. Yet you do it with a belief that the sacrifice will be rewarded.

"There was one positive thing. I think my boys came up feeling that reading and having a lot of books in your presence all the time was a good thing. I had a special room for study. There were times when you couldn't walk in there for all the books and papers all over the floor. All the time I was going to graduate school my oldest son would take a book with him, even when he was going to the barber shop.

"But when you tell your kids that the solution to success is through hard work and preparing yourself, and you have to come back and eat those words — that's the most difficult thing of all."

In May of 1992, McIlveen wrote to the Texas A&M University System chancellor requesting assistance. The chancellor is chief executive officer for all the agencies and colleges that make up the statewide Texas A&M system. McIlveen recounted the fact that he had been verbally rebuked by the interim director of graduate studies and was told never to call back. Nevertheless, McIlveen did call back. This time he was politely referred to the Office of General Counsel which in turn informed him that his case was closed. Since the Office of General Counsel falls under the direct purview of the chancellor, McIlveen explained that he had no choice but to appeal to the highest office of the Texas A&M University System.

The chancellor immediately returned the matter to the College Station campus president, ignoring McIlveen's plea for a meeting. Thirty days later, the senior vice-president and provost of the College Station university informed McIlveen by "confidential" correspondence that there was nothing to be done. "Your application has been processed according to university policies."

In an open records request filed by *The Texas Observer*, this reporter asked for university policies regarding the readmission of graduate students who had been dropped from the rolls for academic difficulty. The Office of General Counsel replied that there were no such policies. *The Texas Observer* also asked for phone records from the Office of Graduate Studies in order to trace the phone traffic on certain key dates. This reporter wanted to find out who was calling whom. The Office of General Counsel replied on behalf of its client, the Office of Graduate Studies, that there were no phone records for half the month of April.

Unfortunately, the stories recounted thus far only begin to convey the kind of experience which McIlveen gracefully suffers as an African-American professional in the Texas A&M University System. He remains optimistic enough, however, to request that certain other "ongoing" matters not be mentioned at this time. In fact, it has taken him quite a while to divulge this much.

McIlveen remains a career professional, even though the calculation of years leaves him precious little of a career. By coming forward, McIlveen performs a public service. His meticulous documentation of bureaucratic paperwork, combined with his excellent record of service, raise profound questions about the management of a multi-billion dollar agency with tentacles that reach into every county. Beyond Texas, McIlveen's story suggests the ominous contours of race discrimination in America during the post-civil rights era.

From the earliest days of his employment with the Texas A&M University System, Garland McIlveen has aspired to be an example. Looking back now on almost thirty years of experience, he has not quite become the example that he intended. In 1963 Martin Luther King, Jr., brought Southern segregation crashing down from Birmingham, Alabama. As McIlveen entered the extension service, there was a very good chance that he would exemplify the new opportunities that would surely open up for African Americans in an integrated society.

But no. And yes. Yes, McIlveen does exemplify opportunity as we find it to date. But no, it is not the opportunity envisioned by the civil rights age.

"Now here's a real problem," says McIlveen, musing on a long life at the hands of discrimination. His memories reach back to the days when he watched his grandmother and uncles go around to the back door of white folks' homes; when he was made to leave a cafe when he attempted a coffee break with his white coworkers; when books obsolete in the white schools were passed down to the "colored" schools. "When you're subjected to this over a long period of time, you don't really know what's happening to you. It's like somebody starts with warm water, increasing the temperature until it takes a toll. But you don't notice it."

What we don't notice is the way things might have been under different circumstances. What if, for example, African-American professionals did not have to fight for every last inch of opportunity denied them because of the color of their skin?

"It seems like A&M is the only agency that doesn't think I'm worth anything," says McIlveen. He is caught by surprise to see his 1963 application. He never saw the letter of recommendations that were sent by teachers, friends, and a commanding officer. Those records have been in the confidence of university files until this summer — totally neglected, it seems, by any professionals who might be seeking to develop promising talent.

The Texas A&M bureaucracy at College Station is apparently unable to digest the fact that McIlveen has been awarded a Signal Service Alumni award from his alma mater at the Prairie View campus. For those unacquainted with Texas, the Texas A&M system is largely segregated. The white campus is at College Station, while the black campus is located some sixty miles to the south at Prairie View. In fact, when McIlveen entered college, he was not allowed to attend the College Station campus, on account of the color of his skin.

"If I wasn't academically qualified, or if I would have embarrassed the university at some point, I could understand this treatment. It is very difficult for me to balance," McIlveen is thinking aloud, allowing a rare glimpse into the depth of matters at hand.

"If it wasn't for the fact that I am a specialist on the extension service faculty and that I had fifteen or sixteen years of service before I started the doctoral program, with a good record in terms of performance . . . I mean there were no blemishes on my record.

"Given all these things and the fact that I passed the written exams . . . I only had one chance at the orals — an unprecedented occurrence in the Department of Entomology. And I am convinced that I passed those orals. I think of committee members who never returned my research proposals — even after my repeated requests. I think of the laughter of the committee during the oral exams. I think of the fact that all six of my committee members gave me written exams. Not one waived their written exams, not even the last-minute substitutes.

"Given all these things, it's difficult for me to believe that had I been anything but black, they would have granted me the degree.

"What we are trying to do here is make a statement," McIlveen continues. "Either way. Either we make a statement that we do allow opportunity for black students, or we don't. Either way, we make a powerful effect. If we do allow opportunity, it sends a signal to other minorities. If we don't allow opportunity, by virtue of the fact that you are the first black through the system, then this university is not sincere. It's a profound type of message, either way you go.

"So what A&M did, they sent out a message. And I'm not sure if they are aware of the message, or if they really care." After a full summer of filing open records requests concerning this case, this reporter can testify that A&M is aware of the message.

In 1990, Texas A&M doctoral candidate Christine Stanley surveyed African-American doctoral students at Texas A&M University and the University of Texas at Austin to find out why black students were giving up their doctoral studies. Ninety-nine percent reported that discrimination was not absent. Although thirteen percent reported that discrimination had not been a problem for them, twenty percent reported overt discrimination, and sixty-two percent reported subtle discrimination.

At both of the major research universities in Texas, students reported that they might decide to give up their doctoral studies because of dissatisfaction with "various areas of the internal environment, academic environment, social environment and institutional services, as well as levels of racial discrimination, types of relationships with faculty, levels of deterrence and demographic status."

"Many factors appear to account for black graduate students foregoing the pursuit of a doctoral program," concluded Stanley. "Efforts must be made to remove some of these negative perceptions and experiences in order for institutions of higher education to attract and encourage more doctoral candidates."

As recent figures show, prepared by the Texas Higher Education Coordinating Board, at every new level of education in Texas, the percentage of white participation increases as the percentage of minority participation decreases. Most of the first graders today are not white. Yet if current trends continue, nearly all of the doctoral degrees awarded in twenty-five or thirty years will be given to whites.

As we see from the experience of African-American professionals in TAEX, or from the reports of doctoral candidates at A&M and UT, African Americans are being discouraged by very bad management practices. Bright, ambitious, and qualified African-American talent is being turned away — consciously or not in favor of less qualified talent. There is no need to sound any alarm about reverse discrimination in Texas. Discrimination here proceeds unreversed and largely unchallenged.

Among the documents which Texas A&M made public this summer, there was a note which indicated that McIlveen was the only Texas A&M student to ever challenge the university in court for racial discrimination. The 1990 trial in a Houston federal court lasted about one day. By the time the second day was over, the judge had dismissed the jury and declared for Texas A&M. Is this what passes for one's right to a speedy trial?

On July 1, ten days after McIlveen received his last letter from the university, Chancellor Richardson issued a memo to all employees of the system.

"The Texas A&M University System is committed to providing an educational and work climate that is conducive to the personal and professional development of each individual." This is how the memo begins.

"It is our firm commitment to ensure that equal employment opportunity will be provided throughout the Texas A&M University System to all employees and prospective employees." This is how the memo ends.

Optimistic that the memo surely meant something, I called McIlveen at home late one evening, just before the Fourth of July holiday. He was processing ears of sweetcorn that he had gathered from a farmer in Wharton. McIlveen is trying to determine which varieties of sweetcorn are naturally resistant to the corn ear worm. The more resistant the sweetcorn variety, the less pesticide will be needed. Integrated pest management. Remember?

McIlveen spent the better part of two days stripping more than five hundred ears of corn, measuring their length, and testing for damage from the corn ear worm. He was in his usual good spirits when I read him the memo.

"You know," Garland paused as the phone line crackled, "it ought to be a misdemeanor to publish a memo like that." His giggle still rings in my ears.

Corps Women

COLLEGE STATION — You have heard how the Aggies are feuding amongst themselves over the future of the famous Fighting Aggie Corps. And you have seen the stupidity of the spectacle from afar. As you know, the clumsy rhythm of Aggie history will not be stilled. And so the best the Aggies can hope for this year is that you'll not concern yourself with anything so trite as the latest Aggie joke.

Having watched a few football games, you know the corps represents Texas A&M's pride and prestige. The corps is A&M's central metaphor of self-identity. Thus, a crisis in the corps signifies a crisis of identity for the university. This is not necessarily a tragic state of affairs, but it deserves serious consideration by all taxpaying Texans. Please do not mistake these events for a laughing matter.

You see, Aggie jokes and clumsy rhythms have convinced you from your distance that nothing but foolishness ever comes from Texas A&M. And this is where the power of the Aggie begins. In all his foolishness you watch him yell, "Farmers fight!" After one hundred years of this, you finally notice there is hardly a farmer left. And this is how the Aggie uses his foolishness against you. You help him laugh your own values to death. After all, it's just a cow college out there. Why bother with such a thing? Isn't it just too funny?

Nevertheless, there are a few farmers yet worth fighting for, and you suspect the Aggies are capable of being sincere. And so you admit that you are able to laugh at Texas A&M's shenanigans in the generous hope that a university can't help but teach itself some lessons, especially such simple lessons. But the stupidity of Texas A&M — its Texas-sized idiocy — is suddenly not at all funny anymore. Either we've been mistaken in our idea of a university, or Texas A&M is no university at all. Fools we need. Frauds we do not. Any hint that the Aggies are not sincere about having a university at College Station is a matter of extreme gravity.

But you have always believed that the world would get better as soon as Texas A&M put itself out of business, so why not be pleased at the hint that the Aggies are finally losing all legitimate claim to management of the state's university at College Station? After all, the prospect is not without obvious promise. You have always felt that the Aggies were an embarrassment to Texas A&M. That maroon-and-white mob of clannish bullies — how could you be expected to mistake them for scholars?

And this brings us to questions to keep warm by in the blustery weather brewing at College Station: Are we subsidizing a university or what? Are we paying for the college or the college prank? Will we teach young men how to be scholars and lovers, or will we encourage them to tyrannize themselves and others? Will we allow Texas A&M to follow this state down or will we call upon it to lead this nation up?

The identity crisis at Texas A&M offers all Texans a rare opportunity to involve themselves in the shaping of a very important public institution. The meaning of the corps allows for broad debates about the meaning of our history and the construction of our future. Please do not stand far away and grin at these events. Demand that Texas get the university it has been paying for. Consider that 9,000 degrees were awarded last year by the state university at College Station. The identity of Texas A&M is too important to treat as a matter of merely local concern.

The style of this dispatch is necessarily wary of specific facts for two reasons. First of all, the Aggie writer constrains himself patiently among conflicting interests. Secondly, the leading edges of the darkest waters in this affair are still too distant to fathom. But there is a clear truth, nevertheless, and it is quite specific. One woman on campus has been unconscionably, and systematically, abused. She remains anonymous to the public and a stranger to the writer, but you will know her as the "liar."

Because of accusations by this one woman the Texas A&M cavalry was indefinitely disbanded. Because of her speedy recantation the same cavalry was hastily reassembled and cheered back into prominence. Because she made the accusation, she was shunned for being weak and talking out of school. Because she later recanted, she was vilified as the "liar" of "lies." You have read about these things in *The New York Times*.

The recantation episode was suspicious enough to be treated with cautious accuracy by *The Times* and *The Houston Chronicle*, but it may be years before the positive truth of the affair is published, and it will be much longer than that before the local press gives any Texas A&M press release a critical reading:

> Texas A&M President William H. Mobley confirmed today that he has been informed by university investigators led by Director of Security and University Police Bob Wiatt that a female cadet said she had falsely accused members of the Corps of Cadets of two physical assaults.
>
> "The young woman met yesterday with university officials and said that the claimed assaults, beating and abduction never happened," said Wiatt . . .
>
> "Significant disciplinary action has been taken against six members of Parsons' Mounted Cavalry, of which she was a member, for incidents of harassment which were verified independent-

ly of the retracted assault charges," said Maj. Gen. Thomas Darling, corps commandant.

Believe it or not, these were the facts given reporters in order that they might loosely report a "lie" and restore the cavalry's reputation to *status quo*. This is how a "university" behaves the day after a traumatized student meets for the nth time with its very own "officials." These "officials" run to the press, sacrifice the student, and, in a most bizarre and desperate reversal, save the cavalry from the woman. And all this happens shortly after Texas A&M acquires a public relations specialist with White House experience. Perhaps there is a joke in this. Perhaps Aggie stupidity is Aggie style. This is really funny — not?

No reporter was able to publish a satisfactory account as to why six cavalry members were disciplined. No editor was able to pull the obvious contradictions of the official language into the form of a critical sentence or headline. The truth was hog tied and dragged off campus. By sunup, it was widely apparent that truth had wised up and left town. Reporters and anchors dutifully stepped in to cover up the drag marks that authorities had suspiciously left behind. White House public relations, it seems, arrived just in time to save the cavalry from any immediate danger from truth.

All this stuff happens on Monday. By Friday there is a press conference hosted by the Texas A&M Association of Former Students at its very own Clayton Williams headquarters on campus. Two former journalists from the student newspaper proclaim that the truth is being suppressed. What's really happening, they insinuate beneath the beaming approval of powerful alumni — what's really happening is that there is some gay-related conspiracy to undermine the credibility of the cavalry and the corps.

They release notes and snippets from tapes indicating that certain faculty and journalists are conspiring to give the corps a bad name: "We have not been given the truth." It would take an Orwellian genius to map the contours of these double reversals. One hears the rattling of a cage, a flick of little bitty claws on steel, a melody piped in. Yes, you heard it right. These two former journalists and these powerful former students have nothing but the highest praise for the official line. They make clear what they will have at any cost. What they want is a corps, a cavalry, and their traditional Aggie identity. They will fling a wide net to tangle up any "liars" or "sympathizers." No question about it — a witch hunt has begun.

In fairness to President Mobley, I am told that he warned the alumni not to sponsor the Friday press conference. He tried to stop the stampede he started. For this, he was able to save face among thinking people on campus. But as good an individual as Mobley may be, this is no healthy season for good individuals at Texas A&M. And this is why taxpaying Texans need to know, wherever you are, that Mobley needs all the help he can get.

Rednecks

In the middle of the presidential landslide, a student I know throws his football into the television so hard that he breaks it. At about that time, two other students I know meet in front of another television set on the Texas A&M University campus.

"How's the election going?"

"Not well."

"How many electoral votes does Clinton need?"

"Thirty something."

"Darn!"

And "unreal" is what I hear all day Wednesday, two hours east of Austin, where Texas is experienced as the color which marked it on election day — Bush country, still.

Say what you want about the Bill Clinton landslide, I know better. As with most Aggies, plenty of Americans are angered at the results of last week's election. As we used to argue that Ronald Reagan never attracted a majority of registered voters, so we must realize that Clinton didn't even get a majority of votes cast.

Nothing of lasting importance has yet been settled by this election, and this is what Clinton supporters need most to know. For all that we have accomplished so far, I worry that we may have begun just another swing in the pendulum, naturally headed already in reverse. I pray against fate that this time's victory will be next time's, but I wonder. What will secure our future against those who are angered?

The day after the election I spoke to a dozen students who had managed to show up to an evening class. There were perhaps sixty empty seats in class that day. After all, it was cold and rainy, everyone was mad, and it had been announced that I would be speaking on the topic of affirmative action, so you can see how there was little incentive for anyone to come to class that day.

Those who came to class, of course, were determined to walk away with their opinions intact, just as I was determined to move them in a new direction. And so the first question I asked was this: "What is affirmative action?"

"Affirmative action is where you set quotas and hire less qualified minorities, depriving white folks of equal opportunity," answered a student I know.

Say what you want about Aggies, you can read similar sentiments these days at the University of Texas West Mall Free Speech Area in the middle of liberal Austin. Where students once built, and rebuilt, a shanty to stand harbinger for a day of South African liberation, there now stands an ugly exhibit opposing affirmative action at the University of Texas Law School.

Jubilant as one may wish to be in the days after the Clinton landslide, make no mistake. Texas is all around us. Much the same as it ever was.

Hard times don't help ease the tension. Racist habits of mind attach like parasites to our self interested, racist institutions. In times of stress, white imaginations invent nightmares designed to scare a body to death. And the Clinton years begin in a time of stress which may very well get much worse before better.

So watch, people, at that sound. Our Texas racists aren't going down. They are mad, frightened, and dead serious when they say white folks are being treated unfairly in America. If Clinton's coalition actually means to reconstruct Civil Rights in the midst of all this, we'll have to hang together like never before.

Thoughts out of season for a post-election binge: We have met the lame ducks and they are us. What we propose to do in the next four years will be bone-breaking work. Our bones. Thus, we will be caught thinking twice in the near future. Is civil rights worth the risk? Do we really want to face it?

As we prepare for inauguration day, then, let's not neglect our souls. Let's gather the seriousness of our challenge into ourselves where it will not be forsaken for midterm elections. Let's understand the deepest level of commitment that will have to be sustained on each street corner in Texas if the Clinton victory is to push back the pendulum that is already swinging against it.

After listening to the sentiments of turned-off rednecks in the wake of the Clinton landslide, I have gathered a few early thoughts. First of all, the Bush folks were looking for someone who would run the country. They are correct to see that Clinton cannot meet their expectations.

Not even the most avid of Clinton's voters expect their president to run the country. What they want from Clinton is some incentive to hope that if we all work hard at America, the president will support our sway.

No president is going to get us out of the trouble we're in. What we expect, then, is a president who is going to sustain the massive struggle that we have begun with the Clinton election. As Clinton himself said time and again, this election was not about him, but about vision and policy. President Clinton can't fix civil rights, but the former governor of Arkansas can articulate the value of integrating our Southern institutions.

President Clinton can't integrate Texas A&M or the University of Texas, but he can sustain our massive resolve to integrate our schools and neighborhoods by any means necessary. The president can see to it that we have new tools to work with, because integration is America's enduring hope. Either there will be one America, or there will be none.

Clinton can't force the South to reinvigorate affirmative action. Clinton can't make people open their hearts or minds. If the president does employ carrots and sticks in behalf of civil rights these next four years, he will have to rely on all the people back home who ushered him in. It will simply not work if we say: I agree with the goal, but we can't force people to change.

As we gaze into the anger of the Bush voter, our task is to see a way through. Our duty is to stand firm, but to think quick, how do we help him see why we can't be moved. If we wimp out on Clinton, or if he wimps out on us, the next election will surely belong to — and yes, some Texan will probably lead — the counter swing.

Living in Austin, these concerns may now seem thin as the paper they are printed on, but the fact is that Texas rednecks are back in force, and unless we are willing to get out there amongst them when they are angry, we've done little more as Travis County voters than to hang President Clinton — and Ann Richards — out to dry. Indeed, unless we figure some way to make these rednecks into our fellow Americans, there is a pendulum that shall return to divide us.

Chapter 11

A History of Higher Education for African-American Texans, 1872–1977

by David A. Williams

Introduction

This essay presents an account of the institutions of higher education founded in Texas for African-American Texans. Whereby, we may come to know and appreciate this segment of the history of people of African descent in Texas.

There have been many unanswered questions, such as: (1) Where did they develop the capacity and hunger for enlightenment? (2) What was their legitimate role in the history of Texas? (3) Who were the founders of these educational institutions which have existed and do now exist in Texas? (4) What has been the social, political, economic, and cultural upsurge in Texas for the past one and one-third centuries? (5) What are the strengths and weaknesses of these Texans? and (6) How secure is their future in the Lone Star state?

These were some timely questions which this publication proposed to answer truthfully, objectively and professionally. Realistically, there has not been a segment in Texas history which has been more ignored or completely overlooked, as has been the cultural history and institutional development of the African-American Texans. Some historians have from time to time emphasized small segments of the general history of these Texans but rarely, if ever, in a qualitative and quantitative manner. Some references cite the role of the African slave in Texas history as a servant and childlike figure. Others present them as docile, impish characters, who were never remorseful regardless of their circumstances. Some who have written about these darker Texas citizens have never known them as real people. It shows in their presentations. Often the historical picture presented is distorted because they are images borrowed from the bias of the past. Stereotypes are usually unreal; they are always unfair. However, they have been used, and far too often, to characterize the African Americans' cultural and institutional development in Texas.

On the pages which are to follow, much painstaking care was taken in scholarly pursuit so as to present the African-American Texans' roles as developers and contributors to their own cultural history.

In this narrative, no effort was made to glorify any person or overemphasize any event. Only the facts were presented in tracing and recording the history of the development of these cultural institutions which were concerned with higher education.

By the presentation of these facts the author was hopeful that the reader would come to know some cultural and institutional history of the African-American in Texas.

As we have come to learn the history of Texas, we have also come to realize that many people of various ethnic origins helped to make Texas a state very rich in cultural history. The history of some ethnic groups is well-known. However, the surface has been only slightly penetrated where history of the African-American Texan is concerned.

How the reader views and interprets what is written on the pages which follow will, in a significant way, determine in some measure how African-American Texans are viewed in the future.

Here the quest for truth has been diligently pursued in the belief that the truth told is freedom given.

In the Old Testament of the Bible, in the book of Daniel, God is reported to have said to the king of Babylon, Nebuchadnezzar, with handwriting on the wall, through the interpretation of Daniel, that he (Nebuchadnezzar) had been "weighed in the balance and found wanting." The same could be said of the historical accounts of many publications which deal with past events in the life of Texas. African Americans are noticeably missing. This is strange because the history of the African Americans is as much a part of the saga of Texas as is the longhorn cow or the mustang horse.

African Americans have come to Texas as explorers, some are descended from the first Texans — the Indians. Some helped settle the first colony in Texas. They served and fought at the Alamo and at San Jacinto. They were always loyal, helpful and productive. Therefore, all history of Texas should include the deeds of these Texans too. This history, perhaps the most incredible story ever told about the African Americans in Texas, is the one which relates the facts of the development of higher educational institutions for African Americans. The story of these institutions' development is certainly a story of "bricks without straw."

There is an interesting parallel of the story of the Hebrews in Egypt being required to manufacture their quota of bricks, without the traditional straw, and African Americans of Texas founding and developing higher institutions of learning without money or traditional background or formal education. In both instances faith and determination played a significant role.

When the Hebrews exceeded all expectations in the production of bricks, the straw was taken from them and the task of meeting their quota was thought to have been impossible. By the same token, when African-American Texans were showing progress in the development of higher educational facilities, whereby they could train a new generation to become proud, productive men and women, their major ingredients were taken away. The black codes were designed to strip the lowly people of Texas of any legal rights or social privileges. There were many ignorant and hostile whites who resented even the mere mention of a black person having any educational advantages. This attitude made philanthropic donations, the "straw" which goes into the building of higher educational institutions, almost nonexistent. Only faith and determination were left. From 1872 to 1947, having little else but faith and determination, ex-slaves, ignorant masses of ministers, laborers and farmers, founded more than twenty-one colleges for the education of their young people. How they did this is still an awesome, mysterious miracle. Sometimes the miracle came in the image of a Northern philanthropist or a white zealous missionary. Other times circumstances would produce the miracle. Still other times the legislature, in spite of itself, provided the miraculous happenings.

Through divine guidance and inspired leadership the Hebrews were inspired beyond their human capacities, and their accomplishments astonished their taskmasters.

Through faith and determination the ex-slaves and the disenfranchised freedmen were of the opinion that they could succeed at their task, difficult though it may be, if they trusted in the same God who permitted the Hebrews to make their "bricks without straw."

When the children of Israel were required to produce bricks without the customary use of straw, biblical historians proclaimed the resulting outcomes a miracle. If this proclamation has truth, then the other great miracle was one which seemed technically and practically impossible. It was the development of institutions of higher education in the state of Texas by and for African Americans.

When the Civil War ended and when at long last the slaves were allowed their freedom (belatedly) on June 19, 1865, there was so much to be done. The matter of enfranchisement was far more than just getting the right to vote, being free, and not having to answer to the slave masters. It was incumbent upon these ex-slaves now to create for themselves some vehicle sufficient to the task of undergirding the institutional process which must assure them of a secure foundation, upon which they could build a productive future. The citizens of the colonies placed a supreme value on education. So did the freed slaves and free persons of color. They all realized that if they were going to survive it would be through education. Consequently, every effort was exerted to provide institutions of learning beyond the high school level.

The church was the first to establish an institution of higher private education for African Americans in Texas. Public higher education was established in 1878. The first college was indirectly the result of prompting by the federal government. Texas accepted the provisions of the Morrill Act in 1866 for the establishment of an agricultural and mechanical college; however, because of the provisional status of the Texas government, formal acceptance was delayed until 1871, when Texas was readmitted to the Union. Once accepted, the state had five years in which to establish the school. The Agricultural and Mechanical College of Texas was organized in 1875 in time to retain the federal endowment.

The Constitution of 1876 directed the legislature to establish and provide for the maintenance of a branch university for colored youths "when deemed practicable."

Texas authorities apparently came to the conclusion, and with some justification, that by implication the Morrill Act intended for provisions to be made for the agricultural and mechanical education of black youths as well as white youths. This was to be the only effort on the part of the state legislature to establish or provide for higher education for African-American Texans until February 1947, when it was forced to act under pressure from the National Association for the Advancement of Colored People and the Sweatt case. The only other source of higher education for African Americans in Texas was provided by the various church organizations. Specifically, these were the African Methodist Episcopal Church Conferences, the Christian Methodist Episcopal (formerly the Colored Methodist Episcopal Church), the United Methodist Episcopal Conferences (formerly the Methodist Church North and South), Baptist Conventions and Associations, the Presbyterian Synod, the United Christian Church Boards, and a Catholic diocese.

It was the purpose of this research to, among other things, (1) determine the forces that gave rise to the development of the educational institutions of higher learning for African Americans in Texas; (2) ascertain what significant roles the whites of the North and South assumed and consummated in this institutional development; and (3) determine the part African-American legislators and church personalities took in the development of these institutions.

This research was intended also to answer the following questions: (1) What forces gave rise to the development of institutions of higher education for African-American Texans? (2) What effect did the white Northern and Southern missionaries and philanthropists have on the efforts to establish higher education? (3) Were there divergences of opinions and fluctuating attitudes reflected in the legislative enactments from 1866 to 1876? If so, why? (4) Did the African-American legislators contribute significantly to the higher education of blacks in Texas? (5) How have the black people of Texas generally aided their own causes in higher education?

This study was needed to provide those interested with an understanding of the origin and development of higher education in Texas for persons of Afro-American heritage. The early efforts of blacks and whites in this very significant undertaking need to be known so an appreciation of these institutions can be established and can finally become a part of the history and folklore of the citizens of Texas. This study was necessary because of the need for thorough historical research on the development and service of institutions of higher education for Texans. Research in this area has been limited.

This study was limited to the institutions of higher learning which were founded for African Americans. Public or private elementary and high schools were not considered. Particular emphasis was placed upon the historical development from 1872 to the decade of the 1990s.

Background of Higher Education
for African Americans in Texas

Out-of-State Facilities

A progressively increasing interest in the education of the black people of Texas was evidenced in the various Texas Constitutions, from 1836, when no mention of the subject was made, to 1876, when specific provisions required for the black Texans' impartial and equal educational facilities. The process of legalizing higher education became a long drawn-out process which lasted more than a hundred years. While these unending legal battles were attempting to clarify the legal status of the black Texans in higher education, various segregation states were expanding the opportunity for professional and specialized training for black people, by providing funds for tuition at out-of-state educational institutions which accepted blacks as students.

After the *University of Maryland v. Murry* decision in 1935 and the Missouri ex rel. *Gaines v. Canada* decision in 1938, Southern states developed the practice of granting financial aid to blacks to permit them to secure graduate work outside the state. The system usually provided scholarships for the difference in cost between study at the state's institutions for whites and study at the designated out-of-state school. Sometimes the grant was for the difference in tuition only; sometimes it also included the cost of transportation. Even before the court decisions which established the principle that a state must provide within its own borders equal educational opportunities for blacks and whites, certain segregation states had begun to foster out-of-state schooling for blacks who could not acquire the courses they needed in the state's black schools.

In 1927, West Virginia became the first state to set up a scholarship plan for black students. Other states soon adopted the plan, and within the next twenty-one years all seventeen segregation states had developed some kind of out-of-state program. Eight, or almost half, of the plans were instituted during the five-year period from 1943 to 1948.

Texas, in 1939, became the seventh state to provide funds for such differential scholarships. Fields most frequently included in the programs were education, law, medicine, social work, dentistry, pharmacy, library science, physical education, home economics, agriculture, music, business, engineering, and architecture.

The feeling grew among officials of Southern states that they might pool their resources and efforts and make greater progress in satisfying the educational needs of their black citizens. There were seventeen segregation states involved in this cooperative effort: West Virginia, Missouri, Kentucky, Virginia, North Carolina, Texas, Oklahoma, Maryland, Tennessee, Arkansas, Georgia, Alabama, Florida, Louisiana, South Carolina, Delaware, and Mississippi.

The results were the Regional Educational Program, developed as a means of overcoming some of the tremendous cost barriers to providing specialized and advanced study educational opportunities for both whites and blacks.

Elaborating on earlier individual state programs for out-of-state study, the Regional Conference of Southern Governors developed in 1947 a plan, "regional universities," which would furnish both black and white students with educational opportunities not available in their own states; but provided in one or more of the Southern states.

Obviously, this arrangement was much more significant for black students than for white, since educational facilities were much more highly restricted for blacks in each state concerned. On February 8, 1948, the governors of fourteen Southern states (Louisiana, Alabama, Mississippi, Tennessee, Arkansas, Virginia, North Carolina, South Carolina, Texas, Oklahoma, Georgia, Florida, Missouri, and West Virginia) pledged support to the establishment of regional graduate, professional, and technical schools by signing the Regional Compact for the Board of Control for Southern Regional

Education. Favorable action by at least six state legislatures was required to establish the Board of Control.

By April 1, 1950, the Compact had been approved by thirteen legislatures, and the board was formally established on June 11, 1949. Though the governor of Texas signed the Regional Compact, the Texas Legislature did not approve it. A resolution of approval was passed by the Senate in the 1949 session, but was never brought to a vote in the House of Representatives.

The Compact recognized the area within boundaries of the contracting states as a geographic district in which a plan of regional education would be carried on and supported by public funds derived from taxation by the constituent states and from other sources. The Board of Control for Southern Regional Education, a joint agency of the participating states, was designed by the governing board. The board's membership consisted of four representatives from each of the participating states: the governor, who served ex-officio, and three members appointed by the governor, who served staggered terms of four years each.

Approximately $1.5 million was appropriated by the various states in the first biennium of the agency's operation. Two forces influenced the development of the plan: (1) an effort to provide by regional cooperation the professional and specialized education for blacks which would otherwise have to be provided by admitting black students to existing state institutions for whites; and (2) a feeling of long standing that the Southern states, poorer in economic resources than the rest of the nation, could get high quality in expensive fields of higher education only by pooling resources.

A primary motive of the governors who signed the Compact and the legislators who approved the initial arrangement was probably an attempt to avoid what seemed an otherwise inevitable breakdown of segregation in graduate and professional education. It now seemed clear that the regional education arrangement was not a method of affording the equal education for black citizens required by the Fourteenth Amendment. If educational opportunity was to be offered within the state to members of one race, it must be offered equally within the state to all races.

The Board of Control established by the Compact made it clear that the agency was not to be considered a means by which a state may escape its responsibility under the *Gaines, Sipuel,* and *Sweatt* decisions. In a landmark Maryland case, the state of Maryland offered its participation in a regional program as a defense in a suit brought by a black resident to gain admission to the nursing school of the University of Maryland. The Board of Control for Southern Regional Education entered the suit to declare that the Compact was not intended for that purpose. The courts held that the offer of the state to provide a place in the nursing school of Meharry Medical College in Nashville, Tennessee, under regional arrangement did not excuse it from the obligation to furnish equal nursing training within the state.

Over a period of years, the Texas Legislature appropriated money to provide out-of-state scholarship aid to black residents who wished to pursue graduate or professional study not available to them in Texas. In 1948, $50,000 biennially had been appropriated for out-of-state aid. In the 1949–50 biennium, $90,000 was appropriated. The funds were used to make up the difference between the Texas and out-of-state school tuition and to pay travel expenses for one round trip to the out-of-state school. Approximately $425 was allotted to each Texas student at the Black Medical College at Nashville, Tennessee. Although the 1949 session of the legislature appropriated $350,000 for a medical school at Texas State University for Negroes, the Board of Regents apparently determined that the amount was insufficient for the purpose; consequently, no action was ever taken. In the meantime, Texas Agricultural and Mechanical University officials contracted with the board to provide places for students of veterinary medicine in return for payments of tuition to the states providing the places.

The Texas Constitution did not prevent the state's participation in contracting for services and regional center programs. However, there were some constitutional barriers to the state's full participation in the program.

Texas had entered into a number of interstate compacts, one of which concerned the joint operation of an educational facility with New Mexico, but there had been no decision by Texas courts relating to the compacts. Opinions of the attorney general concerning interstate compacts, until 1949, did not deal directly with the legality or validity of the compacts nor with the problems that could have developed in relation to the plan for regional education.

The United States Constitution says that "no States shall, . . . without the consent of Congress . . . enter into any agreement or compact with any other state or with a foreign power." However, many interstate compacts have been made and carried out without congressional approval. While there had been no decision directly on the point prior to 1949, there were directives in Supreme Court opinions to the effect that only those compacts which increased the states' political power or were "political in nature and involve a promise" required congressional consent.

It was not clear (according to the seventeen regional states) whether or not the Compact concerning Southern regional education was an arrangement which required congressional consent. It was thought of, at the time, as being a worthwhile plan. However, the 1954 Supreme Court ruling in *Brown v. Topeka* made this idea invalid.

Provisions of the Texas Constitution

The Texas Constitution of 1876 provided that:

> The Legislature shall also, when deemed practicable, establish and provide for the maintenance of a college or Branch University for the instruction of the colored youths of the State, to be located by a vote of the people; provided, that no tax shall be levied, and no money appropriated, out of the general revenue, either for this purpose or for the establishment, and erection of the buildings of the University of Texas.

As it has been stated elsewhere in this chapter, an escalating interest in the education of black citizens of Texas was evidenced in the various Texas Constitutions, from 1836, when no mention of the subject was made, to 1876, when specific provisions required impartial and equal educational facilities for the black people of Texas. A detailed analysis of educational provisions in the six Texas Constitutions, in the order of their existence, shows more clearly the manner in which this increasing concern for the education of black Texans and the consciousness of responsibility for it has found constitutional recognition.

The first constitution of Texas, in providing for the maintenance of a general system of education and in establishing a perpetual free common school fund, made no provision for the education of black people of Texas. Since black Texans did not at that time have universal freedom, they did not fall within the scope of these constitutional provisions. Their education was left to the discretion of the free white citizens of the state.

After the abolition of slavery, Texas recognized its black inhabitants as citizens in making provisions for their education. The Constitution of 1866 was the first to make specific mention of education for black Texans. It provided that the perpetual public school fund should be used exclusively for education of the white scholastic inhabitants of the state and that an additional tax might be levied for educational purposes, provided "that all sums arising from said tax which might be collected from Africans, or persons of African descent, shall be exclusively appropriated for the maintenance of a system of public schools for Africans and their children." A further significant provision was that "it shall be the duty of the Legislature to encourage schools among these people."

The Constitution of 1869 made further progress by including black persons in the general provisions for education without any discriminatory phraseology.

Specific provision for equal facilities was made in the currently effective Constitution of 1876. Segregation was specifically and simultaneously required: "Separate schools shall be provided for white and colored children, and impartial provision shall be for both." Some degree of higher educational opportunity was provided for the first time by the 1876 document, which authorized the establishment and maintenance of a "College or Branch University for the instruction of the colored youth of the State, to be located by a vote of the People." Although located in Austin by an election in 1882, the authorized institution was never established there by the legislature.

The Republican Party renewed the efforts for the "colored branch university" in 1884. In a resolution adopted at their Annual Convention in Dallas, the Republicans declared they favored not only "the early completion of the University of Texas, but also of 'its colored branch.'" Again in 1892, the Republicans at Fort Worth demanded "that the Legislature comply with the constitutional requirement and establish a branch of the State University for the colored people." At Dallas in 1894, the platform favored "equal school accommodations for all races" and urged the state to, "as early as practicable, take the necessary steps toward instituting the colored branch of the University, thus putting into effect the expressed will of the people."

The most vocal group efforts for a separate branch university for Negroes was the Teachers State Association of Texas. Beginning in the spring of 1896, the black teachers organized a propaganda campaign aimed at achieving the black college. The Negro section of the *School Journal* relayed the appeals for action across the state. In May, the black education leaders announced:

> Now is the time to strike for a colored university. The iron is heating — the political iron — it will soon be red hot. We must prepare to strike. Every teacher who reads this is urged to get to work at once. Call your people together, organize a University club and send the name of the officers to the secretary of the central committee at Austin . . . . The entire state must be organized. Only by organized effort can we hope to accomplish our purpose. Every teacher and preacher in the State must see the importance and necessity of this school. We are now inaugurating a movement to secure the establishment of this university. We must not, we cannot fail. The best and ablest men of the race in Texas are committed to it. The time has come for action. The plan is simple: organize; support your organization and report it to Rev. J. D. Pettigrew; meet, discuss and report your meetings to the press; have your secretary keep up correspondence with the secretary at Austin; draw up and circulate a petition to the legislature, asking for the establishment of this school, and get as many names of parents of school-age children to sign it as possible, and send them to Rev. Pettigrew at Austin, Texas. Get every candidate for State Senator and State Representative, of whatever party, who expects the support of negro votes, to pledge that if elected, he will support a bill for the establishment of a branch university for colored youth; and when he is elected, don't fail to send him letters and petitions to remind him to keep his word, and if he fails to do so, then you will know enough never to support him again under any circumstances.

The pressure continued throughout the summer. In a June editorial, a black educator declared:

> The wise and patriotic men of the Constitutional Convention of 1876 thought the time would come when the colored youth would need higher training. These statesmen present a marvelous contrast to a few upstarts of today, who claim that the negro needs no such training. According to these little fellows there is no need of well-educated teachers, ministers, and doctors in our race; no

need of any literary talent of any higher order. If some negroes had their way, all the schools would be closed and the negro doomed to an ignorant serf.

Later, before the Annual Black Teachers' Convention held at Corsicana in July 1896, President Broyles of the State Association publicly expressed himself in favor of the "branch university for colored youth."

Meanwhile, the state's white educational and political leaders, responding to the blacks' pressure, were busily advocating the expansion of Prairie View A&M College at Hempstead, Texas, as the best solution to the black university issue. Governor Charles A. Culberson and Superintendent of Public Instruction James M. Carlisle said in a joint statement in the late summer of 1896:

> This institution (Prairie View) has done more than any other single institution in the state for the colored schools and the colored people of Texas . . . . It is hoped that at least twice 50,000 acres of public lands will be set aside for the proposed enlargement of the school. It would be well, also, to make provision for an additional number of scholarships.

The Democratic State Convention, meeting at Fort Worth in August 1896, pledged to all races and classes equal protection in the enjoyment of life, liberty, and the pursuit of happiness. Provision had already been made for the control and management of colored schools by colored trustees. The Prairie View Normal School would be enlarged, making provision for industrial features and gradually converting it into a university for the colored people. To this end, they favored setting apart immediately for that purpose 50,000 acres of the unappropriated public domain.

The Prairie View directors in their 1896 report also called for the development of Prairie View.

> The university for higher classical education of the colored youth of Texas will eventually be located at this school. This can be done at comparatively little expense to the state by the addition of a few buildings and teachers, and by this means the colored race could obtain both an industrial and classical education. The former, all will admit, would be of untold advantage in connection with higher education, especially for the negro race. We are informed that the negroes throughout the State are practically unanimous in favor of this university plan . . . . We believe it would be a great

saving to the State, and expedite the establishment of the colored university which has so long been asked for by the negro race.

The Republicans, in the 1896 election year, repeated their insistence "that laws should be speedily enacted extending to our colored youths the opportunities of a university education." Thus, the "colored university" question had become a major topic in the educational and political arenas of the state.

Many black educational leaders viewed with skepticism the suggestion, now sometimes coming from among their own ranks, that Prairie View be made the Negro "branch university." E. L. Blackshear of Prairie View and H. A. Maxwell of Austin, writing in the October issue of the *School Journal*, asked Texas' Negro teachers for clarification of their stand on "the Colored State University question."

> In his annual address, President M. H. Broyles, of the State Colored Teachers Association recommended that, for the present, we request the A and M College board to add some of the college branches or courses to Prairie View, and let it be a nucleus of a university, in embryo. We are of the opinion that, if this were done, it would be the last of the "University," but of course, we do not dare express this as the general opinion. We think that we should strike the iron and keep it "hot" until we accomplish our purpose . . . . We are not in any way hostile to Prairie View; as Texas teachers we could not be. We believe it to be one of inestimable value to Texas as a normal school, but we believe that we should have a university on a broader scale equipped with first-class facilities, such as grand old Texas is well able to afford her citizens of color. Texas is the richest state in this ground southland, and out of her abundant resources can easily afford to help the struggling negro in his attempt to gain higher education.

Blackshear later called for a conference of the state's educators to meet in Hempstead at the end of the year to discuss the problem.

Robert L. Smith, at this time one of the wealthiest and most influential black people in Texas, was born in Charleston, South Carolina, in 1861. He was graduated from Atlanta University, and was afterwards editor of a paper in Charleston. He then moved to Texas, where he became a teacher. In 1895, he was elected member of the Texas Legislature from Colorado County. He was a founder of the Farmers' Improvement Association, which by 1912 owned more than 75,000 acres of land worth considerably more than $1 million. In 1906, the Association, under Smith, founded a school at Ladonia, and in 1911 organized a bank at Waco. Smith was also a trustee of the Jeanes Fund and an aide to Booker T. Washington. At the opening of the Twenty-fifth Texas Legislature, Representative Smith introduced a bill to appropriate 50,000 or more acres of the public domain for the establishment of the colored state university at Austin. Smith's action was immediately applauded by black leaders, who took the occasion to chide those still insisting on Prairie View as the location for the school.

> Some of the teachers of the State are in favor of making the University an annex to Prairie View. We trust the State Legislature will have judgment enough (and we believe it will) to ignore this, and locate the University at Austin where the popular vote has placed it. We think the people's interests ought to be served and not those of a few select political teachers, and the people (want) the University at Austin. It seems strange that some, who a year ago were opposed to Prairie View as a place for its location, now think it just the place. We suppose they are now looking from a different direction.

The lawmakers responded favorably to Smith's bill and enacted a law authorizing the governor and the commissioner of the General Land Office to have surveyed 50,000 acres to

> . . . be set apart and constitute a permanent endowment for a branch university for the colored people . . . it shall be under the control of the Board of Regents for the University of Texas, and held by the board in trust for the benefit of the said branch university for the colored people.

The legislative action produced elation among blacks throughout the state. The editors of the Negro section of the *School Journal* said:

> The teachers of Texas and the friends of education, as well as the colored citizens of the State, owe a debt of gratitude to the 25th Legislature, for its generosity in appropriating 50,000 acres of the public domain toward the establishment and maintenance of a branch university for the colored race. All honor to the Solons, especially the gallant speaker Dashiell, Rep. Smith, the colored member of the House, and to the entire Senate, who championed and favored our cause. We hope to see the matter pushed forward with all possible energy.

The black people's desires and the legislature's good intentions were, however, handed a decisive setback when the Texas Supreme Court (in *Hogue v. Baker*) nullified the action by prohibiting Land Commissioner Baker from appropriating any more land for educational purposes. The Court declared that the "one-half of the public domain appropriated for free school purposes had been so appropriated," and that the remaining half was not available for such purposes.

Yet the spirits of black Texans and their lawmaking friends remained undaunted. The legislators, after the Baker decision, reaffirmed their intention to act "in good faith." They adopted a concurrent resolution explicitly stating their intent to circumvent the Court's ruling and to give the black Texans their university. The resolution read:

> Whereas, the people of Texas are pledged by Constitutional provision to establish a university for the colored race whenever it is practicable; and
>
> Whereas, the Democratic Party has acknowledged the necessity for said university through its platform adopted at Fort Worth, 1896; and
>
> Whereas, the Democratic Party in the 25th Legislature carried out in good faith the demands of said Fort Worth platform by appropriating and setting apart 100,000 (actually 50,000) acres of the public domain for the establishment of said university for the colored race; and
>
> Whereas, the Supreme Court of Texas has nullified the action of the Legislature . . . by its decision in declaring that Texas had no public domain unappropriated;
>
> and . . .
>
> Whereas, the Legislature is prohibited by the Constitution (Article 7, Sec. 14) from levying any tax or making any appropriation out of the general revenue to establish said university; therefore, be it resolved by the House of Representatives, the Senate concurring, that it is the duty of the state, as well as the expressed will of the democratic party to faithfully carry out this obligation, which was voluntarily taken by our Party in convention assembled.
>
> Resolved further, that as soon as the commission appointed to investigate and ascertain the exact status of the public domain and the public free school lands of Texas shall make its report to the Governor (stating) the amount of said land belonging to the state, that steps shall be taken to establish said university for the

colored race, either by appropriating public domain, if there is any public domain, or by appropriating lands regained to the state from railway corporations that have refused to comply with their charter grants or to obey the laws of Texas.

While the legislators were trying to figure a way to give the black Texans their state university, the blacks, themselves, were still arguing about its location and character. As the years passed, more and more influential black educators switched to the so-called Prairie View expansion plan. One Brenham black educator, H. M. Tarver, said that he opposed the establishment of any "colored university," unless it was an expanded Prairie View. Principal Blackshear, who had long been in the camp of the militant group working for a separate school at Austin, then announced that he heartily agreed "with the remarks made by Professor Tarver." He claimed to believe that the "colored youth of Texas will be more benefitted by the additional facilities which will be afforded by the (Prairie View expansion) plan." The statements of Tarver, who had headed the committee of the State Colored Teachers Association campaigning for a separate university, and of Blackshear took most of the steam out of the blacks' drive for a separate school at Austin. At the same time, M. H. Broyles, Prairie View mathematics teacher and one-time head of the Teachers Association, expressed the blacks' appreciation for the efforts of the legislature to provide a black university, despite the unfavorable court ruling. He said the action showed that "the Democratic Party, in pledging the establishment of a branch university for 'colored youths' in 1896 and in appropriating 50,000 acres of land during the session of the 25th Legislature, acted in good faith."

Thus, with an unfavorable court decision blocking action and with growing black acquiescence in the so-called Prairie View expansion plan, the legislature allegedly set out to make Prairie View a "classical college." The statutes of 1899 and 1901 were adopted in an effort to carry out this plan.

It was 1915 before the legislators took any new action on the "colored university" question. During that year, they sought, through constitutional amendment, to get around the prohibition against levying any tax or making any appropriation of "general revenue to establish or maintain the University of Texas or its branches," in order to secure new funds for Negro higher education. The proposed amendment provided for the allocation to the A&M College of Texas 600,000 acres of land from that set apart to the

University Permanent Fund. From this amount, 150,000 acres were to be allotted to Prairie View. The amendment was defeated at the polls on July 24, 1915, "by a vote of 81,658 to 50,318." Four years later, on March 18, 1919, House Joint Resolution Twenty-nine proposed an amendment to those sections of the state constitution dividing the "University Permanent Fund between the University of Texas and A and M on a two to one basis." The proposal would have required the "A and M Board to apportion to Prairie View an equitable part of A and M's one third. The amendment was defeated by a vote of 36,560 to 76,422."

In 1945, Prairie View was made a "university" until such time as a permanent "colored university" could be "legally" established. In 1947, the "branch university for colored youth" — Texas Southern at Houston — was finally established. It came, however, a little too late, for a black man named Heman Marion Sweatt had already filed a suit that would soon open the doors of "the university of the first-class" — the University of Texas — to all qualified students, black as well as white.

Black Legislators' Input

Beginning in 1868 and extending into 1898, more than thirty black legislators served in the Texas Legislature. Small in number, the black legislators did not constitute a bloc vote of any significance. Together they represented twenty-nine counties, almost without exception from the Black Belt areas. Although none made an outstanding record as a legislator, most were fairly well-respected by their white colleagues. The quality of these black legislators appeared to be no higher or lower than those of other states during the Reconstruction period. Some were illiterate, but approximately 30 percent attended high school, and about 25 percent had some college training. In the case of many blacks and whites, however, the schools from which they graduated offered more work on the high school than on the college level. Among legislators with college training, blacks also fell somewhat below the white educational level, primarily because of the blanket of restraints against teaching slaves to read or write before the Civil War. Since only two had been born in the Northern states, black Texas legislators compared favorably with their white counterparts in Southern background. In comparison to black legislators in other Southern states during the late nineteenth century, black lawmakers in Texas included fewer individuals born in the North and fewer lawyers and skilled artisans.

Black legislators were relegated to service on unimportant and minor committees. To some extent, this was due to their lack of education, experience, and training, but more because of their race and party affiliation. Usually they were assigned positions on the education, penitentiary, and road and bridge committees. A few served on the claims and accounts and county boundaries, insurance and statistics, privileges and agriculture and stock-raising committees. Some of these assignments were of importance to the black legislators, such as those on the education committee.

Two black senators who were reported to have been especially active in the Twelfth Legislature were Matt Gaines of Washington County and the Sixteenth District and G. T. Ruby of Galveston, Brazoria and Matagorda counties. These senators introduced bills, offered resolutions, and presented petitions. Gaines was vehement in his denunciation of the separate school law providing separate schools for white and black students, and made many speeches in the legislature against the law. For the most part, black legislators were restricted to introducing and reading petitions from their constituents. Few pieces of significant legislation were sponsored by any of the group. On March 21, 1879, Burton, senator from Fort Bend County, introduced a bill calling for the establishment of a mechanical college of Texas for the benefit of "colored" youths. He also introduced a bill entitled an act to provide for the organization and support of a normal school at Alta Vista College in Waller County for the preparation and training of "colored" teachers, which was read the third time and adopted. Another resolution offered by Senator Burton shows his interest in the youth of his race and their advancement. The resolution is as follows:

> Resolved — That the Committee on Education be instructed to inquire into the practicability of the state establishing a Manual School in connection with the Agricultural and Mechanical College for colored youths, whereby students at said college may be enabled to pay all or part of their tuition and other expenses by labor on the farm and report by bill or otherwise. The Resolution was adopted.

Senator Burton was highly respected by his fellow members.

The last black legislators to attempt to sponsor an education bill for higher education during this period were N. H. Haller and R. L. Smith. They served in the Twenty-third and Twenty-fourth legislatures. Haller cosponsored a bill to establish a Negro branch of the University of Texas, which was defeated. Smith and Haller were the last black legislators to serve in the Texas Legislature until 1966.

There were seventy years between the departure of R. L. Smith and N. H. Haller from the legislature and the entrance of three other blacks — Senator Barbara Jordan (Harris County), Representative Curtis Graves (Harris County), and Joseph Lockridge (Dallas County). By 1977, there were thirteen black legislators, and they continued to work diligently for the advancement of black people of Texas through the quality of a free and equal higher educational system.

Philanthropic Interests

Northern missionaries and philanthropists have been instrumental from the beginning in the development of organized education for black people in the South. The work of the major denominations, especially that of Baptists, Methodists, and Congregationalists, is well-known. So also is the work of the General Education Board of the Rockefeller Foundation, of the Phelps-Stokes Fund, and of the Carnegie Foundation. Most of these groups were oriented toward higher education for black people.

Black Americans had to overcome traditional ideas about the scope and purpose of higher education before they were able to create a place for themselves in America's colleges and universities. In each case, philanthropy was primarily responsible for opening college doors. The achievement of philanthropy in regard to the black American, as well as the black American in Texas, commanded special attention in view of the artificial barriers raised by his social situation and his relatively low economic status. The result of the latter was that nearly all the philanthropic support of his higher education had to come from Northern whites.

Before the Civil War no attempts were made in Texas to provide higher education for black people. Nationwide, especially in the free states, concern over the black man's welfare was restricted, for the most part, to efforts of abolishing slavery. After emancipation, the emotional excitement generated by the condition of the slave was transferred to a preoccupation with "uplifting the freedman and extending to him the same opportunities for self-improvement other citizens enjoyed." Providing education for the blacks seemed the proper way to implement these plans. However, it seemed that white Texans did not share this point of view.

The situation that existed in 1865 posed an immense challenge to Americans and Texans with philanthropic interests. There were about four million former slaves in the country, and in Texas there were near 200,000, but only a tiny fraction was literate. In the areas of heaviest black concentration, not even a primary school system existed.

The black Americans were unable and the white Southerner unwilling to create and support black people's educational opportunities similar to those others enjoyed. If anything were to be done, Northern philanthropists and the federal government would have to take the initiative.

As an individual, the Northerner with a desire to help educate the Texas freedman was, alone, helpless. There were no colleges to which he could send contributions, and the total Southern resistance and black poverty precluded the possibility of their arising in Texas. Organizations were desperately needed that were capable of creating the objects of Northern benefactions and then channel financial aid to them.

The major religious faiths quickly formed philanthropic agencies to direct Northern finances toward the black people of Texas and the South. The Home Mission Society took an active part in founding institutions of higher learning, both for black Texans and black Americans, throughout the Southern states.

Another channel through which the Northern dollars reached the black colleges in the South and in Texas was the philanthropic foundation. The first American foundation in the educational field dated from 1867, as the result of a $1 million gift from George Peabody, international merchant and financier. The second million dollars followed two years later. The philanthropist placed his money in the hands of white trustees from the North and the South with the stipulation that it be used for improving education among the poorer classes of the South without regard to race. While most of the money went to white primary and normal schools, black teachers' colleges received a few grants. The greatest significance of the

Peabody Education Fund was as a model in educational philanthropy for subsequent benefactions. In 1914, the Peabody Fund dissolved, after having disbursed more than $3 million. In the final disposition of its resources, $350,000 went to the John F. Slater Fund, which had been established in 1882 as the first philanthropic foundation devoted exclusively to the education of black Americans.

John F. Slater was a Rhode Islander who became rich in the manufacture of textiles. His reason for giving $1 million to black education in 1882 stemmed from his conviction that schooling was essential if the ex-slave was to become a responsible citizen. Slater appointed an eminent board to administer his gift and gave them a free hand. It was his belief that their collective wisdom and experience acquired from direction of the fund would be a far better guide to policy than anything a single philanthropist could propose in advance. Slater was concerned, however, that his money be distributed "in no partisan, sectional, or sectarian spirit" and that it should promote rather than discourage self-help on the part of the black people in the South. In the first year of operation the Slater Fund benefited institutions of higher learning as well as public school systems. After receiving the $350,000 from the Peabody Fund in 1914, it was equipped to play (for several decades) a major role in the development of education for black people of the Southern states, Texas included.

Other philanthropists followed the example of Peabody and Slater. In 1888, the American Missionary Association announced the receipt of $1,000,894 from a native of Connecticut who had made a fortune as a merchant in Augusta, Georgia. The Daniel Hand Educational Fund for Colored People was to be administered by the American Missionary Association. Hand made no restrictions in the deed of trust, and the association was able to advance its work on all educational levels. The Hand Fund, along with the Negro Rural School Fund, which a Philadelphia Quakeress named Anna T. Jeans established in 1907, was not directly concerned with higher learning. Its significance lay in freeing the existing colleges for development as true institutions of higher learning, instead of serving as preparatory schools.

The establishment in 1902 of John D. Rockefeller's General Education Board was a major event in the history of American philanthropy. No agency, public or private, exerted a comparable force in shaping black higher education. At the prompting of his son,

John Jr., Rockefeller created the board with a gift of $1 million. Ultimately his gifts totaled over $129 million. "The object of this Board," declared the initial gift-bearing letter, "is to promote education in the United States of America without distinction of sex, race, or creed." By 1918, black colleges had received $1,141,282 from the General Education Board, but this only hinted at what was forthcoming. From 1924 to 1929, Texas black institutions received $596,700.

The various means by which the early black colleges received financial support had in common their near-total dependence on the philanthropy of Northern whites. But there were also liabilities inherent in a situation in which control, or at least direction, of the institutions rested in non-colored and non-Southern hands. All too frequently philanthropic support for black higher education stemmed from zeal and pity, rather than from careful appraisal of needs and circumstances. Many of the early schools, which their supporters chose to call colleges, had students with at best a primary education. Nevertheless, many of the idealistic white benefactors and faculty members were determined to teach a classical college curriculum even on a dirt floor and to scarcely literate students. The competitive spirit among the sectarian societies caused much overlapping of educational facilities with a resultant lowering of quality. Distorted claims were made, and in some cases, solicitations were conducted for nonexistent colleges. Institutions that had sprung up in the first bloom of philanthropic concern for the black American withered when the enthusiasm and support declined.

It appears that Northern philanthropy had clearly undertaken too much too soon for its efforts to be completely effective. The General Board recognized in 1915 that "the number of institutions now struggling for existence is of all relation to the number of qualified teachers and students . . . the financial resources available . . . and the service to be performed." What had resulted from the early philanthropy, the board contended, was a rash of inferior institutions that called themselves colleges but offered in all but a few cases a level of training far below college standards. It was imperative "that under existing conditions only a few efficient colleges for Negroes can and ought to be maintained." The board directed its disbursements with an eye to this need.

The delicate social situation that existed in Texas and throughout the South in regard to the black citizens posed another pitfall for

Northern philanthropy. Southern whites were suspicious of the attempts of Northerners to give higher education to black people. In 1890, Jabez Lamar Monroe Curry, a Southern administrator of several educational foundations concerned with the South, commented that all the Northern education dollars bought for the Negro was "unsettling, demoralizing, pandered to a wide frenzy for schooling as a quick method of reversing social and political conditions." More forthright was Senator James K. Vardaman of Mississippi: "What the north is sending south is not money but dynamite. This education is ruining our Negroes. They're demanding equality."

These comments were very representative of what white Texans felt and said during this period in history. A rapid survey of the world of philanthropy reveals that since 1938, philanthropy did not change much, for black Texans in particular. That revolutionary change which seemed to have characterized the 1930s was gone. Needs seemed to have changed. In the earlier period, the needs of black colleges were unique. The problem of philanthropy was to create a system of bona fide higher education from the indiscriminate mass of lower-grade institutions that chose to call themselves colleges and even universities. The needs of the black colleges more nearly paralleled those of other colleges. As a consequence, philanthropy had to return to less revolutionary but equally important developments: the support of scholarship programs, improvement in the training and pay of faculty, the creation of new departments and the strengthening of older ones, and provision of better buildings and equipment.

The foundation, which had undertaken the task of making black higher education a reality, maintained its important sources of economic aid during and after World War II. However, black education in Texas, and elsewhere in the Southern states, was rapidly becoming too complex and too large a business for even the wealthiest foundations to support. Also, many of the foundations that had been of great service to the development of higher education for black people began to cease their operations. Rockefeller's General Education Board, which had given generously to higher learning for black Americans in the South, was considering closing out its philanthropic activities.

The Rosenwald Fund brought its operations to a close in 1948, and the resources of the Slater and Jeanes funds, which had merged in the Southern Education Foundation, were declining.

The Baptist Home Mission Society, which had at one time exerted great influence on black education, watched its financial resources approach the vanishing point. The horde of veterans who flooded the campuses immediately following the end of World War II increased the urgency of the situation. In attempting to meet the financial crisis, the black colleges were handicapped by the composition of their student bodies. Since most students came from lower economic groups, tuition could not be raised to increasingly higher levels, as had happened in the white colleges in Texas and throughout the South. As it had so often been in the past, philanthropy appeared to be the only means available to solve the financial difficulties of black higher education.

In January 1943, Frederick Douglas Patterson, president of Tuskegee Institute, addressed a letter to the presidents of other private black colleges. Patterson was deeply troubled over black education's bleak prospects for financial support. He proposed that the colleges unite in a joint fund-raising campaign — an educational community chest in the name of black people. The General Education Board and the Rosenwald Fund agreed to underwrite a portion of the expenses of the first campaign. In 1944, twenty-seven private accredited black colleges (later the number rose to thirty-three and finally stabilized at thirty-two) launched the initial campaign for the United Negro College Fund. It was a pioneer effort in joint campaigning by educational institutions in America, and subsequently had many imitators. In addition, the fund represented a philanthropic declaration of independence by which blacks made clear the direction and application of the funds. Shortly after its fifteenth campaign, the fund reached an important milestone, when the amount it had raised for its members surpassed the $41 million that the General Education Board had dispensed to black higher education over the years.

The United Negro College Fund organized for its first campaign with a board of directors composed of all the college presidents and sixteen outside members. It also brought to its support, in advisory capacities, many men and women prominent in finance, education, and the professions. Headquarters were established in New York City and campaigns were conducted in 120 communities. The initial campaign was a striking success, whereas in 1943, the last year before the joint effort, the member colleges had separately raised a total of $300,000. The fund, in 1944, collected $765,000.

About 75 percent of the donors had not previously given to black education. Except for a slight drop in income during 1946, the fund gradually increased its harvest, reaching $1.21 million in 1950 and surpassing $2 million for the first time in 1960. New York City usually contributed 25 to 30 percent of the total. In 1977, the goal was set at $15 million. Texas college members, nine in all, were the recipients of a very large share of this amount.

Today, the United Negro College Fund remains the largest supporter of higher education for black Americans and for black Texans. In 1977, not only did white businesses and individuals give to support higher education for black people, blacks of substantial means were giving increasing amounts. Such private institutions as Bishop, Huston-Tillotson, Wiley, Paul Quinn, and other colleges were the recipients of such fundings.

Black Teachers Organization

The organization of the "Colored Teachers State Association of Texas" in 1884 did much to influence the public mind and to give black teachers a more reputable standing. Thirteen professional educators and businesspersons, including L. C. Anderson, E. L. Blackshear, and Norris Wright Cuney, met at Prairie View A&M and founded the Association, with Anderson as its first president. The early history of the Association revealed that it began "as a social movement, a political movement, and for the most part, an economic movement." Its original purposes "were based upon politics of equalitarianism and politics of compromise."

Membership in the Association was open without restriction to all persons interested in education. This gave the Association a political flavor, since politicians tried to use the organization as a vehicle for political advantage. Teachers misunderstood the real purpose of a teachers association, because of the political implications; but by the end of the century, the Association divested itself of political complications. The Association grew slowly during the first few years, but by 1893, sufficient members had joined to create a need for district organizations. A district was formed for East Texas in 1893, and a decade later, another was set up for South Texas. In succeeding years, membership increased, and the Association became one of the more important factors in the progress of black education in the state.

Bishop College, Marshall, Texas, 1952.

Institutions Established by Religious Organizations

Baptist Conventions and Associations

Bishop College

Bishop College had its genesis when President Rufus C. Burleson of Baylor University, at Waco, Texas, interceded with the American Baptist Home Missionary Society of New York City for funds to found a college for Negroes in the Southwest. Col. Nathan Bishop, a former secretary of the society, supported the move and became the chief benefactor of the college. He said:

> I expect to stand side by side with these freedmen in the day of judgment. Their Lord is my Lord. They and I are brethren; and I am determined to be prepared for the meeting.

Bishop College was established in 1881 in Marshall, Texas, by a band of illiterate ex-slaves and a group of missionaries from the

Home Mission Society of the Northern Baptist Convention (now the American Baptist Convention). The college was named for Colonel Bishop, who died before the college opened. The school was established as a liberal-arts college but provided educational opportunities for children and adults from the kindergarten through the undergraduate years.

During the administration of its first president, S. W. Culver, the institution was chartered in 1886, under the laws of the state of Texas. Incorporators were representatives of Northern, Southern, and Negro Baptist Conventions. The academic program was geared to prepare teachers and preachers, and to provide professional training for lawyers, physicians, and dentists.

In 1892, during the administration of N. Wolverton, the college's second president, an affiliation was effected with the Richmond Theological Seminary, Richmond, Virginia, making it possible for advanced students to enter the seminary, and with Shaw University, Raleigh, North Carolina, to accept the pre-professional students at Bishop College for admission to the schools of law and medicine.

In 1894, the college received a legacy from ex-Governor Colby of Maine; and a gift of eleven acres and several residences from W. A. Cauldwell of New York City.

Albert Loughridge, A. A. Chaffee, and C. H. Maxson became Bishop's third, fourth, and fifth presidents.

In 1929, after the interim presidency of A. B. Gilmore, Bishop College elected its first black president, Joseph J. Rhoads, a native of Marshall, Texas, and a graduate of the college. The same year the high school department was discontinued, and Bishop College was given unconditional rank as a senior college by the Texas State Board of Education. Bishop became one of two black colleges west of the Mississippi to be rated at that time by the Southern Association of Colleges and Schools.

A junior college branch was opened in Dallas (1947), and a graduate program leading to the master of education degree was initiated in 1947. President Rhoads also organized the Lacy Kirk Williams Ministers' Institute, which did become nationally known as one of America's largest short-term training centers for in-service ministers and lay church leaders. The college joined the United Negro College Fund in 1944.

Bishop College, Dallas, Texas, 1975.

In May 1951, Earl L. Harrison, pastor of Shiloh Baptist Church, Washington, D.C., and a member of the Board of Trustees, was named interim president during the illness of President Rhoads. Following the retirement of President Rhoads in August of that year, Harrison assumed full duties of the office, but declined permanent appointment. He served until February 29, 1952. During his short tenure, Harrison succeeded in realigning the Baptist Missionary and Educational Convention of Texas with Bishop College.

In December 1951, the Board of Trustees elected M. K. Curry, Jr., president. He assumed office on March 1, 1952. Eventually, steps were taken to move the college to Dallas. The Board of Trustees approved the recommendation to move the college in 1956. The college was moved to Dallas in September 1961.

Through the leadership of Carr P. Collins, Sr., chairman of the Development Committee, the first capital funds campaign for the college was successfully conducted in Dallas in 1960–61. He was supported by other campaigns sponsored by the Baptist Missionary and Educational Convention of Texas headed by Ernest C. Estell, Sr., and the Christian Higher Education Challenge sponsored by the American Baptist Convention, Ronald V. Wells, director. In 1967, Travis T. Wallas and P. W. Gifford directed the first joint UNCF-Bishop Sustentation Campaign.

Early in January 1964, the college participated in the organization of the Dallas-Fort Worth Metropolitan Inter-University Council, which was composed of administrators from nine of the colleges and universities in the area and the Southwest Center for Advanced Studies to promote inter-institutional cooperation.

The college also became a member of The Association for Graduate Education and Research (TAGER), a consortium of private colleges and universities in the Dallas-Fort Worth metropolitan area which were committed to improving and expanding programs in graduate education.

In 1967, Bishop College participated in the organization of the Texas Association of Developing Colleges, a consortium of six traditionally black colleges which were committed to improving the quality of undergraduate instruction, reducing unnecessary duplication of course offerings, and promoting cooperation among the participating institutions.

In 1977, the college's physical plant consisted of twenty-six buildings valued in excess of $18.1 million. All except one have been constructed since the college moved to the Dallas campus from Marshall in 1961.

Two major capital fund drives (1960–1961, 1964–1965) contributed to the construction and equipage. A third capital effort, sanctioned by the Board of Trustees and approved by the Dallas County Screening Committee, was launched in the spring of 1974. Its goal of $5.4 million in the 1974–1976 period was to provide three additional facilities:

(1) An all-purpose classroom building for expanding programs in Business, the Humanities, and the Social Sciences;
(2) An Administration Building in which all administrative activities will be combined;
(3) A Health and Physical Education-Recreation Building, including a natatorium and field house.

In March of 1975, President Curry announced to the meeting of the Board of Trustees that the capital fund goal had been subscribed. A total of $5,422,000 had been pledged, with more than 51 percent of the amount pledged coming from black-oriented individuals and groups. The total pledged to this effort through June 1976 exceeded $7 million, with over $4 million from black contributors.

The college had strong support from a number of private foundations, and in October 1972 was included in the Ford Foundation "five-year program to increase opportunities in higher education." Bishop College received three major Ford grants, and was one of eight predominantly black institutions chosen by Ford to receive grants over a five-year period expected to total $3.5 million each.

According to President Curry, Bishop's efforts, substantial growth, and good stewardship of its resources have attracted increased federal monies. The last such major grant came in 1974 — the Advanced Institutional Development Grant under the authority of the Title III Strengthening Developing Institutions Program. The program netted Bishop a total of $3.15 million over a five- or six-year period.

The Bishop College program was consistent with the institution's high academic, social, ethical, and religious standards. Bishop was recognized by educational authorities as standing in the front rank of colleges in the Southwest. The college had gained national recognition for its program of citizenship training and community service.

In 1947, the institution was accredited by the Association of Texas Colleges and Universities and the Southern Association of Colleges and Schools. The teacher-education program at the college was approved in 1947 by the Texas Education Agency. The college had met all the pre-medical requirements of the American Medical Association. The graduates were admitted to the graduate and professional schools of American universities which required the bachelor of arts degree, or its equivalent, for admission.

In 1977, Bishop College held membership in the American Association of Colleges for Teacher Education, the Association of American Colleges, American Association of Collegiate Registrars and Admission Officers, American Council of Education, Cooperative College Development Program, National Association of Collegiate Deans and Registrars, Independent Colleges and Universities of Texas (ICUT), The Association for Graduate Education and Research, Texas Association of Developing Colleges, Council on Social Work Education, National Association for Equal Opportunity in Higher Education, a consortium of over 100 private and public black colleges and universities, and Positive Futures, Incorporated.

Bishop College had pledged to help young men and women to develop their potentialities for scholarly achievement, professional competence, and effective participation in the general processes of democratic society. This kind of philosophy became a part of the spirit of Bishop College in its infancy, and it was fortified with the leadership of J. J. Rhoads, its first black leader.

Rhoads, being a man of conviction and courage, led the fight for equal teacher salaries in Texas. As chairman of the Commission on Democracy in Education, he achieved equal salary decisions in several school districts and the eventual establishment of state policy which supported equal compensation based upon professional preparation and qualification. He directed the Sweatt case, which resulted in admission of blacks to state universities and colleges. It was similar events, which were an outgrowth of his leadership, which inspired a group of college students to participate in a protest demonstration in Austin, Texas, April 27, 1949.

In the spring of 1949 (early in April), the efforts to integrate state universities and colleges were going slowly. President Rhoads summoned some students and the president of the Southwestern Regional National Association for the Advancement of Colored People (NAACP) college chapters (Texas, Louisiana, Arkansas, New Mexico, Arizona, and Oklahoma) to his office, where they met with the local campus NAACP president and the student body president. In this meeting, they were informed of the attempt to enroll Herman A. Barnett in the University of Texas at Austin's Graduate School as a medical student. The students informed the president of their desire to be on hand for the occasion, and he agreed. The group met with Donald Jones, state NAACP director, and it was decided that they would stage a demonstration at the State Capitol in support of Barnett's attempt to enter the University of Texas as a medical student. Plans were finalized, and several bus loads of students from Bishop, Wiley, and Jarvis colleges departed April 27, 1949, for Austin. When they arrived in Austin, W. Astor Kirk and a large number of students from Tillotson and Samuel Huston College met with them at Tillotson College. They were later joined by a number of white students from the University of Texas NAACP Chapter, led by the chapter president.

The morning of April 27, the group accompanied Barnett to the registrar's office, where he attempted to enroll as a graduate student. His application was rejected. Following Barnett's rejection, the students assembled and marched in protest, from the campus of the University of Texas along University Avenue and on Congress to the State Capitol. When they reached the Capitol grounds, they went to visit with Governor Beauford H. Jester. After having the students wait in the Capitol Rotunda for a while, the governor arranged to see them. They were able to present their grievances to him. The governor denied them the privilege of registration at the University of Texas at Austin. He suggested instead that they apply at the University for Negroes at Houston. The students informed the governor that: "We represent 300 senior Negro students desiring further professional study without facilities to obtain it in Texas." Jester said their petition would be turned over to the proper authorities. He asked what they would think of separate facilities. At that point, the governor was told that these students had come seeking admission to the University of Texas and other state institutions, as citizens of the state who are entitled to attend, not as beggars seeking special arrangements.

In August, the medical school accepted Barnett to sit in regular classes; even so, a facade of separation remained, because Texas State University for Negroes issued his degree.

In 1977, perhaps the most outstanding attribute of the college was its presidential leadership. President Curry, who became the administrative head of Bishop on March 1, 1952, was also the president of the forty-one-member college United Negro College Fund, Inc. The future for Bishop College did look bright indeed. However, mismanagement and lack of financial aid combined to lead to its untimely demise in 1988.

Butler College

A co-educational black college was established as Texas Baptist Academy in 1905 by the East Texas Baptist Association. After the death of President C. M. Butler in 1924, the name was changed to Butler College and the status was raised to junior college level. According to various Baptist ministers, in 1932 the Texas Baptist Convention became a partner in ownership and operation of the college. At the close of World War II, the school enlarged its program to include such vocational courses as tailoring, photography, and secretarial science, particularly to benefit veterans. In 1949, the plant consisted of a thirty-three-acre campus and eleven buildings; the college also owned a farm of 103 acres on the Tyler-Kilgore Highway. Presidents of the college have been: R. C. Bledsoe, C. M. Butler, J. V. McClennan, Isaiah Jackson, William M. Butler, M. K. Curry, and R. W. Puryear.

With a new charter in 1951 and Claude Meals as president, the school made plans to become a four-year college with curricula leading to a bachelor's degree. An emphasis of the educational program was teacher preparation. Declining enrollment hindered the school's plans. A succession of new presidents included John W. Williams, Leon Fernandez Hardee, and Millard J. Smith. The physical plant in the 1960s consisted of fourteen buildings, three of which were faculty dwellings.

Student enrollment declined from 203 in 1954 to 58 in 1969. The college was closed prior to the fall term of 1962, never having attained the status of an accredited four-year college.

Conroe Normal and Industrial Bible College

A predominantly religious institution, Conroe College was founded in 1903 by the American Baptist Missionary and Educational Association. It was chartered by the state of Texas in 1904. J. Johnson served as president from 1903 to 1906, David Abner from 1906 to 1909, William A. Johnson from 1909 to 1946, W. S. Brent from 1946 to 1951, C. H. Durden from 1951 to 1953, A. L. Bradley from 1953 to 1963, J. S. Curry from 1963 to 1967, A. L. Bradley from 1967 to 1968, I. S. Spencer from 1968 to 1971, and P. J. Walker from 1971 to 1977.

During its early history, the school secured 105 acres of land. A number of its teachers, who were from Guadalupe College, were employed by David Abner during his administration. They worked toward the training of ministers and Christian workers to serve in the state of Texas and throughout the nation.

The purpose of Conroe College was to meet the needs of students in all walks of life. The college's primary purpose was to provide courses of study for persons preparing to serve in various aspects of the work of the church and especially the Christian ministry. It also was structured to serve those who needed to further their studies of Christian theology.

In implementing its aims, Conroe College made the study of the Bible and theology the center of its curriculum. The objective was that the student who graduated from the college would be well-prepared, well-adjusted, a stable element in society, and a capable, constructive worker.

Conroe College was a coeducational institution of higher education. The administrative government of the school was planned by the seventeen members of the Board of Trustees elected at large from the state of Texas.

The college has depended upon Christians everywhere who have felt the need for trained Christian leadership. This group was composed of a Board of Trustees, American Baptist Convention of Texas, and other state and national organizations. The school's endowment was faith in God and courage. It did not turn away anyone who wanted a Christian education.

Guadalupe College

According to tradition, on September 11, 1871, W. B. Ball was sent to Texas by Northern white people to engage in the work of educating the black people of Texas. Ball, a black man, was supposed to have organized the first school for black people in Seguin, Texas.

Ball was a teacher in the community, and his contact with the young people of the community led to his being in contact with the ministers of the city and country. One of those ministers was Leonard Isley, a white minister from the northern United States. Isley, according to tradition, was a constant worker among the black people of Seguin and his work was reported to have been effective. Isley preached to the black people supposedly under an oak tree each second and fourth Sunday in the month. Ball came to know Isley and eventually was baptized by him on the first Sunday in August 1873.

In that same month, Isley, Hiram Wilson, Napoleon Pruett, Aaron Tilman, A. Jones, and others organized the Guadalupe Missionary Baptist Association. It seems that the association's most urgent need at the time was trained religious and educational laborers. Ball was one of the persons to meet the criteria for service in the community. Isom McKnight later teamed with Ball to assist in the educational and religious work. These two men seemed to have been an ideal team.

In 1884, at an annual session of the association, Isley told of his plans for organizing a college at Seguin for black people. The plan was accepted by the association and later they purchased a Catholic school building in which the school was begun. Despite complications and intimidations which arose in various ways, there was support which came from the people of Seguin, Texas, and Guadalupe

County. The moral and financial support of many white citizens in and around Seguin was a factor in the success of the founding and growth of Guadalupe College.

The college received a significant contribution from George Brackenridge of San Antonio, Texas. He gave the college $7,550. This he gave to Guadalupe College to be used as an agricultural farm.

W. B. Ball was president of Guadalupe College from 1884 to 1892. He was succeeded by D. J. Hull. Other administrative heads of Guadalupe College from 1892 to 1936 were: P. J. Mays, D. Abner, C. H. Griggs, and P. B. Oldham.

In 1936, the college was destroyed by fire. The college was moved to San Antonio following the fire, where it was still in operation in October 1977. After the move to San Antonio, the leadership of the college was provided by D. Manning Jackson (1937–1948), George A. Johnson (1948–1951), A. A. Lucas (1951–1952), and C. C. Brown (1952–).

According to the records of the Guadalupe Missionary Baptist Association and the minutes of the Sweet Home Baptist Church of Seguin, Texas, Guadalupe College was the second oldest black church-related institution of higher education in the state of Texas. In 1977, Guadalupe College of San Antonio, Texas, operated as an institution which trained ministers and church workers.

Catholic Diocese

St. Phillips College

St. Phillips College was founded in 1898 in San Antonio, Texas, by Bishop James Steptol Johnston. The school began in an adobe house in what later became La Villita. The institution was under the direction of Mrs. Cowan, a missionary, for two years. The school developed from an industrial school for girls to a high school and later a college.

In September 1927, St. Phillips opened its doors as a junior college, serving the immediate needs of the Negro community of San Antonio and vicinity.

In August 1942, St. Phillips ceased to function as a private institution, becoming a municipal junior college through an affiliation with San Antonio College under the auspices of the San Antonio In-

St. Phillips College

Jarvis Christian College

dependent School District. While the name of St. Phillips Junior College was continued in use for certain legal purposes, the school was referred to in its new capacity as St. Phillips College.

In October 1945, the citizenry voted to place San Antonio and St. Phillips colleges under a newly created district board of trustees. The new district was known as the San Antonio Junior College District. Effective September 1, 1946, San Antonio and St. Phillips colleges came under the administration of the Board of Trustees of the San Antonio Union Junior College District. The year 1977 marked the seventy-ninth anniversary of the founding of St. Phillips College.

United Christian Church

Jarvis Christian College

In 1904, Jarvis Christian College was no more than a dream in the minds of missionary women of the Christian Church (Disciples of Christ). By 1910, however, a gift of 456 acres of land by Maj. and Mrs. J. J. Jarvis provided the site upon which the college was built. Subsequently, women of black Christian churches presented cash contributions totaling $1,000, an amount augmented by $10,000 pledged and raised by the Christian Women's Board of Missions.

The college was begun in 1912, as a Christian Institute modeled upon Southern Christian Institute of Edwards, Mississippi. T. B. Frost, superintendent, was soon joined by Charles Berry in the task of clearing grounds and erecting buildings for the institute, which proposed, through its largely elementary program, to educate "head, heart, and hand," to the end that its students would become "useful citizens and earnest Christians."

In 1977, Jarvis retained its affiliation with the Christian Church (Disciples of Christ) and had developed into a four-year college of arts and science with an autonomous board. It became affiliated with Texas Christian University in 1964, and was a member of a five-college consortium, the Texas Association of Developing Colleges.

Five presidents have provided leadership, which wrought the transformation from an institute to an accredited senior college.

J. N. Ervin, who was president between 1912 and 1938, effected the beginning of high school work in 1914, the beginning of state accreditation in 1921, junior college work in 1928, the senior college program in 1937, and the elimination of high school work in 1938. Of the buildings constructed during his tenure, the Emma B. Smith Building (1936) is all that has remained.

Between 1938 and 1949, during the administration of P. C. Washington, the original college charter was granted (1939), a Bible chair was established, and additional structures were completed, of which the Florence Robinson Building remained.

John B. Eubanks, executive vice-president between 1949 and 1951, was president from 1951 to 1953. He and his advisory consultant, Cleo W. Blackburn, were responsible for the introduction of a program of general education and for changes leading to the inclusion of Jarvis on the Southern Association's "Approved List of Colleges and Universities for Negro Youth." Blackburn became president in 1953 and continued in office until 1964. He introduced the concept of fundamental education (1953) and saw the establishment of an autonomous board (1958) to replace the Texas Board of Trustees representing "prominent members of the Christian Churches." He brought John O. Perpener to Jarvis as resident executive (1959) with the title executive vice-president.

Blackburn was strongly influential in the establishment of the affiliation between Jarvis and Texas Christian University (1964). During his administration, the Fellowship Center (1955), the James A. Aborne Health Center (1961), the Barton-Zeppa Agro-Industrial Building (1961) and four dormitories (1962) were constructed, and plans were initiated for the construction of the Olin Library and Communication Center.

Perpener, after a period as the first provost and chief administrative officer (1964–66), subsequently became president (1966). His administration saw the elimination of inter-collegiate football and the Agro-Industrial Program (1964). He saw the addition of: affiliation with the Association of Developing Colleges, a consortium (1967); achievement of membership in the Southern Association of Colleges and Schools (1967); and achievement of Texas Education Agency approval of the Teacher Education Program (1969). In addition to the removal or razing of older frame structures, such as the Physical Education Building, Woolery Courts, the Commons Building, and some older faculty housing, improvements were made in campus lighting, roadways, and sewage facilities (1965–67). Several buildings were also completed: the Meyer Science and Mathematics Center (1969); Phase I of Faculty Housing (1970); and four new dormitories along with a section of the Women's Common Building (1970). There was also a renovation of the Emma B. Smith Building (1970).

John P. Jones became the sixth president of Jarvis Christian College in 1972. During his four years in office, he was responsible for reaffirmation of accreditation by the Texas Education Agency and the Southern Association of Colleges and Schools, and the establishment of a modern water purification system and sewage disposal plant. Jones was succeeded by E. W. Rand in 1976.

Churches of God

Southwestern Christian College

Southwestern Christian College was established in Fort Worth under the name Southern Bible Institute in the fall of 1948, with forty-five students. The board of trustees planned to purchase property in Fort Worth for a permanent school plant; however, an opportunity arose in 1949 to buy the site formerly occupied by Texas Military College in Terrell. The move to Terrell was made in 1950, at which time the name of the school was changed to Southwestern Christian College.

Although founded primarily for the education of Negro youth from the Churches of Christ, Southwestern Christian College was open to anyone. The Bible-centered junior college offered basic academic courses leading to the associate of arts degree. In 1974, the fall term enrollment numbered 235 students, and the faculty consisted of approximately twenty members. Jack Evans was president of the college in 1977.

Congregational Church

Tillotson College

Tillotson College, a senior college for Negroes built and maintained in Austin, Texas, by the American Missionary Society of the Congregational Churches, was chartered in 1877. The school was named for George Jeffery Tillotson, who planned the school, selected the site, and raised $16,000 for its establishment. Called

Tillotson Collegiate and Normal Institute, it opened on January 17, 1881, with 250 students, chiefly in the lower grades. Allen Hall was the first building; Beard Hall was constructed in 1894. In 1947, there were fourteen buildings on a campus of twenty-three acres.

William E. Brooks, first president (1881–1885), was succeeded by John Hershaw (1886), Henry L. Lubbell (1886–1889), William M. Brown (1889–1893), Winfield S. Goss (1894–1895), Marshall R. Gaines (1896–1904), Arthur W. Partch (1905–1906), Isaac M. Agard (1907–1918), and Francis W. Fletcher (1919–1923). J. T. Hodges, the first black to be president (1924–1929), was followed by Mary E. Branch (1930–1944), and William Jones, who became president in 1944.

In 1925, the school was recognized as a junior college. It became a women's college in 1926, and enrollment dropped to 130 in 1930. In 1931, the high school was dropped, and senior college standing was achieved. Coeducation was restored in 1935, and in 1943 the college was granted an "A" rating by the Southern Association of Colleges. In 1946, enrollment was 650 for the long session, and the faculty numbered 35. Three degrees were offered: bachelor of arts, bachelor of science, and bachelor of science in home economics.

African Methodist Episcopal Church

Paul Quinn College

Paul Quinn College was founded in Austin by a small group of African Methodist circuit-riding preachers in 1872. The institution later moved to Waco, as a one-building trade school, and taught newly freed slaves blacksmithing, carpentry, tanning, saddlery, and other skills.

As the African Methodist Episcopal Church developed throughout the South, funds became available for a larger school. The first two acres of the present twenty-two-acre campus in Waco were purchased in 1881. That same year, Paul Quinn College (named for Bishop William Paul Quinn, an A. M. E. Missionary of the Western states for almost 30 years), was chartered by the state.

The oldest liberal arts college for black people in Texas began with a faculty of five and an early-day curriculum which encompassed mathematics, music, Latin, theology, English, printing, carpentry, sewing, and "household work." Facilities on the new campus included the brick main building, one frame building, and "three shed rooms for young men."

Additional buildings were made possible through contributions from interested patrons of the college. In 1950, the college entered an extensive expansion program, completing a church, student union, gymnasium, and administration building by 1954. Major renovations of other buildings on campus were also made. In 1954, the Waco Chamber of Commerce launched a successful $100,000 drive to replace a girls' dormitory destroyed by fire. The campus included fifteen permanent structures by 1964.

The college was accredited by the Texas Education Agency and affiliated with the Council for Small Colleges and the Association of Texas Colleges and Universities. Ten departments of instruction were organized into three divisions: humanities, natural sciences, and social sciences. Bachelor of arts and bachelor of science degrees were granted. A member of the South Central Athletic Conference, Paul Quinn maintained varsity teams for intercollegiate competition in basketball, baseball, and track.

The library contained 28,718 volumes in 1969. In the fall of 1974, enrollment was 496. The president of the college was Stanley E. Rutland. The 1977 fall registration was 561.

United Methodist Conferences

Samuel Huston College

Samuel Huston College, a coeducational school for Negroes in Austin, Texas, developed from a plan projected in 1876 by the Methodist Episcopal Conference. In 1883, an agreement with the Freedman's Aid Society resulted in the purchase of a six-acre plot on which the college was built. A gift of $9,000 was received from Samuel Huston of Marengo, Iowa, for whom the institution was named. In 1898, a contract was let for a one-story building.

The first president of the college, R. S. Lovinggood, arrived in Austin in the fall of 1900, and the first term opened with an enrollment of eighty. H. S. White of Romeo, Michigan, gave a library of 500 volumes.

*E. T. Burrows, of Maine, gave
$5,000 to complete building
of Samuel Huston College.*
— TAAHO Collections,
Austin, Texas

Cheerleaders, Samuel Huston College in the 1920s.
— TAAHO Collections, Austin, Texas

By 1905, the enrollment was 419; in 1906, it reached 517. Courses ranged from elementary grades through college, including instruction in blacksmithing, bookkeeping, teaching, and preaching. In 1916, the school plant was enlarged to fifteen acres, and substantial buildings including a laboratory, a laundry, and an industrial building were added.

In 1927, Samuel Huston was recognized by the State Department of Education as a class "A" senior college. The teacher placement bureau was an added department; the premedical course was accepted by the American Medical Association as meeting its requirements.

Texas College

Texas College was located at Tyler, Texas, 100 miles east of Dallas and 116 miles west of Texarkana. Tyler had a population of approximately 60,000 and was the major city of East Texas. The college was so strategically located that it was within a two-hundred-mile radius of one-half the black population of Texas.

Texas College was organized in 1894 by a group of ministers of the Colored Methodist Episcopal Church (now Christian Methodist), and instruction began at the institution in 1895. The name of

Texas College

this institution was changed in 1909 to Phillips University, in honor of the presiding bishop, who was chairman of the Board of Trustees; however, the name of Texas College was restored in 1912.

The institution has had an extended number of scholars who have served as its presidents. The first president was O. T. Womack, who served from 1895 to 1903. Much credit has been given this first president, who with patience and thoughtful care directed the activities of Texas College through its first eight years. Following President Womack for a brief period of two years was W. B. West, 1903-1905. S. W. Broom was elected president in 1905 and served in that capacity until 1910. G. L. Tyus served as president from 1910 to 1914 and was followed by C. C. Neal, who held the office for one year, 1914–1915. The first significant period of unparalleled educational growth and development was experienced during the administration of W. R. Banks. It was during the presidency of W. R. Banks that Texas College was fully accredited as a junior college by the Texas Department of Education.

In 1931, D. R. Glass was elected president of Texas College. His term as president spanned thirty years, until 1961. With the advent of Glass, the second significant program of academic growth and physical expansion was consummated. Texas College was accredited in 1932 by the State Department of Education as a senior college; and in 1933, the college was granted a "B" rating by the Southern Association of Colleges and Secondary Schools. This rating by the Southern Association of Colleges and Secondary Schools attracted unusual attention, because Texas College had initiated and developed a community-centered program for the in-service development of teachers. As a result, Texas College was able to strengthen and enrich educational offerings, augment physical facilities, improve the quality of instruction, and increase student enrollment to such an extent that the institution was granted an "A" rating in 1948. Likewise, it was during the Glass administration that Texas College became one of the first members of the United Negro College Fund.

Two short administrations followed the presidency of D. R. Glass; they were those of President Robert L. Potts, 1961–1963, and Horace C. Savage, 1964-1967.

In June 1967, Allen C. Hancock was elected as the eleventh president of Texas College. First-time formal academic accreditation by the regional body, extensive campus renovation, and the construction of two dormitories and a science building subsequently took place as the college experienced a resurgence in growth and development.

Texas College was a church-related institution under the supervision, care, and ownership of the Christian Methodist Episcopal Church. It provided a program of study and experience which was designed to contribute to the intellectual, social, physical, emotional, and spiritual development of each student.

Texas College endeavored to develop individuals who were concerned and active participants in various communities, the state, the nation, and the world. To accomplish this goal, the college provided the following: (1) basic programs in the arts and sciences; (2) basic requirements for entering various occupations and professions; and (3) programs for the preparation of teachers for elementary and secondary schools. These programs were designed to culminate with the acquisition of a bachelor's degree.

Texas College was a small residential college, and its purpose was to provide opportunities for involvement among the administration, faculty, and students which would greatly enhance the student's progress toward total development. Texas College adhered to an open admission policy. Retention, however, depended upon satisfactory personal development and performance. Special programs were provided to assist each student in the elimination of various difficulties which would tend to impede progress toward total development.

Wiley College

Wiley College was founded in 1873 and chartered in 1882, by the Freedman's Aid Society, which later became the Board of Education for Negroes, now merged with the Board of Education of the Methodist Church.

Wiley College was a Christian coeducational institution named for Bishop Zac W. Wiley, an outstanding minister, medical missionary, educator, and bishop of the former Methodist Episcopal Church. He was born in Lewistown, Pennsylvania, on March 29, 1825. He became interested in the Christian ministry while a boy. He joined the church and served as an exhorter for four years. Because of voice difficulties, he had to leave the ministry. He decided

Wiley College

to study medicine and upon graduation became a medical and educational missionary to China. In 1864, he was made editor of the *Ladies Repository,* and during the same year was elected bishop. While bishop, he organized a conference in Japan and later returned to China, where he died November 22, 1884.

Originally, the college was located in two frame buildings just south of Marshall's city limits. In 1880, it was moved to its present site.

Bishop J. W. Walden and R. S. Rusk were closely identified with the college during the early days. Rusk, with the assistance of the leading members of the Board of Trustees, selected the grounds and planned the buildings. The wisdom of the initial arrangements perhaps paved the way for present achievements.

Individuals who have taught at Wiley College have been some of the outstanding men and women of the United Methodist Church. Among the first presidents were F. C. Moore, W. H. Davis, N. D. Clifford, George Whitaker, and P. A. Cool.

In 1894, the United Methodist Church saw fit to change its policy in the management of the institution, and Isaah B. Scott was made president. His administration was characterized by increased efficiency in all departments. The General Conference in 1896 elected Scott to the editorship of the *Southwestern Christian Advocate,* and M. W. Dogan was made president of the college. During the forty-six years of his presidency, the college grew tremendously. His successors have diligently pursued the goals he set, by maintaining high standards and keeping abreast of modern trends and objects in education.

Under the guidance of J. S. Scott, who became the ninth president in 1948, the college continued to move forward with its physical plant and its intellectual and spiritual program. E. C. McLeod was president from 1942 to 1947.

T. W. Cole, Sr., became the tenth president in 1958. He was the first graduate of the institution to be elected president and also the first layman to be president of the institution. R. E. Hayes succeeded Cole as president in 1975.

Wiley was the first black college west of the Mississippi River to be granted the "A" rating by the Southern Association of Colleges and Secondary Schools. The rating was awarded in 1933. In 1977, the institution still maintained the rating.

Wiley College was also recognized by the State Board of Examiners of the Department of Education of Texas, the Methodist University Senate, the Association of American Colleges, the Association of Colleges for Negro Youth, and the American Medical Association. Wiley College was awarded full membership in the Texas Association of Colleges and Universities.

United Church of Christ and the United Methodist Conference

Huston-Tillotson College

Huston-Tillotson College, Austin, Texas, was a coeducational college of liberal arts and sciences operated jointly under the auspices of the American Missionary Association of the United Church of Christ and the Board of Education of the Methodist Church. It was formed by merger of Samuel Huston College and

Mary E. Branch became president of Tillotson College in 1930.
— TAAHO Collections, Austin, Texas

King-Seabrook Chapel, Huston-Tillotson College.
— TAAHO Collections, Austin, Texas

Tillotson College, which was effected October 1952. Huston-Tillotson remained primarily a Negro college after the merger, although there were no restrictions on race.

The college was accredited or approved by the following bodies: Southern Association of Colleges and Schools, University Senate of the Methodist Church, American Association of Colleges for Teacher Education, Association of American Colleges, National Committee on Accrediting, Council for Higher Education of the United Church of Christ, Texas Education Agency, and Association of Texas Colleges.

Bachelor of arts and bachelor of science degrees were offered, with major concentration in fifteen areas. In 1966, the twenty-three-acre campus contained an administration building, science building, two residence halls, student union-dining hall, gymnasium-auditorium, music hall, lounge, and two other halls. Its library housed 47,420 volumes by 1969. By the early 1970s, new buildings included a classroom-administration building, a chapel, an addition of three wings to the women's dormitory, and an addition of two wings to the men's dormitory.

Mary E. Branch and William H. Jones, last presidents of Tillotson College, and Karl E. Downs, Robert F. Harrington, and Willie J. King, past presidents of Samuel Huston College, undertook cooperative sponsorship of several academic activities beginning in 1945. M. S. Davage served as interim president during the transition period. He retired in 1955 and was succeeded by J. J. Seabrook, the first permanent president of Huston-Tillotson College. Upon Seabrook's retirement in 1965, John Q. Taylor King became president.

Presbyterian Synod

Mary Allen Junior College

Mary Allen Junior College (originally Mary Allen Seminary) at Crockett, Texas, was founded in 1866 for the education of Negro girls. The institution was established largely through the efforts of Samuel Fisher Tenney, for fifty-four years pastor of the First Presbyterian (Tenney Memorial) Church of Crockett. Tenney learned from a Northern newspaper that a fund had been established to erect a school for "colored" girls as a memorial to Mary Allen, the deceased wife of the secretary of the Board of Missions for Freedmen of the Presbyterian Church. Since it was announced that the school should be located somewhere in the South, Tenney contacted the board and secured the cooperation of local businessmen in making an offer for the location of the school. The offer was accepted and work was started immediately.

The campus was located on the site of the first home of the original grantor of the land, Andrew E. Gossett. The first building was an old Presbyterian church, which J. B. Smith, the seminary's first president, purchased and moved to the campus. The other buildings were constructed of brick, which were made in a brickyard Smith had purchased for that purpose.

Smith and the next two presidents, Byrd R. Smith and J. B. Jones, were black men. During Byrd Smith's administration, the school was converted into Mary Allen Junior College. The Presbyterian Board withdrew its support, and the school was closed during World War II. In 1948, the institution was owned and operated by a Black Baptist Church Association. Due to declining enrollment and acute financial problems, Mary Allen closed its doors May 1971. There seemed little hope of it ever opening again.

Institutions Originating From
State Governmental Decree

Prairie View A&M University

The Fifteenth Legislature of Texas met in the year 1876. One of the acts of that legislature provided for the establishment of "an agricultural and mechanical college" for Negro citizens to be located in Waller County. L. M. Minor was elected first teacher of the school (Alta Vista Agricultural College). He served in this capacity from 1878 to 1879. In the last year of his principalship a legislative act provided for reorganization of the college and made funds available for the training of public school teachers. The teaching of military tactics was initiated in compliance with the Legislative Act of 1876.

The second principal, E. H. Anderson, served from 1879 to 1884; and L. C. Anderson, the third principal, held the position for the next twelve years. The gray stone administration building,

*John B. Coleman
Library, Prairie View
A&M University.*
   — TAAHO Collections,
      Austin, Texas

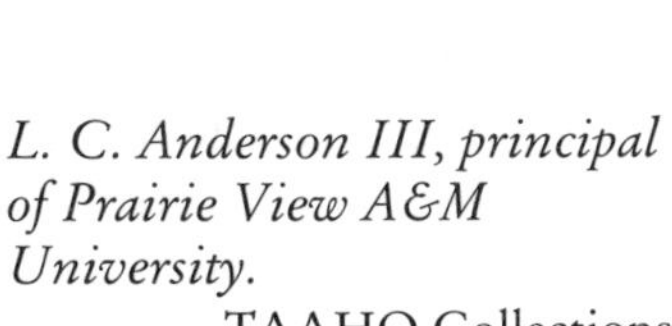

*L. C. Anderson III, principal
of Prairie View A&M
University.*
   — TAAHO Collections,
      Austin, Texas

whose architectural design was widely admired, was erected in 1890. During L. C. Anderson's administration, the Twentieth Legislature agreed to an "Agricultural and Mechanical Department" to be attached to the Normal School. Under the provisions of the Hatch Act the college was made a branch experiment station.

For the next nineteen years, E. L. Blackshear served "Prairie View Normal" as principal. During his administration significant growth was made in the curriculum and the physical plant. In 1899, the name was changed to "Prairie View State Normal and Industrial College," and the new name indicated the enlargement of the curriculum. A four-year college course was authorized by the state legislature in the session of 1901. Some additions to the plant were: two dormitories for men, Foster Hall (1909) and Luckie Hall (1909); a dormitory for women, Crawford Hall (1912); and a combination auditorium-dining hall building (1911).

I. M. Terrell, the fifth principal, held the position during the war years, 1915-1918. Despite the world conflict, the school plant expanded. Some additions were the mechanical arts building, more than sixty cottages for families, and the laundry, erected in 1916. In 1918, the Spence Building, for the Division of Agriculture, was erected. The close of World War I brought the activation of a recognized Reserve Officers Training Corps to the campus. The Cooperative Extension Service was also launched at this time.

During the administration of the sixth principal, J. C. Osborne (1918-1925), six buildings were added. In 1924 and 1925, the veterinary hospital, science building, the College of Exchange, the elementary training school, a Home Economic Practice College, and music conservatory were added. The Nursing Division was founded in 1918.

In 1926, W. R. Banks became the seventh principal of Prairie View. He served until August 31, 1947, at which time he became principal emeritus. He held the position longer than any of his predecessors, and Prairie View developed along several lines during his tenure. The physical plant doubled in size by the addition of six buildings valued at more than $100,000 each. The dining hall and the hospital, three apartment houses for male teachers, three dormitories for women, a greenhouse, an incubator house, a classroom building, a new auditorium-gymnasium, a new mechanical arts building, and cottages for families were added to the physical plant.

One of the significant studies of the Banks administration was

*W. R. Banks became
seventeenth principal of
Prairie View A&M
University.*
— TAAHO Collections,
Austin, Texas

a comprehensive evaluation of the objectives and purposes of Prairie View in 1933–34. Out of the study emerged Principal Banks' most often quoted statement: "Prairie View College must serve the State of Texas at the points of her greatest needs." The establishment of the Prairie View Conference on Education in 1931 was an important event in the history of the university. In the years that the conference met, Prairie View was host to educators, ministers, doctors, businessmen and women, housewives, social workers, and farmers.

In the establishment of the Division of Graduate Study in 1937, Prairie View University added another page to its expanding history.

In 1936, the first buildings were constructed to house the National Youth Administration resident center, and a new chapter in vocation training for youth was opened. The project was enlarged and made a training center for Negro men in critical occupations for support of the war effort. The men filled positions as welders, mechanics, pipe fitters, machine operators, and moulders in shipyards, foundries, and machine shops all over the nation. The project terminated in July 1943. The facilities are now used for vocational trade courses.

In July 1943, a training unit of the Army Specialized Training

Program was established with 200 trainees enrolled in Basic Engineering Curriculum. They were trained for special services with the Army Corps of Engineers.

In 1943, when the Forty-eighth Legislature met in January, it appropriated $160,000 for the erection of a library building. This amount was supplemented by $20,000 for equipment and books.

The name of the college, Prairie View Normal and Industrial College, was changed to Prairie View University in 1945, by an act of the Forty-ninth Legislature. The legislature passed the bill permitting Prairie View University to offer, as the need arises, all courses offered at the University of Texas.

On September 1, 1946, E. B. Evans became the eighth principal of Prairie View.

In 1947, the Fiftieth Legislature of Texas, through a special legislative act signed by Governor Beauford H. Jester on February 27, 1947, changed the name of the school from Prairie View University to Prairie View Agricultural and Mechanical College of Texas. The act provided that courses be offered in agriculture, the mechanical arts, engineering, and the natural sciences connected therewith, together with any other courses authorized at Prairie View at the time of the passage of the act. All of the courses were to be equivalent to those offered at the Agricultural and Mechanical College of Texas.

In March 1947, the old academic building which housed the principal administrative offices was destroyed by fire. The Fiftieth Legislature, which was then in session, made an emergency appropriation of $300,000 for the erection of the present Administration Building, which was completed in March 1949.

The title of the principal was changed to dean by the Board of Directors, and became effective during the 1947–48 school year. On September 1, 1948, the title of dean was changed to president, and on December 3, 1948, E. B. Evans, the eighth principal, was inaugurated as the first president of Prairie View Agricultural and Mechanical College of Texas.

The Divisions of Agriculture, Arts and Science, Home Economics, and Mechanical Arts, were changed to School of Agriculture, Arts and Science, Home Economics, and Engineering, effective September 1, 1950. The directors of the respective schools were named deans.

A new women's dormitory was completed in September 1950, at a cost of $350,000, and was named for the late dean of women,

Miss M. E. Suarez. The dormitory housed 247 women and had facilities for recreational and social activities. A similar building for male students, named in honor of a former teacher, J. M. Alexander, was completed in 1952. The E. B. Evans Animal Industries Building, valued at $284,000, was completed in 1951, and the Gibb Gilchrist Engineering Building was constructed in 1952, at a cost of $258,170.

Construction of still more adequate housing for the rapidly growing student body was completed in early 1955, with additions to Suarez Hall and to Alexander Hall, costing approximately $550,000. These additions provided space for an additional 240 female students and 250 additional male students.

Dairy and utilities warehouses were completed at a cost of $32,000. Also, $15,000 worth of water and sewer line installations were added to the college system. Construction of an exchange store and single faculty women's and single men's dormitories were also completed in 1955. The latter was named in honor of George W. Buchanan, former manager of the exchange and ex-teacher of mathematics. The faculty women's dormitory was named in memory of the late Lucille B. Evans, wife of President E. B. Evans. The hospital, constructed in 1939, had been named for J. C. Osborne, the sixth principal of the college. A new and completely modern Home Economics Building, named for Mrs. Elizabeth C. May Galloway (Elizabeth C. May Building), former dean of the School of Home Economics, was added in 1957. The old Home Arts structure was renovated into a modern music building.

The Board of Directors of the Texas A&M University System approved a $3 million building and improvement program for the college in 1957. The new $1 million Memorial Student Center was completed early in 1960, and construction on a $2 million science building was completed in 1961. Other construction during this period included building utilities, street extensions, and storm sewers. An underground Education Building, with a seating capacity of 5,000, was completed in 1964. In 1965 two new air-conditioned dormitories valued at $2.5 million were completed to house 900 students (450 males and 450 females). During the spring semester of the 1966–67 academic year, construction was begun on a half-million-dollar addition to the W. R. Banks Library.

The college was accepted for membership in the Southern Association of Colleges and Secondary Schools in December 1958, and later received reendorsement and full approval of the National

Council for Accreditation of Teacher Education. Improvements in offerings and facilities for science, mathematics, and engineering also resulted during the years from 1958 to the present time.

President E. B. Evans, who in 1959 became eligible for modified retirement, was asked by the Board of Directors to continue as president of the college. This tribute came in the midst of many other state and national honors for Evans in recognition of outstanding service to education. His services continued until August 31, 1966, at which time he was named president emeritus.

On September 1, 1966, J. M. Drew, who had served as dean of instruction and dean of graduate studies, became the second president of Prairie View Agriculture and Mechanical College. Shortly after taking office, he became ill, and as a result of his asking to be relieved of his office, the Board of Directors asked President Emeritus Evans to serve as acting president.

On November 22, 1966, the Board of Directors elected as the third president Alvin I. Thomas. Prior to his elevation to the presidency, Thomas had served as dean of the School of Industrial Education and Technology. Thomas introduced, for Prairie View A&M College, the concept of the residential college.

Forces Giving Rise to Establishment

Since 1876, the Texas Legislature had been interested intermittently in providing higher educational opportunities for black people of the state. The Constitution of 1876 had authorized establishment and maintenance of a "college or branch university for the instruction of 'colored' youths of the State, to be located by a vote of the people." This mandate was the first legal recognition of the responsibility of the state for black higher education. In the same year, 1876, the legislature provided for the establishment and maintenance of the state's first public institution of higher education for black people, the Agricultural and Mechanical College of Texas for the benefit of "colored" youth, near Hempstead.

Focus

In one of his early addresses, President Thomas said:

Resting on some 1400 acres of beautiful countryside . . . thirty minutes from the largest city in the South and 5th largest city in America, Prairie View can create an environment which will contain only those influences which will affect a student for good and we can lock out the intellectual pollution of the cities and give the students a refreshing, undistracted experience aimed at maximum personal, social, and intellectual growth.

At Prairie View A&M University, practically all of the students lived in residential halls. Because of this arrangement, the university had the ability to provide a special kind of learning situation; the residence halls as well as the library and the classrooms were learning centers. As a residential university, Prairie View used all of its resources to provide the greatest number of influences which served to develop students in the fullest possible manner. Curriculum orientation of the university was primarily agriculture, engineering, military science, and natural science. The college offered bachelor degrees in agriculture, arts and sciences, engineering, home economics, industrial education and technology, and nurse education. The graduate school offered the master's degree in several areas of study. The university also offered training in the Army and Naval Reserve Office Training Programs.

There were three separate and distinct functions of Prairie View A&M University that were clearly set forth in state and federal acts for its establishment and support.

First, it was an institution for the preparation and training of teachers.

Second, it was to offer liberal arts and scientific curricula.

Third, it was a Texas Land Grant institution providing opportunities for training in agriculture, home economics, engineering, and related branches of learning.

In addition, the institution offered training in health education so that it may give the state professionally trained nurses and provide opportunities for observation and practice for newly graduated students of medical colleges.

Prairie View proposed to serve the citizens of Texas at the points of their greatest needs and endeavored to bring the student's training into closer relationship with life's occupations.

The central theme of the philosophy of the institution was that education must have the objective of making a worthwhile and respectable living.

Contemporary Status (1977)

Prairie View A&M University in 1977 had grown to an annual enrollment of 6,000 coeducational students from Texas, forty other states, and twenty-five foreign countries.

The faculty was well-trained and experienced. There were more than 250 faculty members. Doctorates were held by 102 faculty members and they held 147 master's degrees. The administrative and clerical staff consisted of fifty people.

The university is accredited by the Texas Education Agency, the Southern Association of Colleges and Secondary Schools, the Association of Texas Colleges, and the National Council for Accreditation of Teacher Education.

In 1977, Prairie View was 100 years old and was still a part of the Texas A&M University System. Its annual operating budget exceeded $25 million and its enrollment (as mentioned before) was approximately 6,000. The physical plant had grown to more than 150 buildings, valued at an estimated $40 million. Its services covered the length and breadth of Texas through a professionally trained alumni.

Texas Southern University

Inception

"The Legislature shall also, *when deemed practicable*, establish a college or branch university for colored youth . . ." So said the Constitution of 1876. For many years, however, black and white citizens of Texas found difficulty in determining just how the constitutional provision was to be implemented. Some contended that the establishment of Prairie View had fulfilled the constitutional requirement. Others held that Prairie View was only a "normal school" or, at best, an A&M college, and that the constitutional convention had intended that the colored youths should have a "classical" university similar to the University of Texas. Some advocated the expansion of Prairie View so as to include a "classical" division, while still others insisted that a new, separate university be constructed, like the University of Texas at Austin. The controversy over the issue was to be one of the most heated in Texas educational history.

Time after time, the Texas Legislature failed to act on the uni-

Texas Southern University, Houston, Texas.
— TAAHO Collections, Austin, Texas

versity issue. Usually, the appropriation blockade was the limit of their activity. The black people of Texas were uncompromising in their efforts to have a university established.

As a stop-gap measure to provide higher educational facilities for black Texans until a black university might be established, the legislature of 1945 changed the status, function, and name of Prairie View Normal and Industrial College. It was provided that Prairie View University should:

1. Be authorized, in addition to the courses of study then authorized, to conduct courses in law, medicine, engineering, pharmacy, journalism, and any other generally recognized college course taught at the University of Texas, such courses to be substantially equivalent to those offered at the University of Texas.
2. Remove the obligation to teach in the Negro public free schools for one year in case students of law, medicine, engineering, pharmacy, journalism, and any other generally recognized college courses taught at the University of Texas.

Hiding behind the constitutional and practical restriction on funds for the University of Texas, legislators claimed that these restrictions made it impracticable to establish a respectable branch of the university for black Texans.

The legislature in 1947 provided for the establishment of "an entirely separate and equivalent university of the first class for Black Texans." The provisions of this act are:

> **Sec. 1.** The Legislature of Texas deems it impracticable to establish and maintain a college or branch of the University of Texas for the instruction of the colored youth of this State without the levy of taxes and the use of the general revenue for the establishment, maintenance and erection of buildings as would be required by Section 14 of Article VII of the Constitution of Texas, if such institution were established as a college or branch of the University of Texas. Further, the Legislature of Texas deems that establishment of a Negro University with such limitations as to funds and operation would be unfair and wholly inadequate for the purpose of providing an equivalent University of the first class for Negroes of this State. Therefore, it is the purpose of this Act to establish an entirely separate and equivalent University of the first class for Negroes with full rights to be the use of tax money and the general revenue for establishment, maintenance, erection of buildings and operation of such institution as provided in Section 48, Article III, of the Constitution of the State of Texas.

> **Sec. 2.** To provide instruction, training and higher education for colored people, there is hereby established a University of the first class in two divisions: the first, styled, "The Texas State University for Negroes," to be located in Houston . . . ; the second, to be styled "The Prairie View Agricultural and Mechanical College of Texas," at Prairie View . . . . At the Prairie View Agricultural and Mechanical College shall be offered courses in agriculture, the mechanical arts, engineering, and the natural sciences connected therewith, together with any other courses authorized at Prairie View at the time of the passage of this Act, all of which shall be equivalent to those offered at the Agriculture and Mechanical College of Texas. The Texas State University for Negroes shall offer all other courses of higher learning . . . all of which shall be equivalent to those offered at the University of Texas. Upon demand being made by an qualified applicant for any present or future courses of instruction offered at the University of Texas, or its branches, such courses shall be established or added to the curriculum of the appropriate division of the schools hereby established in order that the separate Universities for Negroes shall at all times offer equal educational opportunities and training as that available to other persons of this State . . .

Section 11 of the act provided for the establishment of an interim School of Law of the Texas State University for Negroes and made an emergency appropriation for that purpose.

The emergency clause declared that:

The fact that the people of Texas desire that the State meet its obligation of equal educational opportunities for its Negro citizens from State-supported institutions, and the fact that a separate and equivalent University of the first class for Negroes cannot be established and maintained under the limitations and restrictions contained in Section 14, Article VII, of the Constitution of Texas if such institution were made a college or branch of the University of Texas, and the fact that the only means of establishing an equivalent University of the first class for Negroes with use of tax money and the general revenue is to create a separate University entirely independent of the University of Texas, and the fact that interim courses must be established immediately by existing schools for the education of Negroes prior to the establishment and operation of said separate University of the first class for Negroes, creates an emergency and imperative public necessity . . . .

It is important to understand that this act guarantees to the Negroes of Texas in unmistakable terms "an equivalent University of the first class, courses . . . equivalent to those offered at the Agricultural and Mechanical College of Texas," and "all other courses of higher learning . . . all of which shall be equivalent to those offered at the University of Texas," and "at all times . . . equal education opportunities and training as that available to other persons of this State . . . ."

This disparity between the legal educational rights and privileges of the black Texans and the actual educational benefits afforded them gave rise to some significant court action in the Lone Star State. The first case came September 30, 1946. This case ended in a dismissal.

The second and most important case was the *Sweatt v. Painter* case. Heman Sweatt opened the doors for graduate and professional study with his case against the University of Texas. This suit moved legislators, who resisted all previous appeals, petitions, and prayers, to establish two universities "of the first class" for black citizens. The intended maintenance of segregated Jim Crow colleges and universities, however, did not materialize. In the spirit of Heman

Sweatt, in his rejection of the "basement law school," black Texans insisted that state-supported institutions should be color blind; there was not to be any institution labeled "for Negroes."

Establishment

Heman Marion Sweatt applied in February 1946 for admission to the law school at the University of Texas, the only public institution granting a law degree in Texas at that time. His application was refused by the university registrar and by President T. S. Painter, pending an opinion by Attorney General Grover Sellers, which had been solicited by the president of the University of Texas. Attorney General Sellers' opinion intimated that Sweatt was not eligible to enter the university law school at that particular time, but if equal educational advantages were not available within the state within a reasonable amount of time, he must be admitted.

Sweatt prepared and filed a suit in the District Court of Travis County and obtained an interlocutory writ to enter the School of Law. There was to be a period of suspension for six months to give the state an opportunity to establish a law school for black Texans as contemplated in the 1945 act of the legislature creating Prairie View University.

In December 1946 Sweatt's request for a writ of mandamus to enter the University of Texas Law School was denied. The denial was contingent upon the opening of a law school for black people at Houston. The law school was to be a branch of Prairie View University and the school was to have been opened in time for the second semester. The judgment claimed that such a school would make available to Sweatt legal training substantially equivalent to that offered at the University of Texas. Sweatt's attorney gave notice of an appeal to the Texas Court of Civil Appeals.

After the legislature, on March 3, 1947, had passed an act establishing a state university for Negroes in Houston, Attorney General Price Daniel asked the Court of Civil Appeals to remand to the trial court the case of Heman Marion Sweatt. The attorney general recited that in compliance with this law, the university Board of Regents had established an interim law school in Austin to function until the new university in Houston could assume that assignment. Sweatt resented the indignity, and rejected "separate education" as amoral in intent, grossly discriminatory in its provisions, and in no sense equal. His attorneys seized the opportunity to convert his case into a frontal attack on segregation. The Court of Civil Appeals remanded the case, and a new trial was set for April 28. Both the plaintiff and the state welcomed the opportunity to complete the records before appeal. There were several trials before the Third Court of Civil Appeals, but all failed to permit Sweatt to enter the University of Texas Law School.

The case went to the Supreme Court. On June 5, 1950, the U.S. Supreme Court ruled that Heman Sweatt "be admitted to the University of Texas Law School."

The Sweatt case attracted and united black groups outside the teaching profession — the National Association for the Advancement of Colored People, Voters League, political leaders, ministers, businessmen and women. All joined the cause and made contributions. There was general recognition by black people that the State of Texas was committing grave injustice in its refusal to provide them with the opportunity for graduate and professional study within the state's borders.

The constitutional provision for a university "when the Legislature deemed it practicable" was completely ignored for seventy years; no efforts had been made to give "colored youth" the university envisioned by drafters of the 1876 Constitution. Announcement of the lawsuit for admission to the University of Texas created a shock that immediately awakened the legislators. Within a year, the legislature had appropriated $2 million to establish two universities of the "first class." It was that kind of "turmoil" and "confusion" that ushered into being, in 1947, Texas Southern University.

Development

The growth and development of Texas Southern University depended largely upon the appropriation of the state legislature. A check of these appropriations reveals that from the outset, Texas Southern University received less support than the majority of state institutions of comparable size. To compensate for the fact that Texas Southern does not share in the University of Texas Systems Permanent Educational Fund, the university has always had to rely upon local contributions and alumni support. The university has periodically received small grants from individual businesses and from industrial foundations. These grants were, by and large, made in token amounts, large enough to be "respectable," but miniscule in comparison with grants from some businesses and industries to majority institutions. Business and industry have, thus far, simply not seen the wisdom or the fitness of their making sizable investments in a Texas Southern University, presumably because it was a minority institution, and did not seem capable of a major impact in the world of business and industry.

In 1977, as in the past, Texas Southern engaged in a fund-raising effort to supplement its budget. The Texas Southern University "Campaign 77" set a fundraising goal of $2 million. The campaign was launched April 2, 1977. According to Austin Coleman, public relations director at the university, "Texas Southern University has never received enough money in state appropriations to operate its programs. For years, we have needed to seek outside sources."

Accomplishments and Aspirations

Texas Southern has moved forward steadily since its beginning in 1947. By 1955, the university had gained accreditation from the Association of Schools and Colleges for Teacher Education. Its School of Law was approved by the State Board of Law Examiners and by the American Bar Association. The School of Pharmacy has been accredited by the American Council of Pharmaceutical Education. In 1955, the School of Business became an institutional entity, and the university had sponsored the beginnings of a modest extension program.

Certain of its faculty members, notably John T. Biggers in art, Henry A. Bullock in sociology, and John R. Sheeler in history, have achieved national and international reputations in their respective fields.

In 1955, there was a change in the university leadership, which underscored the commitment of the institution to continuing academic excellence as well as to viable community service. Samuel M. Nabrit, distinguished biologist and dean of the Graduate School at Atlanta University, became Texas Southern's second president. Nabrit's professional and administrative qualifications were impeccable, and his appointment did not have political overtones, which, fairly or unfairly, had insinuated themselves into the operations of the previous administration. The president brought to his office a prestige and pattern of educational accomplishment which made possible important new and meaningful connections for the university in the total academic community. Under Nabrit's leadership, the university grew as a special purpose university. Texas Southern, then, was "a special purpose institution of higher education" from the time of its establishment. The university's history supported with considerable weight the idea that the institution's philosophical and functional guideline had been the phrase "university of the first class," rather than a legal description rooted in the racial customs of a bygone period in the nation's history.

According to Lash, in a distinctive and particularly unique way during the recent years of turbulence in American society, the university served as an agency of educational involution and resolution of distinctive and unique societal prospects. The beginnings of a reordering of ethnic affairs in the nation gave birth to the institution, and its capacity for appropriate institutional responses to the reordering process shaped and conditioned the development of its academic and service programs. In a modern national and international society which would validate and implement cultural pluralism as an avowed and viable goal, a special-purpose institution of higher education — Texas Southern — was an available resource of power and promise.

In 1977, Texas Southern University was one of America's leading minority-oriented higher institutions. It was steadily gaining in leverage and credibility as a center of academic activities related to international education. The university's location in Houston, Texas, placed it in a strategic site of overseas trade, commerce, and cultural diversity. The institution's growing programmatic and service connections with elements of the international community identified the university more and more with those interests and concerns which focused on dynamic components of growth and development in those awakening nations which are seeking to actualize what were their latent and incipient national assets. The university's international associations and commitments were being steadily verified and credentialed in Middle East, African, Caribbean, and South American nations, and Texas Southern's name and program were known at least nominally in Japan and in The People's Republic of China. The university had experienced a quadrupling of the number of its international students in residence over the past half-decade, and the institution has had sizable numbers of both intern students and committed graduates on overseas assignments.

Texas Southern's international connections had brought the institution nearer and nearer to the forefront of international educational activities, especially with reference to its status as a predominantly black American higher education establishment with definite and substantive overseas involvements. The size and extent of these involvements, while modest and still unfolding, were enough to suggest that the university possessed great potential as something of a unique agency of international education, and that it had particular promise for educational training and service to Third World countries and entities.

This suggestion was borne out by several cases. The university had sponsored a continuing Teacher Corps/Peace Corps Program which had supplied trained professional workers to designated African countries. Texas Southern was the key institution in a Texas-based consortium of higher institutions allied in an International Studies Program. In 1976, Texas Southern was selected as one of eight American minority-oriented institutions to conduct special training programs for Nigerian nationals as part of the plan of the Nigerian government to effectuate a substantial increase in the availability of higher education to the citizens of that country. It was significant here that the university had, in effect, become a "professional training ground for professional trainers" of sophisticated Nigerian manpower, so that the given training programs had a built-in ripple effect on the meaning of a trained workforce in that developing nation.

These and other relevant persuasives did suggest to the university administration that Texas Southern was to give more thought and attention to the status and prospects of the institution's international involvements. A pattern of significant university out-of-country activities emerged and was verified and certified by institutional cooperations and joint engagements with overseas governments and other entities. Texas Southern officials were convinced, then, that their university had reached a critical point in both its philosophical and its implemental commitments to appropriate structures and programs in international education at the collegiate, graduate, and professional levels. Texas Southern, a minority-oriented American higher institution, was in position to utilize its history. The experiential expertise, the present and potential training know-how in the specific behalf of developing countries, all made possible a new and substantial era in international higher education.

In 1973, through a special act of the Texas Legislature, Texas Southern was designated a "special purpose institution of higher education for urban programming." The bill making the university a special purpose institution was signed into law by Governor Dolph Briscoe on June 17, 1973.

In 1977, Texas Southern, led by Granville M. Sawyer, had assumed full leadership as a special-purpose institution of higher education. As such, it had provided instruction, research programs, and services as they were appropriate to its designation of "special-purpose."

By 1977, Texas Southern University had experienced an almost unexponential pattern of growth. In 1947 the student body numbered 2,300. By 1968, twenty-one years later, the enrollment had grown to more than 4,600, double the 1947 figure. More than 9,100 students were enrolled for the spring semester 1977 and a projected enrollment for fall 1980 was 11,000.

Summary and Conclusions

It was the purpose of this study to trace the development of higher education for black Texans from the time of inception of the first institution in 1872 to the year of 1977. The forces which gave rise to the development of higher education for black Texans were primarily twofold.

The most prolific forces which gave rise to higher education for blacks in Texas were religious organizations. The oldest college to be established in the state of Texas by Methodist churches was established by the African Methodist Episcopal Church Conferences. Paul Quinn College was founded in Austin, Texas, by a small group of African Methodist preachers in 1872. The college was later moved to Waco, Texas, where it continued as an institution of higher education in 1977.

There were three other colleges founded by various Methodist Conferences in Texas. Texas College was founded by the Christian Methodist Episcopal Church at Tyler, Texas, in 1894. In 1977 Texas College had an enrollment of more than 500 students. Samuel Huston College was founded in Austin, Texas, by the United Methodist Conferences in 1876. In 1953, Tillotson College was merged with Samuel Huston and the merger of the two denominational schools (Samuel Huston, the United Methodist Church; Tillotson, the Congregational Church) established the coeducational college known as Huston-Tillotson. In 1977, the college reported an enrollment of 696 students.

Wiley College was founded in 1882 by the Freedman's Aid Society. The school was later merged with the United Methodist Church. Wiley College was the first black college west of the Mississippi River to be granted an "A" rating from the Southern Association of Colleges and Secondary Schools.

The Baptist Conventions and Associations were responsible for the establishment of four institutions which were included in this study. The oldest Baptist college was Bishop College. Bishop College was founded in 1881 by a group of illiterate ex-slaves and a group of missionaries from the Home Mission Society of the Northern Baptist Convention. Bishop College operated in Marshall, Texas, from 1881 to 1961. The college was moved to Dallas, Texas, in September 1961. In 1977, Bishop College was the fastest growing, church-related, predominately black college in Texas.

Guadalupe College was established in 1884 at Seguin, Texas, by the Guadalupe Baptist Missionary Association. The college operated in Seguin from 1884 to 1936. In 1936, the college was destroyed by fire. The school was moved to San Antonio following the fire, where it was still operating in 1977, as a Bible seminary.

Conroe College, a predominately religious institution, was founded in 1903. In 1977, the college continued to operate but without state certification. Its only students were minister trainees.

Butler College, the youngest Baptist-sponsored, black educational institution, was founded in 1905 at Tyler, Texas, by the East Texas Baptist Association. Butler College did not develop beyond the status of a junior college. Due to financial problems the school closed in 1969.

The Catholic Diocese of Texas founded a school for black students in 1898. Bishop James Steptol was the founder. The school was named St. Phillips College. In 1942, St. Phillips ceased to function as a private institution, becoming a municipal junior college through an affiliation with the San Antonio College under the auspices of the San Antonio Independent School District.

In 1904, Jarvis Christian College was founded through a cooperative effort of black and white missionary women of the United Christian Church. In 1977, Jarvis Christian College was the second most rapidly growing black church-related school in Texas.

The Churches of Christ founded Southwestern Christian College in Fort Worth in 1948. The school moved to Terrell in 1949. The school operates today as a junior college.

Mary Allen College was founded in 1866 for the training of black girls. The Presbyterian Synod founders of the school withdrew their support during World War II. In 1948, the institution was owned and operated by a black Baptist association. Due to declining enrollment and acute financial problems, Mary Allen closed its doors in 1971. The school never really reached full college status and was included in this study only because of its cultural and historical value. Since this is true, Paul Quinn and not Mary Allen is considered the oldest institution of higher education for black Texans.

The other forces which gave rise to the development of higher education for black people in Texas was found in the state government. The two schools established were Prairie View A&M University in 1876 in Waller County, and Texas Southern University, established in 1947, in Houston, Texas, thus becoming the last educational institution established for the higher education of black people "only" in Texas.

·The Northern white missionaries and philanthropists were significant forces which gave rise to higher education for blacks in Texas. The aid from white Southern missionaries and philanthropists did not come in any significant amounts until early in the 1960s. Since 1960, support by whites in Texas has increased but not in any monumental proportion. Private schools seem to have received more support than did the public or state-supported schools.

Black legislators who have served in the legislature from 1868 to 1977 have all shown an interest in education for the black people of Texas. It would seem that they did exert sincere effort with minimal success.

There were divergences of opinions and fluctuating attitudes reflected in the legislative enactments, particularly from 1866 to 1876, because of the opposition of whites to any kind of education for blacks at that time, because of the bitter fighting between the "Radical" Republicans and the Democrats, and a general feeling of prejudice toward the freed slaves.

The black people of Texas seem to have been willing to try to provide for the future of their race through higher education. During the period from the 1870s to the 1930s, Texas black people had very little or no money, but through unexplainable efforts, they were able to establish more than twenty-three educational institutions of higher education. These institutions of higher education were founded by people who were illiterate, people who through church organizations and individual effort significantly aided the cause of higher education for black Texans.

In 1977 there were thirteen schools of higher education which were founded by church organizations still in operation. Two of these schools have shown significant growth and progress: Bishop College, Dallas, Texas, and Jarvis College, Hawkins, Texas. The growth and progress of the other colleges has been stable. They seemed to be meeting a special need in a unique manner.

The two state schools, Prairie View A&M University at Prairie View, Texas, and Texas Southern University at Houston, Texas, have both exceeded all contemporary expectations. In 1977, Prairie View was one hundred years old and was still a part of the Texas A&M University System. Its annual operating budget exceeded $25 million and its enrollment was approximately 6,000. The physical plant had grown to more than 150 buildings valued at an estimated $40 million. Its services covered the length and breadth of Texas.

By 1977, Texas Southern University had become an international and intercultural university with the "special purpose" designation. The university was experiencing, it did seem, above-average growth. The enrollment increased from 2,303 in 1947 to over 9,100 in 1977. The contemporary framework of Texas Southern University seems to have addressed itself to the urban society and to international affairs.

In 1977, Texas had more institutions of higher education either founded by black people, operated by black people, or designed predominately for black people than any other state in the United States of America.

Among black Texans, there seemed to have been an optimism about the future of those institutions, which have somehow survived many adverse circumstances for the past century. With good leadership, increased support from business, industry, philanthropists, the state legislature, and the United Negro College Fund, Texas black higher educational institutions should survive to serve and meet special needs of those Texans, black or white, who have a particular need for years to come.

Chapter 12

A History of African-American Higher Education in Austin and Travis County, Texas

by David A. Williams

Introduction

This chapter traces the development of higher education for African Americans in Austin and Travis County, Texas. Forces which gave rise to the development of higher education for African Americans in Austin and Travis County were singular in origin. There were no overt attempts made by state, federal, or local governments to provide for such education in Austin and Travis County. The Methodist and Congregational churches (American Missionary Association) were the two organizations after the Civil War to successfully provide institutions of higher learning for persons of African descent.

Private higher education for African-American Texans was first established in Texas in 1866 with the founding of Mary Allen College at Crockett, Texas. Mary Allen (originally Mary Allen Seminary) was founded to provide training for girls of African descent. The college was founded largely through the efforts of Samuel

Dr. Rueben Shannon Lovinggood, second president of Samuel Huston College.
— TAAHO Collections, Austin, Texas

Samuel Huston, philanthropist for whom the school is named.
— TAAHO Collections, Austin, Texas

Fisher Tenney. Due to declining enrollment and acute financial problems, Mary Allen closed its doors May 1971.

From 1866 to 1912, a total of thirteen institutions of higher education were established in Texas by religious organizations. Two of those institutions were located in Austin, Texas; namely, Tillotson College and Samuel Huston College.

Rev. George Jeffrey Tillotson moved to Texas from Connecticut in the early 1900s. He sought to establish a school somewhere in the South where young people of African descent could be trained to become schoolteachers. Reverend Tillotson observed the intense struggle that was the African-American Texan's following the dark days of slavery. He felt the need for their being well educated beyond public school. His concerns led to the founding of Tillotson College in 1877.

Samuel Huston College was founded in Dallas, Texas, in 1876 by Rev. George W. Richardson, a Methodist minister. The school was first located in Dallas. The Methodist Episcopal Church West Texas Conference supported the school. In 1898 Samuel Huston was moved to Austin and began operating in 1900. In 1952, Tillotson College and Samuel Huston College were merged into one institution. This historical narrative relates the development of these two institutions of higher education.

It was the purpose of this study:

1. To determine the role of African-American church personalities in the development of these institutions;
2. To determine the forces that gave rise to the development of the higher educational institutions for African Americans in Austin and Travis County; and,
3. To ascertain significant roles of Anglo-American church personalities in the development of these institutions.

It was the purpose of this narrative to answer the following questions:

1. When did each institution begin and what are some influential factors? What are some significant related events?
2. Who were the significant individuals involved?
3. What institutions, events, or organizations were involved in the early history?
4. Where are the institutions cited in the narrative?

Left:
*Dr. John Q. Taylor King, Sr.,
chancellor, president emeritus, Huston-
Tillotson College.*
   — TAAHO Collections, Austin, Texas

Below:
*Left to right: Dr. J. J. Seabrook, president retired, Huston-Tillotson College;
Florence Temple; V. C. Dallas; Henry
Wilder.*
   — TAAHO Collections, Austin, Texas

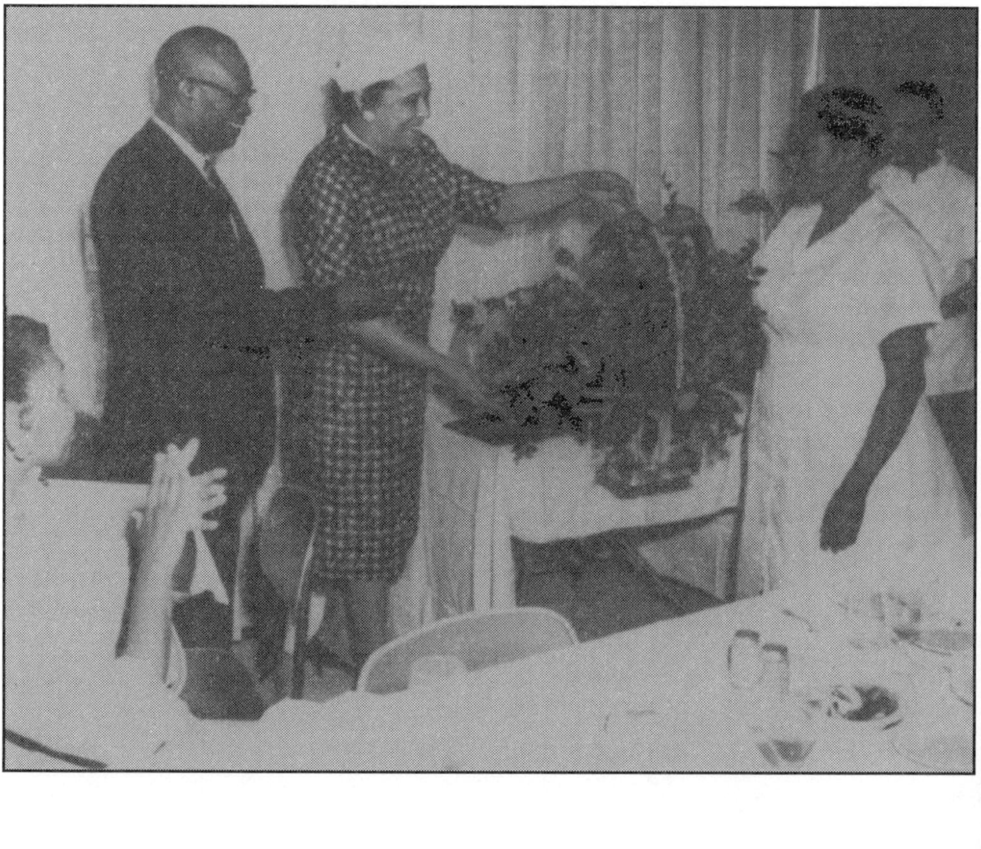

1965, Huston-Tillotson President Seabrook's retirement reception. Left to right: Dr. J. J. Seabrook; Mrs. J. J. Seabrook; Mrs. Marcet King; Dr. John Q. Taylor King, Sr.; Dr. McKrakin; unidentified trustee.
— TAAHO Collections, Austin, Texas

5.   How was each institution related to the community, region, county, and state?

This narrative was needed to provide the Travis County Historical Commission with an understanding of the origin and development of higher education for African Americans in Austin and Travis County so that a state historical marker could be obtained in recognition of such. The early efforts of African Americans and Anglo Americans in this very significant undertaking need to be recognized so an appreciation of these institutions can be established and can finally become a part of the history and folklore of Austin, Travis County, Texas, and beyond.

The focus of this narrative was limited to the institutions of higher education which were founded by or for African Americans and were located in Austin and Travis County.

Sources of Information

To determine the historical development of higher education for African Americans in Austin and Travis County, research studies which have been written regarding such institutions were examined. Many valuable sources were found at the Downs-Jones Library on the Huston-Tillotson College campus, Carver Library, and Texas State Historical Commission. A review of the collection of *College Catalogs* of the two institutions studied was made to ascertain valuable historical information. Visits were made to the library of Huston-Tillotson College to collect data and conduct personal interviews.

Some general works concerned with the history of higher education in Austin and Travis County were used to provide background for the narrative. Six particularly valuable sources in this area were: Chrystine I. Shackles, *Reminiscences of Huston-Tillotson College*; Williams, *Bricks Without Straw: A History of Higher Education for Black Texans 1877-1977*; Webb, *Handbook of Texas*; Walker, Doty, and Freeman, *Evans Industrial Hall, Huston-Tillotson College, November 1981*; United States Department of the Interior, National Park Service, *National Register of Historic Places Nomination Form*, submitted July 28, 1985; Trammell, Crow, *Huston-Tillotson College, Use Plan for the Renovated Old Administration Building*, 1985. These were all excellent sources and are highly recommended.

A number of other sources were also used to obtain information regarding the general history of higher education in Texas as well as Austin and Travis County. They were as follows: Alwyn Barr, *Black Texans*; Vernon McDaniel, *History of the Teachers State Association of Texas*; Fredrick Eby, *The Development of Education in Texas*; Fred L. Brownlee, *New Day Ascending: Our American Missionary Heritage*; Tillotson College, *Catalogues of Tillotson College, 1911-1912*; Basil Matthews, *Booker T. Washington, Educator and Interracial Interpreter*; Huston-Tillotson College, *Ram's Guide: Helpful Information for Better College Living*; Frank W. Johnson, *A History of Texas and Texans*; and W. C. Nunn, *Texas Under the Car-*

*Dr. T. R. Downing, president,
Samuel Huston College.*
— TAAHO Collections, Austin, Texas

petbaggers. All of these proved to be very good sources of useful material. Complete bibliographic information on these sources may be obtained in the bibliography section.

Tillotson College

Tillotson College was founded in 1875 upon an earlier secondary school sponsored by the American Missionary Association. The college was made possible by Rev. George Jeffrey Tillotson, a retired minister of Wetherfield, Connecticut. Tillotson selected the site where the college was to be built.

The same year Tillotson was founded, two significant African Americans were born. They were Mary McLeod Bethune and Carter G. Woodson. Both made monumental contributions to African-American education in the United States. Also in 1875, the Fisk Jubilee Singers raised enough money to construct the first important building at Fisk University. That same year saw the expansion of the railroad network which would be the primary source of transportation used by many students who would travel to Austin to attend Tillotson College.

When the college was chartered in 1877, it was known simply as Tillotson Collegiate and Normal Institute. The school for persons of African descent was built and maintained by the American Missionary Association of Congregational Churches. Tillotson Institute was the brainchild of Rev. George Jeffrey Tillotson, a Congregational minister who had been educated at Yale College and Yale Divinity School, and who served congregations in Connecticut and Massachusetts some forty-five years before deciding to establish a school for African Americans in the Southwest.

The purpose of the institution was the training of African-American teachers, and after consulting with the American Mis-

Evans Hall under construction, Tillotson College, 1911.
— TAAHO Collections, Austin, Texas

Evans Hall, completed 1912.
— TAAHO Collections, Austin, Texas

sionary Association, Tillotson chose to focus his attention on Austin, Texas, where a Mrs. Garland had cooperated with the Association in running Austin's first African-American school. Tillotson bought acreage east of the State Cemetery and opened Tillotson Collegiate and Normal Institute, the first African-American college in the Southwest.

The Institute opened on January 17, 1881, with most of its 250 students coming from the Austin area. Initially, instruction was directed towards the primary grades, but the intention of the founders and faculty clearly was to develop "a strong college-preparatory course with some attempts to build up a collegiate department." Industrial training was introduced and taught in a two-and-one-half-story frame building which had been constructed in 1887; religious and moral instruction was emphasized in a program that was intended to "develop the best in life and character."

In these and other particulars, Tillotson Institute was very much like other black schools such as Tuskegee in Alabama or Hampton in Virginia, where the first students knew how to read but had received nothing approximating a college-preparatory education; and where industrial and technical training was not only emphasized for its practical benefits but also used as a pedagogical vehicle. However, the resemblance between Tillotson and other, older black institutes in the South stopped at this point. New buildings appeared on the campus with regularity — Allen Hall in 1881, Beard Hall in 1894, Evans Industrial Hall in 1912, and the Administration Building in 1914. But the programs which occurred in those buildings and, indeed, the constituency of the students changed dramatically between 1881 and the 1950s. While the school announced a full four-year college course as early as 1888, it was not recognized as an accredited junior college by the Texas Department of Education until 1925. A year later, Tillotson became a woman's college, and in 1930, after the high school was discontinued, Tillotson was given senior college standing. In 1935, Tillotson changed once again to a coeducational institution, and in 1943, it was granted an "A" rating by the Southern Association of Colleges.

One of the most significant changes in the organization of Tillotson College was initiated when a representative of the Tillotson-affiliated American Missionary Association and a representative of the Methodist Board of Education discussed the possibility of a merger between Tillotson and nearby Samuel Huston College, founded in 1900 by the West Texas Conference of the Methodist Church. The merger was completed on October 24, 1952, and the name of the resulting institution became Huston-Tillotson College.

Tillotson College and the Issue of Industrial Education

While the overall development of Tillotson College reflected economic uncertainties common to colleges in general as well as varying opinions about the necessity for specific programs, the commitment of the school to industrial education was unwavering until the 1920s. A facility for teaching industrial classes had been constructed by 1887, and Evans Industrial Hall was largely completed in 1912.

Like many African-American colleges around 1900, Tillotson made no secret of its interest in manual training:

> We believe that industrial training should have a large place in our scheme of education. It teaches careful observation and accuracy in calculation and expression, forms habits of industry, strengthens confidence and decision and cultivates a correct estimate of values in life. It not only tends to usefulness and thrift, but has an important part in the development of mind and character.

Contained within this statement in the 1911–12 college *Catalogue* were most of the concepts and key words which typified the state of American industrial education in the first decade of the twentieth century. Industrial training, the *Catalogue* proclaimed, not only produced students with practical skills; it also helped to inculcate proper attitudes, a sense of values, and the habits of industry and thrift. Additionally, industrial training was, like any academic course of study, a vehicle for learning and a method for the development of such mental skills and "accurate, intelligent and truthful observation." As historian August Meir wrote in 1963, such a program generally was thought to

> [supply] a pedagogical aid for mental development; ... [serve] as a moral discipline inculcating habits of thrift and industry, a sense of the dignity of labor, and a feeling of economic independence; [and] ... [prepare] students to earn their living through the trades ...

Also included within the brief description of the objectives of

Tillotson College's industrial program were many of the salient points raised by two radically different philosophies of African-American education current around the turn of the century. Expressed simply, a great many African Americans in late nineteenth-century and early twentieth-century America believed that industrial education was the key to economic prosperity and general social and moral improvement. Other African-American leaders believed that members of their race, like those of other more privileged groups, should be able to acquire a broad liberal arts education. Furthermore, they believed that it was only by the creation of an indigenous leadership of businessmen and scholars that the greater number of African Americans would advance economically and culturally.

The attraction of industrial training, though well-established in American African-American colleges by 1900, was neither a twentieth-century nor a strictly African-American issue. European educational theories which espoused agricultural and industrial training had found favor in the United States by 1850, and those theories became the foundation for sweeping educational changes in black and white colleges after the Civil War, when industry entered an era of explosive growth.

Black interest in industrial education occurred as early as the 1830s, and certain African-American leaders, motivated by economic realities, stated at the Rochester Convention of 1853 that economic progress, "based on mutual self-help and racial cooperation, was a practical program for racial elevation and the achievement of citizenship rights." White technical schools such as Rensselaer, Lawrence, and Sheffield found their African-American counterparts in Hampton Institute in Virginia (1868), Tougaloo College in Mississippi (1870), and Atlanta University in Georgia (1871), all of which offered programs which had been inaugurated by the American Missionary Association. Undoubtedly, the most widely known of the programs was that initiated by Booker T. Washington at Tuskegee in 1881 where, thirty years later, the Institute *Catalogue* noted that the purpose of the Department of Mechanical Industries was to provide opportunities for young men to study a trade or vocation, to achieve a sense of the dignity of labor, obtain aid in paying all or part of their educational expenses, and to acquire the training necessary to be industrial leaders. Courses included carpentry; brick masonry, plastering, and tile setting; brickmaking; and tinsmithing.

Simultaneously, many black leaders and their white supporters were anxious to demonstrate that African Americans possessed the capacity for the most advanced intellectual endeavors. At a meeting in Washington, D.C., in 1890, black educators insisted on the need for higher as well as industrial education, and after 1900, blacks such as W. E. B. DuBois became increasingly critical of industrial education and impassioned about the need to educate and develop the African-American race's exceptional men.

That both concerns — for industrial and for "cultural" education — were topics of considerable local discussion well after 1900 was demonstrated on the editorial pages of *The Austin Statesman*. In March 1912, during the time when Evans Industrial Hall was nearing completion, five separate editorials appeared about the subject. While most of the comments stemmed from activities at white educational institutions, nonetheless they probably reflected public opinion about industrial programs in general. Coming down heavily on the side of "cultural" education initially, the *Statesman* editor noted colleges and universities were a significant factor in the development, enlargement, and elevation of American life. Such institutions had the potential for "giving currency to higher ideas and ideals, laying emphasis on character and service," and training students to be "at home in the wor[l]ds of nature, industry, art, history, literature and philosophy." Woe be to those schools which placed "undue stress . . . on vocational effort and proper attention is not paid to cultural subjects that tend to develop the student's ability to think clearly and reason sanely."

On the national scene, passions waxed hot between the two camps as the New York City Board of Education voted unanimously to revise the public school curriculum to eliminate trade classes. Apparently the board agreed with the opinion of Dr. Henry VanDyke, who believed that true education "aims not at a marketable product but as a vital development," and that "the important question about our educational institutions is, 'Not what they teach, but how do they prepare us to learn.'" In Texas, Dallas businessman G. W. Owens also opposed the new courses of study in that city such as domestic science and manual training, and lobbied against them passionately.

A summary editorial in *The Austin Statesman* of March 19,

1912, attempted to reconcile these varying viewpoints, again point-ing to the differences between colleges such as Amherst, which was reaffirming its belief in a strictly "cultural" course of study, and other institutions which were revising their programs to include vo-cational training. However, rather than insist that the two extremes were irreconcilable, the paper noted that schools such as the Univer-sity of Texas were attempting to achieve workable compromises so that students could "get cultural elements into and cultural values out of an education which shall prepare men and women for some definite contribution to the world's work and welfare."

Industrial Training at Tillotson College: The Construction of Evans Industrial Hall

The planning and construction of Evans Industrial Hall on the Tillotson campus in the fall of 1911 and spring of 1912 was an ex-pression of the college's belief in the value of manual training. How-ever, the college *Catalogue* made it clear that industrial training was not an end in itself, nor was it offered to the exclusion of other, more "cultural" subjects. "Industrial training and academic studies," the *Catalogue* stated, were to be "joined closely head and hand and one in spirit."

The construction of Evans Hall was made possible by the mon-etary gifts of an Austin resident and member of the Tillotson Board of Trustees. Born in 1844 in Piermont, New Hampshire, Ira Hobart Evans was typical of many capitalists and philanthropists who may or may not have entertained ideas of racial equality, but who did believe in African-American education and/or manual training.

Educated in Vermont, Evans served in the Union Army during the Civil War and then was detailed in a two-year term on the border of Texas and Mexico. After a brief and unsuccessful venture at stock raising about 100 miles northwest of Corpus Christi, Evans worked for the United States Internal Revenue Service along the border. Then, at the urging of friends, he began a brief but illustrious career as a politician, serving as the Republican representative of the West-ern District of Texas and then as Speaker of the Texas House of Representatives in 1870. In December 1871, Major Evans left politi-cal life and became involved with the various business enterprises which occupied his attention for the next half century. In chrono-

Woodworking class, Evans Industrial Building, Tillotson College.
— TAAHO Collections, Austin, Texas

logical order, he was elected general manager of the Texas Land Company, secretary of the Houston & Great Northern Railroad Company, secretary of the Consolidated International & Great Northern Railroad Company, and president of the New York & Texas Land Company. He was an organizer and director of the Austin National Bank and, after 1881, he served on the Tillotson Board of Trustees until 1920, just three years before his death in Austin on April 19, 1923.

At some point before 1912, a fund-raising drive by Tillotson College culminated in a conditional gift from Ira Evans sufficient to begin construction on a new industrial hall. *The Austin Statesman* reported in the middle of November 1911 that "an industrial building of concrete blocks to cost $6,000 has been started on the Tillotson College campus . . ." One month later, the walls began to rise until, by January, the walls, front porch, and chimneys were completed. In February, the roof was added, and a month later, the *Statesman* noted that "the three-story addition to Tillotson College which was begun some months ago is nearing completion. The

Ira H. Evans gave large contributions for construction of Evans Hall at Tillotson College.
— TAAHO Collections, Austin, Texas

structure is of cement blocks and will cost something like $7,000. It is to be used as a manual training building."

While detailed information about the planning, design, and construction of Evans Industrial Hall is not known, at least two features of its creation deserve attention. First, it seems likely that the superintendent of the Boys' Industrial Department at Tillotson College, Clement Laird Wild, was the architect and general contractor for Evans Hall. Oral tradition that Wild was brought from Tuskegee or Hampton Institute to perform such services could not be substantiated by an examination of enrollment or faculty lists at either school, but the fact that Wild was present in Austin only during the year when the hall was begun and completed tends to support the conclusion that he was at the college specifically to direct construction of the building.

The second salient feature of the construction of Evans Hall was the fact that students participated in the project. Articles in *The Austin Statesman* and Tillotson *Catalogue* of 1911-12 noted that industrial students had participated in the fabrication of the cement blocks which later were used in the construction of the walls as well as in the building itself. Such participation extended to the completion of other buildings on or near the Tillotson campus, such as the Durden House at 807 Comal, built for a faculty member, and the Administration Building.

By 1912, Evans Industrial Hall was incomplete on the interior, but it was usable for classes. In general, the layout of each floor was open and spacious, suitable for the industrial classes which were held there. On the first floor a door on the west end gave entrance to

Typical biology classes at Tillotson College between 1910 and 1920.
— TAAHO Collections, Austin, Texas

a broad central hallway, on either side of which were large workshop rooms. One large workroom was located across the back or east end of the building in which students worked with the various types of mechanical machinery and automobile parts in repair and engineering classes. This pattern of rooms was followed on the second floor as well, where the woodworking room was located. Until additional interior partitions were made and ceilings enclosed, rafters were exposed and the roof structure of the two lower floors was supported by free-standing wooden columns. Since there were no interior restrooms, facilities were located outside the building on a ridge where Jackson-Moody Humanities Building is presently sited.

Photographs, personal reminiscences of individuals long-associated with the college, and lists of classes in college catalogues suggest that most significant changes to Evans Industrial Hall occurred after 1925, when the college became a women's school, and in the 1930s and 1940s, when less emphasis was placed on industrial arts and more on subjects such as home economics and various formal sciences. President Mary E. Branch (1930–45), for example, was responsible for moving home economics, chemistry, and biological

Stenography class at Tillotson College.
— TAAHO Collections, Austin, Texas

sciences into Evans Hall. During her administration, many out-standing black dentists, pharmacists, doctors, home economics teachers, and tailors received their initial training in Evans Hall.

Changes in the content of the classes taught in Evans Industrial Hall resulted in a number of interior alterations to the building. On the first floor, partitions of cement block, fiberboard, and gypsum board were added as bathrooms were installed and smaller class-rooms were required. The south room was divided up, and typing and business classes were taught there. Photographs indicate the presence of chemistry and electronics laboratories on the first floor as well.

Tillotson College's fine Home Economics and Home and Family Life courses were taught on the second floor of Evans Hall beginning in the 1930s, when domestic arts classes, such as sewing, were located in rooms on the south side of the building, and domes-tic sciences, such as cooking, were located on the north side. On the northwest side of Evans Hall, a demonstration dining room was cre-ated where special dinners were served and receptions were held. On the northeast side, a kitchen was installed; and after 1952, when Tillotson and Samuel Huston colleges were joined, custom-made furnishings and equipment were taken from Eliza Dee Hall at the latter school and reinstalled in Evans Hall.

In June 1942, a fire damaged portions of the southeast room on the second floor of the Hall and use of the building decreased. In the following years, some courses were discontinued while some were moved to other buildings on campus. However, the structural soundness of the Hall made it appropriate for certain incidental uses, and so in the 1970s a Black Heritage Exhibit was housed there and, more recently, a portion of the first floor served as a book depository.

By 1980, despite a decrease in actual use of Evans Industrial Hall, the administration of Huston-Tillotson College had realized that Evans could be renovated, and that it was the oldest structure still standing on the campus. Subsequently, the Hall was nominated to the National Register of Historic Places in 1981, and plans were formulated for its preservation and adaptive re-use. These plans not only reflected an awareness of the original commitment of Tillotson College to industrial training, but also demonstrated an appreciation for the evolution and changing emphasis of the school as reflected in classes taught in Evans Industrial Hall. The College had expressed in a substantive way its interest in the preservation of the most historically significant building on the Huston-Tillotson campus.

Tillotson College first opened its doors on January 17, 1881, with 250 students, chiefly in the lower grades. Allen Hall was the first building; Beard Hall was constructed in 1894. In 1947, there were fourteen buildings on a campus of twenty-three acres located in historic East Austin, an area lying east of downtown and north of the Colorado River, between East Seventh and Eleventh streets.

William E. Brooks was the first president (1881-85). His successor was John Hershaw (1886). Henry L. Lubbell succeeded Hershaw (1886-89). In 1889, William M. Brown became president and his term of service as president ended in 1893. The other presidents were: Winfield S. Goss (1894-95), Marshall R. Gaines (1896-1904), Arthur W. Partch (1905-06), Isaac M. Agard (1907-18), and Francis W. Fletcher (1919-23). J. T. Hodges was the first African American to serve as president (1924-29), and was followed by Mary E. Branch (1930-44), and William H. Jones (1944-52).

The Old Administration Building — Tillotson College

The Old Administration Building has prominent historical significance as one of the two original buildings remaining from the Tillotson Campus. It was built between 1913 and 1914 with concrete blocks manufactured by Tillotson College students in Evans Industrial Hall as part of an industrial training program.

The Old Administration Building is proposed for renovation as an administrative facility for Huston-Tillotson College. The building will represent an aesthetic and architectural complement to Evans Hall and serve as the new focal point and symbolic finial of the expanded thirty-acre campus described in the college's comprehensive master plan. It will serve as a memorial to the college's rich heritage and a symbol of the college's commitment to renewal of educational opportunity for the twenty-first century.

The exterior of the renovated building will be restored to its original subtle but majestic splendor depicting the distinctive "modified prairie" architecture typical of the urban Southwest during the early twentieth century. The college will seek the appropriate historical designations of the city of Austin, the state of Texas, and the federal government. The interior of the building will be renovated to preserve the distinctive character of the building, with high-pressed metal ceilings, hardwood floors, and prominent wooden staircases and door trims. The renovation will also promote state-of-the-art accessibility, office technology, and energy efficiency.

The building will provide office space for various central administrative functions which are currently housed in Agard-Lovinggood Classroom-Administration Building.

The first floor of the building will house the offices of Enrollment and Retention Services, along with a Heritage Room. Many of the larger spaces will be divided into smaller office areas for the dean of enrollment and retention services, student recruiters, clerical staff, and the financial aid director and assistant director. The Heritage Room will function as an archive where photographs, historical documents, and recognition plaques for major donors will be on display.

The second floor will consist of a large meeting room for the Board of Trustees, community organizations, and campus groups. It will also include a small kitchen area. Office space for the vice-president of institutional advancement and for the programs within that

Administration Building, Huston-Tillotson College, 1968.
— TAAHO Collections, Austin, Texas

administrative unit will be provided, including the Alumni Affairs director and administrative assistant, the director of College Development, and clerical staff.

The top floor is designed as the Presidential Suite. It will include the offices of the president, the vice-president of planning and research, the dean of administrative services, and the president's secretary, receptionist, and administrative assistant.

Huston-Tillotson College

Huston-Tillotson College, chartered in 1952, represents the merger of Samuel Huston and Tillotson College. Tillotson College was founded in 1875 upon an earlier secondary school sponsored by the American Missionary Association. The college was made possible by Rev. George Jeffrey Tillotson, a retired minister of Wetherfield, Connecticut, who selected the site.

Allen-Fraizer women's dormitory, Huston-Tillotson College.
— TAAHO Collections, Austin, Texas

Samuel Huston College was organized by Rev. George Warren Richardson in 1876 at Dallas, Texas. The school was adopted as the educational institution of the West Texas Conference of the Methodist Episcopal Church. In 1890, it moved to Austin and was renamed for Samuel Huston, a farmer from Marengo, Iowa, who donated gifts to erect the first building, Lovinggood Hall.

The proposal for a merger between Tillotson College and Samuel Huston College was completed on January 26, 1952, by the trustees of both colleges, and the charter document was signed on October 24, 1952. Huston-Tillotson College was established on the site of the Tillotson College campus, located between Seventh and Chicon streets in East Austin. The capital city of Texas is a rich, urban area which affords access to numerous cultural enterprises, state government, research and development, military installations, and a variety of businesses and industries.

Huston-Tillotson College, committed to the historical traditions of its predecessor institutions, provides a quality of education which comprehensively prepares its students for academic achievement, career exploration and preparation, public and community service. It is a private, coeducational institution which reaffirms its mission as a four-year baccalaureate degree granting college of liberal arts. The student body represents a microcosm of the multiethnic, international community. The college is dedicated to its purpose of providing a program which addresses the necessary skills, knowledge, experiences, and attitudes essential for success in the twenty-first century.

Industrial building, Samuel Huston College.
— TAAHO Collections, Austin, Texas

Samuel Huston College

The saga of Samuel Huston College is one of adventure, drama, and vicarious undertaking. Perhaps the entire development of this wonderful institution would have been dramatically different had not the spirit of concern and Christian charity consumed one Rev. George W. Richardson and his devoted family.

In 1876, Samuel Huston College was founded in the basement of Saint Paul Methodist Episcopal Church, Dallas, Texas. The Reverend Richardson, a member of the Minnesota Annual Conference, became the school's first executive officer.

The formative years of the college in Dallas were years of uncertainty and peril. In retrospect, one can see that in 1876 the clouds of "separate but equal" were forming over the nation and even more so in the Lone Star State. Following reconstruction, practically all political rights given the African American resulting from the Civil War were retracted.

In Texas, the public education of the African American was disgraceful. Higher education, comparatively speaking, was even worse. Consequently, the Methodists, black and white, in the West

Texas Conference felt an urgent need in these critical times to establish a suitable college to educate young people of color.

The school fund for blacks in Texas was slightly more than that of other Southern states, approximately $5 per pupil. For Massachusetts, it was $27 per student. In those critical years, if public education had been the only source of public education for those poor blacks, it would have been almost disastrous in Texas, for while there were many cities with well-regulated schools, many blacks lived in the Colorado and Brazos river bottoms, where too often the teachers themselves were poorly prepared. One only had to observe the kinds of boys and girls who had come from these public schools to be thoroughly convinced of the need of a well-regulated school such as Samuel Huston College, with trained Christian teachers to teach African-American boys and girls the fundamental skills and prepare them with a liberal, well-rounded, normal education and return them to their various communities for them to enrich and raise the standards of the public schools.

The Methodists felt that a church-related college was essential to the preparation of teachers. From 1876 to 1900, there were only a limited number of high schools in the church conference jurisdiction that actually offered courses sufficient to prepare teachers for children of color. Much of the work that was to be accomplished became the task of Samuel Huston College because there was a direct church following of almost 15,000 members and 500 Sunday school pupils. The school was so popular with the masses that it was patronized by all denominations.

The members of the West Texas Conference of the Methodist Episcopal Church nurtured monumental concerns for the success of Samuel Huston College. They struggled the better part of thirty years to establish Samuel Huston College for the education of African-American youths. These Methodists believed that it was the duty of the wealthy, patriotic men and women of the nation to help in this work. If they could not engage in it personally, they should give the means so the work could be done.

There were many who were concerned with the slow progress of the college in the city of Dallas. There were serious concerns about the location. Some even expressed concerns that the location was too remote. There were ministers, laymen, and friends of the Dallas Methodist supporters who expressed concerns about the ever-present potential for violent reaction to the school's presence in that North Texas city. Geographically it was not centrally located, and some annual conferences wanted the college in a city that was more to the center of the West Texas Conference. The city also needed to have a social and political climate that was tolerant of the idea of higher education for people of black African descent.

According to George O. Richardson, his wife, Emma, and his father, George W. Richardson, the early days of development of Samuel Huston into a functional institution were uncertain and gloomy.

In the fall of 1875, Rev. George W. Richardson was in ill health. He had been very ill for five years; his son, George O. Richardson, felt that he would not survive another winter in Minnesota. Therefore, he decided to relocate in Texas and have his father come to live with him for the winter. The move to Dallas seemed to have caused the health of Father Richardson to improve remarkably. When Father Richardson's health was improved, he began to observe the schools provided for people of African descent in the Dallas area. Reverend Richardson had been a chaplain for the colored regiment, the Seventh United States Artillery, 1864–66, during the Civil War. According to his son, this made him attentive and sensitive to the educational needs of those freed slaves and their young children. He found the conditions so utterly unsatisfactory, according to his son, he decided to open a private school.

He leased the St. Paul Methodist Episcopal Church for five years and opened the school on February 22, 1876, with six pupils. The school enrollment increased daily. At the end of February, the son began to help with the school. There was no help from the Freedman's Aid Society; the Richardsons had to run the school on the small tuition of only $1 per month per pupil and what they could afford to give of their personal possessions. On April 21, 1876, the school had sixty students.

One Saturday morning near 4:00 A.M., the Richardsons were awakened by the cry of fire. When they reached the door, they saw the church, where the school was housed, engulfed in flames. Reverend Richardson, partly dressed and bareheaded and barefooted, ran to the rear of the building and found that it had been kerosened by white vandals. There was no chance to save the building, but they were able to save most of the tables and seats.

The Richardsons said, "It was a pitiful sight to see the despair written on the face of that faithful colored pastor, Rev. J. G. Webster, and the members of his flock as they stood around the smoking brands."

The black people in this community had labored hard and had sacrificed much to build their church, and they had hoped that this school would be the beginning of a permanent institution for their children's education; and now everything seemed lost.

Early that same day, the Richardsons (the father and son) went to see the pastor of the Tabernacle Church, Rev. L. H. Carhart. He was a personal friend and he understood, better than they did, that this was an attempt to drive them out, but he was determined to help them stay. They decided to erect a temporary structure for immediate use and rebuild the church as soon as possible.

They bought the lumber and had it delivered to the site where they were to build. They hired two carpenters and rounded up as many black volunteers as they could find who could use a saw or drive a nail.

According to Reverend Richardson, "That was a busy afternoon, and the sound of the hammers did not cease till nine o'clock; then we carried in the seats that we had saved from the fire, and the building was ready for dedication." Reverend Richardson went on to say, "Then we sang the Doxology, in which the great crowd of men and women joined, feeling much more joyful than they had in the dim light of the early dawn."

On Sunday the church school and Sunday services were held as usual. On Monday the school opened as though nothing had happened.

The mayor of the city of Dallas and the better class of white citizens attempted to show their regrets and shame for the low, cowardly acts of the hateful whites who had burned the church school. Richardson reported that one of the daily papers commended their efforts and condemned, in strong terms, the outlaws who would try to break up that kind of benevolent work for the African Americans who lived in the area.

In less than a month following the fire, the school had grown so large that the Richardsons had to rent the church which belonged to the Colored Methodist Episcopal (CME) Church. Half of the students were taught at the CME Church.

The quarterly conference met at the St. Paul Methodist Episcopal Church on November 7, 1876. Rev. Dr. William Brush, the presiding elder of the Austin District, was in charge.

The following resolutions were adopted:

Whereas the Rev. G. W. Richardson and his son George O. Richardson have leased from the Trustees of this church their church property for school purposes for five years, and have met with such success that this list of registered scholars is above two hundred, and

Whereas we are thoroughly identified by the losses we have suffered in common with these brethren and by the benefit we receive from their school and their help in the Sunday School, and

Whereas we have the utmost confidence in the ability of these brethren to build up and conduct a first class institution of learning; therefore

Resolved that we request the West Texas Conference to adopt the above-described school as a conference school; and therefore are

Resolved that we request the appointment of Rev. Geo. O. Richardson as President and Rev. A. J. Burris as Local Agent of said college.

(Signed) William Brush, P.E.

On November 19, 1876, the teachers of the school requested (by formal resolution) recognition and support from the West Texas Conference as it met in San Antonio. Their request was granted and the school was given the name Andrews Normal College. Rev. L. H. Carhart, Rev. Melvin Wade, Mr. George Mickle, Rev. William Brush, Rev. J. G. Webster, Mr. E. Stare, Mr. Alanzo Jones, Rev. G. W. Richardson, and Rev. A. J. Burris were appointed trustees of Andrews Normal College. The Rev. George O. Richardson was appointed president.

The school survived the first full year in Dallas and opened the 1877 term with renewed optimism; however, there was speculation that the Dallas location, in many respects, was unfortunate. The matter of relocation was discussed in open conference, and it was decided that the school should be moved to Austin, Texas. The Committee on Education made the recommendation and it passed unanimously on November 26, 1877, at the West Texas Conference in Waco. A committee consisting of Samuel Gates, Charles L. Madison, and A. M. Gregory were appointed to select and purchase property for the school in Austin.

According to accounts given by Rev. G. W. Richardson, the school opened in Austin, Texas, the first Monday in September 1878

*Rev. M. C. B. Mason,
strong supporter of Samuel
Huston College.*
— TAAHO Collections,
Austin, Texas

Samuel Huston ensemble, early 1900s.
— TAAHO Collections, Austin, Texas

Samuel Huston baseball team, early 1900s.
— TAAHO Collections, Austin, Texas

in Wesley Chapel Methodist Episcopal Church. In December 1878 at the sixth session of the West Texas Conference which met in Columbus, Texas, one and one-half acres were purchased in Austin for the school at a cost of $1,350.

On December 1, 1878, the conference changed the name of the school to West Texas Conference School. The primary supporters were the Methodist Episcopal Church and the Freedman's Aid Society.

The college struggled for approximately thirty years. Dr. R. S. Rusk, secretary of the Freedman's Aid Society, purchased a large lot of almost six acres in 1883. The same year Samuel Huston, of Marengo, Iowa, gave the school $9,000. Some accounts report the amount to be $10,000, but they are unverifiable. Because of this generous gift, the school was given his name. The stone foundation for the first building was laid, but due to acute financial problems construction was not resumed until 1898. Finally, following setback after setback, the school opened on November 1, 1900. Dr. R. S. Lovinggood, with his wife, was sent to Austin to become president of the college.

When the school was opened in 1900, aged black washerwomen came with bedding and made beds ready for students with their own hands. Saturday after Saturday, washerwomen came with their small earnings tied in a small piece of cloth, shared it with the school, got down with the president and prayed for the school, and went their ways. Week after week, an aged black laborer came by and gave his meager earnings until his gift grew to more than $250.

Week after week, humble poor people paid installments out of humble weekly earnings and gave it proudly to the school. With this kind of faithful support, the school grew and the enrollment reached as high as 517. The faculty grew to number eighteen total. The progress and accomplishments of Samuel Huston College from 1900 to 1952 are legendary.

The Samuel Huston campus consisted of approximately sixteen acres and was located about a quarter of a mile east of the state capital. A main city thoroughfare divided the campus. The college had one of the best locations in the Southwest.

Leadership for the school from 1876 to 1952 includes:

George W. Richardson, Founder	1876
Presidents	
George O. Richardson	1876-1900
R. S. Lovinggood	1900-1916
M. S. Davage	1916-1920
J. B. Randolph	1920-1922
R. N. Brooks	1922-1926
T. R. Davis	1926-1930
Willis J. King	1930-1932
Stanley E. Grunnum	1932-1943
Carl E. Downs	1943-1948
Robert S. Harrington	1948-1952

Summary

Samuel Huston College was founded by Rev. George W. Richardson in 1876 at Dallas, Texas. The school was supported by the West Texas Conference of the Methodist Episcopal Church and the Freedman's Aid Society. In 1878, the school was moved to Austin. A gift of $9,000 was made to the school by Samuel Huston of Ma-

Left to right: Attorney Kenneth Lamkins; Dr. E. H. Givens (Austin dentist); Jackie Robinson (famous baseball player who attended Samuel Huston briefly in the 1940s); Dr. Karl Douens, president of Samuel Huston College, 1943–1948.

— TAAHO Collections, Austin, Texas

rengo, Iowa, and the school was named after the donor. By 1905, enrollment had reached 419; by 1906, the enrollment was 517. Courses ranged from elementary grades through college. The curriculum included blacksmithing, bookkeeping, teaching, and theology. In 1916, the school property was increased to more than fifteen acres, and several buildings were erected.

Through the years, Samuel Huston College produced many outstanding and productive members of the state and of the nation. They are listed prominently in science, military science, medicine, education, the performing and creative arts, and religion. Through them and their descendants, the legacy of Samuel Huston College will live forever. A special thanks should go to the Richardson family: George W. Richardson, George O. Richardson, Caroline A. Richardson, Earl M. Richardson, and Clara A. Richardson. We should all be grateful that their labors and sacrifices were not in vain.

Chapter 13

A History of African-American Catholicism in Texas

Compiled by Ada Simond

(Courtesy of Luther C. Simond)

Introduction

The tale of African-American Catholicism in Texas is a story of heroes — largely unknown heroes. The early heroes were the slaves who clung to religion even though prayers offered no protection from a cruel system of servitude. Later, newly freed slaves would attend Mass even though it meant submitting to the indignity of sitting in the back of the church.

The sacrifices parents made to send their African-American children to Catholic schools were surely heroic. Enduring threats of Klan violence was a true test of faith. The African-American men and women who chose a vocation as a priest or nun were indeed heroes. The men and women who founded chapters of the Knights and Ladies of Peter Claver and youth groups were heroes as well.

This paper will address the history of African-American Catholics, noting these heroes along the way but recognizing that any study of African-American history is limited because of a lack of reliable research and documentation.

Black Catholic bishops in the United States in 1985. Top row: Walton D. Gregory, Auxiliary of Chicago; Emerson J. Moore, Auxiliary of New York; Moses B. Anderson, S.S.E., Auxiliary of Detroit; James T. Steib, S.V.D., Auxiliary of St. Louis; John H. Ricard, S.S.J., Auxiliary of Baltimore. Front row: Joseph A. Francis, S.V.D., Auxiliary of Newark; Harold R. Perry, S.V.D., Auxiliary of New Orleans; Joseph L. Howze, Bishop of Biloxi; Eugene A. Marino, S.S.J., Auxiliary of Washington; James P. Lyke, D.F.M., Auxiliary of Cleveland.

— Courtesy U.S. Catholic Historical Society, New York
Courtesy Luther C. Simond, Austin, Texas

African-American Catholicism in Texas

It began with Estevan.

That the roots of African-American Catholicism in Texas can be traced so directly to a black man from North Africa is one of the many twists that makes the history of African-American Catholics in Texas so fascinating.

The first blacks to arrive in what is now the United States came with the Spaniards and were Spanish-speaking Catholics. The best known example and the one who is most closely identified with the roots of African-American Catholicism in Texas is Estevan from Morocco. Estevan Dorantes, also called Estevanico, or Little Steven, was a guide and interpreter who accompanied the explorer Cabeza de Vaca to the Texas shores in about 1528, nearly 100 years before the slaves landed at Jamestown.

When the de Vaca ship crashed into the Texas Gulf of Mexico, it was Estevan who led the group of survivors inland. One by one, however, they died. Estevan was admired for his linguistic and medical skills, which he may have acquired by studying with the Spanish priests and brothers. These skills allowed him to live among the Indians for eight years. In 1539 the Indians killed him.

To call Estevan the Father of African-American Catholicism in Texas is an oversimplification. He lived for such a short time and made no known or lasting contribution that would later enhance the development of Catholicism or, more importantly, African-American Catholicism, in Texas.

Although it is speculated that Estevan fathered children during the eight years he lived along the Texas coast, any of these children would have grown up Indian. However, his historical role is still very significant.

First of all, it attests to the enduring nature and divergent history of African-American Catholicism in Texas. And it is more than coincidence that the shores where Estevan died would later become one of the state's busiest slave ports (Galveston) and the port where Texas slaves were notified when they were freed.

More important is the fact that Estevan is the first hero among the many heroes and heroines of the tale of African-American Catholicism in Texas. And because there is no way to name the thousands of other black men and women who are also heroes and heroines, the memory of Estevan stands as an important reminder that such people did exist.

Catholicism in Africa

To begin any study of black Catholicism, one must first go back to Africa. Ancient Ethiopia was converted to Christianity in about 380 A.D., which is sooner than Catholicism reached Ireland, Poland, or any other northern European country. Traces of ancient Catholicism are still evident today in the Coptic churches, which at one time were unified with the Church of Rome. Today, the Ethiopian devotion to the Blessed Virgin is a remnant of the Roman Catholic Church in Europe and elsewhere.

Africans were involved in laying the very groundwork of the Catholic church. Among early African contributors to the church in areas of theology, governance, and martyrdom are St. Augustine, African popes Victor (ca. 186-197), Melchiades or Miltiades (ca. 311-314), and Gelasius I (ca. 492), and the martyrs Felicity and Perpetua. These historical contributions were not properly noted by the European church hierarchy.

In the seventh century, Arab Muslims swept across North Africa, killing Catholics and destroying the churches. These Islamic invasions further destroyed records of African religious accomplishments as well as artifacts and statues in the likeness of Africans. In modern times, archaeologists and historians have found remnants of Catholicism in Nubia through the fourteenth century, before Columbus discovered America. This broken link, separating the African and the European branches of the Catholic church, made it easier centuries later for the Spanish, European, and American branches of the Catholic church to enslave blacks. Estevan was, after all, a Catholic slave owned by Catholic Spaniards.

Catholicism and Slavery in America

Although unknown numbers of slaves were converted to Catholicism, many were Catholic when they were enslaved. Although it is often accepted that African Americans became Catholic by way of their slave masters, in fact it is very likely that many blacks were Catholic in their native Africa and brought their faith with them when forced to come to this country.

While Europeans may have envisioned that the faith that sustained slaves was based on worship of idols, it is not unreasonable

Father Augustine Tolton (1854–1897), the first black priest whose parents were slaves.
— Courtesy Josephite Archives

that these displaced Africans were praying to the same God we pray to today. And although it is more traditional to consider that while slave holders generously converted slaves to Catholicism, it is not unreasonable to wonder how many white souls were saved by slaves who influenced their masters to embrace Catholicism.

Although there may have been centuries of African Catholicism, there are other forces at work that provide additional evidence that some slaves brought their Catholicism to America with them on slave ships. The nineteenth century, the time the slave trade was burgeoning, parallels the period of increased missionary work and evangelization by the Catholic church in Africa.

By 1800, after years of slave labor on the land owned by religious orders, the church began to split on the issue of slavery and began to question the church's treatment of blacks.

Slavery was adopted in Texas in 1829. The slave trade flourished between the 1820s and the 1860s in Texas. After the Civil War started, slaves were not as easy to come by in Texas. Traders became more aggressive and brought in a larger number of slaves from Louisiana. More than likely, some if not most of these slaves were Catholic.

If Texas had not been so hostile to both African Americans and Catholics, it is not unreasonable to surmise that the Lone Star State could have easily become the seat of African-American Catholicism in America.

The Louisiana/Texas Connection

Historically, two factors that have resulted in the large African-American Catholic population in Texas are slavery and migration from Louisiana. Slaves were baptized by the Catholic French as early as 1699. The numbers would be even greater if Catholicism did not meet the resistance from the early Texas settlers that it did. And the conflicts between slavery and the Catholic way of thinking created some uneasiness that took a while to resolve.

Shortly before the Civil War, 60 percent of the country's African-American Catholics resided in Louisiana.

Growth from this area has remained steady overall, but there have been large spurts of growth. For example, in 1927 a great flood of the Mississippi River sent African Americans fleeing to Crosby, Texas. Because so many of them were Catholic, by 1936, a mission or church, Blessed Martin de Porres, was established for the former Louisianians in Crosby.

In 1951, as industrial opportunities began to increase in Houston, another large influx of African-American Catholics moved to Houston and surrounding areas. That year, the Galveston diocese had the fifth largest African-American population in the United States.

Today, nearly two-thirds of the South's African-American Catholics live in Louisiana. Therefore, Louisiana is a key state in the development of African-American Catholicism in Texas. As migration from Louisiana to Texas increased, so did the numbers of African-American Catholics.

African-American Parishes

Statewide, there are numerous important communities that must be mentioned when looking at the historical roots of African-American Catholicism in Texas. The Houston-Galveston area, Washington-on-the-Brazos, Corpus Christi, Dallas-Fort Worth, Austin, and several East Texas communities have or have had solid African-American Catholic communities, even under the most hostile conditions. There have been at least thirty-five predominantly African-American parishes in Texas during the last century.

The earliest known African-American Catholic community in

Texas was founded in 1849 at Old Washington-on-the-Brazos, the original capital of Texas. However, the mission itself predates the Civil War. This mission dates back to 1840, when plantation owner Malcolm Spain, a Catholic Mississippian, brought a large group of African Americans to the Brazos River country in Washington County.

Initially, blacks and whites worshiped together here. Growth of the African-American community, as well as convenience, created the need for a parish closer than the integrated church, which was closer to where the whites lived.

At that time Masses were said by community priests at private homes of African-American Catholics. An entry from the Josephite Archives reads: "Father Scherty could do more in Washington County if he had a little church. He says Mass on the front porch of a Negro Cabin."

However, harassment by whites nearly destroyed this small Catholic enclave. It was risky enough for whites to be known as Catholics, but to be Catholic and helping African Americans, too, was particularly dangerous. Priests were beaten and the church burned by hostile whites.

The spirit of Catholicism, however, among the former slaves did not die with the church. Later, another church was built on land donated by descendants of Malcolm Spain. This testifies to the enduring spirit of these African-American pioneers. Now the mission, known as the Blessed Virgin Mission, is part of the Diocese of Austin and has about forty families as members.

The emphasis on ministries for African-American Catholics in Texas coincided with the 1889 Third Plenary Council of Baltimore. The council established its annual Negro and Indian missions collections and set up a commission to oversee the distribution of these funds for African Americans and Native Americans.

In Houston, the first known African-American parish was established in October 1887 by the Rt. Rev. Nicholas A. Gallagher, bishop of Galveston. He dedicated a small elementary school in the city's Third Ward for the education of African-American children.

At the time, nearly 10,500 of Houston's estimated 28,000 residents were of African descent. It was fitting, indeed, when nearly 100 years later, Texas' first African-American Catholic bishop was assigned as auxiliary bishop of Houston. Even more fitting is that the Most Rev. Curtis Guillory is a native of Louisiana. Years from now, when others study African-American Catholicism in Texas, Guillory will emerge as one of the modern day heroes.

In San Antonio, St. Peter Claver Church was founded in 1888 by an Irish priest who did not like seeing African Americans seated in pews in the back of the church. Although the number of African-American Catholics in San Antonio was not large, the number of African-American Catholics grew to the point that by 1915 there were three predominantly African-American churches in San Antonio.

In 1889, Holy Rosary Church of Galveston was founded. The Catholics in this community, who undoubtedly walked along some of the same paths that Estevan did more than 300 years earlier, were probably slaves and descendants of slaves who got off slave ships that docked in Galveston Bay.

Bishop Guillory made history when he ordained an African-American deacon here during Centennial Services. It marked the first time a bishop of African-American descent administered the Sacrament of Holy Orders in Texas.

In 1890, an important Texas African-American community was born in Ames. African-American Catholics, former slaves from Louisiana, began migrating into this community. Our Mother of Mercy Church was started in 1910.

From the end of the century until the 1950s, at the same time growth was occurring in South and East Texas from Louisiana, Catholicism was growing in other parts of the state as well. Many African Americans were moving farther northward into Texas, increasing the numbers of African-American Catholics in Central and North Texas. Rural black Catholic communities were losing numbers, but were still in existence.

Among the African-American parishes in Texas and their starting dates:

1905:   St. Peter Apostle Church was founded in Dallas.
1910:   Liberty.
1915:   Blessed Sacrament Church was founded in Beaumont.

(Again, hostility was expressed by the white community in Beaumont. A May 1922 entry in the Josephite Archives said: "A letter signed K.K.K. threatens the dynamiting of our beautiful church and school." Given the fact that the Ku Klux Klan in Texas enjoyed a healthy membership for years, it is likely that the two groups most hated by the Klan — African Americans and Catholics — had a chilling effect on the growth of African-American Catholicism in Texas.)

1915:   Port Arthur.
1917:   Corpus Christi. Corpus became home to an African-American parish priest who took up residence in Texas when Fr. Joseph John, of the Society of African Missions of Lyons (France), arrived in 1926. Fr. John returned to his native Trinidad in 1929.

1929:   Fort Worth.
1935:   Raywood, Orange and Tyler.

In Austin, Holy Cross Catholic Church was founded in 1936. The parish also included a school and a hospital, the first African-American Catholic hospital in Texas. The hospital presented an important opportunity that extended beyond the Catholic community of Austin: It provided African-American women with an opportunity to study nursing and gave African-American doctors a place to practice medicine that did not exist to any large degree before.

These institutions, built by the Rev. Charles Weber, earned him the title "The Carpenter Priest." Even though the Holy Cross Order no longer operated the thriving African-American Catholic parish, its role was crucial in its establishment.

In 1991, the Rev. George Artis, of the Society of the Divine Word, was the parish priest. Rev. Artis is a role model for young Catholics of African descent.

Other historically black parishes and the dates they were established:

1937:   Marshall and Weimar.
1938:   Dayton.
1939:   Texarkana.
1940:   Amarillo.
1942:   Bryan.
1944:   Denison.
1945:   McNair.
1952:   Waco.

Despite the fact that growth occurred, support for survival of these churches and institutions of African-American Catholicism was spotty. Although incidents of active racism were not uncommon, resistance was generally expressed by lack of support. These

Father John Dorsey, S.S.J. (1873–1926), the second black Josephite priest.

— Courtesy Josephite Archives

missions relied on support from whites and white Catholics, who were not always eager to help. African-American Catholics in conservative North and West Texas were particularly hard-pressed to receive white support.

Ministries: Orders, Organizations, Individuals

It is difficult to talk about African-American Catholics without talking about the priests and nuns and religious orders — black and white — who ministered to the needs of these Catholics.

Many orders made significant contributions to the development of African-American Catholicism in Texas, namely the Dominicans, the Society of the Divine Word, the Jesuits, and the Oblates. But particularly noteworthy in the earliest years were the Josephites and the Holy Cross Order.

The Josephite Order was established in England in 1870. In 1893, a U.S. headquarters was established in Baltimore with a mission to aid African Americans. In the late 1880s, schools and missions were started in Texas, and as early as 1901, a Josephite, the Rev. Francis J. Tobin, was working with African-American Catholics in Texas.

Statewide, the Josephites were responsible for the establishment of churches, schools, and nursing homes for African-American Texans. College campus ministries were pioneered at colleges, such as Prairie View.

The Holy Cross Brothers and Sisters have a long and impressive history of establishing and sustaining black missions, parishes, schools, and hospitals. The order, established in France, is now headquartered at Notre Dame University in Indiana. The order has been present in Texas since 1872. In addition to establishing parishes and programs for Hispanics and blacks, it was instrumental in the establishment of St. Edward's University in Austin.

In a 1987 interview, Brother Joe Houser explained the climate in which his order toiled in Texas: "Nobody else cared if the blacks and Hispanics got an education. The Anglos just wanted them to pick cotton."

An organization that has been equally instrumental in the development and sustenance of African-American Catholics is the Knights and Ladies of Peter Claver, which dates back to the 1920s. The organization is named after the Spanish Jesuit who devoted more than half a century working on behalf of slaves.

Claver leaders such as Joseph Cochran of Galveston, A. E. Woodley of Houston, Bertha Balque, and Della Brooks were the early leaders of the Knights and Ladies. People such as these and others provided support for the NAACP and for African-American men and women pursuing vocations.

The first African-American priest in America, the Rev. Augustine Tolton, was born a slave in 1859. Tolton was ordained in 1886. Tolton once preached in the cathedral in Galveston. Other individuals who have made outstanding contributions include the Rev. John Henry Dorsey, second African-American Josephite priest in America and the first known African-American priest in Texas, and the Rev. Fr. Joseph John of the Society of African Missions of Lyons, who, as previously mentioned, came to Corpus in 1926 but returned to his native Trinidad in 1929.

These men are among the growing list of black heroes in the tale of African-American Catholicism in Texas. Undoubtedly, to be a black Catholic in these early days was to be a minority in a minority in Texas. But to be a black priest and administer to the many needs of African-American Catholics must have been an extraordinarily difficult task, a heroic task.

Integration

It is unknown what effect integration had on the development of African-American Catholicism in Texas, positive or negative. Although segregation played an important part in where, how, and why black parishes began in Texas, it is not as clear to explain the effect integration might have had on either predominantly black parishes or African-American Catholicism in Texas in general.

Although segregation led to separation of white and black churches, there were reasons this system benefited African-American Catholics. For example, such a system allowed them some control of these institutions. Also, there was more of an opportunity for them to express their unique cultural differences.

In the early years, all churches were segregated. It is impossible to say that earlier integration of Catholic churches or schools would have made any difference in the number of African-American Catholics; however, for many early African-American Texans, trying to be Catholic was indeed a test of faith.

Ada DeBlanc Simond, an Austin black octogenarian rooted in Catholicism, recalls that the first time her parents took the family to Mass in Austin in the 1920s, "there was general unrest" among the white parishioners in the church. She also recalls that even though there was a pew reserved for blacks at the rear of the church, they were not welcome.

"I remember that the little white children would snatch and break our rosaries and tear up our missals," she recalled. Until a parish for African Americans was established in Austin, the LeBlanc family attended a church of another faith.

When Catholic schools and churches integrated, the effects integration had on enrollment varied from place to place. Some African-American churches and schools welcomed integration; others did not. One result of integration, however, that negatively affected African-American churches and schools is that when it was determined that there were too many facilities once all resources were pooled, it was generally the African-American institutions that became obsolete.

Even with integration and changing demographics, the majority of African-American Catholic parishes in Texas remain predominantly black and proud of their rich traditions.

In areas where growth was nurtured, additional growth and stability of African-American Catholics endured. In African-American communities that lacked broader support, the spirit floundered or the number of black Catholics merely survived.

Less than four percent of the 53.4 million Catholics in the United States are African Americans, and fewer than 300 of the 54,000 priests. About 1,000 of the 20,000 parishes have mainly black congregations, but most are run by white pastors.

African-American Catholic ranks in Texas are being gradually supplemented by Yankee migration that grew particularly heavy in the late 1960s through the early part of this decade.

The climate for African-American Catholicism in Texas has been greatly enhanced by growth, the Northern migration, and the church's recent encouragement of the cultural infusion into black services.

The next century is likely to see increased growth in African-American Catholicism in Texas. And during the next century, it will be easier to identify more of the African-American heroes and heroines of Catholics in Texas.

Conclusion

African-American Catholicism in Texas is alive and well. It has survived slavery. It has survived racism within the church and from the community at large. It has survived Klan violence and hostility and lack of support from all groups: black, white, Catholic, and non-Catholic. It has survived cultural repression. Not only has African-American Catholicism survived, it has flourished, quietly and with dignity.

The Vatican has now stated that racism is morally wrong. The Pope has also welcomed the cultural gifts black Catholics bring to the faith.

In the next century, African-American Catholicism will be a positive and productive spiritual force that will benefit the church in Texas as a whole.

Section III

Reconstruction Legislators

Through mandate of Reconstruction, African-American Texans were able to participate freely in the political process. Not only were they allowed to vote, they could also seek, through free elections, seats in the legislature in Austin. From 1868 to 1898, approximately sixty African Americans were elected to the Texas Legislature and were selected as delegates to the 1868-1869 and 1875 Constitutional Conventions. A list of the participants follows.

Constitutional Convention, 1868-1869

Delegate	*County(ies) Represented*
Charles W. Bryant	Harris
Stephen Curtis	Brazos
Wiley W. Johnson	Harrison
Mitchell M. Kendall	Harrison
Ralph Long	Limestone
James McWashington	Montgomery
Sheppard Mullins	McLennan
George T. Ruby	Galveston, Brazoria, Matagorda
Benjamin O. Watrous	Washington
Benjamin F. Williams	Colorado

Twelfth Legislature, 1870-1871

Name, Elected To	*District*	*County(ies)*
Richard Allen, H.R.	14	Harris, Montgomery
Silas Cotton, H.R.	18	Robertson, Leon, Freestone
Goldstein Dupree, H.R.	14	Harris, Montgomery
Matthew Gaines, Senate	16	Washington
Jeremiah J. Hamilton, H.R.	26	Fayette, Bastrop
Mitchell Kendall, H.R.	7	Harrison
David Medlock, H.R.	19	Fall, Limestone, McLennan
John Mitchell, H.R.	17	Burleson, Brazos, Milam
Henry Moore, H.R.	7	Harrison
Sheppard Mullens, H.R.	19	Fall, Limestone, McLennan

George T. Ruby, Senate   12 Brazoria, Galveston, Matagorda
Benjamin F. Williams, H.R. 25 Lavaca, Colorado
Richard Williams, H.R.   15 Madison, Grimes, Walker
      H.R. — House of Representatives

Thirteenth Legislature, 1873

Legislator, Elected To	*District*	*County(ies)*
Richard Allen, H.R.	14	Harris, Montgomery
Edward Anderson, H.R.	14	Harris, Montgomery
Matthew Gaines, Senate	12	Washington
Henry Moore, H.R.	7	Harrison
Henry Phelps, H.R.	13	Austin, Fort Bend, Wharton
Meshack (Shack) Roberts, H.R.	7	Harrison
George T. Ruby, Senate	12	Brazoria, Galveston, Matagorda
James H. Washington, H.R.	15	Grimes, Madison, Walker
Allen Wilder, H.R.	16	Washington
Richard Williams, H.R.	15	Grimes, Madison, Walker

Fourteenth Legislature, 1874

Legislator, Elected To	*District*	*County(ies)*
David Abner, Sr., H.R.	7	Harrison
Thomas Beck, H.R.	15	Grimes, Madison, Walker
Edward Brown, H.R.	7	Harrison
Walter M. Burton, Senate	13	Austin, Fort Bend, Wharton
Jacob Freeman, H.R.	13	Austin, Fort Bend, Wharton
John Mitchell, H.R.	17	Burleson, Washington
Meshack (Shack) Roberts, H.R.	7	Harrison

Constitutional Convention, 1875

Delegate	*District*	*County(ies)*
David Abner, Sr.	7	Harrison
B. B. Davis	13	Austin, Fort Bend, Wharton
Melvin Gaddin	15	Grimes, Madison, Walker
Lloyd McCabe	13	Austin, Fort Bend, Wharton
John Mitchell	17	Burleson, Washington
William Reynolds	15	Grimes, Madison, Walker

Fifteenth Legislature, 1876

Name, Elected To	District	County(ies)
Walter M. Burton, Senate	17	Fort Bend, Wharton, Waller
William H. Holland, H.R.	37	Fort Bend, Waller, Wharton
Walter Ripetoe, Senate	4	Harrison
Meshack (Shack) Roberts, H.R.	10	Harrison
Henry Sneed, H.R.	37	Fort Bend, Waller, Wharton
Allen Wilder, H.R.	39	Washington

Sixteenth Legislature, 1879

Name, Elected To	District	County(ies)
Thomas Beck, H.R.	30	Grimes, Madison
Walter M. Burton, Senate	17	Fort Bend, Waller, Wharton
R. J. Evans, H.R.	29	Grimes
Jacob Freeman, H.R.	37	Fort Bend, Waller, Wharton
Harriel G. Geiger, H.R.	27	Robertson
B. A. Guy, H.R.	39	Washington
Elias Mayes, H.R.	28	Brazos
Walter Ripetoe, Senate	4	Harrison
Andrew Sledge, H.R.	40	Washington
Benjamin F. Williams, H.R.	37	Fort Bend, Waller, Wharton

Seventeenth Legislature, 1881

Name, Elected To	District	County(ies)
Thomas Beck, H.R.	30	Grimes, Madison
Walter M. Burton, Senate	17	Fort Bend, Waller, Wharton
R. J. Evans, H.R.	29	Grimes
Harriel G. Geiger, H.R.	27	Robertson
Robert A. Kerr, H.R.	42	Bastrop
Doc Lewis, H.R.	37	Fort Bend, Waller, Wharton

Eighteenth Legislature, 1883

Name, Elected To	District	County(ies)
R. J. Moore, H.R.	71	Washington
George W. Wyatt, H.R.	53	Fort Bend, Waller

Nineteenth Legislature, 1885

Name, Elected To	District	County(ies)
R. J. Moore, H.R.	71	Washington
James H. Steward, H.R.	48	Robertson
Benjamin F. Williams, H.R.	53	Fort Bend, Waller

Twentieth Legislature, 1887

Name, Elected To	District	County(ies)
H. A. P. Bassett, H.R.	52	Grimes
R. J. Moore, H.R.	71	Washington

Twenty-first Legislature, 1889

Name, Elected To	District	County(ies)
Alexander Asberry, H.R.	48	Robertson
Elias Mayes, H.R.	50	Brazos

Twenty-second Legislature, 1891

Name, Elected To	District	County(ies)
Edward Patton, H.R.	2	San Jacinto, Polk

Twenty-third Legislature, 1893

Name, Elected To	District	County(ies)
Nathan H. Haller, H.R.	64	Brazoria, Matagorda

Twenty-fourth Legislature, 1895

Name, Elected To	District	County(ies)
Nathan H. Haller, H.R.	64	Brazoria, Matagorda
Robert L. Smith, H.R.	63	Colorado

Twenty-fifth Legislature, 1897

Name, Elected To	District	County(ies)
Robert L. Smith, H.R.	67	Colorado

To learn more about African-American Reconstruction legislators, read Merline Pitre's book, *Through Many Dangers, Toils and Snares* (Austin: Eakin Press). Also see Chapter 3 of this book.

Modern Legislators

In 1967, African Americans returned to the Texas House of Representatives for the first time since 1897. Two African Americans won elections to the House of Representatives. One of the two was Joseph E. Lockridge, a Dallas attorney and son of a Baptist minister. Representative Lockridge was named "Rookie of the Year" by his colleagues in the House in 1966. Lockridge died in an airplane crash in May 1968. The other African American elected to the House of Representatives in 1967 was Curtis Graves, a public relations consultant from Houston. Graves was born in New Orleans and graduated from Texas Southern University. He was elected a state representative from Harris County.

By the late 1960s, the influence of African Americans in Texas politics began to increase significantly. African Americans in general were free to register to vote, and they exercised the right as freely as any other group in the state. Each election year, voters elected twelve to fourteen African Americans to serve in the state legislature.

Sixtieth Legislature, 1967-1968

Name, Elected To	*District*	*County(ies)*
Barbara Jordan, Senate	11	Harris
Curtis M. Graves, H.R.	23	Harris
Joseph E. Lockridge, H.R.	33	Dallas

Sixty-first Legislature, 1969-1970

Name, Elected To	*District*	*County(ies)*
Barbara Jordan, Senate	11	Harris
Curtis M. Graves, H.R.	23	Harris
Joseph E. Lockridge, H.R.	33	Dallas

Sixty-second Legislature, 1971-1972

Name, Elected To	*District*	*County(ies)*
Barbara Jordan, Senate	11	Harris
Curtis M. Graves, H.R.	23	Harris
Zan W. Holmes, Jr., H.R.	33	Dallas

Sixty-third Legislature, 1973-1974

Name, Elected To	*District*	*County(ies)*
Anthony Hall, H.R.	85	Harris
Samuel W. Hudson III, H.R.	33C	Dallas
Eddie Bernice Johnson, H.R.	33O	Dallas
George Mickey Leland, H.R.	88	Dallas
Paul Ragsdale, H.R.	33N	Dallas
Senfronia Thompson, H.R.	89	Harris
Craig A. Washington, H.R.	86	Harris

Sixty-fourth Legislature, 1975-1976

Name, Elected To	*District*	*County(ies)*
Anthony B. Hall, H.R.	85	Harris
Samuel W. Hudson III, H.R.	33C	Dallas
Eddie Bernice Johnson, H.R.	330	Dallas
George (Mickey) Leland, H.R.	88	Harris
Paul B. Ragsdale, H.R.	33N	Dallas
G. J. Sutton, H.R.	57A	Bexar
Senfronia Thompson, H.R.	89	Harris
Craig A. Washington, H.R.	86	Harris
Wilhelmina Delco, H.R.	37	Travis

Sixty-fifth Legislature, 1977-1978

Name, Elected To	*District*	*County(ies)*
Wilhelmina R. Delco, H.R.	37D	Travis
Anthony W. Hall, H.R.	85	Harris
Samuel W. Hudson III, H.R.	33C	Dallas
Eddie Bernice Johnson, H.R.	33O	Dallas
George (Mickey) Leland, H.R.	88	Harris
Paul B. Ragsdale, H.R.	33N	Harris
Lou Nelle Sutton, H.R.	57E	Bexar
Senfronia Thompson, H.R.	89	Harris

Craig A. Washington, H.R.	86	Harris
Albert J. Price, H.R.	7A	Jefferson
Clay Smothers, H.R.	33G	Dallas

Sixty-sixth Legislature, 1979-1980

Name, Elected To	District	County(ies)
Reby Cary, H.R.	32B	Tarrant
Lanell Cofer, H.R.	33O	Dallas
Wilhelmina Delco, H.R.	37D	Travis
Al Edwards, H.R.	85	Harris
Samuel W. Hudson III, H.R.	33C	Dallas
El Franco Lee, H.R.	88	Harris
Albert J. Price, H.R.	7A	Jefferson
Lou Nelle Sutton, H.R.	57A	Bexar
Senfronia Thompson, H.R.	89	Harris
Craig A. Washington, H.R.	86	Harris
Bobby Webber, H.R.	32A	Tarrant
Ron Wilson, H.R.	81	Harris

Sixty-seventh Legislature, 1981-1982

Name, Elected To	District	County(ies)
Reby Cary, H.R.	32B	Tarrant
Lanell Cofer, H.R.	33O	Dallas
Wilhelmina Delco, H.R.	37D	Travis
Al Edwards, H.R.	85	Harris
Samuel W. Hudson, H.R.	33C	Dallas
El Franco Lee, H.R.	88	Harris
Albert J. Price, H.R.	7A	Jefferson
Paul B. Ragsdale, H.R.	33N	Dallas
Lou Nelle Sutton, H.R.	57E	Bexar
Senfronia Thompson, H.R.	89	Harris
Craig A. Washington, H.R.	86	Harris
Bobby Webber, H.R.	32A	Tarrant
Ron Wilson, H.R.	81	Harris

Sixty-eighth Legislature, 1983-1984

Name, Elected To	District	County(ies)
Reby Cary, H.R.	32B	Tarrant
Larry Evans, H.R.	147	Harris

Wilhelmina Delco, H.R.	37D	Travis
Al Edwards, H.R.	85	Harris
El Franco Lee, H.R.	88	Harris
Albert J. Price, H.R.	7A	Jefferson
Paul B. Ragsdale, H.R.	33N	Dallas
Lou Nelle Sutton, H.R.	57E	Bexar
Senfronia Thompson, H.R.	89	Harris
Craig A. Washington, H.R., Senate	13	Harris
Ron Wilson, H.R.	81	Harris
Jesse Oliver, H.R.	111	Dallas

Sixty-ninth Legislature, 1985-1986

Name, Elected To	District	County(ies)
Craig A. Washington, Senate	13	Harris
Wilhelmina Delco, H.R.	50	Travis
Al Edwards, H.R.	146	Harris
Larry Evans, H.R.	147	Harris
Sam Hudson, H.R.	100	Dallas
El Franco Lee, H.R.	142	Harris
Albert J. Price, H.R.	22	Jefferson
Paul Ragsdale, H.R.	110	Dallas
Lou Nelle Sutton, H.R.	120	Bexar
Senfronia Thompson, H.R.	141	Harris
Ron Wilson, H.R.	131	Harris
Jesse Oliver, H.R.	111	Dallas
Harold V. Dutton, H.R.	142	Harris
Ron Givens, H.R.	83	Lubbock

Seventieth Legislature, 1987-1988

Myra A. McDaniel, Appointed Secretary of State

Name, Elected To	District	County(ies)
Craig A. Washington, Senate	13	Harris
Wilhelmina Delco, H.R.	50	Travis
Harold V. Dutton, H.R.	142	Harris
Al Edwards, H.R.	146	Harris
Larry Evans, H.R.	147	Harris
Ron Givens, H.R.	83	Lubbock
Samuel Hudson, H.R.	100	Dallas
Jerald Larry, H.R.	111	Dallas
Fred Blair, H.R.	110	Dallas

Name, Elected To	District	County(ies)
Lou Nelle Sutton, H.R.	120	Bexar
Senfronia Thompson, H.R.	141	Harris
Ron Wilson, H.R.	131	Harris
Albert J. Price, H.R.	22	Jefferson
Garfield Thompson, H.R.	95	Tarrant

Seventy-first Legislature, 1989-1990

Name, Elected To	District	County(ies)
Eddie Bernice Johnson, Senate	23	Dallas
Rodney Ellis, Senate	13	Harris, Fort Bend
Fred Blair, H.R.	110	Dallas
Wilhelmina Delco, H.R.	50	Travis
Samuel Hudson, H.R.	100	Dallas
Jerald Larry, H.R.	111	Dallas
Albert J. Price, H.R.	22	Jefferson
Karyne Conley, H.R.	120	Bexar
Garfield Thompson, H.R.	95	Tarrant
Senfronia Thompson, H.R.	141	Harris
Ron Wilson, H.R.	131	Harris
Harold V. Dutton, H.R.	142	Harris
Al Edwards, H.R.	146	Harris
Larry Evans, H.R.	147	Harris
Ron Givens, H.R.	83	Lubbock
Sylvester Turner, H.R.	139	Harris

Seventy-second Legislature, 1991-1992

Name, Elected To	District	County(ies)
Eddie Bernice Johnson, Senate	23	Dallas
Rodney Ellis, Senate	13	Harris
Fred Blair, H.R.	110	Dallas
Karyne Conley, H.R.	120	Bexar
Wilhelmina Delco, H.R.	50	Travis
Harold V. Dutton, H.R.	142	Harris
Al Edwards, H.R.	146	Harris
Larry Evans, H.R.	147	Harris
Samuel Hudson, H.R.	100	Dallas
Jerald Larry, H.R.	111	Dallas
Albert J. Price, H.R.	22	Jefferson
Garfield Thompson, H.R.	95	Tarrant
Senfronia Thompson, H.R.	141	Harris
Sylvester Turner, H.R.	139	Harris

Seventy-third Legislature, 1993-1994

Name, Elected To	District	County(ies)
Rodney Ellis, Senate	13	Harris
Royce West, Senate	23	Dallas
Garnet Coleman, H.R.	147	Harris
Karyne Conley, H.R.	120	Bexar
Yvonne Davis, H.R.	111	Dallas
Wilhelmina Delco, H.R.	50	Travis
Harold V. Dutton, H.R.	142	Harris
Al Edwards, H.R.	146	Harris
Samuel Hudson, H.R.	100	Dallas
Jesse W. Jones, H.R.	110	Dallas
Albert J. Price, H.R.	22	Jefferson
Garfield Thompson, H.R.	95	Tarrant
Senfronia Thompson, H.R.	141	Harris
Sylvester Turner, H.R.	139	Harris
Ron Wilson, H.R.	131	Harris

Seventy-fourth Legislature, 1995-1996

Name, Elected To	District	County(ies)
Ron Wilson, H.R.	131	Harris
Rodney Ellis, Senate	13	Harris, Fort Bend
Albert J. Price, H.R.	22	Jefferson
Garnet Coleman, H.R.	147	Harris
Yvonne Davis, H.R.	111	Dallas
Dawnna Dukes, H.R.	50	Travis
Harold V. Dutton, H.R.	142	Harris
Helen Giddings, H.R.	109	Dallas
Samuel W. Hudson III, H.R.	100	Dallas
Jesse W. Jones, H.R.	110	Dallas
Glenn O. Lewis, H.R.	95	Tarrant
Senfronia Thompson, H.R.	141	Harris
Sylvester Turner, H.R.	139	Harris
Royce West, Senate	23	Dallas

Biographies of modern African-American legislators follow, prefacing biographies of other notable African-American Texans.

Biographies

Barbara Jordan, Senator, Harris County.
— Courtesy TAAHO Archives,
Center for American History,
University of Texas at Austin

BARBARA JORDAN

When Barbara Jordan of Houston was elected to the Texas Senate in 1966, she became the first African American to serve in that assemblage since Walter M. Burton in 1882, and the first African American woman to be elected senator in the history of the state. The daughter of a Baptist minister, Senator Jordan graduated from Texas Southern University and the Boston University Law School. She practiced law in Houston and was the president of Houston Lawyers Association. Barbara Jordan was the first African American woman from the South to serve in the United States House of Representatives. She delivered the keynote address at the Democratic National Convention in 1976. She later became a tenured professor in the LBJ School of Public Affairs at the University of Texas at Austin.

*Curtis M. Graves,
Representative, Harris County.*
— Courtesy TAAHO Archives,
Center for American History,
University of Texas at Austin

CURTIS M. GRAVES

Curtis M. Graves, a graduate of Texas Southern University and a Houston public relations man, was elected to the House of Representatives in 1966, at the age of twenty-seven. He served in the House from 1966 to 1971.

When Graves' political career ended, he went to work for the National Aeronautics and Space Agency in Washington, D.C.

Joseph E. Lockridge,
Representative, Dallas County.
— Courtesy TAAHO Archives,
Center for American History,
University of Texas at Austin

JOSEPH E. LOCKRIDGE

Abraham Lincoln provided the leadership which generated the Emancipation Proclamation. In 1964, President Lyndon B. Johnson furnished the leadership which gave African Americans (through the Civil Rights Bill) what the 15th Amendment to the U.S. Constitution was supposed to have given in 1869. He gave them the ballot. On May 5, 1966, Joseph E. Lockridge, a quiet attorney, was elected to place five, Dallas, of the Texas House of Representatives. Lockridge joined the Texas House at the age of thirty-four. He was supported by an integrated, conservative, and business-oriented Democratic Committee for Responsible Government. The African-American communities in Dallas County and around the state were astonished when news came that State Representative Joe E. Lockridge was killed in an airplane crash on May 3, 1968. Lockridge went down in a Braniff aircraft that crashed in Dawson, killing eighty-five people. Lockridge was the first African American to represent Dallas County in the Texas Legislature.

Zan Wesley Holmes, Jr.,
Representative, Dallas County.
— Courtesy TAAHO Archives,
Center for American History,
University of Texas at Austin

ZAN WESLEY HOLMES, JR.

After the tragic death of Joseph E. Lockridge, Zan Wesley Holmes, Jr., a young

Methodist minister and a Southern Methodist University graduate, won a special election to the same seat with similar support. Holmes served one term in the Texas Legislature. He later became the first African American to be appointed to the powerful University Board of Regents.

*Samuel W. Hudson III,
Representative, Dallas County.*
— Courtesy TAAHO Archives,
Center for American History,
University of Texas at Austin

SAMUEL W. HUDSON III

Samuel W. Hudson III was born in Dallas, Texas, on November 6, 1940. He and his wife, Henri, have eight children: Samuel IV, Cynric, Lelalois, Samzie, Stacie, Tracie, Trenchella, and William. Samuel grew up in North Dallas, attended public school at J. W. Ray Elementary, B. F. Darrell Elementary, Phyllis Wheatley Elementary, H. S. Thompson Elementary, Lincoln High School, and James Madison High School. He earned his B.S. and Juris Doctor of Law at Texas Southern University in Houston, and was admitted to the State Bar of Texas in 1967. Mr. Hudson was elected to serve in the Texas House of Representatives in 1973 and had served thirteen terms at the 1995-1996 biennium. He was the chairman and co-founder of Minorities Organization for Business Opportunities (MOBE), founding board member of Interracial Council for Business Opportunities of Dallas, chairman of Mustang District Boy Scouts, vice-president of Black Chamber of Commerce of Dallas, regional chairman of Coalition for Urban Environmental Studies, vice-chairman of Dallas Legislative Delegation, and chairman of Small Business Interim Study Legislative Committee. His legislative accomplishments in the last two decades include authoring and passing the following bills in the Texas Legislature:

✳ Single member districts for Dallas Community College elections.
✳ Pauper's Oath for cost of appeal.

* Authority of district courts to hear poverty agency election disputes.
* Inclusion of an Indian as a member of the State Indian Commission.
* Extension of the statute of limitations in civil suits to include weekends and holidays.
* Expansion of wrongful death statutes.
* Peace officer status for Dallas Housing Authority Guards.
* Established the means for incorporation and organization of Urban Co-ops (signed into law 5-27-75).
* Provided more effective and liberal operation and administration of federally funded day care programs (signed into law 6-21-75).
* Made it possible for small businessmen to get larger contracts without restrictive bonding.
* Permitted a person to appeal from forcible entry and detainer evictions by filing Pauper's Oath rather than a bond.
* Provided better notice and protection for property owners under forced sheriff's sale of real estate (signed into law 6-21-75).
* Made it possible to seal the delinquency file of juveniles.
* Author of prison furlough law.
* Made it illegal to violate use of channel 9 CB emergency channel.
* Fasted sixty-nine days to get ninety-six bills heard in committee.
* Expungements of juvenile records.
* Acknowledgment of paternity on birth certificates.
* Prevented intimidating signs outside entrance of polling places.
* Prohibited lead smeltering plants from locating near residential areas (signed by the governor).
* Established state-supported day care centers (signed by the governor 6-19-87).
* Court fees to be collected by Dallas County for the enhancement of the county law libraries.
* Made it possible for individuals carrying personal identification cards to enjoy the same privileges as those who have driver's licenses (signed by the governor 6-19-87).

Eddie Bernice Johnson, Representative, Senator, U.S. Representative, Dallas County.
— Courtesy TAAHO Archives, Center for American History, University of Texas at Austin

EDDIE BERNICE JOHNSON

Born in Waco, Texas, December 3, 1935, Johnson is a mother of one, and received a bachelor of science degree in nursing from Southern Methodist University. Johnson began her career in elective office in 1972 with an upset victory over the favored candidate for a seat in the Texas House of Representatives. She won overwhelmingly. Johnson served three terms in the Texas House of Representatives before resigning to become President Carter's regional director of the Department of Health, Education and Welfare. After nine years away from elective office, Johnson ran successfully for the Texas State Senate and she became the first African American to represent Dallas since Reconstruction. Eddie Bernice Johnson was elected to the United States Congress from the 13th District of Texas in 1992. After her election, the *Dallas Morning News* reported that Johnson "was instrumental in winning a monumental victory for Dallas African Americans when she got the legislature to finally agree to a fifty percent African American district in Dallas County . . . She is tough, shrewd, and unswervingly devoted to her principles."

George (Mickey) Leland, Representative, U.S. Congress.
— Courtesy TAAHO Archives, Center for American History, University of Texas at Austin

GEORGE "MICKEY" LELAND

George "Mickey" Leland was born in Lubbock, Texas, on November 27, 1944. He received a bachelor of science degree in pharmacy from Texas Southern University in Houston in 1970. He was an instructor of clinical pharmacy at TSU for several years.

Leland first ran for public office in 1972. He was elected to the Texas House of Representatives. He was a member of the House for three two-year terms. In 1978 Leland declared his candidacy for the U.S. Congress as successor to Barbara Jordan. Jordan had announced her intention not to accept reelection. Leland was elected to the U.S. Congress from the 18th District of Texas. He served on the Energy and Commerce Committee, the Post Office and Civil Service Committee, and the Select Committee on Hunger. He was chairman of the Committee on Hunger and chairman of the Subcommittee on Postal Operations and Services. He also served as chairman of the Congressional Black Caucus.

Leland sponsored the Homeless Persons' Survival Act. A number of its provisions were incorporated into the $1.058 billion Stewart B. McKinney Homeless Assistance Act. His active role in the legislative process varied, ranging from policy toward South Africa, Central America and the Middle East, to unemployment and the preservation of the traditional predominantly African-American colleges.

In 1989, Congressman Leland was killed in an airplane crash in the remote hills of Ethiopia while visiting a refugee camp for the starving people of that region.

Senfronia Thompson, Representative, Harris County.
— Courtesy TAAHO Archives, Center for American History, University of Texas at Austin

SENFRONIA THOMPSON

Texas native Senfronia Thompson was born in Booth, Texas, and raised in Houston. A Houston attorney, Thompson was in 1995 serving her twelfth term in the Texas House of Representatives. She became the longest-serving female House member in Texas history on December 23, 1985.

Representative Thompson was in the forefront of every campaign against discrimination in the '70s, '80s, and '90s. She has been placed among the highest ranks of any legislators for her voting record on issues of concern to women, minorities, labor, consumers, reform advocates, the elderly, teachers, and civil libertarians. During the 70th Legislature, she was chair of the first legislative standing committee to have a female majority. During the 73rd Legislature, her Judicial Affairs Committee heard and passed more bills than any other House committee, including many reforms in child support enforcement, simplified probate proceedings, and judicial elections. She has authored and passed the Durable Power of Attorney Act, the Uniform Interstate Family Support Act, the Sexual Assault Program Fund, and numerous other reforms benefiting women, children, and the elderly. Representative Thompson is a leading advocate for alimony, judicial election reform, and simplified legal proceedings on minor civil matters. A former public schoolteacher, Thompson has three adult children and one grandson.

Craig A. Washington, Representative, U.S. Congress, Harris County.
— Courtesy TAAHO Archives, Center for American History, University of Texas at Austin

CRAIG A. WASHINGTON

Craig A. Washington was born in the East Texas city of Longview in 1941 and attended Prairie View A&M University, where he earned a bachelor of arts degree in 1966. In 1969, he graduated from the Thurgood Marshall School of Law at Texas Southern University. He was elected to the Texas House of Representatives in 1973. That same year, Mickey Leland was elected to the state legislature to serve in the House of Representatives. In 1983, Washington was elected to the Texas Senate. While in the Texas Legislature, he distinguished himself in both Houses through his ability to get significant bills passed. He was successful in causing the state to limit its investments in companies doing business with apartheid South Africa. While in the Texas Legislature, Washington served on numerous important committees.

Craig Washington replaced the very popular George "Mickey" Leland, who had become a U.S. congressman and who died in a tragic plane crash in Ethiopia in 1989. Washington was the leading vote-getter in the primary, and won the special election in December 1989. While in Washington, Congressman Washington served on the Education and Labor Committee and the Committee on the Judiciary. He was defeated in his quest for reelection to Congress in 1994.

Wilhelmina R. Delco,
Representative, Travis County.
— Courtesy TAAHO Archives,
Center for American History,
University of Texas at Austin

WILHELMINA R. DELCO

Preparation for her future role as a dynamic and successful public servant began early for Wilhelmina Ruth Fitzgerald Delco. She attended high school at Wendell Phillips Senior High School in Chicago, Illinois, and college at Fisk University, where she earned a B.A. in sociology. She and her husband, Dr. Exalton Delco, are parents to four children and four grandchildren, and they call Austin home.

Mrs. Delco's civic and volunteer activities, as well as political involvements, are legendary. As a state legislator, she was cited as one of the "bright spots in the House" during the 68th Legislative Session by the *Texas Observer,* "a dedicated and forthright leader" who campaigned for the creation of a comprehensive constitutional construction fund. From 1975 to 1994, Delco achieved many firsts and served with merit on numerous committees. She served honorably as Speaker Pro Tempore in the House of Representatives. Mrs. Delco retired from the House and politics in 1994.

ALBERT J. PRICE

Albert J. Price was born April 6, 1930, in Port Arthur, Texas. He has one daughter, Anita Juandalyn, and one son, Albert J. Price, Jr. Price graduated valedictorian of his class in 1946 from Hebert High

Albert J. Price,
Representative, Jefferson County.
— Courtesy TAAHO Archives,
Center for American History,
University of Texas at Austin

School in Beaumont, Texas. He earned his B.A. in sociology in 1950 at Morehouse College in Atlanta, Georgia, and did graduate work at Atlanta University from 1950 to 1951.

Throughout his tenure as a state representative, Price introduced legislation that was focused on upgrading the living conditions of the elderly, low-income families, children, and the handicapped. In 1995, Price became a ten-term veteran in the Texas House of Representatives, representing District 22. He also served as vice-chairman of the State, Federal and International Relations Committee, and was a member of the Transportation Committee.

From 1977 to 1995, Price served on the following committees: <u>65th Session</u>: Transportation, Higher Education, Select Committee on Minority Business Enterprises; <u>66th Session</u>: Energy, Liquor Regulation; <u>67th Session</u>: Higher Education, Liquor Regulation; <u>68th Session</u>: Higher Education, Federal and International Relations; <u>69th Session</u>: Higher Education, Labor and Employment Relations; <u>70th Session</u>: Insurance, Financial Institution; <u>71st Session</u>: Higher Education, Elections; <u>72nd Session</u>: Ways and Means, Science and Technology; <u>73rd Session</u>: Public Safety, Investments and Banking; <u>74th Session</u>: vice-chairman State, Federal and International Relations, Transportation.

In 1980, Price was appointed by President Carter to be a member of the official delegation from the United States to join in the celebration of the independence of Zimbabwe in Africa. He is best known as "Al Price."

LOU NELLE SUTTON

Lou Nelle Sutton, a native Texan, was educated in the public school system at San Angelo, Texas. She earned her undergraduate degree from Samuel Houston College in Austin, Texas.

Lou Nelle Sutton,
Representative, Bexar County.
— Courtesy TAAHO Archives,
Center for American History,
University of Texas at Austin

Mrs. Sutton was a successful businessperson, having owned Sutton and Sutton Mortuary in San Antonio, Texas. Following the untimely death of her husband, State Representative G. J. Sutton, she sought election to the office he held. Voters of District 129 cast a record number of votes for Mrs. Sutton, and she became the first woman from Bexar County to be elected to the state legislature. Representative Sutton served on the Appropriations Committee for two terms. She was successful in getting millions of dollars appropriated for Bexar County, San Antonio, and several other Texas cities. Her awards and honors were numerous, and she held memberships in many important civic and social organizations. Her political career spanned approximately twelve years.

Ron Wilson,
Representative, Dallas County.
— Courtesy TAAHO Archives,
Center for American History,
University of Texas at Austin

RON WILSON

Representative Ron Wilson had the distinction of being the youngest member of the Texas House of Representatives during the 65th Legislative Session. The young native of Houston was elected to the House in 1976 at the age of twenty-two. Ron Wilson was the recipient of an academic scholarship to St. Stephen's Episcopal School, where he completed his formal high school education. Upon graduation from St. Stephen's, he enrolled in the Plan II Program at The University of Texas at Austin. In August 1977, Wilson received his bachelor of arts degree from the Plan II Honors Program. He received his Doctor of Jurisprudence from The University of Texas School of Law in 1988.

The 73rd Legislative Session was Wilson's ninth term and he is currently in the top ten percent of seniority membership. Since coming to the House, he has served on a number of committees and as chairman of the Legislative Black Caucus. During the 72nd Session, Wilson served as chairman of the Liquor Regulation Committee, was a member of the Ways and Means Committee, the Legislative Council, the Committee on Redistricting, and was chairman of the interim Select Committee on Rules.

Significant legislation highlighting Representative Wilson's successes as a voice for Texas citizens have been bills establishing the Texas Human Rights Commission and declaring the Reverend Dr. Martin Luther King, Jr.'s birthday as an official state holiday. He initially introduced during the 68th Session a bill relating to the establishment and operation of a state lottery. What has affectionately become known as "The Lottery Bill" had been reintroduced by Representative Wilson since the 68th Session. The lottery measures successfully passed the House and Senate during the 72nd Legislative First Called Special Session. The constitutional amendment was passed by Texas citizens on November 5, 1991. The State of Texas became the thirty-fourth state to operate a lottery.

For the past two sessions, Representative Wilson has taught a class for The University of Texas at Austin's Plan II Department and for Texas Southern University's Honors Undergraduates on Politics. The class is entitled "Texas State Government: An Insider's Perspective." Representative Wilson was appointed chairman of the House Committee on Licensing and Administrative Procedures for the 73rd Legislative Session. He is a member of the Committees on Redistricting and State Affairs and the Legislative Council. His chairmanship of the Committee on Liquor Regulation during the 70th, 71st and 72nd legislative sessions and his chairmanship during the 73rd makes him the only African American ever appointed to chair business committees in the history of the Texas Legislature.

In 1995, Wilson was in private practice at Wilson and Associates. Representative Wilson is the eldest son of Henry Wilson III and Carrie Wilson. He and his wife, Treina, have two sons, Erik Brandon and Colby Ehren.

*Al Edwards,
Representative, Harris County.*
— Courtesy TAAHO Archives,
Center for American History,
University of Texas at Austin

AL EDWARDS

Al Edwards was first elected to the Texas House of Representatives in 1978 from the 146th District, Harris County, and is a native of Houston. His family consists of wife Lana, sons Albert Edwards III and Jason, and one daughter, Alana. Edwards is a real estate broker and a public relations executive. He earned his B.S. at Texas Southern University, and did further studies at Tuskegee Institute, the University of Houston, and Houston Bible Institute.

From 1978 to 1995, Edwards chaired the Texas Legislative Black Caucus and the House Rules and Resolutions Committee. He also served on the Public Safety and Transportation Committees. As early as 1882, efforts were made to make June 19 an official state holiday. The idea did not become reality, however, until it was introduced in 1979 by Al Edwards and received interracial and bipartisan support. Because of his effective leadership in efforts to pass the "Juneteenth Bill" (H.B. 1016), he is referred to as the "Father of the Juneteenth Bill."

---

*Sylvester Turner,
Representative, Harris County.*
— Courtesy TAAHO Archives,
Center for American History,
University of Texas at Austin

SYLVESTER TURNER

Sylvester Turner, born in 1954, the sixth of nine children, was raised by his father, a commercial painter, and mother, a maid at the Rice Hotel. In 1968, his father died of leukemia and his mother shouldered the family responsibilities. Turner showed promise at an early age by becoming valedictorian and senior class president of Klein High School. At the University of Houston, he was speaker of the Student Senate and graduated magna cum laude. At Harvard Law School, he was a finalist in the Ames Moot Court Competition. After graduation from law school in 1980, he became an associate with Fulbright and Jaworski. Later, he formed his own firm, known as Barnes & Turner. In addition to his successful law practice, Turner is an adjunct professor at the Thurgood Marshall School of Law, and seminar lecturer at the South Texas College of Law and University of Houston Law School Continuing Legal Education Programs.

Turner has been and is active in several civic, religious, and educational causes, including the United Negro College Fund, Houston Metropolitan Ministries, Houston-Galveston Area Food Bank, Acres Homes Citizens Chamber of Commerce, and the Acres Homes War on Drugs Committee. He is an active member of the Brookhollow Baptist Church, as well as a popular speaker at schools and churches.

Turner is acknowledged for his rapid rise in the Texas House of Representatives. Soon after he won the Harris County District 139 seat in 1988, he established a reputation as a consensus builder. During the 73rd Legislature, Turner served as vice-chair of the Calendars Committee and was an active member of the State Affairs and Corrections Committees. For the 74th Session, Representative Turner served as vice-chair of the State Affairs Committee and member of the Calendars and Appropriations Committee.

His awards are numerous: Rookie of the Year from *Texas Monthly*, Legislator of the Year from the Houston Police Patrolman's Union, and Rising Star from the Harris County Democrats. In 1990, he was named one of the Five Outstanding Houstonians by the Houston Jaycees. Later, his Harris County legislative colleagues made him delegation chair. Turner is best known for his candidacy for mayor of the city of Houston in 1991, where he demonstrated his sharp intellect, his clarity of vision, and his strong commitment to education, youth, and spiritual concerns. He has one child, Ashley Paige.

RODNEY ELLIS

Rodney Ellis is an investment banker and a lawyer from Houston.

Rodney Ellis, Senator, Harris County.
— Courtesy TAAHO Archives,
Center for American History,
University of Texas at Austin

He is the director of Apex Securities, Inc., a Texas-based investment banking firm specializing in municipal finance. Senator Ellis came to the Texas Senate in 1989, after serving for six years on the Houston City Council. In his first session, Senator Ellis received the Sierra Club's Legislative Service Award for Clean Air, and was named a "Superhero of the 72nd Legislature" by a coalition of civil rights, environmental, and consumer groups. In the 73rd Session, Senator Ellis passed legislation making Texas the first state in the nation to require tax-exempt hospitals to perform a reasonable amount of charity care. He also made Texas the first state in the country to offer school lunch programs for poor schoolchildren during summer vacation. Senator Ellis passed a Hate Crimes bill that increases the penalties for violent crimes motivated by bigotry. In addition, he passed legislation creating the Texas Council on Workforce and Economic Competitiveness, to help meet the demand for highly skilled workers in the new global economy.

Senator Ellis is an advocate of judicial reform that would ensure diversity, quality, and impartiality in the judiciary. He seeks to create new opportunities for minority-owned and women-owned businesses. In 1994, he received the Texas Outstanding Public Service Award for his ongoing effort to ensure that all Texans have access to affordable insurance.

Senator Ellis holds a bachelor's degree from Texas Southern University, a master's degree from the Lyndon B. Johnson School of Public Affairs, and a law degree from The University of Texas Law School. Before entering public office, he was chief of staff to the late Congressman Mickey Leland and former Lieutenant Governor Bill Hobby. Senator Ellis has a daughter, Nicole Ellis.

HAROLD V. DUTTON, JR.

A native of the Fifth Ward and a lifelong Democrat, Harold Dutton's roots began in the Kelly Courts. After graduating from

Phyllis Wheatley High School, Dutton attended Texas Southern University. Representative Dutton graduated from TSU in 1966 with a BBA in accounting and has been designated by the TSU School of Business as a "Distinguished Alumnus." Other than during 1971-72, when Dutton was executive director of Julia C. Hester House, his principal employer upon graduation from TSU was Conoco Inc., where he held numerous management positions. In June 1985, Dutton became president of Four Star Broadcasting, Inc. and part-owner of TV-67, an independent UHF television station in the Houston area that began airing in early 1986. He later became an independent investor and broadcasting consultant. Currently, Representative Dutton operates his own law firm in Houston.

Representative Dutton has served in a number of community activities, and in 1981 was cited as an Outstanding Young Man of America. A member of Kappa Alpha Psi Fraternity and a 32nd Degree Mason, Dutton has been a member of the Texas House of Representatives since 1984. During the 73rd Legislature, he served as co-chairman of the Joint Select Committee on Historically Underutilized Business and was vice-chairman of Urban Affairs. In the 74th Legislature, Dutton served on the Calendars Committee, the Energy Resources Committee, the Insurance Committee, and as chairman of the Subcommittee on Insurance Availability. In addition, Dutton serves as vice-chairman of the House Democratic Caucus, is a member of the Steering Committee for the House Research Organization, a member of the Legislative Study Group, the Legislative Black Caucus, and the Harris County Delegation. He is also a member of the Texas Bar Association, the Houston Bar Association, and the Texas Trial Lawyers Association.

Dutton is a graduate of Thurgood Marshall School of Law, where he was inducted into "Who's Who in American Colleges and Universities," and he has been recognized as Legislator of the Year by the *Forward Times* newspaper, the Houston Police Officers Association, Harris County Deputy Sheriff's Association, and the Afro-American Deputy Sheriff's Association. In November of 1994, Representative Dutton was elected to his sixth term for House District 142.

*Larry Q. Evans,
Representative, Harris County.*
— Courtesy TAAHO Archives,
Center for American History,
University of Texas at Austin

LARRY Q. EVANS

Representative Evans was first elected to serve the people in the 147th State House District in 1982. There were approximately 100,000 residents in the district, which included the University of Houston, Texas Southern University, Jack Yates High School, Third Ward, Fourth Ward, MacGregor Park, and Riverside General High School. Representative Evans had prior legislative experience as a former staff assistant to Senator Craig A. Washington, and as an administrative assistant to former Congresswoman Barbara Jordan and State Senator Chet Brooks. Evans is a practicing attorney with the law firm of Washington & Randle in Houston.

He received his B.A. in political science from The University of Texas, his M.A. from Texas Southern University, and his Doctor of Jurisprudence from the Thurgood Marshall School of Law. Evans and his wife, Charlene, have two sons, Larry Q. Evans II and Jon Alan Evans. Representative Evans is a member of the National Bar Association, the Texas Trial Lawyers Association, the Houston Lawyers Association, and the Thurgood Marshall Law School Alumni Association. Evans is also licensed by the Texas Supreme Court, the United States District Court for the Southern District of Texas, the United States Court of Appeals for the Fifth Circuit, and the United States Supreme Court. Representative Evans' committees and responsibilities include the Harris County Delegation (vice-chairman), Local and Consent Calendars, the Legislative Black Caucus (chairman), Criminal Jurisprudence (Budget and

Oversight), Ways and Means (Budget and Oversight — vice-chairman), the House Research Steering Committee, and the Democratic Caucus Nominating Committee.

Garnet F. Coleman,
Representative, Harris County.
— Courtesy TAAHO Archives,
Center for American History,
University of Texas at Austin

GARNET F. COLEMAN

State Representative Garnet Coleman was born September 8, 1961, in Houston. He is the son of Dr. John B. and Mrs. Gloria Coleman. Coleman and his wife have one son, Garnet Austin Coleman. He attended Howard University in Washington, D.C. He graduated cum laude with a bachelor of arts in political science from the University of Saint Thomas at Houston in 1990. Coleman possesses multiple entrepreneurial skills and has been successful in several business ventures.

Representative Coleman served District 147 in Texas as a member of the House of Representatives during the 72nd and 73rd Legislatures. Coleman is the only legislator to have been appointed to the House Appropriations Committee during his first regular legislative session. He served as a member of the Committee on Public Health. He was elected vice-chairman of the Harris County Legislative Delegation, and became a member of the Texas Legislative Black Caucus. Garnet's political activities include Apportions Committee, Environmental and General Government Subcommittee, Public Health Committee, vice-chairman of Harris County Legislative Delegation, Texas Task Force on Smoking and Health, Texas Legislative Black Caucus, Appropriations Interim Subcommittee, Gangs and Juvenile Crime Prevention, Texas Commission on Children and Youth, Retirement and Aging Committee, Judicial Affairs Committee, and delegate to the Democratic National Convention in 1988 and 1992.

*Royce West,
Senator, Dallas County.*
— Courtesy TAAHO Archives,
Center for American History,
University of Texas at Austin

ROYCE WEST

State Senator Royce West, D-Dallas, is a successful attorney and Texas legislator. He was installed as state senator, District 23 (Dallas County), in January 1993. He took his second oath of office on January 10, 1995. His agenda for the district and throughout his first and current terms as a state senator include school safety, economic development, crime, and education. Significant strides occurred in each of these areas during his first term. During the 73rd Legislature, Senator West was instrumental in derailing legislation that would have allowed Texans to carry weapons openly in holsters by his successful filibuster of Senate Bill 1776. His action stalled the bill long enough to delay its consideration by Governor Ann Richards until after the end of the regular session, thus avoiding any action by the Senate or the House to override the governor's veto. Other key legislative measures sponsored or cosponsored by Senator West during the 73rd Session created the enhancement of penalties for hate-crimes, increased penalties for randomly shooting guns inside the city limits, prohibited the public consumption of alcohol within 600 feet of a public or private school, and increased penalties for violent crimes such as gang-related violence and crimes against women and children. Senator West was a major voice in the first revision of the Texas Penal Code in over twenty years. The *Dallas Morning News* wrote that Senator West was a lawmaker to watch.

West currently serves on the State Affairs, Criminal Justice, Jurisprudence (vice-chair), Administration, and Committee of the Whole on Legislative and Congressional Redistricting Committees. He served on the Labor Committee of the Assembly on the Legislature for the National Conference of State Legislators (NCSL) and was an alternate member of the Justice and Consumer Affairs Committee for the State Legislators Conference (SLC). Lieutenant Governor Bob Bullock nominated Senator West for the NCSL and SLC committees. He also served on the following interim committees: Joint Select Committee on Historically Underutilized Businesses and Senate Interim Committee on Domestic Violence.

He is a graduate of the University of Texas at Arlington with bachelor's and master's degrees in sociology. While attending UTA, he served as president of the student body. He later earned his Doctorate of Jurisprudence from the University of Houston, receiving his license as an attorney and counselor-at-law from the State of Texas in 1979. He was certified by the Federal Bar of Texas (Northern District) in 1980.

From 1979 to 1984, Royce West worked in the Dallas County district attorney's office and specifically served as chief felony prosecutor from 1982 to 1984. He was the first African American to hold this position in Dallas County. In addition, he was the Democratic nominee for district attorney in 1986. He has developed a reputation in political and civic circles as a "coalition builder" of multiethnic groups to address community issues. The prevailing issues of crime, discrimination in the workplace, safe schools, economic development, education, and health care have been and will continue to be addressed by Senator West.

His experience and civic affiliations speak to his commitment to serve the public. He has served the following boards, commissions, and memberships: Dallas Bar Association; Dallas County Democratic Party — Finance Council; Dallas County Dental Health Board; J. L. Turner/Dallas Black Bar Association; Mayor's Criminal Justice Task Force; NAACP — life member; National Bar Association; Texas Association of African American Lawyers; Texas Criminal Justice Task Force; Texas Defense Lawyers Association; Texas Turnpike Authority; UNCF Volunteer Leadership Committee — general co-chair/honorary chair; UTA Development Board; UTA Alumni Association — University Society member; UTA Minority Scholarship organizer; West Dallas Community Centers — president; and Wilmer Hutchins ISD Scholarship organizer. He has received numerous awards and honors, including the following: Torch of Consciousness Award, American Jewish Congress — 1994; Dreamer Award, I Have A Dream Foundation Inc. — 1994; Legislative Crime Fighter of the Year, Greater Dallas Crime Commission — 1994; Delta Xi and Theta Theta Appreciation Award (Omega Psi Phi) — 1994; Appreciation Award by Daniel "Chappie" James Learning Center — 1993; Distinguished Texas

Senate Political Achievement Award by BOSS VI — 1993; Christian Community Leadership Award by Cathedral of Faith Missionary Baptist Church — 1993; The Jonathan Jasper Wright Award by Dallas Chapter of the National Association of Blacks in Criminal Justice — 1993; Appreciation Award by the National Black Chamber of Commerce — 1993; 100% Attendance Record during 73rd Legislative Session — 1993; Southeast Dallas Business and Professional Women's Man of the Year — 1993; Certificate of Appreciation by the Texas Municipal League — 1993; CB Bunkley Award by the J. L. Turner Legal Association — 1992; Political Representation Award by the Texas Peace Officers Association — 1992; Outstanding Service Award by the Successful Student Learning Center — 1992; African American History Month Award by David W. Carter High School — 1990; Service Award by Phyllis Wheatley School — 1989; Outstanding Leadership Award by the United Negro College Fund — 1987-1992; Outstanding Service Award by Wilmer Hutchins High School — 1987; Mayor's Criminal Task Force Award — 1987; Distinguished Service Award by the New Hope Baptist Church — 1986; Chief Felony Prosecutor (283rd Judicial District Court) — 1982. Royce West is an active deacon of Good Street Baptist Church, and a devoted father and husband.

Dawnna Dukes,
Representative, Travis County.
— Courtesy TAAHO Collections,
Austin, Texas

DAWNNA DUKES

Dawnna Dukes, elected in 1994 as state representative for District 50, Northeast Travis County, is a third-generation native of Austin. During her elementary school years she attended St. Mary's Parochial School and lived in East Austin with her six brothers and sisters. She attended Pearce Junior High and graduated from John H. Reagan High School. She completed her studies at Texas A&M University in 1986, receiving a bachelor of science degree in psychology. Upon graduation from college she was employed by a development, management and construction firm in College Station. She returned to Austin in 1987 to be closer to family and pursue other business interests. In 1988 she began employment at Maxey & Associates, Inc., a criminal justice planning and architectural firm, as a receptionist. Within three months she moved into the planning and marketing division, traveling through Texas and Mississippi developing and performing criminal justice planning methodologies for more than 3,000 jail beds totaling over $80,000 in construction value. After seventeen months she was offered the position of corporate secretary, member of the board of directors, and shareholder in the firm. In May of 1992 she entered into a partnership in the planning of Maxey & Dukes Associates. In 1995, Dawnna Dukes owned DM Dukes & Associates, an African-American, female-owned, sole proprietorship based in Austin. DM Dukes & Associates consults in the areas of legislative issues, criminal justice planning, business resource development, research planning, business marketing/outreach, grant writing and acquisition, employee recruitment, employee training, technical assistance, and education. Dawnna Dukes has served on legislative committees including Environmental Regulation and State, Federal and International Relations.

Ron Givens,
Representative, Lubbock County.
— Courtesy TAAHO Archives,
Center for American History,
University of Texas at Austin

RON GIVENS

Ron Givens was first elected to the Texas House of Representatives in 1984. Serving District 83 constituents, he was responsive to the needs of Lubbock and the South Plains. He served on the State, Federal and International Relations Committee, the House Public Health Committee, and the House Cultural and Historical Resources Committee. Givens was appointed by Governor Bill Clements to serve on the Texas Commission on the Celebration of the Bicentennial of the United States Constitution.

Givens grew up in Lubbock and attended Huston-Tillotson

College in Austin. His lifelong commitment to Lubbock was the catalyst behind his election as the first African-American Republican to the Texas House since Reconstruction. Givens' civic involvement includes service with the Lubbock Board of Realtors, Lubbock County General Assistance Agency, and the Texas National Guard. He was also a lieutenant in the U.S. Army Reserves.

*Fred L. Blair,
Representative, Dallas County.*
— Courtesy TAAHO Archives,
Center for American History,
University of Texas at Austin

FRED L. BLAIR

Since 1968, Fred L. Blair was engaged in general real estate practice. He specialized in sales, management, and appraisal of all types of real estate property. Blair was born in Corsicana in 1940. He is married to Evelyn, and they have four children: Fred, Jr., Sandra, Reginald, and Tiffany. Blair attended El Centro Junior College in Dallas. He was elected Dallas city councilman, 1980-1984, deputy mayor pro tem, 1980-1983, mayor pro tem, 1983-1984, and representative of District 110 to the Texas House in 1986.

*Jerald H. Larry,
Representative, Dallas County.*
— Courtesy TAAHO Archives,
Center for American History,
University of Texas at Austin

JERALD H. LARRY

Born and raised in Dallas, Jerald H. Larry is a graduate of Lincoln High School. Remaining in the Dallas Metroplex to receive his college education, Larry studied at North Texas State University in Denton, as well as

El Centro College and Bishop College, both in Dallas. After completing his college education, Jerald Larry embarked upon a career as a tax consultant, first owning and managing Larry's 4-J's Professional Business Services, and later supervising investigations for the Texas State Treasury. He is also a licensed real estate agent.

Larry was officially elected to serve in the Texas House of Representatives for District 111 of Dallas on November 4, 1986. Representative Larry's civic and organizational activities include the Dallas Black Chamber of Commerce, the Texas Coalition of Black Democrats, the Dallas County Democratic Progressive Voters' League, and the Dallas County Democratic Party. Jerald H. Larry resides in Dallas and is the father of two sons, Jerald Andre Larry and Jerrod Enrique Larry.

Yvonne Davis,
Representative, Dallas County.
— Courtesy TAAHO Archives,
Center for American History,
University of Texas at Austin

YVONNE DAVIS

Yvonne Davis, a woman who believes an individual should succeed because of her ability and not her ethnic identification or gender, was born in Odessa on February 4, 1955. She graduated from Odessa Ector High School and earned a bachelor of science in political science at the University of Houston. She became the owner and CEO of YD Associates, a political/governmental relations consulting firm in Dallas. In 1993, she was elected a state representative to the Texas House of Representatives for District 111 in Dallas County. Davis also served as a research assistant for the Texas State Senate, staff assistant to the U.S. House of Representatives in Washington, D.C., and administrative assistant for the Dallas County Commissioners Court. Her political and civic experiences include:

✳ Texas Democratic Party executive committeewoman, 23rd Senatorial District (two terms).
✳ Precinct chair, Precinct 4444, Dallas.
✳ Member of Oak Cliff Democrats.

✳ Member of Texas Coalition of Black Democrats.
✳ Board of Directors, Greater Oak Cliff Citizens Council.
✳ Board of Directors, Bryan's House.
✳ Women's Council of Dallas.
✳ Business and Professional Women's Club, Inc.
✳ Who's Who in American Politics.
✳ Public Relations Society of America.
✳ National Association of Black Meetings Planners.
✳ Oak Cliff Chamber of Commerce (Dallas).
✳ Dallas Black Chamber of Commerce.
✳ President of Democratic Women of Dallas County.
✳ NAACP Board of Directors.
✳ Dallas Assembly.
✳ Women Legislators Lobby.
✳ League of Women Voters.

*Charlie and Isabella Brown,
wealthy ex-slaves.*
— Courtesy Bob Lee, Texas
Trailblazer, Houston

CHARLIE AND ISABELLA BROWN

It was an ironic twist of fate when ex-slave Charlie Brown purchased a plantation and his wife became mistress of the house she once served as a slave. And when Charlie Brown died, a *Houston Post* headline noted that he was "The Wealthiest Negro in Texas."

Brown began purchasing property in West Columbia, Texas, in Brazoria County not long after slavery ended, according to Morris Richardson, who became interested in Brown's life when he taught at the school named for Brown beginning in 1951. Richardson read that Brown bought about 900 acres of land and eventually owned about a third of the land in West Columbia — some 3,000 acres. During a guided tour of the area, Richardson pointed out miles of road winding through land that Brown once owned. Descendants still own some of the land and three of his grandchildren still live there, but much of the land has been sold and some was lost in legal disputes. Richardson and his wife purchased four acres of the land and live in the home that one of Brown's daughters once owned.

Nature has reclaimed much of the evidence of a thriving community known as Cedar Grove, where Brown farmed with the help of his family and tenant farmers. Gone are the homes they lived in, as well as the church and the school for which Brown donated property. All that is left of the first home that Brown purchased is a brick chimney surrounded by trees and shrubbery. He and his wife, Isabella, are buried in the family cemetery not far from the old homestead. It is a tranquil spot shaded by hundred-year-old cedar, pecan and live oak trees on a little hill just above Dance Bayou, named for the family that Brown bought the land from long ago. One of Brown's granddaughters, Valda Tolbert, lives across the bayou from the cemetery. She did not remember her grandfather, but always heard that he purchased the land for twenty-five cents an acre. Family members also still attend St. Mary's AME Church, founded in the 1860s and built on land donated by the Brown family.

Charlie Brown later moved his family to downtown West Columbia into a two-story mansion. It was an old plantation home that Brown had moved from the Brazos River to the town's main thoroughfare. There he had a grist mill, cotton gin, and syrup mill. Descendants say that Brown's home had the first electric lights in the city and that he was the first Negro who owned a car. He was probably also one of the first to have a telephone. Today, Brown Street, named in his memory, goes right through the area where his mansion stood. An old, faded photograph is the only record that there was ever a home on the now vacant property; however, the memory of Charlie Brown is still evident. He donated the land for the Charlie Brown Intermediate School, located on Brown Street not far from where the family home stood.

There are hundreds of descendants of Charlie Brown, and each summer they return to West Columbia for a family reunion on Juneteenth. They celebrate on the land that their family has owned for more than 120 years. No one knows how Charlie Brown got the money to begin buying property in 1869, but everyone knows that he became one of the most influential men in the area — quite a legacy for a man who spent nearly half his life in slavery.

T. P. FOWLER, JR.: Grandson of 80 John Wallace

T. P. Fowler, Jr., whose full name is Thaddeus Postelle Fowler, Jr., was born to Thaddeus Postelle Fowler, Sr., and Mrs. Eula (Wallace)

Fowler at Neylandville, Texas, which is located in northeast Texas, midway between Greenville and Commerce in Hunt County. Neylandville, located on the Cotton Belt Railroad, is successor to "Jim Town," an all-black town, which was founded by James "Free Jim" Brigham more than 125 years ago. Brigham was called "Free Jim" after he purchased his freedom, his wife's freedom, and the freedom of two of his ten children during the 1850s before slavery ended in 1865. T. P. Fowler, Jr.'s paternal grandfather, A. G. Fowler, was born a slave on February 22, 1859, in South Carolina. A. G. Fowler came to Texas in 1875, and after his marriage to Mary Arbella Enox in 1877, they became the parents of sixteen children. During the 1880s, A. G. Fowler and four Neylandville residents — Professor Benjamin Freeman (Neylandville's first teacher and first postmaster), George Washington Brigham, Thomas Brigham, and John Houston — formed a farmers' co-op, which built a general store, constructed a cotton gin, and purchased a wheat drill and a wheat-harvesting machine. The Neylandville post office was located in the general store from about 1886 to 1924, when the post office was discontinued and closed by the U.S. Post Office Department.

During the 1890s, A. G. Fowler, Professor Benjamin Freeman, John Houston, George W. Brigham, and Thomas Brigham joined the Farmer's Improvement Society, an organization established by Robert Lloyd Smith, a free black who was born in South Carolina in 1861. After attending Avery Institute in South Carolina and the University of South Carolina, Smith received his degree from Atlanta University. After migrating to Texas, Smith was principal of the Oakland Normal School in Colorado County in 1885. As an aide to Booker T. Washington and an advocate of the Tuskegee Line of Accommodation and Self-Help, Smith's Farmer's Improvement Society encouraged black farmers toward economic independence with home and farm ownership, cooperative buying, cash purchases instead of credit buying, and raising much of their own food. The Society, which sponsored agricultural fairs and paid sick and death benefits, spread over Texas, Oklahoma and Arkansas, and branched out to include a truck growers' union, an agricultural and normal college located between Wolfe City and Ladonia in 1906, and the Farmer's Improvement Bank in Waco. The woman's barnyard auxiliaries specialized in better egg, poultry, and butter production, and the raising of improved swine for the market.

A. G. Fowler, Professor Benjamin Freeman, John Houston,

Thomas Brigham and George Brigham served as bank directors and as trustees of the college at various times. The St. Paul School District was located in Neylandville from the 1880s until the district merged with the Commerce (Texas) Independent School District during the 1960s. Prior to the 1940s, the St. Paul School District was one of the few black public schools in the area which offered such vocational courses as homemaking, industrial shop, and agriculture. The school was one of the first to teach typing in the area. Fowler, the Brighams, Houston, Freeman, and other Neylandville residents served as St. Paul Trustees at various times.

After graduating from Texas College in 1934, T. P. Fowler, Jr. spent the next four years with his grandparents near Loraine. He worked on the Wallace headquarters ranch under the supervision of his grandfather, 80 John Wallace. His uncle, Carson Wallace, operated the family's Silver Creek ranch, which is located fourteen miles south of the headquarters ranch. From 1934 to 1938, he (Fowler) pursued summer courses and agricultural seminars at Prairie View A&M University. From 1938 to 1941, he taught in Greenville before returning to the family ranch after the death of his grandfather. Since Carson Wallace had moved to the ranch headquarters and had assumed the position of ranch manager, Fowler and his wife moved to the Silver Creek ranch, which he operated until 1946 when they moved to their stock farm near Loraine. From 1946 to 1981, his involvement in the D. W. Wallace ranch operation was part-time. After 1981, his involvement increased. He was one of the three co-managers of the ranch as of June 1, 1988.

In 1943, Fowler's wife began teaching in the Loraine Colored School, which held classes in a church. He and his wife erected a building which was used for school until 1949, when a building from the Shepherd School District was moved to Loraine. The school was closed in 1965, when classes were integrated. He became principal in 1949, but moved to Sweetwater in 1953 to become principal of Washington High School. In 1963, he became principal of D. W. Wallace High School in Colorado City. From 1966 to 1981, he filled other administrative positions in the Colorado City Public Schools. His wife was a special education supervisor and reading teacher during that time. At retirement in 1981, he and his wife had thirty-five and forty-two years of service, respectively. They received their master of education degrees from McMurry College in 1959. She had previously received her B.A. from Wiley College. Both were life members of the Texas State Teachers Association, the Texas Retired Teachers Association, and the National Education Association.

In Sweetwater, T. P. Fowler, Jr. worked with the Red Cross and United Fund organizations. After leaving Sweetwater, he served four years (1970-72 and 1978-80) as president of the Mitchell County Cancer Unit and three years as treasurer (1986-89). He was secretary-treasurer of the Colorado City Lions Club from 1982 to 1986. He was president of the Mitchell County Retired Teachers Association (1982-84). He held membership in the West Texas Historical Association and other historical organizations.

Other honors and community service activities included: counselor of Washington Hi-Y Club, Greenville, Texas, 1938-41; scoutmaster, Loraine (Texas) Boy Scout Troop, 1944-53; chairman, Boy Scout Committee, Sweetwater, 1953-63, and Colorado City, 1963-66; Boy Scout Service Appreciation Award, 1955; member, Texas State Fair Achievement Day Advisory Committee, 1955; C.M.E. Church Layman Award, 1972; American Cancer Society Appreciation Certificate, 1978; member of Texas College Board of Trustees; member of General Connectional Board of the Christian Methodist Episcopal (C.M.E.) Church; and life member of the Texas African American Heritage Organization. T. P. Fowler, Jr. was elected delegate to the C.M.E. Church General Conference five times, and served once as an alternate delegate. He was a member of the Mitchell County Soil and Water District Advisory Committee. He died October 22, 1991, and was buried in the family cemetery on the D. W. Wallace Ranch near Loraine in Mitchell County.

*80 John Wallace on the ranch
in Mitchell County.*
— Courtesy Institute of Texan Cultures,
San Antonio, Texas

DANIEL W. WALLACE:
A Texas African-American Cowboy

Strangely enough, one of the most honored residents of Mitchell County achieved success the hard way without benefit of adequate educational opportunities or beneficent legislation. Although he had it harder than most, he became a greater success than most.

The life story of Daniel Webster "80 John" Wallace has been an exciting subject of conversation in thousands of homes throughout Texas and the Great Southwest for many years. He has been frequently highlighted in the media and more recently in literature. In 1960, his youngest daughter, Hettye Wallace Branch, wrote *The Story of 80 John*, a brief book which tells the life story of her colorful father. His unique story has received favorable comment in more than a dozen books of historical significance, including college and secondary school textbooks, and in many magazine and newspaper articles. His picture and life story have been featured on calendars and in historical brochures, exhibits, and displays.

Daniel Webster Wallace was born of slave parents (William Wallace and Mary Barbry Wallace) on September 15, 1860, near Inez in Victoria County, Texas. He was born in a log house on a small farm owned by Mrs. Mary (Miles) Cross. The farm consisted of about 200 acres, a few cows, and other livestock. The house, which contained two rooms and a small hall, had dirt floors. Although both of his parents were born in Virginia, they did not meet until they came to Texas. William Wallace lived in Mississippi before he was brought to Texas by a slave owner named Wallace. Mary Barbry lived in Missouri before she was sold to Jonathan Miles, who brought her to Texas in about 1859. Although their names are not available, she gave birth to three children in Missouri. The youngest came to Texas with her and was two years old when mother and child were sold by Miles to his sister, Mary Cross, for the sum of $1,000.

Mrs. Cross was the widow of Thomas S. Cross, who died in 1857 after they moved from Missouri to Texas in 1853. They had three children: Jack Cross, Thomas B. Cross, and Mary Cross. Mary Barbry's child, who was listed on the June 1860 Census as a two-year-old boy, died sometime during the year 1860. His death probably occurred before the birth of his brother, Daniel Webster. Mrs. Cross married Josiah Dial O'Daniel, a captain in the Army of the Confederate States of America, on July 4, 1861. Three children were born to this union: James Dial, Milton Howard (Mitt), and Lillie. When the Civil War ended on April 9, 1865, it sounded the death knell of slavery in the United States of America. Mary Barbry, however, continued to work for the O'Daniel family.

Mr. and Mrs. O'Daniel always spoke highly of Mary as being different from the other slaves. They sometimes spoke of her as an "up-to-date" or "high-class" slave. Her attractiveness was mostly in the way she held her head in walking, and in the neatness of the coil of long black hair at the nape of her neck. She immediately became the maid or house girl in her new home when she was purchased by Mrs. Cross in 1860. She did her work so well that her mistress was very pleased and permitted her to bring her son to the "Big House," where she could attend him while working. When Webster grew older, he was left alone to amuse himself in his mother's home. Since he was a precocious child, he needed very little outside attention. He could and would always entertain and keep himself busy riding the stick horses his mother made for him. They pitched, bucked, and sometimes stampeded from room to room until he grew tired and fell asleep on the floor.

After Mrs. Cross married Captain O'Daniel and the O'Daniel family moved to a farm near Flatonia in Fayette County in 1866, Mary Barbry Wallace and Webster went along with them to live. During the period from 1866 to 1876, when Webster was growing up in Fayette County, school was provided for African-American boys and girls in three of those years. When school was provided, the three-month term was held in the winter time, the coldest three months of the year. The teacher kept the children bringing in wood periodically to keep the building warm. Since Webster was taller than the other boys, the teacher asked him to make more trips for wood than the others. This caused him to have an aversion for the teacher and the school. He tended to become sullen and stubborn when he thought he was imposed upon. Due to the failure to provide an adequate school in the community, Webster received very little academic training during his formative years.

While growing up in Fayette County, Webster played with Tom Cross, who was four years older than he was, and with James Dial O'Daniel, who was born about two years after Webster (in 1862). He also played with several Anglo and African-American boys who were about his age. One of the African-American boys was named Joe Scallion, who was one year older than Webster. When Scallion later moved to Mitchell County during the early 1880s, he found that Webster Wallace was a Mitchell County resident and had been for several years. Webster and his playmates often amused themselves by participating in footraces and horseraces.

They fished and swam in the area creeks and hunted small game. They also engaged in such manly sports as boxing and wrestling. Webster was best in boxing among his peers, and was a very close second to Joe Scallion in wrestling events. Sometimes Webster excelled Joe on a particular day, but overall Joe was acclaimed tops in wrestling events by a slim margin.

As a youngster, Webster worked for a number of people and received little or no pay in return since most of the people in those days did not believe in rewarding children handsomely for their labor. When they were paid wages, it amounted to about thirty cents per day. He worked in the fields during the planting, growing, and harvesting seasons. In the spring, he helped to plant corn and cotton. Since there were no mechanical planters, seeds were dropped by hand into furrows opened by a plow drawn by one horse or mule. In the beginning, he usually dropped the seeds while another worker covered them up with a hoe. After the seeds came up and the plants started growing, he helped to keep the rows clean by chopping grass and weeds. During the harvesting season, he helped to gather corn and pick cotton. When he grew older, Webster began to plow the furrows during planting season, and then plow the middles to cultivate the soil during the growing season. He was able to earn up to fifty cents per day when he learned how to plow.

Some people who were good cotton pickers preferred the harvesting season to the others, since their earnings were based on their ability to perform rather than on a fixed wage. Since he was not proficient in the art of picking cotton, Webster's earnings during the cotton picking season amounted to about thirty-five to forty cents per day. Although he did not like any kind of farm work, he disliked the chopping of grass and weeds most of all. He always seemed to be thirsty, and would take his hoe and go to the tree where an old canteen and gourd cup swayed back and forth rhythmically with water. Actually, he was thirsty, but also was thinking of ways to join the cowboys he heard singing and yelling as they drove cattle to and fro.

Webster's mother was a very devout Christian believer of the Baptist faith. As a consequence, he was well-acquainted with religious activities. On some Sundays, they attended church services with the O'Daniel family. On other Sundays, he and his mother attended services at a segregated black church. On one Sunday, the minister of the church the O'Daniel family attended selected a text from the book of Genesis. As he discussed the story of Cain and

Abel, he said, "Abel was a keeper of sheep, but Cain was a tiller of the ground. When the two brothers brought their offerings to God, the Lord had respect for Abel's offering, but not for Cain and his offering. Because of this, I exhort you to begin concentrating on livestock raising instead of spending all of your time tilling the soil." After mentioning several successful stock raisers in other parts of South Texas, he cited Jonathan Miles as a prime local example. Continuing, he said, "Mr. Miles has accumulated a very large and profitable livestock operation out in West Texas. This proves that God is blessing him because of his wise choice of a respected occupation." This sermon stimulated and encouraged O'Daniel and the other male members of the congregation to begin spreading their livestock operations.

Tom Cross rode horseback to Runnels County and began working for his uncle, Jonathan Miles. Tom's older brother, Jack Cross, was already employed by Miles. In 1872, Miles formed a ranching partnership with Sam Gholson, who had dissolved a partnership with George Kindred (Kin) Elkins in Coleman County. Although Jack Cross moved to Central Texas, Tom continued to work for Gholson and Miles. About 1873, Gholson and Miles moved their operation to Taylor County and located their headquarters on Jim Ned Creek near Buffalo Gap. When Gholson and Miles dissolved their partnership, Tom Cross chose to continue working for Gholson. Gholson later became the managing partner of the Gholson-Dunn ranch operation. Tom Cross became the ranch foreman.

Following the Sunday that the white minister delivered the sermon on Cain and Abel, Webster and his mother heard a similar sermon by the minister of the black Baptist church. This minister summed up his sermon by saying, "It's better to work for white folks who are in the cattle business than it is to work for those who don't do anything but till the soil." These sermons impressed young Webster to the extent that he wanted to be a cowboy instead of a plowboy. Thereafter, when he worked in the fields, he was always thinking of ways to join the ranks of the cowboys.

During the month of December 1875, he overheard a conversation which made him think that the opportunity to become a cowboy might come sooner than he had expected. Maj. Robert Carr, a former Confederate Army officer, told O'Daniel, "I want to move my cattle to Lampasas County. Then I want to pick out some big steers and old cows to send up the trail to Ellsworth, Kansas. Since I don't want to go up the trail myself, I am in the market for a trail driver."

"My stepson, Tom Cross, just might be able to help you. He's coming home for Christmas and stay about two months before going back to Buffalo Gap," O'Daniel replied. When Tom Cross arrived in Flatonia about two days before Christmas Day, he readily agreed to help Major Carr move his herd to Lampasas County. But he hedged on accepting a job as trail boss for the cows and big steers Carr wanted to send north to the Kansas markets. "Since I am working for Gholson and Dunn," he said, "I want to talk with Sam Gholson before taking the job. You might want to contact drovers like Shanghai Pierce and Mark Withers and make a deal with one of them. On the other hand, they might buy your cattle on credit and pay you after they have sold them in Kansas. If you want to wait until I get back to Buffalo Gap and talk with Gholson," Cross continued, "Gholson might work out a deal to take your cattle along on his trip next month."

Major Carr responded that they would get together on it after they reached Lampasas County.

Despite the fact that Tom Cross was about four years older than Webster, they were very close to each other before Tom rode away to West Texas to become a cowboy. They regained that closeness later (January and February 1876). Tom visited in Flatonia after Christmas of 1875. Webster asked Tom many questions about riding, roping, trail driving, and herding cattle. Webster listened eagerly as Tom explained and described his life on the open range. Although it was evident that Webster wanted to be a part of the trail drive to Lampasas and a possible trip upon the Western Trail, nothing definite was actually put into words. The two of them, however, had a mutual understanding about certain things which would develop later.

During the second week in March 1876, Tom Cross, Major Carr, and the latter's cowboys began gathering the Carr horse and cattle herds for the drive to Lampasas County. On Saturday morning, the eleventh day of March, Webster learned that the drive would begin Monday, March 13. He walked quickly to the field and began to work vigorously, fully determined that this would be his last day in that field.

On Sunday morning, he arose at 3:30 and dressed in the dark, fearful that he might awake his mother. He treaded silently down the hall and out the door with his hat on his head and an old coat under his arm. As soon as he closed the door, he began running in the direction of the corrals, where the cattle were penned. Tired and gasping for breath, Webster confronted Major Carr and said, "Sir, please take me with you." Carr asked Webster if he could ride, and hearing that he could, Carr called one of the wranglers and told him to saddle a horse for Webster. When that was done, he told the youngster to mount. Webster had some misgivings about riding a real cow horse that he had never ridden before, but he was determined that he could. With screwed-up courage, he climbed into the saddle and expected the worst. Suddenly, the horse lowered his head and went into his act. Young Wallace grabbed the saddle horn with both hands, planted his feet firmly in both stirrups, and held on for dear life. After a few pitches, the horse became docile, as if he knew its rider was desperate to become a cowboy. After the horse quit pitching, Webster was hired and assigned to riding drag when the cattle drive got under way. According to some sources, Webster was hired in spite of his inexperience because the boss (Major Carr) remembered the wild horse he was forced to ride when he was a tenderfoot. Others subscribe to the theory that Tom Cross had interceded for Webster prior to the date that the cattle drive was scheduled to begin.

The cowboys gathered around the chuck wagon for their final orders. Ranch owner Robert Carr made it clear that every man was expected to do his job well and cooperate with the other cowboys on the drive. Each man would be required to obey orders at all times. Then he announced that Tom Cross would serve as trail boss. "Although he is only twenty years old," Carr said, "Tom has been up the trail several times, including one trip when he took over as trail boss after the regular trail boss took sick on the drive. I could be trail boss from here to Lampasas, but I think you might as well start taking orders from him now so you will be used to it if you have to go up the trail from Lampasas without me."

On the morning of March 13, 1876, the Carr trail herd crew swung into action by pointing the herd in the direction it was supposed to go. Ranch owner Carr and his foreman positioned themselves as point riders. About a third of the way back of the point riders were the two swing riders. The two flank riders were stationed about a third of the way back of the swing riders. The drag riders had the most disagreeable job of all because they had to ride in the dust kicked up by the entire herd. Since the least experienced trail hands were placed on drag, Webster was one of the two cowboys assigned to the drag positions.

Although the act of moving cattle up the trail was called "trail driving," the few times they were actually driven were: (1) to get them away from familiar territory when they first left their home range, (2) to tire them down in an effort to avoid stampedes, and (3) to reach feed and water in sections where these were scarce. At other times, they were merely trailed or kept in the direction the drover or trail boss wanted them to go as they grazed along at the rate of about ten to twelve miles a day. The Carr trail herd made about twenty-five miles the first day. After the second or third day, the trail herd started making ten to fifteen miles a day.

One day the trail crew drove the herd hard for a few hours in a successful effort to avoid a stampede. The next day was another story, however, when a massive stampede was caused by a band of wild horses. After several hours of hard riding which tested the mettle, strength, and endurance of the trail crew, the stampeding herd was brought under control. Despite his inexperience, Webster Wallace "pulled his freight" during the stampede and won his spurs as a trail hand. Moreover, his performance as a night guard continued to be satisfactory. He was complimented by Carr, Cross, and some of the trail hands. After the cattle left the bedground the next morning and were strung out in a thin line, Carr and Cross, who were stationed on opposite sides of the herd, began counting the cattle. As each hundred head was counted, each man tied a knot in his lariat rope. When the herd had passed, Carr and Cross counted their knots. When each announced his tally to the other, both agreed that no animals were missing.

During the remainder of the journey to Lampasas County, the drive proceeded more or less on schedule without incident. Eventually, the lead cattle entered Lampasas County, their destination, followed by the rest of the herd. When Carr and Cross viewed the tall grass growing on the land the former had selected for his new ranch site, they agreed that Carr should let his old cows and big steers graze the area for at least two months before starting up the trail to Kansas.

After the cattle were turned loose on the free range, the trail hands who were not on Carr's regular payroll received their pay in cash and were told that they could go home. Tom Cross received

$30 for his work; Webster received fifteen silver dollars, the largest amount of money he had ever received at one time. Strangely enough, he did not keep it very long. Major Carr sold him a bridle, saddle, blanket, and a slicker for $13.50, leaving him the paltry sum of a dollar and a half. Placing his newly acquired purchases on a pony owned by Tom Cross, Webster joined Cross in riding to Buffalo Gap, where he hoped to get a job working for Sam Gholson on the Gholson-Dunn spread.

When they reached Buffalo Gap, Cross told Gholson that Major Carr would like to send some cattle up the trail with Gholson and Dunn and associates when the next drive to Kansas took place. Gholson agreed to include the Carr cattle in the next cattle drive, but frowned on the idea of hiring an extra cowhand. He reminded Cross that the ranch policy was to limit employees to twelve. James Isaac (Jim) Greene, a Gholson-Dunn cowhand who lived nearby and owned a small herd of cattle and a string of horses, overheard Gholson. He said he had been building up his livestock and planned to start his own operation. When he quit, he knew there would be a spot for Webster.

After working for Sam Gholson at Buffalo Gap in Taylor County, Webster helped John Nunn's NUN outfit drive the first herd into Scurry County. Seventeen months later, he began working on Clay Mann's "J D" ranch, which was located in southeastern Mitchell County and southwestern Nolan County. Mann ruled a cattle empire, which at its peak had vast herds roaming and grazing the luxuriant, grassy slopes and ranges of southeastern Montana, north central Wyoming, eastern New Mexico, western Texas, and southwestern Chihuahua in the Republic of Mexico. Impressed by Wallace's performance as a top hand, Mann decided to teach the hard-working youth the economics of the cattle business. In 1881, after saving most of his monthly wages for two years, Webster purchased his own herd, which was permitted to graze on the Mann Ranch. At this time he acquired his famous nickname, "80 John." Mann's famous "80" brand provided the "80" half of Wallace's nickname. He had acquired the "John" part when he worked for John Nunn.

During the years from 1879 to 1884, Mann sent trail outfits to Powder River, Wyoming; Ogallala, Nebraska; Chihuahua, Mexico; and to the Kansas railheads at Dodge City, Caldwell, Abilene and Coffeyville. Eighty John Wallace was involved in each of the trail drives. His trail-driving experiences included service on the Chisholm, Goodnight-Loving, Shawnee, Western, and Cut-Off trails.

In 1885, encouraged by his employer, Wallace began accumulating his own grazing land, and eventually owned twelve and a half sections (8,000 acres) in Mitchell and Nolan counties. At the age of twenty-five, realizing that he needed a better education, he rode to a Navarro County school and entered the second grade. After two winters of studying, his basic skills improved greatly. While attending school in Navarro County, he met and married Miss Laura Deloach Owen, who planned to teach school in Falls County. Instead, she married 80 John Wallace and went to West Texas as a bride. Her father, Francis Green Owen, and her maternal grandfather, Henry Lawrence Carruthers, were among those ex-slaves who purchased land after slavery ended and continued to farm after 1865.

Owen and Carruthers and other Navarro County African-American farmers secured a charter for "The Colored Men's Land and Commercial Joint Stock Company." Chartered with a capital stock of $25,000, the company's aim was to enable blacks to buy and improve lands in Navarro. During the 1890s, Green Owen, Henry Carruthers and his son, George Carruthers, and two of Henry Carruthers' grandsons, William Porter and Squire C. Porter, Jr., were among those who joined Robert Lloyd Smith's Farmer's Improvement Society. George Carruthers and the Porter brothers were stockholders in the Farmer's Improvement Bank in Waco. George Carruthers was a member of the Trustee Board of the Farmer's Improvement College located between Wolfe City and Ladonia.

At the time of 80 John's death, his four children and three of his four grandchildren had received college educations. His youngest grandson finished high school and attended college later. Wallace's interest in education caused two schools to be named for him. The first, built in 1937 on land he donated, is now used as a neighborhood center. The second, a modern brick structure erected in 1953, served as a public school until 1975, when it was designated as the "Wallace Community Education Center."

When he died March 28, 1939, at the age of seventy-eight, Wallace was the oldest resident pioneer of Mitchell County. Rated as one of the most progressive ranchers and farmers in the county, white or black, his Hereford cattle, numbering more than 500 at times, were of the best. Listing among his friends nearly all of the old-time cattlemen in the area, he was always a central and respected figure at pioneer gatherings in Colorado City each year. His wife died in 1950 at the age of eighty. A membership in the Texas and Southwestern Cattle Raisers Association for more than thirty years, four signal honors, including one during his lifetime, and three that came more than a quarter-century after his death, commemorate Wallace's contributions to the history of the West Texas cattle industry. During the Texas Centennial Celebration in 1936, his "DW" brand was one of 778 brands shown with brief historical sketches on white pine plaques in the cattle brand exhibit, and his branding irons, "D" and "W," were among the 491 branding irons donated by Texas and Southwestern cattle raisers to the livestock division of the Texas Centennial Exposition.

On April 3, 1966, the Mitchell County Historical Society Committee dedicated a Texas Historical Marker honoring 80 John Wallace. In 1968, the photo and story of this colorful pioneer were displayed on the Negro Histo-wall at the Institute of Texan Cultures during the Hemisfair Exposition in San Antonio. In March 1979, Wallace's "DW" brand was one of nine Mitchell County brands selected to be placed on the stairway of the newly opened Kleberg Animal Science Center at Texas A&M University at College Station. His branding irons are also on display in the Center. On July 25, 1981, the "DW" brand was one of fifty-eight registered Mitchell County brands which were burned into wooden panels at a branding ceremony held on the courthouse lawn as a special event of the Mitchell County Centennial Celebration. These panels are displayed under the canopy outside the north wall of the Colorado City Museum. The "DW" brand was first run in Scurry County on the open range during the 1880s, and on leased land in Scurry and Fisher counties during the 1890s and the first two decades of the twentieth century. The brand has been run in Mitchell and Nolan counties since 1889. He also ran the "D Triangle" brand in Mitchell and Nolan counties during the 1880s and 1890s.

The photo-story of Wallace's wife, Mrs. Laura Deloach Owen Wallace, is located in the "Pioneer Women's Exhibit" at the Institute of Texan Cultures in San Antonio. For one who had been reared in the thickly settled farming community of Antioch in Navarro County, Mrs. Wallace adjusted remarkably well to the hardships of the pioneer West Texas environment. She willingly faced the hardships and dangers of frontier life with her husband

and shared in the triumphs and joys involved in creating a better life for their family. At her insistence, her husband established an orchard containing peach and plum trees, berry vines and grape arbors, and purchased a flock of chickens and several dairy cows and swine. As a result, the usual pioneer diet of beef, beans, potatoes, canned tomatoes, and bacon was supplemented with eggs, chicken, milk, butter, and ham. One of the first in the area to plant a garden, Mrs. Wallace grew vegetables, which added to the family diet during the growing season. While growing up in Navarro County, she learned to can and dry fruits, make plum and grape jellies, and cure bacon, ham, and other pork meat cuts. Consequently, her family was able to enjoy, on a year-round basis, many foods that were considered seasonal before the advent of food locker plants and freezer units in homes and grocery stores. Peach cobbler and berry pie were favorite desserts in the Wallace household. Surplus foods, including eggs, chickens, peaches, plums, grapes and cream skimmed from milk, were sold as produce.

When her husband found it necessary to spend time away from home on cow hunts, roundups and other business, Mrs. Wallace was equal to the task of overseeing the ranching operation during his absence. This was especially true during the droughts of 1894 and 1917-18, when she looked after the welfare of the cattle and horses that were left on the ranch after most of the livestock were shipped to out-of-state pastures for grazing purposes. She kept the ranch records of the livestock and farming operations, and handled the business and social correspondence. She was always knowledgeable about cattle numbers and the bale count of each of the farm tenants during the cotton harvest. At various times, she served her church as Sunday school teacher, superintendent, and as president of the Women's Missionary Society. To show appreciation for her contributions to her community, which included both Loraine and Colorado City, and to her church at all levels, a posthumous honor was bestowed upon her when a church building was erected in Loraine in 1953 and named the "Wallace Memorial Christian Methodist Episcopal Church."

Daniel W. "80 John" Wallace's life story appears in *If I Can Do It Horseback,* which is a collection and publication of a group of articles by John M. Hendrix that originally appeared in *The Cattleman,* the official organ of the Texas and Southwestern Cattle Raisers Association. In "Abilene . . . On Catclaw Creek," Katharyn Duff cites 80 John Wallace as one of the first to install windmills in the Colorado City area. He is one of Effie Kaye Adams' "Tall Black Texans."

Besides being one of the first to install windmills in the Colorado City area, he was also among the first to grow feed crops, including maize to feed horses and mules, and grain sorghum, which was put up in bundles for supplemental feeding of cattle during the winter. After his first land purchase, he periodically added to his landholdings and increased his livestock herd. During the 1920s and 1930s, he had 1,200 acres in cultivation. Five hundred acres were planted to cotton and the remainder in feed. He practiced crop rotation, built cross fences in his pastures, and secured the best available herd bulls.

His biography, written by Martha Earnest, a Colorado City native, appears in Volume III of the *Handbook of Texas.*

> During the more than twenty years he worked for Mann he saw every phase of open range cow work. He saw the Texas and Pacific Railroad built beyond Colorado City and worked for such cattlemen as Christopher Columbus Slaughter, Isaac L. Ellword, A. B. "Sug" Robertson, C. A. "Gus" O'Keefe, and for the Bush and Tillar Cattle Company (see Benjamin Johnson Tillar).

A. C. Greene, in his book *A Personal Country,* describes how a delegation of white men requested Wallace's assistance in constructing a badly needed church. His response was the donation of a site and financial assistance. He also assisted in the construction of a church for a Negro congregation in Loraine that served as the first school for Negro pupils there. These gifts and many other acts of charity provided justification for the epitaph on his tombstone: "He was always ready and willing to respond to the call for help."

— Contributed by T. P. Fowler,
Grandson of "80 John," in 1991, shortly before his death

HIRAM WILSON

After emancipation, there were several physical manifestations of the residence and cohesion of African Americans in Texas. The Central Texas community of Capote is a classic example. The most notable were Capote Baptist Church (1872) and H. Wilson & Co.

Hiram Wilson, pottery maker.
— Courtesy TAAHO Archives,
Center for American History,
University of Texas at Austin

(1870), both founded by Hiram Wilson. The men at H. Wilson & Co. produced a line of high-quality stoneware vessels. The vessels were processed by salt glazing, the use of lids on vessels instead of tie-down rims, and the presence of an unusual horseshoe-shaped handle. Vessels from the Wilson's pottery still exist and can be found throughout Central Texas in barns, homes, and antique shops. They are tributes to gifted craftsmen using skills learned in slavery and amplified by creativity to establish a viable business.

Julius W. Becton, Jr.,
Lt. Gen. (U.S. Army, Ret.)
— Courtesy TAAHO Archives,
Center for American History,
University of Texas at Austin

JULIUS W. BECTON, JR., LT. GEN. (U.S. ARMY, RET.)

Lt. Gen. Julius Wesley Becton's public service career includes two key federal positions after nearly forty years of active commissioned service in the U.S. Army, and rising to the rank of lieutenant general. He is the first graduate of Prairie View A&M University to attain star rank in the military. In November 1989, the Texas A&M University System Board of Regents unanimously elected him president of Prairie View A&M University.

After receiving his B.S. degree in mathematics from Prairie View A&M University in 1960, he later earned his M.A. degree in economics from the University of Maryland in 1967. He is also a graduate of top military schools, including the U.S. Army Command and General Staff College, the Armed Forces Staff College, and the National War College. He holds honorary degrees from Huston-Tillotson College in Austin, and Muhlenberg College in Pennsylvania.

Becton enlisted in the U.S. Army in July 1944 and graduated from Officer's Candidate School in 1945. A veteran of World War II and the Korean and Vietnam conflicts, he has served in various positions at scores of posts in this country. Overseas duties carried him to Germany, the Philippines, France, the Southwest Pacific, Korea, and Japan. His active duty assignments included deputy commanding general, U.S. Army Training and Doctrine Command; commander, VII U.S. Corps in Germany; and commander, 1st Cavalry Division. He served almost two years as director of the Office of U.S. Foreign Disaster Assistance before being nominated by then President Ronald Reagan and confirmed by the Senate as director of the Federal Emergency Management Agency, a position he held for nearly four years before moving into the private sector.

Prior to his acceptance of the position of president of Prairie View A&M University, he served as chief operating officer for American Coastal Industries, Inc. A native of Bryn Mawr, Pennsylvania, he served during the late 1980s on the National Board of the American Red Cross and the World Board of Governors for the United Services Organization (USO). He is first vice-president of the U.S. Armor Association and a member of the Federal Emergency Management Agency Advisory Board, the Defense Equal Opportunity Management Institute Board of Visitors, the Fund for the Improvement of Post-Secondary Education Board, the Commission on Colleges of the Southern Association of Colleges and Schools (SACS), the 1st Cavalry Division Association Board of Governors, the Texas A&M Research Foundation Board of Trustees, the Marine Spill Response Corporation Board of Directors, *Right Choices* Editorial Advisory Board, the Boy Scouts of America — Sam Houston Area Council Board of Directors, the National Academy of Public Administration Advisory Panel on the National Transportation Policy — Department of Transportation, and the Editorial Advisory Board of *The Washington Times*.

Becton has been listed in several *Who's Who* directories, and was named by *Ebony Magazine* several times as "One of the 100 Most Influential Blacks in America." Other honors include the Distinguished Service Award (Association of the U.S. Army), the Distinguished Service Award (Federal Emergency Management Agency), Distinguished Knight (Gold) — Order of St. George, and Honorary Colonel — 17th Cavalry Regiment. He is married to the former Louise Thornton, and they have five children — Shirley, Karen, Joyce, Renee, and Wesley. They also have eight grandchildren and one great-grandson.

Bessie Coleman, first African American female pilot.
— Courtesy Texas State Historical
Association,
Austin

BESSIE COLEMAN

In 1922, Bessie Coleman received her air pilot's license from the Federation Aeronautique Internationale in France, to become the first black woman pilot. Born in Atlanta, Texas, on January 26, 1893, she had a driving force to learn and better her position. She finished high school and wanted to go to college, but her mother could not afford to send her. Bessie earned money from washing and ironing to attend college, but her money lasted only one semester. She went to Chicago, where she attended beauty school and worked as a manicurist at the White Sox Barber Shop.

Although her dreams of college had been shattered, she was still an avid reader. She began devouring everything she could find on aviation. By the time World War I was over, she had made a firm decision to learn to fly. Bessie's quest to obtain flying instruction in the U.S. was fraught with blatant prejudice for two obvious reasons: her race and her sex. But Bessie Coleman was not to be denied; she met both obstacles head-on. Persistent in her efforts, she went to Robert S. Abbot, editor and publisher of the *Chicago Weekly Defender,* for help. After extensive investigation, he informed her that the French were more liberal in their attitudes toward women and people of color, and he encouraged her to go to France. With money she had earned, she made two trips to Europe, studying under the best European flyers. In 1922, she returned as the only black female pilot in the entire world.

Bessie's perspective was: "What use is an achievement if it cannot be shared?" Her primary goal was to open a flying school to teach other blacks. Since money was a problem, she began giving flying exhibitions to raise funds to open her school. Her first exhibition, in 1922, was at Chicago's Checkerboard Field. Between exhibitions, she lectured on aviation in churches and movie houses.

At the threshold of opening a school, Bessie suffered a fatal accident. On April 30, 1926, she had been asked to give an exhibition by the Jacksonville, Florida Negro Welfare League. At 7:30 P.M., flying at 110 MPH at an altitude of 3,500 feet, Bessie put her plane into a nosedive and never came out.

A most eloquent comment on the life and death of the world's first black woman pilot was made in the *Chicago Weekly Defender* on the tenth anniversary of her death: "Though with the crashing of the plane, life ceased for Bessie Coleman, enough members of her race had been inspired by her courage to carry on in the field of aviation, and whatever is accomplished by a member of the race in aviation will stand as a memorial to Miss Coleman." It is said that every year on Memorial Day, pilots fly over Bessie Coleman's grave and drop flowers in her honor.

John Q. Taylor King, Sr., Lt. Gen.
(U.S. Army Ret.), chancellor and president
emeritus of Huston-Tillotson College.
— Courtesy TAAHO Archives,
Center for American History,
University of Texas at Austin

JOHN Q. TAYLOR KING, SR., PH.D.
MAJ. GEN., ARMY OF THE
UNITED STATES (RET.)
LT. GEN., TEXAS STATE GUARD

Gen. John Q. Taylor King, chancellor and president emeritus of Huston-Tillotson College, a college related to the United Church of Christ and the United Methodist Church, is a graduate of Anderson High School, Austin, holds a B.A. degree from Fisk University

(Nashville, Tennessee), a B.S. degree from Huston-Tillotson College (Austin), an M.S. degree from DePaul University (Chicago, Illinois), and a Ph.D. from The University of Texas at Austin. He received the Honorary Degree Doctor of Laws from both Southwestern University (Georgetown, Texas) and St. Edward's University (Austin), and the Honorary Degree Doctor of Humane Letters from both Austin College (Sherman, Texas) and Fisk University, and the Honorary Degree Doctor of Science from Huston-Tillotson College. He holds a Phi Beta Kappa Key.

Although born in Memphis, Tennessee, he was raised in Austin, where he has been active as a lay leader of Wesley United Methodist Church. He has been a delegate to each General and Jurisdictional Conference of the United Methodist Church from 1956 through 1988. He is a former lay leader of the Southwest Texas Conference and was president of the General Council on Ministries of the United Methodist Church from 1972 to 1980.

He entered World War II as a private, served as a captain in the Pacific Theater of Operations, and retired from the Army of the United States as a major general on August 22, 1983. Since WW II, General King has served in Alaska, Japan, Korea, Okinawa, Germany, Hawaii, and at many other U.S. Army and U.S. Air Force installations. He has completed courses at several Senior Service Schools, including the Command and General Staff College, the Air War College, the Industrial College of the Armed Forces, the Logistics Executive Development Course, and the SROC at the Army War College.

General Taylor has received many military awards and decorations. Former Texas Governor Mark White promoted him to the rank of lieutenant general in the Texas State Guard in 1985. He joined the faculty of Huston-Tillotson College in 1947, was professor of mathematics for several years and dean of the college for five years, then was appointed president in 1965 and chancellor in 1987. He retired on June 30, 1988, and now serves as director and chair of the Center for the Advancement of Science, Engineering, and Technology (CASET), a research component of the college.

Participating actively in civic, professional, and fraternal organizations, he is a life member of the Alpha Phi Alpha Fraternity, Inc., a member of Sigma Pi Phi Fraternity, Inc., Phi Delta Kappa Fraternity, Inc., several professional and honor societies, and is a 33rd Degree Mason and a Shriner. A licensed mortician, he is president of King-Tears Mortuary, Inc. Among his many honors are Alumni Awards from Huston-Tillotson College and Fisk University, the Carl Bredt Award from The University of Texas College of Education, Brotherhood Award from the National Conference of Christians and Jews, the Distinguished Service Award from Texas Lutheran College in Seguin, Texas, Roy Wilkins Meritorious Award from the NAACP, the Arthur B. Dewitty Award from the Austin NAACP Branch, the Martin Luther King, Jr. Humanitarian Award and Frederick D. Patterson Award from Alpha Phi Alpha Fraternity, Inc., the Minority Advocate of the Year Award from the Austin Chamber of Commerce, the Military/Education Award from the San Antonio League of the National Association of Business and Professional Women's Clubs, Inc., the Whitney M. Young, Jr. Award from the Austin Area Urban League, the 1990 Distinguished Alumnus Award from the Ex-Students' Association of The University of Texas at Austin, and the 1991 Philanthropist of the Year in Austin Award from the Austin Chapter of the National Society of Fund Raising Executives.

Well-known as a writer, collaborating with others on four textbooks in mathematics and contributing many articles to professional and religious journals, Dr. King is coauthor with his wife of two books: *Stories of Twenty-three Famous Negro Americans* and *Famous Black Americans,* and a booklet on the life of Mrs. Mary McLeod Bethune.

General King is a member of the board of directors of several organizations, including Texas Commerce Bank-Austin, Austin Chapter National Conference of Christians and Jews, the Capitol Area Council, Boy Scouts of America, former chair of the Lone Star District. He is a director and secretary of the Foundation for Insurance Regulatory Studies in Texas. A former chairman of the Austin Civil Service Commission, he is a trustee of Austin College, a former trustee of Fisk University, and is a member of the Philosophical Society of Texas. He is listed in *Who's Who in America, Leaders in American Science, Leaders in Education,* and eight other biographical publications. General King was married to the former Marcet Alice Hines of Chicago, Illinois. They have three sons, one daughter, and nine grandchildren.

Dominion Robert Glass, educator.
— Courtesy TAAHO Archives,
Center for American History,
University of Texas at Austin

DOMINION ROBERT GLASS:
The Man and His Deed

In Forsyth, Georgia, Benjamin and Minnie Glass became the parents of a son they named Dominion Robert Glass. The exact reason for Benjamin and Minnie choosing this particular name for their son is unknown; however, we do know that "dominion" is a noun denoting power, authority, rulership. Young Dominion spent his early childhood in Atlanta, Georgia, living with his aunt and her family. He was educated in the Atlanta public schools and attended Atlanta University, where he earned his bachelor of arts degree. He then furthered his study at Harvard University in Cambridge, Massachusetts.

Dominion R. Glass was now ready to begin his professional career. He chose teaching as a profession, and obtained his first job as a teacher in the Georgia public schools. His next venture in the educational arena was in higher education. He served as academic dean of Paine College in Augusta, Georgia. Dr. Glass was the president of Haygood College, Pine Bluff, Arkansas. In 1928 he became the registrar at Prairie View A&M College. After serving three years as Prairie View's registrar, he succeeded C. C. Owens as president of Texas College in 1931, a position he held successfully until July 1961.

When Dr. Glass came to Texas College in 1931, he found an indebtedness of $28,445.48, with $9,930.52 of that due teachers for salaries. He paid off that debt and met each future payroll on time each month throughout his administration. Texas College under Dr. Glass steadily grew numerically and physically. The school gained memberships in the Association of American Colleges, the Association of Church Related Colleges, the National Association of Collegiate Deans and Registrars, the United Negro College Fund, Inc., the National Institute of Science, and the Association of Texas Colleges. Dr. Glass stimulated growth at Texas College. The enrollment grew from 233 to 2,274. Graduates increased from 13 to more than 200 at the Spring and Summer Convocations. Its alumni roster contained more than 3,000 graduates with 22,000 ex-students. The faculty grew from 10 members to approximately 100. Thirty-five new buildings were constructed and the college revenue tripled. Dr. Glass was cited as one of the four college presidents with the longest tenure, and was noted as the senior president of service in the organization of the United Negro College Fund, Inc.

The year 1961 marked the end of three decades as president of Texas College for Dr. D. R. Glass. Under his dynamic leadership of thirty years, much progress was made. Dominion Robert Glass died October 8, 1968, in Tyler, Texas. His survivors include his wife, Willie Lee Campbell Glass, sisters Jimmie C. Hayes of New York City, Mamie Justice of Cleveland, Ohio, brother Julian Glass of Cleveland, Ohio, and a host of nieces, nephews, relatives and friends.

Emma Lee Moss, folk artist.
— Courtesy TAAHO Archives,
Center for American History,
University of Texas at Austin

EMMA LEE MOSS

Folk art is common to all cultures. It has been a vital part of America's artistic heritage. With little or no formal training, the folk artist reacts to what is often very localized subject matter, with an innocence, intensity, and directness that is immediately and universally understandable and appreciable. Amidst the intensifying complexity of the modern world, folk art offers an opportunity for contrast, reflection, and enjoyment.

Emma Lee Dunlop was born the third of eight daughters in the small town of St. Bethlehem, Tennessee, on November 3, 1916. Never proceeding beyond the eighth grade, she was employed in the home of the Norfleet Figuers family as a housekeeper. In 1946 she moved with her new family to San Angelo, Texas. Her first paintings were done in the early 1950s using nine-year-old Tommy's paints and brushes while he was in school. It was her fascination with colors that first led her to try painting. Urged on by Mrs. Figuers, Emma Lee approached Tommy's art teacher, Tincie Hughs Heddins, for art instruction. After a few private lessons she joined Mrs. Heddins' class at San Angelo College (now Angelo State University) for approximately two years. Unbeknownst to herself, Emma Lee was the first and only black registered at the college at that time. She had not come to integrate, but to study art: "Everybody was so generous, so nice to me." During these years she was introduced to media, materials, techniques such as mixing colors, and the like, but Mrs. Heddins always strongly encouraged her to continue in her own unique style. One painting, "Snow Scene," was selected for the Texas Spring Circuit and shown in several cities in 1954.

In 1956 Emma Lee married Tucker Moss, and in 1959 the Mosses moved with the Figuers family to Dallas. Emma Lee did not start painting again until 1978, when she was urged to do so and supplied with the paints, brushes, and canvasses by her friend, Dallasite Jim Hodges. Emma Lee's art also helped greatly to sustain her through Tucker's terminal illness in 1983. In 1984 Emma Lee married her and Tucker's long-time friend, James Lee Horne, and returned to San Angelo.

Now retired, she works almost daily on her creations in her comfortable home. "I try to stroke a little bit every day. Then I go at it hard three days a week. I may stop and go sweep the yard or put a piece of meat on the stove, but I work at painting those days." At present, she is mostly painting with oils on canvas or masonite. Over the years, in the majority of her paintings she has used watercolors, house and car paints, art pencils, felt tip markers, and even shoe polish in combination with oils. She has worked on paper, cardboard (at one point she was especially partial to Neiman-Marcus boxes), window shades, cloth, wallpaper, and almost any other surface. More recently, she has begun to experiment with mixed media sculpture composed of "found" objects. Her creativity receives greater stimulus from the discards of Texas' urban civilization than from purchased professional materials.

Most twentieth-century folk artists are no longer isolated or wholly self-taught. But like them, Emma Lee is nevertheless of the same tradition as her fully self-taught, isolated predecessors. She has always worked from her rich, imaginative memory, and her subject matter spans the contemporary scene. In the words of Andre Malraux about folk art, hers, too, is "an instinctive, spontaneous response to the world" around her. Although she continues to experiment, paintings like "Baptizin'" and "Tucker at Home" demonstrate that she is at her unique best when depicting country folk in rural and small town settings. But occasionally, she also strikingly captures aspects of the flamboyant Texas urban lifestyle with works like the mystical "Dream Mall." All of her pictures are bright, busy, and cluttered. Even the landscapes are well-populated. "It's not mine if there's not a lot going on," she has said. Her portrayals are generally whimsical and lacking in perspective, reflecting the folk artist's ignorance of the rules of logic and academic art, but they tellingly grasp the mood of the moment of their subject matter. Her work has a naive vision and a vital freshness. As Janet Kutner, art critic for *The Dallas Morning News,* has written, "Her pictures retain an ingenuous, childlike quality." Emma Lee's painting has been compared to that of the renowned black American folk artist Horace Pippin (1888-1946), even though copies of his work were only recently shown to her.

Emma Lee is black and of the black experience. But her art transcends the black experience: "I paints Black. That's my dignity by saying this is from a Black, and I paints Black. But it does not matter what color, I just like people." Her work is at the same time nostalgic and contemporary. Simply and directly and without pretense she conveys her vision of her surroundings and therewith brings enrichment to the American cultural fabric.

W. J. Durham, civil rights attorney.
— Courtesy Marion Butts
Photo Studio, Dallas

W. J. DURHAM:
"A Lawyer's Lawyer"

It can be, and probably has been, said that W. J. Durham was the best lawyer the NAACP ever had. Durham got his start in life quite unobtrusively with his birth in Sulphur Springs in 1896. He attended Emporia State College in Kansas for one semester before joining the army and serving the country fighting in France. When he returned to civilian life, he studied law under a white attorney named Ben Gafford in Sherman. Durham came up against racial opposition in his attempts to pass his bar exam. He succeeded in 1926 and established his own practice in Sherman, yet white opposition to his lawyering didn't end there. In 1930 a white mob burned down Durham's office along with Sherman's black business district, yet Durham continued to handle civil rights cases.

Throughout the 1930s Durham handled many volatile cases, some of the most significant involving the right of blacks to vote in the Supreme Court's 1944 *Smith v. Allright* decision that outlawed the white primaries. Lulu White referred to the decision as the "second emancipation of the Negro." During this time Durham handled other cases as well. In 1940, after a public housing project in South Dallas forced several hundred black families to move into white neighborhoods, the Dallas City Council passed an ordinance that required residential segregation. The move was blatantly unconstitutional, yet the NAACP had a difficult time finding homeowners who would challenge the law due to the fear of white retribution. For the same reasons, it was hard to find an attorney who would handle such a case. There was, however, W. J. Durham, who gladly filed suit on behalf of the homeowners. The suit soon was dropped after the council rescinded the ordinance.

In 1945 Durham, along with Thurgood Marshall, teamed up to handle the *Sweatt v. Painter* case that took the two from Austin to Washington, D.C. Not only did *Sweatt v. Painter* open up The University of Texas Law School to blacks, it put a black foot in the door, opening it to integrated education. In the 1950s Durham was to team up with Marshall again, along with C. B. Bunkley and U. Simpson Tate, to handle the case between the Association and John Ben Shepperd. Although the case was unsuccessful for the NAACP, it paved the way for its smoother operation in Texas. Successful or not, "Durham always commanded respect," Otto Mullinax recalls. Mullinax, a white attorney, who worked with the Association on several cases, remembers Durham as a hard-working intellect who was the best lawyer in Dallas. Historian Michael Gillette states that Durham's "legal ability" as well as his "unparalleled dedication to his work made him virtually indispensable to the civil rights movement in Texas."

— From *The Dallas I Know*, by William Blair, Jr.

*Madison Kilpatrick, ex-slave,
master politician.*
— Courtesy TAAHO Archives,
Center for American History,
University of Texas at Austin

MADISON KILPATRICK

Mystery shrouds the early life of Madison Kilpatrick. It is not known when or how he came to Texas. Some speculate that he was born a slave in Alabama, perhaps in 1829. It is further imagined that he ran away to Texas, where he probably lived as a free man. Robert Kilpatrick, one of Madison's four sons, believed that his father was brought to Texas from Alabama at some point by his owner, Sam Oliver. Madison was a farmer and blacksmith. Not long after his arrival in Hempstead, Madison hired out to a white blacksmith called Arhenback. His admiration for Madison resulted in him giving Madison three lots in Hempstead. Madison built a house on the lots. He also acquired a farm outside the city of Hempstead in Waller County.

Madison was elected the first treasurer of Waller County after its creation by the 13th Legislature in 1873. At that time Waller County was predominantly African American, and African Americans enjoyed the rights to vote under existing laws. African Americans were a strong political force in Waller County until 1903, when the Texas Legislature passed laws allowing the creation of political parties and party primaries which were strongly anti-African American. Since African Americans had never belonged to the Democratic Party or voted in the Democratic primary before, they were now systematically denied the right to vote.

Madison Kilpatrick married Betsy Bradford, and they had ten children — five girls and five boys, two of which died in infancy. His son Robert served as a Hempstead city alderman for eight years. He and Madison, each in his own time, were party bosses who controlled many facets of the fortunes of Hempstead and Waller County.

L. C. Anderson, educator.
— Courtesy Bob Lee, Texas Trailblazer,
Houston, Texas

L. C. ANDERSON

The quest for public education among Texans heightened after the Civil War. A bill introduced by W. H. Holland, the black legislator from Waller County, was signed into law in 1876 "to establish an agricultural and manual school for colored youths of the State." Two brothers would be among the early leaders of Prairie View Normal and Industrial College. Professor E. H. Anderson served as the second principal of the college, and when he died in 1884 he was succeeded by his brother, L. C. Anderson. Both were graduates of Fisk University in Nashville. When L. C. took the baton, he had been running alongside his brother as his assistant, so he had a head start. That same year L. C. Anderson became a major force in the formation of the Colored Teachers State Association of Texas. The organizing meeting was held on the campus of Prairie View, and L. C. Anderson was elected as the first president. As principal and one of the state's top educators, L. C. Anderson had a full agenda.

A major concern during his early tenure was the mission of the college. Booker T. Washington was a well-known proponent of industrial education, and the Texas A&M board, which had jurisdiction over Prairie View, favored Washington's approach to educating Negroes. Anderson had taught at Washington's Tuskegee Institute in Alabama, but made it known that he viewed industrial education as an adjunct to a creative teaching program, according to George R. Woolfolk in his book, *Prairie View, A Study in Public Conscience.* Anderson apparently saw no need to change Prairie View's mission, since almost all of his graduates found teaching jobs. Nevertheless, he began adding industrial education courses. The school grew under his direction. A two-story dining hall-dormitory costing $5,000 was built. Also, four homes for professors cost $3,000, and a $5,000 blacksmith shop was fully outfitted. By 1895, the school appropriation was a record $39,700. But the following year Anderson resigned.

Prairie View's loss was Austin's gain. Anderson accepted the job as principal of the high school in Austin named for his brother, E. H. Anderson. The school was one of the few high schools for Negro students in the state of Texas. Anderson's reign lasted more than thirty-four years and his influence benefited hundreds of students and teachers. Among his many outstanding contemporaries were E. L. Blackshear, who succeeded him as principal of Prairie View, and H. T. Kealing. Both men also have schools named after them in Austin. I. Q. Hurdle succeeded Anderson as principal of the high school and wrote, "Hundreds of those who studied under the tutorship of Anderson have gone out into the world and become principals and teachers in the public schools of Texas." And, he wrote, "Some have entered law and medical schools while others became carpenters, engineers, scientific farmers and still others have entered the Civil Service as employees of the United States government." His influence was so great that the school name was changed to the L. C. Anderson High School. And, in 1935, Prairie View also honored him by dedicating Anderson Hall. Mr. Anderson attended the dedication services.

When he died three years later, Anderson's funeral was attended by the who's who among Texas educators of his day, including the presidents of both Prairie View and Wiley College and the superintendent of Austin Public Schools. Anderson had been an active member of Ebenezer Baptist Church as well as a member of several fraternities. Anderson was married twice and had four children. Perhaps his most outstanding legacy as founder of the Colored Teachers State Association was that it continued to exist, with top Texas educators at its helm, for more than eighty years.

BOB CHATHAM

Chatham spent his early days as a slave in south central Texas, but by the time he was fifty-seven years old, he was cashing sizeable checks at Houston banks and coming to town from his home base in Hempstead, Texas, via his own private spur track. And he conducted his business by telephone from his railcar. One shipment in 1916 was 169 railcars worth more than $20,000. This was reported in the Prairie View campus newspaper.

Chatham was one of the first graduates of the university after it opened in 1878. The Watermelon King was not only a wizard at

Bob Chatham, ex-slave and agricultural entrepreneur.
— Courtesy Bob Lee, Texas Trailblazer, Houston

growing the fruit but at marketing. His melons were shipped throughout Texas and out of state. His family became famous for developing a watermelon known as the Black Diamond. Old-timers fondly recall the taste, and today the Texas Agricultural Extension Service considers the melon one of the state's major varieties.

Chatham's granddaughter, Bogie Lee Jackson, recalls the days when they were the first African Americans in the Hempstead area with a car — a secondhand Pierce Arrow with plastic curtains, attached by leather straps, to shield them from the rain and cold. She also vividly remembers her grandfather's big house with servants, and that they were considered well-to-do in those days. All of his children knew about Bob Chatham's high regard for education. He founded a school on his Hempstead property. There he taught his eleven children, along with the children of those who worked for him. The Rock West School, commonly called the Chatham School, opened each October and closed each May, before the harvest season.

By the time Chatham died in 1929, most of his cash base had been lost when the Farmers National Bank closed in bankruptcy. But Chatham left his children quite a legacy — nearly thirty acres of land apiece, and a reverence for education. Most of his children attended Prairie View. Three served as principals, one served as vice-principal, and two others were teachers in Houston schools. Five of his sons formed the Chatham Brothers Watermelon Farm, which became widely known in the 1940s. One of their advertising flyers touted the business as having the "largest watermelon farm in the world," with 1,000 acres of land being farmed. The family is no longer in the watermelon business and most of the land has been sold, but the family tradition of education is alive and well with many descendants in the profession. In Houston, the R. C. Chatham Elementary School bears the name of Bob Chatham's oldest son, and there is a scholarship in his memory to help outstanding ex-students with their college education.

The Watermelon King left another bit of history to be learned. He cultivated a fruit that did indeed have a connection with African Americans. The fruit grew wild on the continent of Africa, and the explorer David Livingstone reported vast tracts of land literally covered with the melon in 1858.

Joseph Alvin Chatman, M.D.
— Courtesy TAAHO Archives, Center for American History, University of Texas at Austin

JOSEPH ALVIN CHATMAN, M.D.

Joseph Alvin Chatman was born in Navasota, Texas, in 1902. His father, Sandy, and his mother, Sally, had difficulty providing for their family in Grimes County, so in 1902 they moved to Mexia. Chatman graduated from Dunbar High School in Mexia, Texas, and attended Prairie View A&M, where he was a member of the baseball team. He also attended Fisk University and was an honor student. Chatman graduated from Meharry Medical College, and in 1926 began to practice medicine in Mexia.

In 1933, Dr. Chatman was successful in erecting a thirteen-bed hospital in Mexia. In 1945, he established a hospital and outpatient clinic in Lubbock, Texas. Dr. Chatman practiced medicine in Lubbock from 1945 to 1967. Dr. Joseph Alvin Chatman died January 12, 1967. His activities outside the medical profession were many, and his honors too numerous to mention. After the death of Dr. Chatman, his immediate family, wife Emmaline Shea Chatman and their two sons, Alvin M. and Michael L., continued to live in Lubbock.

THE SHAVERS: Pioneers of Faith

Eli and Myrtle Shavers are living examples of what Hebrews 11:1-10 is all about. They have been examples of these verses for many years — by 1995, he for ninety years and she for eighty. Both have supported and worshiped in the Church of God in Christ most of their lives. As far back as either could remember, they have been "Holiness." Elder Shavers preached and pastored in the Church of God in Christ for many, many years. Myrtle Shavers worked by his side most of those years.

Both Eli and Myrtle experienced the growth and development of the COGIC movement in Texas. They worked personally with leaders such as Mother Lillian Brooks Coffey, Bishop Charles Harrison Mason, and Bishop J. E. Alexander. They heard firsthand the testimony of Bishop Mason, founder of the Church of God in Christ, U.S.A. These were his words: "I was saved in Plumerville, Arkansas eighty-seven years ago when I was seven years old. I received the Baptism of the Holy Ghost in 1906 on Azusa Street in Los Angeles, California during a Holy Ghost Revival conducted by Elder W. J. Seymore. The name of Church of God in Christ was revealed to me in the Spirit in 1897. I founded the First General Assembly of the Church in 1907. I have been in jail many times for the cause of the Gospel. Once in Houston, Texas. I have suffered a many persecution for the sake of the Gospel, but God has always delivered me. I have been through so many things that I can't remember them all now. I've traveled a many miles, also been on foreign soil as far as England to take this great truth." The Shavers were inspired by this testimony many, many years ago, and it started their mission of faith which continued on into 1995.

Augustine C. Williams, first African American to serve as director of examinations for the Texas State Board of Cosmetology.
— Courtesy TAAHO Archives, Center for American History, University of Texas at Austin

AUGUSTINE C. WILLIAMS

Augustine C. Williams was born in O'Donnell, Texas. She received her public school education in San Angelo, Texas. In 1957 she married David A. Williams. She attended Crescent Cosmetology Institute in 1958, where she received her operator's license and her instructor's license. In 1972, she became an inspector examiner III for the Texas State Board of Cosmetology. In 1973, she became the first African American to hold the position of director of examinations for the TSBC. Further training in vocational education was received at Southwest Texas State University, Prairie View A&M University, and Texas State Technical Institute. She left State service in 1984, and became the owner and operator of Style-Rite Beauty Salon, only four blocks east of the State Capitol. Augustine could have been a teacher, a scientist, or a politician, but she chose cosmetology, perhaps because she had always admired women like Madam C. J. Walker, M. E. Coleman, and U. V. Christian. This is why she chose to open the Style-Rite Salon when she left the Texas State Cosmetology Commission.

DR. A. N. POINDEXTER:
Professor of Veterinary Medicine, Prairie View A&M University

Dr. A. N. Poindexter has been a professor of veterinary medicine at Prairie View A&M University since 1945, and is the oldest practicing black veterinarian in the United States. Dr. Poindexter was one of the first black vets to join the Texas Veterinary Medical Association. Among his peers, he is considered a vet's vet. Over the years, he has received a number of teaching, outstanding citizen, and service awards, including a Silver Beaver Award from the Boy Scouts of America. Also, he was the first black to serve as chairman of the board of directors of a local bank in Waller County. A. N. and his wife Rachael have five grown children — Alfred III, Bruce, Paula, Betty, and Yvette.

Earl Campbell, Heisman Trophy winner.
— Courtesy TAAHO Archives,
Center for American History,
University of Texas at Austin

EARL CAMPBELL

In 1978, Earl Campbell graduated from The University of Texas, won the Heisman Trophy, and was the number-one draft choice of the Houston Oilers. In 1978, Earl Campbell was proclaimed by the Texas State Legislature as the fourth official State Hero of Texas, joining Stephen F. Austin, Davy Crockett, and Sam Houston.

After retiring from the National Football League in 1986, Campbell started producing and marketing his special sausage. In 1991, he founded Earl Campbell Foods, Inc. with headquarters in Austin. The sausage is produced in a USDA-approved plant in Waelder. The company has established itself as one of the fastest growing sausage companies in the United States. His sausage is available throughout Texas. Besides hot links and spicy smoked sausages, Earl Campbell also produces his famous barbecue sauce.

W. F. "RED" KITCHEN: Rancher

"Red" Kitchen is a native of Crockett, Houston County. He has been actively engaged in farming and ranching most of his life. Kitchen is presently involved with the Houston County ASCS and the 4-H. He is a member of the board of directors of the Houston County Appraisal District, the Houston County Cattle and Forage Council, and the Texans Natural Beef Cooperative Association. "Red" is married to the former De Etta Miller. They are the parents of three children: Darius, Willie Edward, and Freddie Dean. Both sons are involved in the ranching operation.

J. D. JACOBS:
Owner of J. D. Jacobs Transportation, Inc.

J. D. Jacobs began his agricultural career as a potato grower in West Texas. He purchased his first truck to haul vegetables in 1969, and has since expanded his fleet to fifteen trucks, hauling a variety of agricultural products throughout the U.S. Jacobs' business clients include Frito Lay, ITT Corporation, Kraft Foods, Kroger, Quaker Oats, Southwestern Bell and Texas Utilities. J. D. and his wife Ollie have three children: Donna, Jackie and Jeff. The Jacobs family also operates a cattle ranch, and raise wheat and milo.

MARCUS A. HART:
President & CEO, Delta Food Service

Marcus A. Hart began his company in 1978 to manage food service for cafeterias and dining facilities for public and private institutions, including military installations. With management contracts in Texas and seven other states, the company has grown from 22 employees in 1980 to 500 employees by 1990. Under Hart's leadership, Delta Food Service has devised ways to improve customer satisfaction by offering Healthy Heart Menus in addition to the regular menu, and featuring daily specials. Delta has also incorporated the teachings of Total Quality Management into employee training.

Marcus has received numerous community awards, including Citizen of the Year — Noble Star Masonic Lodge (1991), Certificate of Appreciation — Legislative Black Caucus (1992), Texas Black Entrepreneurs of the '90's — Texas A&M University (1992), and Small Business of the Year — U.S. Coast Guard and U.S. Department of Transportation (1992).

Rev. James B. Sadler.
— Courtesy Bertha Sadler Means, Austin

REV. JAMES B. SADLER

In her book *Portrait of a Pioneer in the Making of America*, Bertha Sadler Means says: "Caught up by the spirit of freedom from slavery, Reverend James B. Sadler founded and built the first colored Cumberland Presbyterian Church in Texas so that his people might be able to worship and govern themselves of their own choice. He was a man of great vision and aspiration. He used both vision and aspiration at a great turning point in American history as a stepping stone toward advancing opportunities for his people."

Andrew R. Melontree, Sr.,
lifelong student of many interests,
a scholar and a political practitioner.
— Courtesy TAAHO Archives,
Center for American History,
University of Texas at Austin

ANDREW R. MELONTREE, SR.

Born in Marlin, Texas, Andrew R. Melontree became a lifelong student of many interests, a scholar and a political practitioner. His wife, Vernice (Crayton) Melontree, served as an elementary schoolteacher in the Tyler Independent School District.

Vernice and Andrew have four children. Cynthia M. graduated from East Texas State University in 1978, and the University of Texas at Tyler in 1979, and became an elementary school teacher in Tyler. Andrew R., Jr. graduated Texas College in 1988, and became production manager for Kelly-Springfield Tire Company at their Tyler plant. Lester A. graduated from Stephen F. Austin University at Huntsville, Texas, in 1982, and became an over-the-road truck driver for Central Freight Lines. Beverly D. graduated from East Texas State University in 1982, and the University of Houston Law Center in 1990, and became a prosecuting attorney in Austin. The Melontrees have three grandchildren. Andrew Melontree earned a bachelor of science degree at Texas College and a law degree from Texas Southern University. He was the first African American to be elected a county judge and county commissioner in Smith County.

Isadore H. Clayborn, devoted Prince Hall Mason, a humanitarian with national and international concerns.
— Courtesy TAAHO Archives, Center for American History, University of Texas at Austin

ISADORE H. CLAYBORN: "Personification of Prince Hall Masonry in Texas"

Prince Hall, the founder of African American Freemasonry, was a self-educated man and a champion of individual rights. His strong convictions and belief in the value of human dignity and worth led him to always seek to serve his country and mankind. Isadore H. Clayborn in many ways was a personification of Prince Hall Masonry, not only in Texas but nationally and internationally. Clayborn's masonic career commenced when he was initiated and became a Master Mason in the late 1930s. He served as Worshipful Master of the Thomas Dryder Lodge Dallas, Grand Secretary, and Most Worshipful Grand Master of the Jurisdiction of Texas, Prince Hall Affiliated. He also served as Sovereign Grand Commander for the United Supreme Council, Southern Jurisdiction. Additionally, he served as chairman of the CCFC and chairman of the Committee of Fraternal Relations for the Ancient Egyptian Arabic Order of the Nobles Mystic Shriners, United States of America, AFPS of the Phylaxis Society. I. H. Clayborn was a loyal Mason until his death on April 9, 1994.

Pilot Norman Wilfred Scales.
— Courtesy wife Lydia Scales, Austin

NORMAN WILFRED SCALES

Norman W. Scales was born in Hillsboro, Texas, on November 11, 1918, and grew up in Austin. He attended Austin public schools — Brackenridge Elementary, Kealing Junior High, and Anderson High School. His higher education was received at Tillotson College in Austin. In 1940, Scales enlisted in the U.S. Army and was stationed at Fort Sill, Oklahoma, where he rose to the rank of sergeant in Battery D 349 Field Artillery. While at Fort Sill, Norman took and passed the necessary examinations for admission to the Army Aviation Cadet Corps. On December 23, 1942, he was assigned to preflight training at the Army Air Force Advanced Flying School, Replacement Training, at Tuskegee Alabama, commencing January 26, 1943. On October 1, 1943, Sergeant Scales was commissioned a second lieutenant in the United States Military Single Engine Fighter Pilots of Tuskegee, Alabama. Lieutenant Scales was assigned to the 100th Fighter Squadron, 332nd Fighter Group, 306th Wing of the 15th Air Force. On October 5, 1944, he was sent to Naples, Italy, as a P-51 pilot. Lieutenant Scales was awarded the Distinguished Flying Cross. Scales was married to Lydia Mackey Scales. The Scales have two sons, Ronnie D. and Norman, Jr., four grandchildren, and one great-grandchild. Lieutenant Scales died May 24, 1981.

Pilot Mack Hopkins.
— Courtesy Texas State Historical Association, University of Texas at Austin

MACK HOPKINS

Mack Hopkins was born in Marshall and was "raised" on the campus of Wiley College. His father taught agriculture at Wiley College in Marshall so that Mack lived on the campus for the first twenty-three years of his life. Hopkins played football while a student at the college and played in the Cotton Bowl in 1936 and 1939. When he graduated from Wiley in 1941, he read an article that said that blacks would now be accepted as pilots in the U.S. Air Force. Until that time, Hopkins had seen an airplane up close only once in his life — when a plane was forced to land in a field behind Dogan Hall on the Wiley campus. "So as soon as Hopkins graduated, he volunteered for the Air Force to fly. At that time, he didn't know it was going to be a black and white [situation]." Hopkins had to wait several months after signing up for the program before he went for training. "They had to build a field for us [blacks] to fly in." He remembers hearing them say "we had to fly alone or not at all." A training field for black pilots was finally established at Tuskegee, Alabama. In fact, during the early phase of their training the black pilots lived on the campus of Tuskegee Institute. The training program lasted nine months. A new class started every five weeks. When Hopkins went into the Air Force it was just in time to see the first class, the 99th Squadron, graduate. When the 99th Squadron graduated in 1942, however, they were not sent overseas like their white counterparts. The black press was furious: "We want our boys to fight, too." It took almost a year before the 99th was finally sent to North Africa in March of 1943.

Mack and the nineteen other men in his class went through three phases of training: basic, primary, and advanced. In the advanced stage of training, Hopkins was transferred out of the class and made a flight instructor. When the black pilot program first started, the Negroes were trained by white instructors. In fact, Hopkins commented that in 1939 there were only eight blacks that had commercial pilots' licenses in the entire United States. The first group of pilots were trained as fighter pilots — they flew P-40s, P-39s, P-47s, and P-51s. The next group, which came after Hopkins' class had graduated, were trained as bomber pilots. This group flew slower planes, mainly B-25s. After the 99th Squadron went into combat, the 332 Fighter Group was formed. It was made up of three squadrons — the 100th, 301st, and 302nd. Although Hopkins was a member of the 301st Fighter Squadron, he did not go abroad with his group. Instead he stayed in Tuskegee and taught other blacks how to fly. He remained in Tuskegee for three years and ten months.

The morale in the Negro Air Force was surprisingly high, despite the separate conditions that existed between the white and

Mack Hopkins, "Tuskegee Airman," flew with the "Red Tail Squadron," World War II.
— Courtesy Texas State Historical Association

black air forces. Hopkins recalled that a white officer on his first day at the base said, "I know most of y'all are from the North but you are in the South and you are going to abide by the customs and laws of the South." Fortunately, none of his northern comrades got in trouble while living in the South. Hopkins believed their education was probably a factor in the black pilots' acceptance of the situation. "They were all college graduates. Most of them had college degrees, some had master's degrees and a few had doctorates. They were all great athletes. They understood what was going on and those of us that were from the South were used to it." Hopkins continued:

> I remember one of my friends was flying and had to set down his plane in a field after he had some trouble. Some people came up

and wanted to know where was the pilot. It was a two-seater plane and he was the only person there. People living twenty miles from Tuskegee didn't know there was an all-black air force there.

And, finally, Hopkins commented: "We thought about the problems but we still felt that we belonged to this country. We felt we should fight for our country. At that time, everything was separate. We accepted separate but equal at that time." In fact, Hopkins described his days in flight training as great. "They brought together all of the top athletes, the top students of the black race. They brought us all together to fly. They said we were the cream of the crop."

In addition to his flight training and his teaching responsibilities, Hopkins was also trained as an aerial photographer. He and several members of his squad took photographs that were later used to map much of the western part of the country.

After he was discharged from the Air Force, Hopkins decided to continue his aviation career. He was accepted into the California Aeronautical Institute, where he took a degree in aeronautical engineering. One of his engineering teachers told him he was going to have to be "twice as good" as all the other fellows in his class to get to the top. Of the 200 students in his class only three were blacks. Wanting to be "top notch" was nothing new to Hopkins, for he and his fellow pilots had been under the same pressure while training at Tuskegee. "We trained that way and they said that we were better. We had generals that came in and watched us fly and they would all say we were the best." In fact, history attests to the skill of the 332nd — in more than 200 missions over Italy and Germany, their group never lost a bomber to enemy aircraft.

Although Californians were more accepting in their treatment of blacks than people in Alabama, black graduates from engineering schools in California still had trouble finding jobs. The few commercial airlines that were in existence after the war had no room for black pilots. Hopkins said that many of his Air Force friends who wanted to continue to fly had to go to Cuba, South America, and Mexico to find jobs. "I went into the post office." Of the 10,000 people who took the civil service test at the same time Hopkins did, he was in the second group of fifty called for employment. He remained with the U.S. Postal Service for twenty-six years. In order to continue flying, however, he and several friends formed the Fleetwing Flying Club in Compton, California. "We flew out there from 1950 to about 1969. That's the last time I flew."

Hopkins retired from the post office in 1972 and went to work for Hughes Aircraft, a satellite manufacturing company owned by the late Howard Hughes. At Hughes Aircraft, Hopkins worked with Greg Jarvis and Ron McNair, two of the astronauts who were later killed in the *Challenger* disaster in 1986. Later Hopkins and his wife, Pauline, returned to Marshall to live. Pauline, his wife of nearly forty-five years, recently died in an auto accident.

Today Mack spends much of his time working in his garden behind his home or in a larger one he planted on some property he owns nine miles out of town. Hopkins is very active in Marshall's civic life. He is on the board of directors of the League of Women Voters, a member of Kilgore's Educational Advisory Committee for the Jobs Training Program, the business manager for the Old Power Mill Cemetery Association, a member of a stamp club, a member of Alpha Phi Alpha Fraternity, Inc., and a member of the Regular Fellows. Although he's been away from aviation for many years now, Hopkins says: "Flying is something you never get over. You feel like you own the world when you fly. I think that is the main thing. You feel like you are over it all."

— From *One of the First Black Air Force Pilots* by Rachel Ann Ealy,
Marshall Junior High School, Marshall, Texas.
Reprinted from the *Texas Historian,* a publication of
Junior Historians of Texas, Volume LI, November 1990, Number 2.
Permission granted by the Texas State Historical Association.

Bibliography:
Books: Robert A. Rose, *The Story of America's Black Air Force World War II,* 1976.
Articles: "School Board Profile: Mack Hopkins," *MISD Communicator,* December 1988.
Newspapers: *Los Angeles Times,* May 25, 1980, and *Marshall News Messenger,* January 31, 1988.
Interviews: Mack Hopkins to Rachel Ann Ealy, November 17, 1989, and Mack Hopkins to Rachel Ann Ealy, December 14, 1989.

JAMES FARMER

To most Americans the civil rights movement began in Montgomery, Alabama, in 1955 when Rosa Parks refused to give up her seat in the front of a city bus. In actual fact, however, the civil rights movement in this country began at least fifteen years before the Mont-

James Farmer, founder of the Congress of Racial Equality (CORE).
One of the big four nonviolent civil rights leaders.
— Courtesy Texas State Historical Association

gomery bus boycott. It started with James Farmer, the founder of
the Congress of Racial Equality (CORE) and the organizer of lunch
counter sit-ins and other forms of nonviolent protests.

Farmer was one of the big four nonviolent civil rights leaders.
The other three were Martin Luther King, Jr., of the Southern
Christian Leadership Conference (SCLC), Roy Wilkins of the
National Association for the Advancement of Colored People
(NAACP), and Whitney Young of the Urban League. Of the four,
Farmer is the only one still alive.

Farmer, the son of a college professor, was born in Marshall in
1920. After living in Holly Springs, Mississippi, and later in Austin,
the family moved back to Marshall. There, in the fall of 1934, at the

age of fourteen, Farmer entered Wiley College. Since he was so much younger than his classmates, Farmer did not partake of the usual college happenings. This left him time to pursue his study of history and philosophy that would later shape and mold him into the man he was to become. While at Wiley, Farmer met Melvin B. Tolson, an English professor, who taught Farmer to use all of his God-given talents of self-expression. With Tolson's encouragement, Farmer joined the debate team and eventually became its captain. The speaking skills he learned while on the debate team taught Farmer how to make inspiring speeches. Later he would put these talents to work for both the FOR (Fellowship of Reconciliation) and the CORE organizations.

Farmer's philosophy of nonviolence was apparent as early as 1941. Excited by the nonviolent resistance movement designed by Mahatma Gandhi to win Indian independence from Britain, Farmer hoped to use similar methods to overthrow segregation in the United States. Farmer presented these ideas to A. J. Muste, the head of FOR. Although Muste heartily approved of this approach, he refused to actively sponsor the movement. FOR did, however, agree to authorize Farmer to start an organization in Chicago encouraging nonviolent resistance to segregation. The Chicago movement, which became CORE or the Congress of Racial Equality, had Farmer as chairman, Bernice Fisher as secretary, and Jimmy Robinson, a white man, as treasurer. The first nonviolent demonstration occurred at the Jack Spratt Coffee House when a group of four blacks and four whites entered the coffee house and sat together. The plan was for the whites to either decline being served until all the blacks had been served or for the whites to order the food and then pass it on to the blacks sitting beside them. The demonstration ended when Jimmy Robinson, a white, paid the bill and the manager threw the money outside the building. Although they were the target of cruel words, there was no violence. The demonstration had been a success, for the group had successfully integrated the coffee house.

Farmer's nonviolent demonstrations continued for a number of years with little or no publicity. Farmer stated: "There was no television to catch the drama, and the press largely ignored it. If we were lucky there might be a small paragraph on a back page of the *Chicago Tribune* saying, in effect, that a few nuts and crackpots sat in a restaurant until they were served, or thrown out, or the place closed — whichever came first." Still, Farmer doggedly continued his campaign of nonviolence. Then, in 1955, Rosa Parks, a black school teacher, made nonviolence a household word when she refused to give up her seat to a white passenger on a public bus in Montgomery, Alabama. "Mrs. Parks' repeated refusal to give in to the status quo led to her arrest and the boycott of public transportation in Montgomery. . . . It brought publicity and attention to the leader of the boycott, Dr. Martin Luther King, Jr." It was King who would receive the attention from the media as the leader of nonviolence. Farmer said "he had labored a decade and a half in the vineyard of nonviolence. Now, out of nowhere, someone comes and harvests the grapes and drinks the wine."

After Farmer and King had met several times, the two nonviolent civil rights activists decided to join forces against segregation. Their efforts increased after Farmer came up with the idea of "Freedom Riders" — or a "small interracial group riding interstate buses through the South with the blacks sitting on front seats and the whites on back seats, refusing to move when ordered." As the black Freedom Riders rode the buses, they would sing:

> *If you can't find me in the backa the bus;*
> *You can't find me nowhere,*
> *Oh-h, come on up to the fronta the bus,*
> *I'll be ridin' up there.*
>
> *I'll be ridin' up there — up there,*
> *I'll be ridin' up there.*
> *Oh-h come on up to the fronta the bus;*
> *I'll be ridin' up there.*

White Freedom Riders would answer:

> *If you can't find me in the fronta the bus;*
> *You can't find me nowhere,*
> *Oh-h come on back to the backa the bus;*
> *I'll be ridin' back there.*
>
> *I'll be ridin' back there — back there;*
> *I'll be ridin' back there.*
> *Oh-h, come on back to the backa the bus;*
> *I'll be ridin' back there.*

The Freedom Riders were in part responsible for passage of the

*James Farmer
around 1987.*
— Courtesy Texas State
Historical Association

Public Accommodations Act and the Civil Rights Act of 1964. After the assassination of Dr. King in April of 1968, Farmer continued to work toward desegregation.

Today, Farmer teaches at Mary Washington College, a predominantly white institution, in Fredericksburg, Virginia. Farmer, now seventy-one years of age, completely blind and fighting diabetes, continues to thwart racism by nonviolent means because he feels that black youths today cannot know where they are headed unless they know from where they have come. In an interview with Farmer almost fifty years after the Jack Spratt Coffee House incident and six years after publication of his book *Lay Bare the Heart: An Autobiography of the Civil Rights Movement,* I asked Farmer why King is viewed by history as the father of nonviolence in the U.S. civil rights movement. Farmer said there was television to broadcast King's efforts while television was not available when Farmer started his movement in the 1940s. He also added that the Montgomery bus boycott shed light on King as a person, while Farmer always remained in the background. And, finally, Farmer commented that King was a Southern Baptist minister who spoke with a Southern drawl. This, he believes, was important to Northerners watching the civil rights movement unfold in the South, for Northern liberals believed segregation and racial discrimination was a Southern problem, not a national one. Thus Martin Luther King, Jr. became the face and the spokesperson for the nonviolent civil rights movement first preached in the United States by James Farmer. In truth, Farmer was the concrete for equality while King was the building. Without both men, the United States might still be a divided and segregated land.

> — From *Farmer Before King: The Non-Violent Civil Rights Movement* by Berenda J. Humble, Marshall Junior High School, Marshall, Texas. Reprinted from the *Texas Historian*, Publication of Junior Historians of Texas, Volume LII, September 1991, Number 1. Permission granted by the Texas State Historical Association.

Bibliography:
Books: James Farmer, *Lay Bare the Heart: An Autobiography of the Civil Rights Movement*, 1985, and Stephen B. Oates, *Let the Trumpet Sound: The Life of Martin Luther King, Jr.*, 1982.
Articles: "Civil Rights Pioneer in a Class Act," *Newsfeature Report*, May 1990.
Newspapers: *Dallas Morning News*, June 19, 22, 1987, Longview *Morning Journal*, June 13, 1986, Marshall *News Messenger*, June 18, 23, 1986, and *The Daily Texan*, June 19, 1987.
Television Programs: Bill Moyers, "A Walk Through the 20th Century," January 1984.
Interviews: James L. Farmer to Berenda J. Humble, January 27, 1991.

Endnotes

**Chapter 4: Freedmantown: The Origins of a Black
Neighborhood in Houston, 1865–1880
by Louise Passey Maxwell**

1. Contemporary accounts written by whites in Houston often referred indiscriminately to all blacks in the city as "freedmen," presumably including former slaves and free blacks. Because of the ambiguity of this term, it will be employed only when in a direct quotation or when the source cited specifically states that the data or examples given refer to "freedmen" — as in this particular case.

2. Byron Porter to William H. Sinclair, 1 September 1866, vol. 1, #3716, "Letters Sent," Bureau of Refugees, Freedmen, and Abandoned Lands, Texas, Record Group (RG) 105 (National Archives). All references will be to the Texas Bureau records in RG 105.

3. For an indication of the rate of illiteracy among registered black voters in Houston, see *Voter Register of 1867–1869, Hardin-Kinney County*, Reel 4, Texas State Archives, Austin, Texas.

4. Foner, 104. The most comprehensive assessment of the importance of land ownership to blacks in the postwar period occurs in Loren Schweninger, *Black Property Owners in the South* (Urbana: University of Illinois Press, 1990).

5. While most blacks remained in the South's rural regions in the years immediately following the war, a significant number left the countryside for the South's urban centers. Richard Wade's work on prewar urban black populations is a seminal work in the study of black urbanization. See Richard C. Wade, *Slavery in the Cities: The South 1820–1860* (New York: Oxford University Press, 1964). Howard Rabinowitz's study of the postwar black populations in Richmond, Montgomery, Atlanta, Nashville, and Raleigh is the most comprehensive study undertaken on the postwar urban black experience. Only a few other local studies have been conducted, and the number dealing with urban blacks in Texas are even fewer. See Howard N. Rabinowitz, *Race Relations in the Urban South, 1865-1890* (New York: Oxford UP, 1978); John Blassingame, *Black New Orleans* (Chicago: University of Chicago Press, 1973); and Don H. Doyle, *New Men, New Cities, New South: Atlanta, Nashville, Charleston, Mobile: 1869–1910* (Chapel Hill: The University of North Carolina Press, 1990). On the black population in Houston, see Howard Beeth and Cary D. Wintz, eds., *Black Dixie: Afro-Texan History and Culture in Houston* (College Station: Texas A&M UP, 1992); and Cary D. Wintz,

"The Emergence of a Black Neighborhood: Houston's Fourth Ward," in *Urban Texas: Politics and Development*, eds. Char Miller and Heywood T. Sanders (College Station: Texas A&M University Press, 1990). Roger L. Ransom and Richard Sutch assert that the trend for blacks to settle in urban areas in the aftermath of the war was the most troubling aspect of black mobility to white contemporaries. See Roger L. Ransom and Richard Sutch, *One Kind of Freedom: The Economic Consequences of Emancipation* (Cambridge: Cambridge University Press, 1977), 62.

6. This population increase was especially remarkable in Houston because of the extremely small number of free blacks in Houston prior to the war — only nine were counted in 1860. Voter registration statistics indicate that more black adult males moved to the city following the war than they did either before or during the conflict: 497 moved after, 393 before, and 315 during the war. The overwhelming majority, however, had lived in Texas prior to the outbreak of the war. On Houston's free black population, see Manuscript Census Returns, *Eighth Census of the United States, 1860, Harris County, Texas, Schedule 1, Free Population*, National Archives Microfilm Series, Roll 282. For discussion of the limited nature of antebellum black community organizations in Houston, see Howard Beeth and Cary D. Wintz, eds., *Black Dixie: Afro-Texan History and Culture in Houston* (College Station: Texas A&M UP, 1992), 18-19. On white Houstonians' attitudes toward free blacks, see Passey, "Freedmantown," 6-12, 17-18. On the attraction of Texas and Houston to emancipated blacks, see M. Louise Passey, "Freedmantown: The Evolution of a Black Neighborhood in Houston, 1865-1880" (master's thesis, Rice University, 1993), 28-29. On Houston's postwar black population, see *Voter Register of 1867-1869*; Manuscript Census Returns, *Ninth Census of the United States: 1870, Texas, Vol. 9, Guadalupe, Hamilton, Hardin and Harris Counties*, National Archives Microfilm Publications (Washington, D.C.: National Archives, 1965); Beeth and Wintz, *Black Dixie*, 89. On the postwar growth in other southern cities, see Rabinowitz, *Race Relations*, 18-20; John Blassingame, "Before the Ghetto: The Making of the Black Community in Savannah, Georgia, 1865-1880," *Journal of Social History*, VI (Summer 1973), 464; John Kellogg, "Negro Urban Clusters in the Postbellum South," *The Geographical Review* 67 (July 1977), 312. On blacks' efforts to purchase land, see Blassingame, "Before the Ghetto," 147-149.

7. On similar patterns elsewhere, see Rabinowitz, *Race Relations*; and Earl Lewis, *In Their Own Interests: Race, Class, and Power in Twentieth-Century Norfolk, Virginia* (Berkeley: University of California Press, 1991), 67-68.

8. On the contemporary perception of Freedmantown, see Rives Taylor, "Fourth Ward and the Seige of Allen Parkway Village," *Cite* 25 (Fall 1990): 6-11, 31. In 1981, Gladys House, a resident of the community also formed the Freedmen's Town Association, Inc. to increase the black community's awareness of the neighborhood's history.

9. For a definition of all of the wards' boundaries, see David G. McComb, *Houston, the Bayou City* (Austin: University of Texas Press, 1969), 72. On the current use of "Freedmantown" as a more general label, see Marguerite Johnston, *Houston: The Unknown City, 1836-1946* (College Station: Texas A&M UP, 1991), 101. Another example of this popular misidentification occurred in a photographic exhibition at the Houston Public Library. See "Caption" for house owned by Ned Jones in *Houston's Forgotten Heritage: Landscape, Houses, Interi-*

ors, 1824-1914, Julia Ideson Building, March 2-June 30; Exhibit of historic photographs from the Junior League Component, Houston Metropolitan Research Center, Houston Public Library (hereafter MRC). The misperceptions concerning the name's original application are magnified by the fact that the area originally designated as Freedmantown in the plat map records is no longer extant, having been subsumed both by the re-channeling of Buffalo Bayou and by the construction of Allen Parkway Village, a United States Housing Authority low-income housing complex of the 1940s.

10. See Housing Authority of the City of Houston, 1983: 11-5; quoted in *Freedmen's Town Historic District*, National Register Department, Texas Historical Commission, Austin, 1984, Item #8. For the report's discussion of the founding of Freedmantown, see *Ibid.*, Item #7; Item #8.

11. There is some indication that the term "Freedmantown" may have been misused by "popular" sources at an earlier date as well. In 1875, an article appeared in the *Houston Daily Telegraph* stating that the stores in Freedmantown did a good business and that the schools were well attended. According to all city records, however, there were no schools located in Freedmantown proper. It is likely that the author of the article was referring to the larger black neighborhood of the Fourth Ward, not specifically to Freedmantown. However, all references in the Harris County deed records and the Houston city directories appeared to delineate clearly between Freedmantown and the surrounding neighborhoods. Only those who lived north of San Felipe Road in the actual Hardcastle Addition were listed as residents of Freedmantown in city directories. See *Houston Daily Telegraph*, 21 December 1875, quoted in Johnnie Therrien, "Newspaper Clippings," WPA Files, MRC; Houston City Directory, 1877-78, (Houston: Mooney & Morrison, 1877). See Index to Real Property Register, G. S. Hardcastle Property, vol. 15: 22-23.

12. *Tri-Weekly Telegraph*, 10 February 1865.

13. Blacks in Houston had greater success in obtaining land than did blacks in rural areas of the state where whites often prevented their purchase of land. Barry A. Crouch, "Hidden Sources of Black History: The Texas Freedmen's Bureau Records as a Case Study," *Southwestern Historical Quarterly* 83 (January 1980): 216, 218-219. For a comparison of the ease of property ownership in urban areas versus rural, see Crouch, "Sources," 219. Reports filed by local officials of the Freedmen's Bureau stationed in the state's urban areas confirm that blacks in Galveston, Austin, and Houston enjoyed a higher standard of living than did blacks in rural areas. For Houston's report, see Byron Porter to Brevet. Col. William H. Sinclair, 1 September 1866, Report for the Month Ending August 31, 1866, Bureau of Refugees, Freedmen, and Abandoned Lands Records, Letters Sent, vol. 1, #3716, Record Group 105, National Archives.

14. Howard Beeth and Cary D. Wintz, eds., *Black Dixie: Afro-Texan History and Culture in Houston* (College Station: Texas A&M UP, 1992), 22. Miller discusses the situation with creditors and Reconstruction governments. See Edmund Thornton Miller, "The State Finances of Texas During the Civil War," in *Collected Papers*, Rice Institute Library, 17. Reprint from *Texas State Historical Association Quarterly*, Vol. XIV, 1.

15. On the economic depression, see David G. McComb, *Houston, the Bayou City* (Austin: University of Texas Press, 1969), 81; See also, Harold L. Platt, *City*

Building in the New South (Philadelphia: Temple University Press, 1983), 48. Schweninger estimates that blacks in urban areas of the South purchased property at a rate three and one-half times faster than rural blacks. He also suggests that blacks may have been aided in their attempts to purchase land by a reduction in the number of white males in the South due to wartime casualties — a factor that would have worked in favor of rural and urban blacks. Schweninger, *Black Property Owners*, 147.

16. Houston blacks had little access to credit other than through individual property owners because of the limited nature of the city's banking institutions. Most of Houston's banks were privately owned and operated — the first private bank being chartered in 1847. The city's first national bank did not open until 1866 and quickly ran into financial difficulties. On banks in Houston, see Margaret Swett Henson, introduction to *Houston's Forgotten Heritage: Landscape, Houses, Interiors, 1824-1914*, eds. Dorothy Knox Howe Houghton, et al. (Houston: Rice University Press, 1991), 9; Marguerite Johnston, *Houston the Unknown City, 1836-1946* (College Station: Texas A&M UP), 51, 87. Also see Beeth and Wintz, *Black Dixie*, 22. On whites' willingness to sell land to blacks on credit, see Deed Records 1836-1904, Harris County, Harris County Court House.

17. According to county tax records, there appeared to be some variation in land values among the different subdivisions of the western portion of the Fourth Ward, with land in the Senechal and Hopson additions being the most valuable, but the values showed great fluctuation and hardly seem to be accurate assessments. Since the register to the deed records for Harris County does not indicate full purchase price, the assessed value of the land provided by county tax records is the only means by which one can attempt to determine variations in the land's worth. However, the tax records surveyed — 1870, 1875, and 1880 — indicate an extremely haphazard method of land valuation. In the Castanie addition, for example, one property owner listed the value of 62 lots that he owned as $500, while another individual indicated that 2 lots were worth $1000. Similar cases appeared in all of the additions' tax records. These values, moreover, do not seem to correlate with the location of the property within the subdivision or with the identity of the owner. It is clear, however, that land in all but the Baker addition (where land clearly was undervalued in the earlier assessments) declined during the decade. While this drop in value in 1875 may be explained by the repercussions of the nationwide depression of 1873, this explanation does not suffice for the values in 1880. Even though a number of wealthy individuals continued to live in the ward, they increasingly located outside of these western additions, suggesting that they had been left largely to blacks and the city's economic unfortunate. While a lot in the Hardcastle addition was valued at $148.52 in 1875 ($158.59 in the Castanie addition), lots in the central part of town were selling for $1,200 to $2,000. On land sales in the central city, see *Houston Daily Telegraph*, 23 July 1875, quoted in Johnnie Therrien, comp., WPA Files. On lot values in the Fourth Ward, see Passey, "Freedmantown," 227.

18. The first horse-drawn streetcar was not put into operation until 1868 and only ran up and down Main Street. Service did not expand until 1874, when eight cars ran along the streets with turn-abouts at the Fairgrounds near Main and Mc-Gowen, at the Market House, on Main Street, and at the Union and Central depots. In November 1874, the *Houston Daily Telegraph* announced the opening of

the streetcar line to San Felipe road, traveling within 150 yards of the old cemetery — approximately to the eastern edge of Freedmantown. On the expansion of the streetcar line to San Felipe road, see *Houston Daily Telegraph*, 11 November 1874, quoted in Ann Wellington, comp., WPA Files. For description of the turn-abouts see Johnston, *Unknown City*, 79, 87; For a more concise history of the streetcar system, see Platt, *City Building*, 32-33, 92-93; Vertical File H-Streetcars, MRC, Houston Public Library.

19. Rabinowitz, *Race Relations*, 103. It is important to emphasize the different usages of the terms "neighborhood" and "community" in this work. Neighborhood is used to refer specifically to a spatial entity. A neighborhood is considered to be a group of streets and banks located together so as to precipitate physical contact between the residents. In contrast to this spatial definition, the term "community" is seen as more of an associational bond between individuals. As used in this work, a "community" is considered to be based upon a spirit of mutuality that arises among a group of people from their shared interests or associations.

20. On postwar black residential development and the role of blacks, see Berlin, *Slaves Without Masters*, 381, 384-385; C. Vann Woodward, *The Strange Career of Jim Crow* (New York: Oxford University Press, 1955; reprint, New York: Oxford University Press, 1966), 13. See also Rabinowitz, *Urban Race Relations*, 329-330. The wide range of residential development in southern cities is illustrated by John Kellogg's study of Lexington, Richmond, Atlanta, and Durham. See Kellogg, "Urban Clusters," 314-317; see also Blassingame, "Before the Ghetto," 481, 484; idem, *Black New Orleans* (Chicago: University of Chicago Press, 1973), 208.

21. On the number of free blacks in Atlanta, see James Michael Russell, *Atlanta, 1847-1890: City Building in the Old South and the New* (Baton Rouge: Louisiana State University Press, 1988), 70. On Houston's free black population, see Manuscript Census Returns, 1860, Schedule 1, Free Population.

22. On blacks' movement into Houston, see Beeth and Wintz, *Black Dixie*, 20. On the Confederate shoe shop, see *Tri-Weekly Telegraph*, 1 December 1865. There is no indication of where this shoe shop was located, although it probably was located somewhere along the banks of the Bayou so as to facilitate transport of the goods produced. On problems with black neighborhoods, see *Tri-Weekly Telegraph*, 19 July 1865. Additional references are found in the *Tri-Weekly Telegraph*, 25, 28 August 1865.

23. Report about the crowded house in Houston in *Tri-Weekly Telegraph*, 19 July 1865. On connection between "negrodom" and "filth," see *Ibid.*, 26 July 1865. For comments about the article in the *Shreveport News*, see *Ibid.*, 21 August 1865.

24. Opposition to black areas of settlement is expressed in *Tri-Weekly Telegraph*, 7, 26 July; 21 August 1865. For descriptions of urban living conditions of the South's black population, see John Blassingame, "Before the Ghetto: The Making of the Black Community in Savannah, Georgia, 1865-1880," *Journal of Social History*, VI (Summer 1973), 469; and Rabinowitz, *Urban Race Relations*, 116.

25. Wintz emphasizes Houston's racially mixed postwar neighborhoods. See Wintz, "Black Neighborhood," 103-104. *Tri-Weekly Telegraph*, 8 September 1865; Writers' Program of the Works Projects Administration (WPA), *Houston: A History and Guide* (Houston: Anson Jones Press, 1942), 81. The health ordinance

authorized the board of health to set restrictions on the number of people allowed in any particular house. For the full text of the ordinance, see *Houston City Directory 1866* (Dallas: R.L. Polk & Co., 1866), 66.

26. Galveston *News*, 19 September 1865.

27. *Houston Daily Telegraph*, 24 September 1866, quoted in Charles Franklin, comp., "Newspaper Clippings," Houston, Texas, WPA Files, MRC.

28. John Kellogg, "The Formation of Black Residential Areas in Lexington, Kentucky, 1865-1887," *The Journal of Southern History*, XLVIII (February 1982), 34-45.

29. No other reference to Hanna & Co.'s "freedmen's bureau" to which the newspaper article refers could be located. However, the local office of the United States Freedmen's Bureau was located close to the area described. See *Houston Daily Times*, 1 October 1868; *Ibid.*, 16 January 1869, quoted in Ruth Denny, comp., "Newspaper Clippings," Houston, Texas, WPA Files, MRC.

30. Kellogg, 3435; idem, "Negro Urban Clusters in the Postbellum South," *The Geographical Review* 67 (July 1977): 313.

31. *Tri-Weekly Telegraph*, 18 August 1865.

32. Whites in Houston had expressed their fears of black residential development even before the war. A housing ordinance passed by the City Council in 1855 to prevent free blacks from sharing their houses with slaves demonstrates that regardless of the size of the city's free black population, whites feared that free blacks would harbor slaves and runaways, thus undermining the city's social fabric. See *Tri-Weekly Telegraph*, 21 May 1855.

33. Galveston *Daily News*, 27 June 1865.

34. This physical separation, however, was not enforced by legal mechanisms during the immediate postwar period; and though it began to occur in a number of southern cities, it remained flexible and sporadic. On whites' perceptions of black postwar gains, see Ira Berlin, *Slaves Without Masters: The Free Negro in the Antebellum South* (New York: Pantheon Books, 1974), 383. Kellogg, "Lexington," 41; Rabinowitz, *Race Relations*, 119.

35. Rabinowitz, *Race Relations*, 98.

36. The Reconstruction government in Houston attempted in the early 1870s to expand the current limits of the city, but the changes made were reversed within two years. Therefore, the limits defined by the 1839 charter and its 1840 supplement in fact remained in effect until the early twentieth century. See Young, *Thumbnail History*, 11; City Planning Commission, *1929, Report of the City Planning Commission*, Houston, Texas, 23. Cary D. Wintz, "The Emergence of a Black Neighborhood: Houston's Fourth Ward," in *Urban Texas: Politics and Development*, ed. Char Miller and Heywood T. Sanders (College Station: Texas A&M University Press, 1990), 99.

37. City directories of the 1860s gave very imprecise address information for blacks, when it was provided at all. The early directories appear to have omitted names sporadically — particularly in the case of blacks. The census provides a better indication of the housing patterns of blacks and whites even though it provides a static picture five full years after the war's end and probably undercounts the number of inhabitants in Houston. I have assumed that the census enumerator proceeded in an orderly fashion through the ward, going house to house or crossing the street at regular intervals. See Manuscript Census Returns, *Ninth Census of*

the United States: 1870, Texas, Vol. 9, Guadalupe, Hamilton, Hardin and Harris Counties, National Archives Microfilm Publications (Washington, D.C.: National Archives, 1965). For a description of the problems with the 1870 census, see Rabinowitz, *Race Relations*, 19 n.2. On the 1870 and other censuses, see Schweninger, *Black Property Owners*, 371-374.

38. Manuscript Census Returns, 1870. It is probable that in some cases, rather than living next door to each other, black and white dwellings were located across the street, or simply on the same block. It is also impossible to know whether or not there were vacant lots between the homes listed next to each other in the census. Because the city directories at this time listed street addresses for only a small number of the city's inhabitants, it is impossible to cross-check the census listings for precise residential location.

39. On free black inhabitants in the prewar period, see Muir, "Free Negro," 214-215; on the emergence of postwar segregation, see Wintz, "The Emergence of a Black Neighborhood," 103-105; and on segregation in Houston during the twentieth century, see Robert D. Bullard, *Invisible Houston: The Black Experience in Boom and Bust* (College Station: Texas A&M University Press, 1987), 216.

40. Susan Jackson, "The People of Houston in the 1850's" (Ph.D. diss., Indiana University, 1975), 89-92.

41. Deed Records 1836-1904, Harris County, Harris County Court House, vol. 3, 525. W. E. Wood, *Map of Houston, Harris County, Texas, 15 January 1866*, MRC, Houston Public Library.

42. There were a number of extremely wealthy white residents in the Fourth Ward, including several prominent merchants. Their names were not listed sequentially in the census manuscript and frequently were preceded or followed by black households, indicating both the merchants' dispersal throughout much of the ward and their proximity to black neighbors. Blacks living around white households often were listed as servants, but this was not always the case. The Fourth Ward, however, apparently was not the central location for the wealthy residents of Houston. Of the seventy-two men listed in the 1870-71 city directory as "prominent" white businessmen in Houston, only six were listed in the 1870 census as residents of the Fourth Ward. See Manuscript Census Returns, 1870; *Houston City Directory 1870-71* (Houston: William Murray, 1870).

43. John Blassingame also suggests the connection between skills learned during slavery and postwar occupations of Savannah blacks. On blacks in Savannah, see Blassingame, "Before the Ghetto," 465-466. On the occupations of Fourth Ward residents, see Manuscript Census, 1870.

44. Newspaper accounts reveal that blacks throughout the city were concentrated in these low-status jobs, and thus that the occupational split between blacks and whites was replicated throughout the city. There seemed to be no direct correlation between foreign-born residents of the ward and specific occupations. Foreigners served in almost every occupation held by Fourth Ward whites. There were, however, no foreign-born residents to hold county or local office — probably due to citizenship requirements — and few were professionals, although this was true for all whites throughout the ward. Foreign-born whites were slightly overrepresented in craft-related and commercial occupations. They comprised, for example, the majority of wholesale and retail merchants (79 percent of the total).

However, foreign-born whites for the most part showed a notable variety in their occupations. See Manuscript Census Returns, 1870.

45. *Daily and Sunday Telegraph*, 16 March 1867, quoted in Charles Franklin, comp., "Newspaper Clippings," WPA Files, MRC. This announcement appeared despite the fact that in 1865 the paper had applauded whites' replacement of blacks as drivers of most of the city's drays. See *Tri-Weekly Telegraph*, 10, 12 July 1865, quoted in Smallwood, *Time of Hope, Time of Despair*, 29.

46. This high incidence of foreign-born whites living among predominantly black neighbors appears to have been common throughout the South's urban areas. For foreign-born population in the Fourth Ward, see Manuscript Census Returns, 1870; For foreign-born population in Houston as a whole, see Houghton et al., *Houston's Forgotten Heritage*, 12; McComb, *Bayou City*, 52. Rabinowitz discusses the prevalence of foreign-born whites in black neighborhoods, see Rabinowitz, *Race Relations*, 112.

47. On the conflicts between black and white laborers, see *Tri-Weekly Telegraph*, 22 December 1865. For a discussion of the growing animosity between black and white workers and black exclusion from trade unions, see Beeth and Wintz, *Black Dixie*, 91-92.

48. By cross-referencing the names of property owners in Freedmantown with the manuscript census it is possible, since so many of the property owners were residents of the area, to delineate with a relatively high degree of specificity the area encompassed by this addition. By separate households, I am referring to individual dwellings. When a second family was living under another's roof, its family head was not counted in this tabulation. See Manuscript Census Returns, 1870; Beeth and Wintz, *Black Dixie*, 22-23.

49. Manuscript Census Returns, 1870. Deed Records 1836-1904, Harris County, Harris County Courthouse. The woman identified as a prostitute represented the only indication found in the census or otherwise during this period that there might be any connection between the Freedmantown neighborhood and prostitution. On the later association of the neighborhood with vice, see Thomas Clyde Mackey, "Red Lights Out: A Legal History of Prostitution, Disorderly Houses, and Vice Districts, 1870-1917," (Ph.D. diss., Rice University, 1984), 192-222.

50. The census records for Harris County in 1870 and 1880 appear to have rarely noted real and personal property holdings of the inhabitants — especially for blacks. The accuracy of the data reported depended purely on the individual's honest disclosure of his assets and the census taker's accurate recording of his or her response. For a copy of the instructions given to the census enumerators in 1860 — presumably those in 1870 were similar — see Lee Soltow, *Men and Wealth in the United States*, 1850-1870 (New Haven: Yale University Press, 1975), 1. See Manuscript Census Returns, 1870.

51. It is impossible to ascertain from the occupational data derived from the census how successful blacks were in obtaining gainful employment and what level of wages they were able to command. Nevertheless, since making this determination for blacks throughout the ward would be equally difficult, one may assume that the opportunities for blacks in any given occupation were basically the same in each of the additions of the ward. See Manuscript Census, 1870.

52. While there were only three households with more than one family, there

were several in which a number of children of different family names were living. These children may have been orphans or extended family members. Unfortunately, there are no existing maps of Freedmantown during this time that show the size of the homes in the area, so the "people-to-space" ratio in these homes is uncertain. See Manuscript Census Returns, 1870. For information on the Fourth Ward as a whole, see Wintz, "Black Neighborhood," 101-102.

53. There is some difficulty in comparing the census returns for 1870 and 1880, since the 1870 census only divided areas of the city by ward for enumeration purposes. The 1880 census, in contrast, identified areas of the city according to enumeration district and then offered a cross-reference by ward. The 1880 census also added street names down the left hand side of each of the pages, facilitating the attempt to locate residents, but many of the outlying residential areas in the Fourth Ward had no recognized street names. Areas within Freedmantown, for instance, are identified only as being "Between San Felipe and the Bayou." Nevertheless, it is possible using old maps and matching names from deed records to identify **parts** of enumeration districts (ED) #85 and #76 as the ones that would have covered most of the subdivisions immediately surrounding Freedmantown. Freedmantown itself appeared to be located in pan of ED #76.

In so narrowing the area of study with the 1880 census, the relevant portion of the census manuscript is more clearly defined and limited than the one used in the analysis of the same neighborhoods in 1870. Compared to the 608 households studied from the 1870 census, only 337 are examined from the 1880. The statistics cited for 1880 therefore are more accurate and more descriptive of the area of the Fourth Ward that comprised the five subdivisions commonly associated with the black community of the Fourth Ward. The statistics cited for 1880 make those for 1870 appear somewhat distorted, since those for 1870 represent the entire ward, not just the western-most additions. However, the ward was less well-developed and thus significantly smaller in 1870 than in 1880, reducing the margin of error.

In addition, figures for the population of the Fourth Ward in 1880 slightly underrepresent the total number of people residing in the ward. One enumeration district in the census combined all of the residents of the First Ward with a portion of those in the Fourth. Since there was no way to delineate the residents of these two wards from one another — many of the street names listed in the census spanned the two wards — for the purposes of this paper, I have simply eliminated this enumeration district from my calculations. Finally, statistics cited for the entire Fourth Ward exclude the residents of Freedmantown. See Manuscript Census Returns, *Tenth Census of the United States: 1880, Texas, Harris County*, National Archives Microfilm Publications (Washington, D.C.: National Archives, 1965).

54. *Ibid.* Among the white residents of the enumeration districts 85 and 76, the 1880 census indicated one instance of interracial marriage. Given the South's traditional disdain of such liaisons, this couple probably chose or was urged to settle outside of predominantly white neighborhoods.

55. Manuscript Census Returns, 1880.

56. *Ibid.*

57. There were three percent fewer in service-related occupations, five percent fewer in craft-related industries, and six percent fewer in commercial occupations. See Manuscript Census Returns, 1880.

58. As noted earlier, despite Freedmantown's later association with prostitu-

tion and its designation as a legal vice district, there was nothing to indicate that at this early date there were any houses of ill repute in the neighborhood. Thus while it is possible that these women who listed their occupations as "at home" were running houses of prostitution, there is no evidence to suggest that this was the case.

59. Manuscript Census Returns, 1880. The average number of occupants per household had increased only slightly to 3.9.

60. *Ibid.*

61. Howard Jones, who sets forth this explanation, even pinpoints the area's foundation to the specific date of January 24, 1866. See Howard Jones, *The Red Diary: A Chronological History of Black Americans in Houston and Some Neighboring Harris County Communities* (Austin: Nortex Press, 1991), 37, 30.

62. Hardcastle's one slave was a male, age 42. See Manuscript Census Returns, *Eighth Census of the United States*, 1860, Harris County, Texas, Schedule 2, Slave Population, National Archives Microfilm Series, Roll 286, p.20 (hereafter referred to as "Slave Population, 1860").

63. WPA, *Guide*, 288. Cary Wintz also retells this account in his essay on the Fourth Ward. See Wintz, "Black Neighborhood," 100. According to the 1869 Wood map, Longcope did own a single lot of property in the Fourth Ward, but it was not located in Freedmantown. See W. E. Wood, *Map of Houston, Harris County, Texas, 1869*, MRC, Houston Public Library; "Slave Population, 1860," 14.

64. Rabinowitz, *Race Relations*, 100.

65. For a description of Harrisburg's location, see McComb, *Bayou City*, 14. For a description of the Confederate camps, see Bill Winsor, *Texas in the Confederacy, 1861-1865: Military Installations, Economy, and People*, (Hillsboro: Hill Junior College Press, 1978), 19, 23, 24, 35. On the location of the Freedmen's Bureau office, see *Houston City Directory 1867-68* (Houston: Gray, Smallwood & Co., 1867). The Bureau's office was located just across the street from the settlement earlier identified as Hanna's Nest, indicating that some of the ward's blacks may have located their residences so as to have easy access to the local agents.

66. Wintz, "Black Neighborhood," 100.

67. Epidemics of yellow fever had been frequent and severe in the city's history. During the 1867 outbreak the Galveston *Daily News* reported that the epidemic had grown worse, particularly within the Fourth Ward. See McComb, *Bayou City*, 88 and Galveston *Daily News*, 27 September 1867. On flooding of the bayou, see *Daily Telegraph*, 6 June 1871, quoted in J. Therrien, comp., WPA Files. There was no direct evidence that there was a hospital in operation on this land adjacent to Freedmantown, but in 1872 a newspaper article reported a proposal to relocate the city hospital from Rusk Street to a ten-acre spot, "near the old graveyard and adjoining the bayou. It was formerly the site of the old hospital, and belongs to the city." See *Daily Telegraph*, 23 July 1872, quoted in Ruth Denny, comp., WPA Files, MRC.

68. Kellogg, "Urban Clusters," 311, 313. The city eventually decided to close the cemetery as of June 1871 and paid to have it refenced, but the white inhabitants of the city continued to view it as a "disgrace to the city." For contemporary newspaper articles concerning the unsanitary and unsightly nature of the city's cemetery, see *Daily Houston Telegraph* 31 January 1871, quoted in Thelma Harris,

WPA Files; *Daily Telegraph* 26 March, 15 December 1871, quoted in J. Therrien and William Dillard, comps., WPA Files.

69. On the Bureau's report, see Crouch, "Sources," 219. For complaints about the rents being charged, see *Tri-Weekly Telegraph*, 9 October 1865; *The Weekly Telegraph*, 14 May 1867, in Franklin; *Daily and Sunday Telegraph*, 19 May 1867, in Franklin, WPA Files, MRC. Similar complaints arose in the 1870s, see Galveston *Daily News*, 7 July 1871, quoted in Margaret Lenox, comp., WPA Files; *Daily Houston Telegraph*, 24 January 1871, quoted in Thelma Hams, comp., WPA Files.

70. In 1872 the *Daily Telegraph* reported average daily wages for a number of occupations. The following wages were reported: Railway engineers, $3.33 1/3; Railway conductors, $4.16 2/3; Railway brakemen, $2.00; Printers (average), $4.00; Bricklayers, $5.00; Plasterers, $4.00; Carpenters, $3.50; Draymen, $3.00; Barbers, $2.50; Clerks, mercantile, $3.00; Clerk, railway, steamboat, etc., $5.00; Day laborers at wharves, $3.00; Mortar carriers, $1.30; Hackmen, $1.50; Stone masons, $5.00; Editors and reporters, $2.30; Common laborers, $1.00. See *Daily Telegraph*, 14 June 1872, quoted in Ava Jo Nowlin, comp., WPA Files, MRC.

71. It is difficult to make a relative comparison of the number of blacks settling in each of the additions in the western portion of the Fourth Ward because they differed so much in size. There were 251 total lots available for sale in the Hardcastle addition, 310 in the Castanie, 330 in the Baker, only 144 in the Hopson and 90 in the Senechal additions. The only way to compare the number of blacks in each is through the deed records. Since most blacks who were property owners in these additions also appeared as residents, this method of comparison probably is fairly accurate. The largest absolute number of blacks appeared in Freedmantown, though the number in the Castanie addition measured a close second. On the increasing number of blacks in the Fourth Ward in the 1870s see Wintz, "Black Neighborhood," 100-104. On the specific characteristics of settlement in each of these additions and for maps showing details of property ownership, see Passey, "Freedmantown," 80-96; 199-220.

72. Deed Records 1836-1904, Harris County, Harris County Court House; vol. P, 570.

73. Index to Real Property Register, Harris County, Harris County Court House, G. S. Hardcastle Property, recorded July 10, 1875; vol. 15: 22. The exact origins of the name "Freedmantown" are unclear. Whether this was a term developed and used exclusively by the white population of Houston, or whether blacks too referred to this area as Freedmantown is uncertain. The county used the designation "Hardcastle Addition" almost exclusively in the registers for the deed records. However, in the actual text of the deeds, there were at least three instances *prior* to 1875 where the clerk identified the property as being located in "Freedmanville." The use of this term before Hardcastle's filing of the plat map with the county suggests that there was a popular perception of this area as the domain of the city's black residents. In addition, a newspaper article in 1871 stated that "nearly the whole population" surrounding the old City Cemetery was black. For cases where area is referred to as "Freedmanville," see Deed Records 1836-1904, Harris County, Harris County Court House, vol. 9B: 531; *Ibid.*, vol. 10: 533; *Ibid.*, vol. 29: 91. For the newspaper reference, see *Daily Telegraph*, 15 December 1871, quoted in William Dillard, comp., WPA Files, MRC.

74. Tax Assessment Rolls 1837-72, Reel 1; 1872-1881, Reel 2, Harris County, Harris County Court House; Subdivision Books, Stewart Title Company. It is difficult to identify all of the property owners in a specific addition using tax records because omissions appeared frequent. A great deal of property also escaped assessment, as is indicated by the numerous suits brought against property owners in later years for their failure to pay their taxes. In April 1861, a change in the tax law allowed non-resident property owners to file land for taxation either in the county in which it was situated or in the county of which the owner was a resident. See Miller, *Collected Papers*, 7. Both tax and deed records have been used in attempting to reconstruct property ownership patterns, so as to reduce the margin of error caused by such omissions. See Wood, *Map of Houston 1869*; and *Bird's Eye View of the City of Houston, 1872*; MRC. Property sales to blacks were highest in 1866 and 1867, but the largest total number of transactions to both blacks and whites occurred in 1875, the year in which Garrett Hardcastle defaulted on a number of outstanding notes — an occurrence that no doubt was precipitated by the city's own financial crisis. "Hardcastle Addition," Subdivision Books, Stewart Title Company. On the city's defaulting on debts, see McComb, *Bayou City*, 125. For references to Hardcastle's economic losses, see "Abstracts of Title Collection," 78-80, 82.

75. The location of black residential areas such as Freedmantown on a major thoroughfare was peculiar in comparison to other southern cities. Kellogg claims that the "cluster settlements" of blacks in the urban South tended to appear where no major streets existed and developed in the interiors of blocks where new streets and alleys had to be constructed. See Kellogg, "Lexington," 33.

76. "Hardcastle Addition," Subdivision Books, Stewart Title Company. There were an additional four blocks in the Hardcastle addition whose development differed from the rest of the addition, even though they were included on the area's original plat map. They were located on the eastern edge of the addition next to the Hopson addition. Hardcastle did not begin selling lots in these blocks until 1875 and almost all were sold to white individuals. Because of their late and seemingly unrelated development, they have not been counted in the calculations for Freedmantown.

77. Jack Yates, the pastor of Antioch Baptist Church, one of the most prominent churches within the black community, urged other blacks to purchase property. According to his descendants, he actively encouraged the establishment of an all-black neighborhood within the section of the Castanie addition where he had purchased land. See Rutherford B. H. Yates, Sr. and Paul L. Yates, *The Life and Efforts of Jack Yates* (Houston: Texas Southern University Press, 1985), 18. None of the historians who have written previously about the development of housing patterns in Houston have suggested the connection between the fall of Reconstruction government and the growth of segregation in the city, but the correlation seems implicit. McComb, for example, claims that by 1875 segregation in Houston was entrenched. Later he suggests that 1875 may have been the year of origin for segregation in the city. The way in which Freedmantown developed, with black residential concentration remaining high throughout the 1870s, and the way that surrounding neighborhoods became increasingly black during the 1870s suggest the applicability of this explanation to the post-Reconstruction situation in Houston. See McComb, *Bayou City*, 86, 157; on a similar development pattern

in South Carolina, see Orville Vernon Burton, "The Rise and Fall of Afro-American Town Life: Town and Country in Reconstruction Edgefield, South Carolina," in Orville Vernon Burton and Robert C. McMath, Jr. (eds.), *Toward a New South? Studies in Post-Civil War Southern Communities* (Westport, Conn: Greenwood Press, 1982), 177-180, 185-186.

78. On the importance of homeownership to neighborhood stability, see Mary Susan Jackson, "Movin' On: Mobility Through Houston in the 1850's," *Southwestern Historical Quarterly* 81 (January 1978), 266. On the importance of homeownership to blacks in the South, see Schweninger, *Black Property Owners*, 169-170.

79. To determine whether or not someone was both a property owner and a resident, a list of all the property owners in each of the subdivisions was compiled. This list then was checked against the census records of 1870 and 1880 to determine whether or not the individuals appeared to be living in the place in which they owned property. A thorough search also was made of the city directories and other secondary sources such as travel accounts and histories of specific institutions during the fifteen-year period to obtain a more complete listing of addresses.

80. While there were a total of thirty-four blacks purchasing property, twenty-seven still owned land there in 1870. See "Hardcastle Addition," Subdivision Books, Stewart Title Company.

81. John Murchison was the first individual to purchase property in Freedmantown in 1866. See Census Manuscripts, 1870 and 1880. Although Murchison appeared in the 1879-80 city directory as "col'd," in the only other issue in which his name appeared, that of 1873, his race was not noted, the usual practice for white citizens. See *Houston City Directory 1873* (Houston: Tracy and Baker, 1873); *Ibid.*, 1879-1880, (Houston: C. D. Morrison & Co., 1879), 166.

82. Rabinowitz claims that white real estate agents in the South quickly saw the profit involved in selling to blacks, although the example he gives dates from the late 1880s. It is unclear whether whites in Houston had similar motives, but it is puzzling that Hardcastle chose to designate his subdivision as Freedmantown — a name that hardly would have attracted white settlers to the area — unless he believed that his best, or only, prospect for developing the land was as a black residential neighborhood. See Rabinowitz, *Race Relations*, 103.

83. The descriptions of the lots in the deed records show that owners occasionally did divide their land and sell a small portion to another individual, but it seems to have happened infrequently prior to 1880. See Wood, *Map of Houston, 1869*; Subdivision Books, Stewart Title Company. The dimensions for the lots in each of the blocks are found on the plat maps. See Deed Records 1836-1904, Harris County, Harris County Courthouse, Hopson plat map, vol. W: 426; Senechal, vol. M: 475; Baker, vol. Y: 351; Castanie vol. M: 571; and Hardcastle, vol. 15: 22-23.

84. On obstacles to property ownership faced by blacks across the South, see Ransom and Sutch, *One Kind of Freedom*, 81. For limited involvement of Freedmen's Bureau, see Crouch, "Hidden Sources," 218. On the high cost of real estate in Houston during the 1870s, see *Houston Daily Union*, 7 March 1871, quoted in Charles Franklin, comp., WPA Files. In other areas of the South such as the community of Hampton, Virginia, the rise in the number of black property owners seems to have been facilitated greatly by the efforts of Rev. George Whipple and the AMA. This, however, clearly was not the case in Houston. See

Edward H. Bonekemper, III, "Negro Ownership of Real Property in Hampton and Elizabeth City County, Virginia, 1860-1870," *Journal of Negro History*, LV (July 1970): 178.

85. Only three of the nineteen who started out with Crane were to become owners of property in the neighborhoods in and surrounding Freedmantown. See *Antioch: Historic Highlights, The Antioch Baptist Church* (Antioch Community Thrust, Inc. Bicentennial Historic Documents Project), 1976. Beeth and Wintz, *Black Dixie*, 24.

86. On Hardcastle's donation of land, see Deed Records 1836-1904, Harris County, Harris County Court House; vol. 10, p. 22. On the trustees' purchase of land in the Senechal addition, see "Senechal Addition," Subdivision Book, Stuart Title Company, Block #3, entry #8. It is uncertain the exact amount the trustees paid for the land since the deed registers customarily only listed the amount of "consideration" given for the property — an amount usually smaller than the full purchase price. The congregation kept the property in Freedmantown until 1910, but there is no indication of how that property was used. The 1869 Wood Map depicts a church at this location, but it is uncertain whether this indicated ownership by Antioch or actual use. No church listing in the city directory ever correlated with this location. See Wood, *Map of Houston, 1869*; On the sale of the land in Freedmantown by Antioch, see "Hardcastle Addition," Subdivision Books, Compilations of the Indexes to Real Property Registers for Harris County, Stuart Title Company, Houston, Texas, Block 11; or see Deed Records 1836-1904, Harris County, Harris County Court House; vol. 64, p. 683. The location of a Methodist Episcopal Church was listed as Freedmantown in the 1877-78 city directory, but deed records indicate that it was in an adjacent block to Antioch's property. See *Houston City Directory, 1877-78*.

87. In the Senechal addition, where a number of whites owned property and where proximity to the city's center ensured a greater degree of contact with whites living elsewhere, Antioch's chances of receiving funds from white sources were much improved. On the importance of black churches and the role of white monetary support, see Rabinowitz, *Urban Race Relations*, 204-205.

88. Mackey, "Red Lights Out," 192-222.

89. On the role of myth making within the African-American past, see Nathan I. Huggins, "Afro-American History: Myths, Heroes, Reality," in Key Issues in the Afro-American Experience (New York: Harcourt Brace Jovanovich, 1971), 5-19.

Bibliography

CHAPTERS 1–2 BY DAVID A. WILLIAMS

Articles and Books

Adair, Anthony. *Heroes of the Alamo.* New York: Exposition Press, 1956.

Anderson, Adrian N., Ralph A. Wooster, David G. Armstrong, and Jeanie R. Stanley. *Texas and Texans.* Websterville, Ohio: Glencoe: MacMillan/McGraw- Hill, 1993.

Arnold, Hendrick. "Request to Texas Government to Remain in Texas as Free Persons." *A Letter* (January 4, 1836). Texas State Archives.

Barker, Eugene C. *The United States and Mexico 1835–1837.* Austin: University of Texas Press, 1928.

———. "Free Negroes in the Republic of Texas." *Southwestern Historical Quarterly* 40 (July 1936 to April 1937).

Barr, Alwyn. *Black Texans: A History of Negroes in Texas 1528–1971.* Austin: Jenkins Press, 1973.

Barr, Alwyn, and Robert A. Calvert. *Black Leaders: Texans for Their Times.* Austin: Texas State Historical Association, 1981.

Brown, Roscoe, and Harry A. Ploski. *The Negro Almanac.* New York: Bell-Weather Publishers, 1969.

Bunkley Anita. *Emily The Yellow Rose.* Houston: Rinard Publishing, 1989.

Carroll, H. Bailey, et al., eds. *Handbook of Texas.* Vol. 1. Austin: Texas State Historical Association, 1952.

Carroll, John M. *The Black Military Experience in the American West.* New York: Liveright Press, 1971.

Curtis, James C. *The Black Experience in America.* Austin: University of Texas Press, 1970.

Ericson, Carolyn Reeves. *"Nacogdoches" Gateway to Texas: A Biographical Dictionary 1773–1849.* Fort Worth: Arrow/Curtis Printing Co., 1974.

Fenn, F. M. O. Family files. Fort Bend County Historical Files, Richmond, Texas.

Florence, Fred S. *Texas.* Dallas: A Republic National Bank Anniversary Publication, 1945.

———. "Free Negroes in Fort Bend County, Texas." *Journal of Negro History* 33 (January 1948).

Garrison, George P. "The Texas Revolution." *Texas State Historical Quarterly* 4 (July 1890 to April 1901).

Greene, Robert Ewell. *Black Defenders of America 1775–1973.* Chicago: Johnson Publishers, 1974.

Hester, Conoly. "The Bill Goyens Legend." *Dallas Times-Herald Magazine* (December 3, 1967).

Holley, Mary Austin. *Texas 1784–1846.* Austin: Texas State Historical Association, 1985.

Hunter, J. Marvin. "Hendrick Arnold, Negro, A Texas Patriot." *Frontier Times* 15 (October 1937).

Jackson, Andrew W. *A Sure Foundation.* Houston: Freedmans Press, 1939.

Johnson, Michael P. *Black Masters.* New York: Norton Press, 1941.

Jordan, Edna Hidell. *Black Tracks to Texas.* Corpus Christi: Golden Banner Press, 1977.

Kilman, Ed. "Negroes at San Jacinto." *Frontier Times, Houston Post* (June 15, 1947).

Kownslar, Allen O. *The Texans: Their Land and History.* Dallas: McGraw-Hill, 1971.

Letters from Texas. Correspondence of the Fredericksburg Arena, Groce's Retreat, March 20, 1836.

"Negro Histo-Wall." Center for Public School Ethnic Studies, University of Texas at Austin, 1968.

Patillo, G. A., to M. B. Lamar, February 24, 1840, Lamar Papers, M.S. No. 1729, Texas State Library.

Ploski, Harry A., and James Williams. *The Negro Almanac.* New York: Wiley Publications, 1983.

Porter, Kenneth W. *The Negro on the American Frontier.* New York: Arno Press and *The New York Times*, 1971.

Ray, Worth S. *Austin Colony Pioneers.* Austin: Pemberton Press, 1970.

Sance, Melvin M., Jr. *The Afro-American Texans.* University of Texas Institute of Texan Cultures at San Antonio, 1987.

Savory, Thomas. "Petition to Texas Government." Austin: Texas State Archives, 1840.

Schoen, Harold. "The Free Negro in the Republic of Texas." *Southwestern Historical Quarterly* 40.4 (April 1937).

Smith, Maxlin. "Petition to Texas Government." Austin: Texas State Archives, 1836.

Stephens, Thomas. "Petition to Texas Requesting Veterans Pension." Austin: Texas State Archives, 1836.

Thompson, Holland. *The Book of Texas.* Dallas: Grolier Society, 1929.

Turner, Martha Anne. *The Yellow Rose of Texas.* Austin: Shoal Creek Press, 1971.

Wade, Houston. *David G. Burnet Letters.* La Grange: La Grange Journal Press, 1836.

Wade, Melvin. "Black Pioneers Had Major Role in Settlement, Growth of Texas." *Austin American-Statesman* (March 30, 1986).

Walraven, Bill, and Marjorie K. Walraven. *The Magnificent Barbarians.* Austin: Eakin Press, 1991.

Wharton, Clarence R. *History of Fort Bend County.* San Antonio: Naylor Company, 1939.

Woodson, Carter G. "The Free Negro in Texas." *Journal of Negro History* 19 (December 1948).

Miscellaneous Sources

Audited Military Claims, Archives Division, Texas State Library, Nos. 145 and 304.

Barker, Eugene C. *History of Texas.* Dallas, 1929.

Blake, Robert B. *Historic Nacogdoches, Texas,* unpublished paper, Nacogdoches, 1939.

Brown, J. H. *History of Texas from 1865 to 1982,* II. Austin: Jenkins Publishing Co., 1970.

Butler, R. L., E. W. Holland, and Ruth Lapham, eds. *William Bollaert's Texas.* Norman, Oklahoma: 1956.

Castañeda, Carlos E. *The Mexican Side of the Texas Revolution.* Austin: Graphic Ideas, Inc., 1970.

————. *Our Catholic Heritage.* 6 vols. Austin: 1950, vol. 6.

Collingsworth, C. M. to Austin, Stephen F., Eugene C. Barker (ed.), The Austin Papers, III. Center for American History, University of Texas at Austin.

"Compendium of The History of Texas," *Texas Almanac for 1859; Texas Almanac: 1857, 1873.*

County Records and San Fernando Archives, Marriage Records, Volume 1, 1798--1856, entry #341, Bexar County Courthouse, San Antonio, Texas.

Daughters of the Republic of Texas. Muster Rolls of the Texas Revolution, Austin, 1986.

————. Defenders of the Republic of Texas, vol. 1, Texas Army Muster Rolls, Receipt Rolls and Other Rolls, 1836–1841. Austin: Laurel House Press, 1985.

Duewell, L. A. "The Story of Monument Hill," *La Grange Journal,* 1936.

Fenn, F. M. O. Family file. Richmond, Texas: Fort Bend County Historical Files.

Handbook of Texas. Supplement, Vol. 3. Texas State Historical Association, University of Texas at Austin, 1976.

House Journal. Third Legislature. Archives Division, Texas State Library, Austin, Texas.

————. Fifth Congress, 34, 35. Archives Division, Texas State Library, Austin, Texas.

————. Seventh Legislature. Archives Division, Texas State Library.

Johnson, F. W. to General Burleson. *Letter,* December 11, 1835.

Katz, William Loren. *The Black West.* Seattle, Washington: Open Hand Publishing Co., 1987.

Kerr, James to Council of War. Congress recognized McCullough as "among the first to shed his blood in the war of independence," Congressional Papers, Fifth Session, No. 1677, File 10, No. 1527, File 17; Memorial 101, File 67, no date.

Kilman, Ed. "Skin Black; Heart True Blue." *Texas Heartbeat, Houston Chronicle,* June 15, 1947.

Lamar Papers. File I, 238, 240, 559. Archives Division, Texas State Library, Austin, Texas.

Martinello, Martan L. *A Personal History: The Afro-American Texans.* University of Texas, Institute of Texan Cultures, San Antonio, Texas, 1982.

Memorial No. 18, File 49, September 18, 1840. Archives Division, Texas State Library, Austin, Texas.

Memorial No. 19, File 49, September 19, 1840. Archives Division, Texas State Library, Austin, Texas.

Miller, Thomas Lloyd. *Bounty and Donation Land Grants, 1836–1888.* Austin: University of Texas Press, 1967.

Morgan, James K. *Papers.* Rosenberg Library, Galveston, Texas.

Moss, A. Henry. *Papers.* Archives Collection, Center for American History, University of Texas at Austin.

Muir, Andrew Forest. "The Free Negro in Harris County, Texas." *Southwestern Historical Quarterly* 39 (July 1942–April 1943).

Muir, Andrew Forest. "The Free Negro in Fort Bend County, Texas." *Journal of Negro History* 39 (January 1948).

———. "Negro Histo-Wall," unpublished paper. Center for Public School Ethnic Studies, University of Texas at Austin, 1968.

Schoen, Harold. "The Free Negro and the Texas Revolution." *Southwestern Historical Quarterly* 40 (January–April 1937).

Shuffler, R. Henderson. "Negro Freedman Hendrick Arnold," *Houston Chronicle Texas Magazine,* Sunday, December 13, 1964.

Telegram and Texas Register. Galveston, Texas, July 8, 1840.

Texas State Historical Marker, erected in 1936, File No. 68-925. "The Bill Goyens Legend." *Dallas Times-Herald,* December 3, 1967.

Their Times. Author unknown. Texas State Historical Association, University of Texas at Austin, 1981.

Tolbert, Frank X. *The Day of San Jacinto.* New York, Toronto, London: McGraw-Hill, 1959.

Wade, Houston. "The Dawson Men of Fayette County." *La Grange Journal,* 1936.

"Who's Who In America, 1952." *San Antonio Express,* January 1, 1956.

Winfrey, Dorman H. "Chief Rules of the Texas Cherokee." *Chronicles of Oklahoma* 32 (Spring 1954).

Wisehart, M. K. *Sam Houston: American Giant.* Washington, D.C.: 1962.

CHAPTER 6   BY CINDY BLAND VERHEYDEN

Bryan, Frank. "On the Jefferson Road." *Texian Stomping Grounds.* Austin: Texas Folk-Lore Society, 1941: p. 16.

Casey, Betty. *Dance Across Texas.* Austin: University of Texas Press, 1985.

Craddock, J. R. "The Cowboy Dance." *Texas Folk and Folklore,* edited by Mody C. Boatright, Wilson M. Hudson, and Allen Maxwell, pp. 183–189. Dallas: Southern Methodist University Press, 1954.

Daniels, A. Pat. *Texas Avenue at Main Street: The Chronological Story of a City Block in Houston, Texas.* Houston, 1964.

Ellis, Anna. "Social Life in Old Texas Days Alive with Thrills — Gaiety, Too." *San Antonio Express,* October 14, 1934: p. D1.

Hart, Katherine. "Austin's Social Season Used to be a Humdinger." *Austin American-Statesman,* January 8, 1972: p. 5.

Pugh, Donald Wagner. *Music in Frontier Houston, 1836–1876.* Austin: University of Texas, DMA Dissertation, 1970.

Sanders, J. Olcutt. "Honor the Fiddler!" *Texian Stomping Grounds.* Austin: Texas Folk-Lore Society, 1941: pp. 78–79.

Steelman, Gloria G. *Musical Activity in Lampasas, Texas: 1880–1929.* Austin: University of Texas, MM Thesis, 1971.
Stone, William Hale. *Twenty-four Years a Cowboy.* Norman: University of Oklahoma Press, 1959.
"They Came from 50 Miles Around and Danced from Sun to Sun." *The XIT Brand Annual.* Dalhart, Texas, 1939: pp. 76–77.

CHAPTER 9   BY MARTIN KUHLMAN

Newspapers
The Austin American.
The Dallas Morning News.
The Houston Informer.
San Antonio Register.
The Texas Observer.

Manuscripts
Moses Leroy Collection. Houston Metropolitan Research Center, Houston Public Library.

Books
Branch, Taylor. *Parting the Waters: America in the King Years, 1954–1963* (New York: Simon & Schuster, 1988).
Crawford, Ann Fears and Jack Keever. *John B. Connally: Portrait in Power* (Austin: Jenkins Publishing Co. 1973).
Reston, James Jr. *The Lone Star: The Life of John Connally* (New York: Harper & Row, Publishers, 1989).

Interviews
Bonner, Booker T. Interview by author. November 11, 1992. Lubbock. Tape recording. In author's possession.

CHAPTERS 11–12   BY DAVID A. WILLIAMS

Books
Ballard, Allen B. *Education of Black Folks: The Afro American Struggle for Knowledge in White America.* New York: Harper and Row Publishers, 1973.
Barker, Eugene C., ed. *Texas History.* Dallas, Texas: P. L. Turner and Co., 1928.
Barr, Alwyn. *Black Texans: A History of Negroes in Texas 1528–1971.* Austin, Texas: Jenkins Publishing Company, 1973.
Benedict, R. Y. *History of the University of Texas.* Austin, Texas: University of Texas Press, 1917.
Bentley, George R. *A History of the Freedman's Bureau.* Philadelphia, Pennsylvania: University of Pennsylvania Press, 1955.
Bowles, Frank, and Frank A. Decosta. *Between Two Worlds: A Profile of Negro Higher Education.* New York: McGraw-Hill Book Company, 1971.

Brawley, Benjamin. *A Social History of the American Negro.* New York: Collier Book Co., 1970.

Brewer, J. Mason. *Negro Legislators of Texas.* Austin, Texas: Jenkins Publishing Company, 1970.

Bryant, Ira B. *Texas Southern University.* Houston, Texas: D. Armstrong Company, Inc., 1975.

Bureau of Educational Research. *The Journal of Negro Education.* Washington, D.C.: Howard University Press, 1963.

Burns, W. Haywood. *The Voices of Negro Protest in America.* New York: Oxford University Press, 1963.

Carnegie Commission on Higher Education. *Between Two Worlds: Profile of Negro Higher Education.* New York: McGraw-Hill Book Company, 1971.

Chandra, Kanahur V. *Black Students Concern in a Black College.* San Francisco: Research Associates, Inc., 1976.

Clark, Joseph L. *A History of Texas.* Dallas, Texas: D. C. Heath and Company, 1940.

Curti, Merle. *The Growth of American Thought.* New York: C. Scribner and Sons, 1935.

Curti, Merle, and Rederick Nash. *Philanthropy in the Shaping of American Higher Education.* New Brunswick, New Jersey: Rutgers University Press, 1965.

Daniels, George M. *Guide to Black Colleges and Universities.* New York: The Third Press, Inc., 1976.

Davis, William R. *The Development and Present Status of Negro Education in East Texas.* New York: Columbia Teachers College Press, 1934.

DuBois, W. E. B. *The Education of Black People: Ten Critiques 1906–1960.* Edited by Herbert Aptheker, Amherst: University of Massachusetts Press, 1973.

Eby, Frederick. *The Development of Education in Texas.* New York: Dodd, Mead and Company, 1925.

Franklin, John Hope. *From Slavery to Freedom.* New York: Alfred A. Knopf Publishers, 1947.

Frazier, Franklin E. *The Negro in the United States.* New York: The Macmillan Company, 1949.

From Isolation to Mainstream: Problems of Colleges Founded for Negroes. (Author unknown.) New York: McGraw-Hill Book Company, 1977.

Galagher, Buell G. *American Caste and the Negro College.* New York: Guardian Press, 1966.

Green, L., and C. G. Woodson. *The Negro Wage Earner.* Washington, D.C.: Associated Publishers, 1902.

Guzman, Jessie P., et al. *Negro Year Book.* New York: William H. Wise and Company, Inc. 1941–1946.

History of Texas. Supplemented with Biographical Mentions of Many Prominent Persons and Families of the State. Chicago: The Lewis Publishing Company, 1896.

Holmes, Dwight O. *Evolution of the Negro College.* New York: American Negro Press, 1970.

Hunt, Robert Lee. *A History of Farmer Movements in the Southwest, 1873–1925.* College Station, Texas: Texas A&M College Press, 1925.

LaGrone, Cyrus Wilson. "A Sociological Study of Negro Population of Marshall, Texas," unpublished master's thesis, University of Texas at Austin, Austin, Texas, 1932.

Luter, Buckner S. "A Historical and Educational Analysis of the Administration and Curriculum of the Hempstead Negro School from 1867 to 1938," unpublished master's thesis, Prairie View A&M University, Prairie View, Texas, 1939.

McKay, Seth Shepard. "Texas Under the Davis Regime," unpublished master's thesis, University of Texas at Austin, Austin, Texas, 1962.

Perry, Douglas G. "Black Populism: The Negro in the People's Party in Texas," unpublished master's thesis, Prairie View A&M University, Prairie View, Texas, 1945.

Sims, Van E. "The Willette Rutherford Banks Administration: A Study in the Historical Development of Prairie View Agricultural and Mechanical College," unpublished master's thesis, Prairie View A&M University, Prairie View, Texas, 1950.

Tarrow, Willie A. "A University for Negroes of Texas, A Promise Unfulfilled," unpublished master's thesis, Prairie View A&M University, Prairie View, Texas, 1946.

Thompson, Esther. "The Influence of the Freedman's Bureau on the Education of the Negro in Texas," unpublished master's thesis, Texas Southern University, Houston, Texas, 1956.

Washington, Samuel N. "The Land-Grant Colleges for Negroes 1914–1945," unpublished master's thesis, Prairie View A&M University, Prairie View, Texas, 1949.

Westbrooks, Johnnie Mae. "The Sweatt Case: A Study in Minority Strategy in Texas," unpublished master's thesis, Prairie View A&M University, Prairie View, Texas, 1953.

Williams, Mabel Crayton. "The History of Tillotson College," unpublished master's thesis, Texas Southern University, Houston, Texas, 1967.

Government Publications

Extensive list of government sources (not included here) in possession of author.

CHAPTER 13   BY ADA C. SIMOND

"A Unique Houston Neighborhood Called Frenchtown." *Houston Chronicle,* Section 5, Monday, September 15, 1986.

Arrington, Carolyn. *Black Explorer in Spanish Texas: Estevanico.* Austin: Eakin Press, 1986.

Barker, Eugene C. "The African Slave Trade in Texas." *Quarterly of the Texas State Historical Association* 6 (October 1902), 145–158.

Bennet, Lerone Jr. *Before the Mayflower: A History of Black America.* Chicago: Johnson Publishing Co., 1982.

Cade, John B. (Prairie View prof). "Out of the Mouths of Ex-Slaves." *Journal of Negro History,* July 19, 1935 (p. 294-337).

Coggins, Richard. *Who's Who in the Bible.* London: Anchor Press Ltd., 1981.

Curlee, Abigail. "A Study of Texas Slave Plantations, 1822–1865." (UT 1932 dissertation.) *Southwestern Historical Quarterly* 26, 10/1922.

Davis, Cyprian. Fr., OSB. "The African Roots of Black Catholics." *The Josephite Harvest Centennial 1888–1988,* Winter 1987–88.

Eugene, Toinette M. "Black Catholic Belonging: A Critical Assessment of Socialization and Achievement: Patterns for Families Black and Catholic." 1983 doctoral dissertation.

Gaillaudet, Frederic. *Sketching Early Texas and Louisiana.* Trans. by James L. Shepherd III, UT 1966.

Hogan, Peter. Fr., SSJ. "The Black Catholic Experience."

"In a Word," *Society of Divine Word Publication* (various issues).

Josephite Archives (various years).

Josephite Harvest Centennial, 1888–1988, Winter 1987–88.

Lathrop, Barnes. *Migration into E. Texas, 1835–1860: A Study from the U.S. Census Texas State Historical Association,* 1949.

Richardson, Rupert N. *Texas: The Lone Star State.* 2nd ed. (Rev. 1964), p. 164.

Contributors

Johnnie M. Armstead

Johnnie M. Armstead, a member of TAAHO and the Hays County Historical Commission, resides in San Marcos, Texas, where she directed restoration work on The Calaboose, a recorded historic landmark in San Marcos. She has been honored as Woman of the Year in San Marcos for her successful history projects.

Thomas A. Britten

Thomas A. Britten earned a Ph.D. in history from Texas Tech University in Lubbock, Texas, in 1994. A Michigan native, Britten received B.A. degrees in history and English from Texas Tech in 1986. He taught both world history and United States history on the high school level for four years, and obtained his M.A. degree in history from Hardin-Simmons University in Abilene, Texas, in 1990. His thesis topic was entitled "The History of the Seminole-Negro Indian Scouts," which was the first attempt at a comprehensive history of the relatively unknown soldiers.

He his wife, Connie, and son, Zachary, currently live in Sioux City, Iowa. Dr. Britten is a professor in the Department of History, Briar College.

Martin Kuhlman

Martin Kuhlman, Ph.D., is a professor in the Department of History and Political Science at West Texas A&M University, Canyon, Texas. He is a member of TAAHO, and has published articles for the *Southwestern Historical Quarterly,* among other publications.

Louise Passey Maxwell

As an Echols Scholar at the University of Virginia, **Louise Passey Maxwell** graduated Phi Beta Kappa with a B.A. in interdisciplinary studies in 1988. In 1993, she received an M.A. in American history from Rice University and is currently working on a Ph.D. at New York University. Her work focuses upon urban development in the South during the late nineteenth and early twentieth centuries.

Greg Moses

Greg Moses attended Texas A&M, where he served as editor of the student newspaper before receiving a B.A. in philosophy and an M.A. in English. He worked as a journalist in the Bryan-College Station area and was awarded "Best Newscast in Texas" for two years in a row in UPI radio contests. For ten years, he was a contributing writer for *The Texas Observer*. He has a Ph.D. in philosophy from the University of Texas, and he currently teaches philosophy at Marist College in Poughkeepsie, NY. His book on Martin Luther King, Jr., and the Logic of Nonviolence is forthcoming from Guilford Press. He is married to Pamela Kaye Harmatiuk, an unreformed Texas native.

Ada DeBlanc Simond

Ada DeBlanc Simond (1903–1989) was a native Louisianian. She moved to Austin with her family in 1914. She received a B.S. from Tillotson College and M.S. from Iowa State University. An educator, historian, writer, and folklorist, she received numerous awards, honors, and citations.

Cindy Bland Verheyden

Cindy Bland Verheyden received a bachelor's degree in journalism from The University of Texas at Austin. She is a native Texan, now living in Austin. Ms. Verheyden is a photojournalist and photo researcher. She has written articles for the *Daily Texan* and *Austin Sun*.

David A. Williams, Ed.D.

David A. Williams completed his public school training at E. S. Doty High School, McKinney, Texas. He served a tour of duty in the U.S. Navy during World War II, spending most of the time in the Southwest Pacific aboard the USS *West Virginia*. He received a bachelor of arts degree in social science and religion from Bishop College, and graduated magna cum laude. The master of education degree was conferred to him in 1970 by Texas Southern University, Houston. Dr. Williams studied for three semesters at The University of Texas at Austin in graduate education, and he received a doctor of education degree from Baylor University in 1978.

Dr. Williams taught social studies for the Austin Independent School District for more than twenty years before retiring in 1989.

He also taught at The University of Texas at Austin for four summers in the Afro-African American Studies Department. He is now executive director of the Texas African American Heritage Organization, Inc., which he founded in 1987. He serves as visiting professor in the Honors Program for Texas history at Huston Tillotson College, Austin, and Howard Payne University, Brownwood.

He is a retired member of the Austin Association of Teachers, Texas State Teachers Association, National Education, and Phi Delta Kappa, and is an active member of several civic and cultural groups including the Travis County Historical Commission and the Heritage Alliance of Austin and Travis County.

Dr. Williams was born in McKinney, Texas. He is married to Augustine Coleman. They have three sons and four grandchildren.